Walter de Gray Birch

The Historical Charters and Constitutional Documents of the City of London

Walter de Gray Birch

The Historical Charters and Constitutional Documents of the City of London

ISBN/EAN: 9783337203788

Printed in Europe, USA, Canada, Australia, Japan

Cover: Foto ©ninafisch / pixelio.de

More available books at **www.hansebooks.com**

THE

HISTORICAL CHARTERS

AND

CONSTITUTIONAL DOCUMENTS

OF THE

CITY OF LONDON.

REVISED EDITION.

𝔚ith an 𝔍ntroduction, 𝔄ppendix, and 𝔈opious 𝔍ndex,

BY

WALTER DE GRAY BIRCH, F.S.A.,

OF THE BRITISH MUSEUM; HONORARY SECRETARY OF THE BRITISH ARCHÆOLOGICAL ASSOCIATION,
ETC., ETC., ETC.

.... "If we exult in the conviction that our free Municipal Institutions are the safeguard of some of our most cherished liberties, let us remember those to whom we owe them, and study to transmit unimpaired to our posterity an inheritance which we have derived from so remote an ancestry."—KEMBLE, *Saxons in England*, ii, 341.

LONDON :
WHITING & CO., 30 & 32, SARDINIA STREET, W.C.

MDCCCLXXXVII.

1887

PREFACE.

For some time now THE HISTORICAL CHARTERS and CONSTITUTIONAL DOCUMENTS relating to the CITY OF LONDON have attracted the attention of those among us who have been interested in watching the growing and by this time universally admitted desire for the revision and augmentation of the Privileges which this ancient Corporation enjoys. Hence the opportunity seems appropriately to have arisen for giving English readers—whether they be citizens, historians, politicians, lawyers, or antiquaries, or simply readers desirous of acquiring general information upon a subject prominently before them, and likely, if we read the direction of popular feeling rightly, to become before long very prominent among the subjects of current legislation—a new and revised edition of the English translation of the City Charters and Documents concerning the constitution of the Corporation.

In proof of this fact, so universally admitted, reference may be made—if, indeed, proof be required—to a speech made as recently as the 9th of November in 1883, by the Lord Chief Justice, on the occasion of the reception of the new Lord Mayor in accordance with the "Fifth Charter of King John" (see page 19), wherein he is reported to have said:—

"What may be in store, if anything is in store, in the way of change, for the great Corporation over which you preside, is yet entirely uncertain. Such things must be left where Homer left them, 'On the knees of the gods;' or as an Englishman would translate it, to the wisdom of Parliament. But this at least may be said, without talking politics, but merely stating facts, that some thirty years ago, when I, from circumstances not necessary to enlarge upon, had official information as to the constitution, the character, and the conduct of that great Corporation, there were some few things which, alike to the friendly inquirer who looked at them with respectful curiosity, and to the hostile critic who subjected them to angry scrutiny, needed, and perhaps demanded, the explanation and defence of which perhaps they were susceptible. Of anything which is very old, and which has lasted for a number of centuries, this must be, and from the necessity of the case must unavoidably be so. I do not doubt, though I have no information on the subject, that in the lapse of time which has taken place since I was more familiarly connected with them, the flaws to which I alluded have disappeared, or are fast disappearing. I do not doubt that the high intelligence which always distinguishes the Corporation of London has taught them that it is only by allowing themselves to be in accord with the spirit of the age, that it is only by approving itself to the high and cultivated intelligence of a great people, that any institution can flourish, perhaps even can survive. I do not doubt that this is perfectly well understood by the Corporation of London, and I have no doubt that if it is so understood by the Corporation of London, that great and illustrious body will continue to flourish in the future as it has flourished in the past, in age as it has flourished in youth, in unabated strength and in undiminished vigour."

Mr. SHAW-LEFEVRE, M.P., speaking on the 29th of November, at the annual dinner of the Gladstone Club, in Holborn, is reported to have said that :—

"It was matter of common information that the Government hoped, intended, and believed that they would carry before they left office the reform of the municipal government of London, the extension of the county franchise, and county government for the rest of England. Those three measures were now struggling for birth. No one could say at present which of them would stand first in order, or which of them would be stillborn; all that they could hope was that, before the present Government went out of office, each and all of them would be carried into law. The extension of the county franchise must inevitably entail, either coincidently or at no great distance of time, a redistribution of seats, and in that

question London had a deep and abiding interest. . . .
. . There could be no nobler, no greater task for any
statesman than to breathe civic life into the inert mass of
London, to bring into harmony its discordant elements of
local government, and to give an organisation and an executive equal to the great duties which lay before it. It was
impossible that we could have a thorough reform of the water
supply, nor could we look forward to the sweeping away of
rookeries in our worst regions ; nor, again, could we raise to
a proper height the lower classes unless a material change in
the government of the Metropolis were effected. He attributed the want of public feeling in London to the absence of
anything like local government in London ; and he believed
that when we had a true local government for London, the
wealthy classes, as in large provincial towns, would begin to
understand that they had duties towards the poorer classes.
Belgravia would feel that it had something in common with
Whitechapel, Tyburn with Pentonville; and when that was
the case, he believed we should see much greater harmony
between all classes of the people of this great Metropolis.
 . . . . . He believed they should achieve the results
they aimed at, and that they would carry these great measures
in a manner which would redound to the benefit of the people
of England."

On the very same day, Sir C. DILKE, M.P., at the annual
dinner of the Eleusis Club in Chelsea, said " they had reached
the time when several great reforms affecting London, for
which the members of this Club had striven for so many
years, were about to be undertaken. There was hope even in
the next Session of no less than three great measures affecting London being introduced. The two were Parliamentary
Reform and Metropolitan Municipal Reform ; the third was
the Reform of the City Guilds. The Royal Commission was
still sitting, and as his colleague, from his position as a
member of the Commission, was unable to speak of its
deliberations, he (Sir Charles) would speak from expressions
which had reached him, although not from Mr. Firth. He
understood they would recommend immediate legislation.
He hoped that that would be the case. The drift of the

evidence was in support of suspensory legislation, and it was likely that the House would be asked to pass a bill by which the 'bad' Companies, if there were bad ones, should be prevented from alienating their property. They did not intend that the property of the City Guilds should be divided, as was the property of Serjeants' Inn. He believed that besides compulsory measures there would be devised some scheme for the appointment of a small Commission to deal with the property in the interests of the inhabitants of the Metropolis. Turning from that question to the two greater questions of further Parliamentary Reform and Metropolitan Municipal Reform, he would say they were pre-eminently reforms affecting the inhabitants of London. . . . . .
He had often tried to show the immense interest of London in the redistribution of political power. There were only two or three towns in the kingdom similarly situated, and Parliament dealt more with the affairs of London than of any other portion of the country. Other towns were allowed to a great extent to legislate for themselves by means of their Corporations, Provisional Orders, and the Local Government Board. Whether the next redistribution of political power would be complete and final, or only a long step towards it, he thought they should claim that the same justice which was meted out to the other large communities of the country should be meted out to the Metropolis. There remained the third great reform—that of the government of the Metropolis. They had heard lately that opposition would be given to the solution of the Metropolitan problem to which his colleague, Mr. Firth, had devoted so much attention. Some maintained that the existing government of London was good enough, while others wished to adopt the City plan of creating new municipalities in various groups of parishes around the Central Municipality of the City of London. He believed the case of both these sets of gentlemen would entirely break down. There were no doubt some parishes in London which had very zealously tried to work the existing law; but, on the other hand, there were some parishes the government of which was a flagrant scandal. These were strong words, but he was prepared, when the time came, to attempt to justify

them. . . . . . . Groups of municipalities would destroy a large amount of existing unity. It would be a retrograde step to create a number of separate municipalities, and it was clear that the general line of the scheme put forward by Mr. Firth must be the line upon which any great measure for the government of London must be founded. . . . . . . He thought it clear that the great majority of the people of London had made up their mind with regard to the passing of measures of Parliamentary and Metropolitan Municipal Reform."

In another place, but at the same time, Mr. G. W. E. RUSSELL, M.P., Political Secretary to the Local Government Board, said :—" With regard to the condition of the squalid portions of London, if the authorities would use the powers they possessed there would be no need for fresh legislation. He deprecated the pulling down of houses unless others were built up to take their places, inasmuch as such a practice tended rather to promote than prevent overcrowding. It was only by a Municipal Government having full control of the whole of London that they could hope to have this question dealt with satisfactorily."

These extracts could be largely added to if it were necessary, but enough has been quoted to indicate the feeling of the times with regard to the Corporation of London and its projected reform.

Several works have from time to time appeared relating to these charters and documents. Among others the following :—*Privilegia Londini*. By W. Bohun, 1723. 3rd edition. (See page 318 for the title and remarks on the book.)

The Charters of the City of London, which have been granted by the Kings and Queens of England since the Conquest, taken verbatim out of the Records, exactly translated into English, with notes explaining ancient words and terms, and the Parliamentary Confirmation of King William and Queen Mary, etc. By J. E. London, 1745. Sm. 8vo.

A Survey of the Cities of London and Westminster, by John Stow, London, 1754, folio, contains extracts and texts of several of the charters printed in the following series.

The History of London from its Foundation to the Present

Time, by W. R. Maitland, F.R.S., London, 1756, folio, contains the texts in English of most of these documents.

A large collection of these Charters and Documents is comprised in the *New History of London, etc.* By John Noorthouck. London, 1773. 4to. This forms the basis of the present work, but considerable revision has been made with regard to the names of persons occurring in the deeds, the editor availing himself of contemporary copies of them among the Manuscripts of the British Museum, and in some instances verifying the texts with the readings of the Charters themselves, by the kind courtesy of the Town Clerk of London, to whom he desires to place on record his deep sense of obligation.

The Charters of London, complete; also Magna Charta and the Bill of Rights, with explanatory notes and remarks. By John Luffman, citizen and goldsmith. 1793. 8vo.

No list of these works would be perfect that omitted mention of the late Mr. George Norton's *Commentaries on the History, Constitution, and Chartered Franchises of the City of London.* London, 1869, 8vo. Third edition revised. Mr. Norton was formerly one of the common pleaders of the City of London, and had an excellent knowledge of the charters preserved in the Town Clerk's office; and, indeed, his *Commentaries* show that he availed himself of his privilege of consulting the records of the City, for he gives a useful abstract of many Corporation charters (with authorities for each, and explanatory notes), which (if not always correct, as in the case of No. II of the present collection, where the note on p. 257 of his work is wrong) in point of completeness has not hitherto been surpassed.

An account of the manuscript copies, both Latin and English, and of the principal printed books in which the Latin texts may be consulted, will be found in the Appendix at the end of the volume.

A careful transcript of most of the early City Charters was made, some time past, under the supervision of the late Sir Thomas Duffus Hardy, D.C.L., Deputy Keeper of the Public Records, and is now preserved in the Guildhall Library.

INTRODUCTION.

THE history of every Corporation is bound up in its documents, and the history of the famous CORPORATION OF LONDON forms no exception to this rule. The gradual growth of all liberties and powers may be traced from the earliest day of their beginning, and as we read Charter after Charter in the series of privileges accorded to the City of London contained in the pages of this work, it is not difficult to acquire a just appreciation of the manner in which that growth has taken place.

"The liberties[1] of the first cities," says Kemble, "must often have been mere favours on the part of the lords who owned the soil and protected the dwellers upon it. Later, these liberties were the result of bargains between separate powers, grown capable of measuring one another. Lastly, they are necessities imposed by an advanced condition of human associations, in which the wishes, objects, and desires of the individual man are hurried resistlessly away by a great movement of civilisation, in which the vast attraction of the mass neutralises and defeats all minor forces. It would, indeed, be but slight philosophy to suppose that any one set of circumstances could account for the infinite variety which the history of towns presents: though there are features of resemblance common to them all, yet each has its peculiar story, its peculiar conditions of progress and decay; even as the children of one family, which bear a near likeness to each other, yet each has its own tale of joy and sorrow, of smiles and tears, of triumph and failure. Yet there is probably no single element of urban prosperity more potent than situation, or which more persuasively modifies all other and concurrent conditions of success. Let the most careless observer only

Saxons ii, 307.

compare London, Liverpool, and Bristol, I will not say with Munich or Madrid, but even with Warwick, Stafford, or Winchester. If royal favour could have made cities great, the latter should have flourished; for they were the residences of the rulers of Mercia and Wessex, the scenes of *witena gemóts*, of Christmas festivals and Easters, when the king solemnly wore his crown; while the *ceorls* or *mangeras* of Brigstow and Lundenwic were only cheapening hides with the Esterlings, warehousing the foreign wines which were to supply the royal table, or bargaining with the adventurer from the East for the incense which was to accompany the High Mass in the Cathedral. But Commerce, the child of Opportunity, brought Wealth; Wealth, Power; and Power led Independence in its train."

First Charter of William I. It is recorded that William the Conqueror, in the second year of his reign over England, made a solemn entry into the City of London by procession, and afterwards, at the instance of William the Norman, Bishop of London, granted the Charter to the citizens which forms No. 1 of the present collection. This is written in the Anglo-Saxon language, and is drawn up in accordance with the conventional usages of Anglo-Saxon diplomatics, and these circumstances are declared by historians to have been looked upon as a great concession to English feelings, seeing that it was issued at a time when the Norman language and Norman forms of legal deeds were supplanting the native language and methods of formulation. "This Charter," writes Noorthouck, "consists of four lines and a quarter, beautifully written on a slip of parchment of the length of six inches and breadth of one; which is preserved in the City Archives as a great curiosity."

The two chief privileges here granted are:—" That the burgesses were declared all to be law-worthy—That their children should be their heirs." Now, there were two ways of being law-worthy, or having the benefit of the law. By the state and condition of men's persons; so almost all free men had the free benefit of the law. But men of servile condition had not, especially such as were *in dominio*, in demesne, for they received justice from their lords, were judged by them in most cases, and had not the true benefit of the law; so neither, as to the second observation in this charter, could their children be their heirs, for they held their lands and goods at the will of the lord, and were not sure to enjoy them longer than they pleased him. The second way of being law-worthy was, when men had not committed any crimes, or done anything for which they forfeited the law and deserved to be outlawed, then they were said to be *legales homines, recti in curia*, or law-worthy, but not so properly as in the first sense of the word.

"From hence we may make a very probable conjecture at the meaning of this protection or charter. It is not to be doubted but that the burgesses of London had obtained of the Saxon kings several liberties and immunities, among which this was one, to be so far free as not to be *in dominio*, or so obnoxious to any lord but that, by reason of their state and condition, they might be law-worthy, that is, have the free benefit of the law; and likewise further obtained (if it was not then a consequent of their personal estate and condition) that their children should be heirs of their lands and goods, and in both these were free from the injuries and unreasonable demands and power of any severe lord. So that all the application made by their Bishop William, and not unlikely by Godfrey the Portreve, to the Conqueror for them was, that their state and condition might be the same as it was in King Edward's days, that their children might be their heirs, and that they might in both be protected from the injury and violence of imperious lords, which by the prevalency of their bishop were granted. Considering, therefore, that by the foregoing instances it is clear that many, or most burgesses of other burghs were *in dominio*, either of the king, or some other lords or patrons in the time of King Edward, and that the Londoners might fear the Conqueror would break in upon their privileges and reduce them to the same condition, this was a great privilege obtained."[1]

Hume,[2] following Dalrymple,[3] says that this famous Charter is nothing but a letter of protection, a declaration that the

---

[1] Brady, *Treatise on English Boroughs*, quoted by Noorthouck, p. 24; Luffman, p. 2.

[2] *Hist.*, Appendix II.　　　　　[3] *On Feudal Property.*

citizens should not be treated as slaves. But even this was a considerable immunity at a time when all persons who were not possessed of land were included in that class. What enhanced the value of these Charters was that they were granted at a time when the feudal system obtained a firmer and more extensive establishment, by the settlement of the Norman barons in England under the military tenure.[1]

The seal, broken, of white wax, was sewn up in a silken bag in Noorthouck's time; it is, unfortunately, no longer appended to the Charter, and its existence is very doubtful.

<small>Second Charter of William I.</small>
The Second Charter of William the Conqueror has been erroneously described and translated by Noorthouck and Luffman, but it is printed (I am informed) at the end of Mr. Alexander Ellis's publication of *The Only English Proclamation of Henry III*. Of it Noorthouck writes:—" Another Charter[2] in the Saxon language, consisting of three lines finely written on a slip of parchment, of the length of six inches and a half, and breadth of three-quarters of an inch, is carefully preserved in the same box with the first Charter. The seal of this Charter is also of white wax, and preserved[3] in a silken bag, but is so much defaced that all that can be made of the impression it bore is something resembling a gate with some steeples or spires. . . . This Charter is conceived in such brief terms that it does not even point out the persons to whom the grant is made!"

Luffman, following Noorthouck, states that it appears extraordinary that no mention is made of the persons to whom the Charter was granted. And well it might be; but the fact is that both these writers have failed to read the name of "Deormanne." The original Charter is preserved in the Town Clerk's Office, at the Guildhall, and I have been favoured with the following correct transcript of it:—

" Will'm kyng gret pill'm b' ⁊ spegn scyrgerefan ⁊ ealle mine þegnas on east seaxan freondlice ᛫ ⁊ ic kyðe eop þ ic habbe ge unnen deormanne minan men[4] þa hide landes æt gyddesdune þe hi of geryden pæs ᛫ ⁊ ic nelle geþolian frenciscan ne engliscan þ him æt ænigan þingan misbeode:"

It will be easily perceived that this Charter is simply a

---

[1] Noorthouck, p. 25.   [2] *Id.*, p. 25.   [3] Also now missing.   [4] *Sic.*

confirmation to Deorman, the king's *homo*, of land of which he had been deprived, and although reckoned by those who have printed the City Charters as pertaining to the City, really having no claim to that position, except as a title-deed to land which must have passed (the Charter itself going with the land) into the possession of the City authorities. Its interest as a Saxon charter is, however, undoubtedly great.

The Charter of King Henry I owes its origin, if we may trust Noorthouck,[1] to the fact that the king having usurped the crown in prejudice to Robert, his elder brother, well knew how difficult it would be to secure himself upon the throne without the assistance and goodwill of London. To engage the citizens, therefore, to support his Government, he conferred upon them the advantageous privileges that are contained in this Charter.

Charter of Henry I.

This Charter[2] not only confirmed to the citizens of London their ancient customs and immunities, but added to their jurisdiction in fee-farm the county of Middlesex, without homage, fealty, or service, on paying a yearly quit-rent of three hundred pounds. It gave them likewise the power of choosing a Sheriff and Justiciary from their own body, and of holding the Pleas of the Crown.

Prior to this grant, the citizens appear to have been wholly dependent on the will of the king; but their privilege being now in a great measure guarded, they aimed at further securing their customs by converting them into written laws; and their arts and mysteries, which had heretofore been kept up by prescription only, were now established into companies. The king, however, kept to himself the appointment of Portreve, or Chief Magistrate. The names of the witnesses, not only in this Charter, but in almost all the succeeding documents, have been very carelessly printed hitherto. In the present series these names have been verified by references to originals and manuscript copies of important character.

King Stephen does not appear to have granted any charter to the citizens of London. His successor, Henry II, however, granted that which forms No. IV of the present series. The date has not been ascertained, but Richard de Belmeis,

Charter of Henry II.

[1] Page 27.   [2] Luffman, p. 9.

xiv INTRODUCTION.

Bishop of London, one of the witnesses, is known to have died A.D. 1162. The date, therefore, may be safely attributed to the period between A.D. 1154 and 1162, and not improbably to an early year of the king's reign.

This Charter[1] confirms the City liberties and immunities, and adds the Acquittal of Murder for the ward of Portsoken, which ward did not properly form part of the City until this time.

Henry II also granted a Charter to the Guild of Weavers of London, on condition of receiving an annual payment of two golden marks at Michaelmas. The witnesses to this Charter, which was given at Winchester, are: T[heobald] Archbishop of Canterbury, who died on the 18th April, A.D. 1161; and Warine, son of Gerard, who was King's Chamberlain[2] from A.D. 1155 to 1158. Mr. Riley, who prints the Latin text of this Charter in his edition of the *Liber Custumarum* for the Master of the Rolls, p. 33, erroneously calls the Archbishop Thomas, who succeeded Theobald, but was not contemporary with Warine the Chamberlain. The date of this deed cannot be later than A.D. 1158.

First Charter of Richard I.

It is stated that the first Charter of King Richard I was granted to the City of London in consideration of the good behaviour of the citizens during his absence abroad; and in all probability their contribution of the considerable sum of fifteen hundred marks, or £1,000, towards his ransom from captivity, influenced the king towards this confirmation of the ancient rights and immunities of the City.

Second Charter of Richard I.

In July, A.D. 1197, Richard I granted to the City a second Charter, which forms No. VI of the series, and for it he is stated to have received a sum of fifteen hundred marks. Luffman writes:—"By[3] this Charter the citizens became Conservators of the River Thames, and their jurisdiction extends westward of London Bridge to Colnie-ditch, near Staines, and eastward of the said bridge to Yenland, including part of the rivers Medway and Lea."

Noorthouck, however, is more precise in his remarks, and declares[4] that as the Charter does not prescribe any bounds,

---

[1] Luffman, p. 13.   [2] Eyton, *Itinerary of Henry II*, p. 315.
[3] Page 19.   [4] Page 36.

or limit the extent over which the City is to take cognisance, but transfers to the City all the right and jurisdiction enjoyed by the king's Keeper of the Tower, it seems clear that the City's right of jurisdiction includes the whole river, from its junction with the sea eastward, so far westward as it is known by the name of Thames. But by the loose expressions of this grant, both the extent of the City's jurisdiction and the objects of the City's power have been so much contested that it has been found needful to explain and amend this Charter at times by others. So that for a long succession of time the extent of the City's jurisdiction on the river Thames has been admitted from Colne Ditch, a little westward of Staines Bridge, to Yendal, Yenland, or Yenleet, east of London Bridge, including part of the rivers Medway and Lea. The reader may refer to Noorthouck for an interesting note on the subject of the soil under the river and its possession by the Corporation of London, made by Lord Burghley.

King John granted at least five Charters to the City. By the first, No. VII, granted at Shoreham in June, A.D. 1199, within a month of his accession to the throne, the citizens, besides having all their ancient rights and privileges confirmed to them, are exempt from the payment of all toll and lastage in the king's foreign dominion. For this the City paid the sum of three thousand marks.[1] *First Charter of King John*

The Second Charter of this king (No. VIII) bears the same date as the previous one. This Charter gives the citizens power to remove all weirs in the rivers Thames and Medway, and right to inflict the penalty of £10 upon those who offend by erecting them.[2] *Second Charter of King John.*

King John's Third Charter, dated at Bonneville-sur-Touque, in Normandy,[3] forms No. IX of this series, only a few days after the issue of the First and Second Charters. The fee-farm of the Sheriffwicks of London and Middlesex is by this Charter confirmed to the citizens of London, at the old yearly rent of three hundred pounds, by which they were held before Queen Matilda took them away; and as a further privilege, it bestows on them the right of choosing the sheriffs *Third Charter of King John.*

---

[1] Noorthouck, p. 37; Luffman, p. 24.
[2] Noorthouck, p. 37; Luffman, p. 25.
[3] Hardy, *Itinerary of King John.*

from their own body.[1] This deed is memorable as being the oldest covenant or conveyance on record in which occurs the legal phrase *to have and to hold*, now esteemed essential in all conveyances of property.[2]

Fourth Charter of King John. The Fourth Charter of King John, No. X of this collection, dated in March, A.D. 1201, is remarkable in many ways. It was granted[3] in consequence of an application made by the Mayor and citizens, to remove the Guild, or Company, of the Weavers from the City—what the offence was which made this fraternity obnoxious to the citizens is not recited—and the king granted their request, on the condition of the yearly payment of twenty marks, an indemnification for the loss of eighteen marks heretofore paid yearly by the Weavers to the king.

Fifth Charter of King John. The Fifth Charter of King John, forming No. XI of the present collection, was issued in May, A.D. 1215. It appears[4] to have been granted about the time of the City being tallaged in the sum of two thousand marks towards taking off the Interdict.

By this Charter[5] the citizens were confirmed in all their ancient rights, and in addition to them was hereby granted the additional and valuable privilege of choosing the Chief Magistrate. This was, in fact, the cause of several of the trades forming themselves into companies, in which they continued for many years, previous to their incorporation by charter; for under the security offered by the Charter, crafts and trades set up fraternities in imitation of those already incorporated.

First Charter of Henry III. According to Noorthouck, King Henry III. extorted from the citizens of London the sum of five thousand marks, and granted them five charters, on condition of their paying him a fifteenth of their personal estate. The king's first Charter, No. XII, appears to be a confirmation of former grants. It is dated in February, A.D. 1227.

Second Charter of Henry III. The Second Charter of Henry III, No. XIII, also a confirmation of former grants, bears the same date as the previous deed.

---

[1] Luffman, p. 29.   [2] Noorthouck, p. 37.
[3] Noorthouck, p. 37; Luffman, p. 30.
[4] Noorthouck, p. 39.   [5] Luffman, p. 33.

The Third Charter of this king, No. XIV, bears the same date. It is a confirmation of the Second Charter of King John, respecting the weirs in the rivers Thames and Medway, to which reference has already been made. *[margin: Third Charter of Henry III.]*

No. XV, the Fourth Charter of Henry III, was issued in March, A.D. 1227, within the space of one month from the issue of the previous documents. This Charter[1] was granted in consequence of the citizens' petition to the king to restore the ancient privileges, given to them by King Edward the Confessor, of keeping the hustings once a week only, "which custom had been greatly encroached upon by the gentlemen of the law (who were at this time considerably increased in number) by litigious fruits." *[margin: Fourth Charter of Henry III.]*

On the 23rd of December, in the eleventh year of his reign, A.D. 1226, King Henry III had granted a charter, not included in this series, "*de non trahendo in consequentiam auxilium quod cives Londoniarum ei fecerunt;*" whereby he undertakes not to draw into a precedent the fact of having received liberal aid from the Barons of London to acquire his inheritance and rights in parts beyond the seas, after the death of Louis VIII, King of France. This was witnessed at Westminster by Hubert de Burgh, Justice of England; Ralph, son of Nicholas; Hugh Dispencer, Henry de Aldithlee, and Luke the Chaplain, Dean of St. Martin's, London. The Latin text is printed in Riley's *Liber Custumarum*, p. 36. There is an early copy in MS. Cotton, Vespasian D. XVI, p. 62.

The Fifth Charter of King Henry III, which comprises No. XVI of this series, is dated in August, A.D. 1227, and was issued by Ralph Neville, Bishop of Chichester, the Chancellor. By this Charter[2] the king granted to the citizens various privileges in the unwarrened and disafforested "Warren of Staines", in the County of Middlesex. *[margin: Fifth Charter of Henry III.]*

On the twenty-seventh day of June, in the twenty-seventh year of his reign, A.D. 1243, the king granted a charter to the Weavers of London, not included in this series. The Latin text is printed in Mr. Riley's *Liber Custumarum*, p. 48. It is an Inspeximus and confirmation of the Charter originally granted to this Guild, or Society, by Henry II, and has been already referred to.

---

[1] Luffman, p. 45.   [2] Noorthouck, p. 43; Luffman, p. 48.

xviii INTRODUCTION.

<small>Queenhithe Charter of Henry III.</small>

The Charter No. XVII of this series, dated at Windsor in February, A.D. 1217, the thirty-first[1] year of the king, is an Inspeximus and confirmation of a covenant made between Richard, Earl of Cornwall, the king's brother, and John Gisors, Mayor of London, concerning the fee-farm of Queenhithe, in Thames Street, sold to the City as a freehold, at the annual rent of fifty pounds.

<small>Sixth Charter of Henry III.</small>

In June, A.D. 1253, King Henry III granted his Sixth Charter to the City of London (No. XVIII), under the following circumstances:—Richard, Earl of Cornwall, and the citizens had a quarrel[2] concerning the exchange of certain lands, which the Earl resented to such a degree that he accused the Mayor of remissness in not punishing the bakers for making defective bread. For this neglect the City's liberties were again seized, and a *Custos* set over the City, until the citizens compromised the matter by making a payment to the Earl of the sum of six hundred marks, and to the king five hundred, under colour of granting this Charter. Previous to the grant of this Charter, the citizens were obliged to wait on the king, at any of his residences in England, to present the Mayor; but this gave them the liberty, when the king was absent from London, to present their Chief Magistrate to the Barons of the Exchequer. It also gave to the Sheriffs of London seven pounds per annum, to be paid at the Exchequer on passing their accounts, in lieu of a piece of land, transferred to the Dean and Chapter of St. Paul's Cathedral.

<small>Charter of Remission by Henry III.</small>

The Seventh Charter, called the "Charter of Remission", granted to the citizens of London by King Henry III (No. XIX of the series), was acquired[3] in January, A.D. 1266, at the cost of twenty thousand marks, or £13,333 6s. 8d. By this means the citizens managed to recover the royal favour after the rebellion of the barons, and the consequent deprivation by Parliament, whereby it had been enacted that the City of London, for the part it had taken against the king,

---

[1] Noorthouck and Luffman are in error in ascribing this to the *twenty*-first year of Henry III.

[2] Noorthouck, p. 48; Luffman, p. 53.

[3] Luffman, p. 55; Noorthouck, p. 55.

should be divested of all its liberties, its posts and chains taken away, and its principal citizens imprisoned and left to the king's mercy.

On the 11th[1] of January, in the fiftieth year of his reign (A.D. 1266), King Henry III granted a charter to the City, not included in the series, whereby the citizens were empowered "to traffic with their commodities and merchandises wheresoever they please throughout his kingdom and dominions, as well by sea as by land, without interruption of him or his, as they see expedient, quit from all custom, toll, and paying; and may abide for their trading wheresoever they please in the same his kingdom, as in times past they were accustomed, until such time as it should be more fully ordered by his Council touching the state of the said city; as by the said letters patent, among other things, more fully appeareth."

The anonymous editor, J. E., in his text of the Great Charter of Charles I, which will be noticed in its proper chronological position, prints the English text of a charter dated 11th January in the same year, which is apparently of a similar nature.

On the 18th of April in this year the king issued a mandate enjoining inquiry by the Sheriff of Surrey as to the title to certain customs paid by the Vill of Southwark. The text of this, with the report of the inquisition held thereupon, is contained in Mr. Riley's *Liber Custumarum*, pp. 278, 279. Customs of the Vill of Southwark.

In March, A.D. 1268, the king granted his Eighth and last Charter, No. XX of the present collection, to the City. This[3] is not only a charter of remission, but of confirmation of all ancient privileges, except the choice of the City Magistrates, and the king selected the sheriffs out of six names put before him by the Mayor, who in turn was shortly afterwards discharged, and Prince Edward, in A.D. 1270, received the government of the City into his hands. Eighth Charter of Henry III.

The Cottonian MSS., Vespasian D. XVI. f. 72, Claudius D. II, f. 131*b*, contain the Latin text of a charter granted by

---

[1] Luffman, p. 56; Maitland, p. 98.   [2] P. 24.
[3] Luffman, p. 64; Noorthouck, p. 56.

King Henry III to the Widows of London, dated at Woodstock, 19th June, fifty-second year, A.D. 1268.

Miscellaneous Charters of Edward I.   Mr. Riley, in his *Liber Custumarum*, has printed several charters of King Edward I to the City, among which may be noticed the following:—

1. Writ[1] to the Mayor, etc., respecting crimes in the City, and the manner of their repression, pesage, etc. 28th November, 10th year, A.D. 1281. (*Lat.*)

2. Writ[2] relating to pesage, etc. 28th March, 10th year, A.D. 1282. (*Lat.*)

3. Writ[3] to the justices itinerant, enjoining further enquiry relating to pesage, etc. 10th June, 14th year, A.D. 1286. (*Lat.*)

4. Writ[4] enjoining the citizens of London to aid his son in the defence of the southern coasts. 15th March, 24th year, A.D. 1296. (*French.*)

5. Writ[5] ordering the sheriffs and aldermen to select a fit and proper person to sell the king's wool and hides beyond the seas. 24th May, 25th year, A.D. 1297. (*Lat.*)

6. Writ[6] ordering inquiry to be made as to the practice of fulling at mills without the City. 23rd January, 26th year, A.D. 1298. (*Lat.*)

7. An Inspeximus[7] of certain charters. 17th April, 27th year, A.D. 1299. (*Lat.*)

8. Letter[8] to the Commonalty of the City of London, naming a day for the perambulation of the Forest. 25th June, 27th year, A.D. 1299. (*Fr.*)

9. Writ[9] enacting the value of coins known as *Pollards* and *Crocards*. 25th November, 28th year, A.D. 1299. (*Fr.*)

10. Writ[10] commanding the citizens of London to send two burgesses to Parliament. 29th December, 28th year, A.D. 1299. (*Lat.*)

11. Writ[11] against the circulation of the *Pollards* and *Crocards*, and against withdrawal of provisions from the markets. 28th January, 28th year, A.D. 1300. (*Fr.*)

[1] P. 329.   [2] P. 330.   [3] P. 332.
[4] P. 72.   [5] P. 132.   [6] P. 127.
[7] P. 255-266, and see List of MSS. at end of the work, No. XXI.
[8] P. 197; translated into English, p. 571.
[9] P. 187; translated into English, p. 562.   [10] P. 136.
[11] P. 189; translated into English. p. 563.

12. Writ[1] for exchange of the *Pollards* and *Crocards* at the Tower. 29th January, 28th year, A.D. 1300. (*Fr.*)

13. Letter[2] to the Mayor and Sheriffs, enjoining the arrest of merchants and others guilty of enhancing provisions and other goods. 10th February, 28th year, A.D. 1300. (*Fr.*)

14. Writ[3] to the bailiff of the fair at St. Botulph's, Boston, co. Linc., confirmatory of the privileges of the City of London. 2nd June, 29th year, A.D. 1301. (*Lat.*)

15. Writ[4] to the Mayor and Sheriffs of London, in reference to the privileges of the wardens, moneyers, and officers of the king's Exchange, and their exemption from tallage. 14th October, 29th year, A.D. 1301. (*Lat.*)

16. Writ[5] to the stewards and bailiffs of the Duke of Britanny confirmatory of the privileges of the citizens of London at the fair of St. Botulph's. 13th July, 33rd year, A.D. 1305. (*Lat.*)

17. Writ[6] to the Mayor, etc., enjoining proclamation to be made of certain statutes in the Court of Hustings. 27th May, 34th year, A.D. 1306. (*Lat.*)

18. Writ[7] to the Sheriffs of London as to observance of the Statute of Winchester. 22 July, 34th year, A.D. 1306.(*Lat.*)

19. Another[8] upon the same subject. 7th December, 35th year, A.D. 1306. (*Lat.*)

No. XXI of this collection is the only charter granted by King Edward I. It is considered to be a charter of confirmation of the City privileges. The Charter,[9] according to Noorthouck, owes its origin to the amercement of those implicated in a riot which appears to have originated in the improper imprisonment of a clerk in the *Tun*, in Cornhill, contrary to the provisions of Magna Charta. Twenty-three thousand marks was paid by the citizens as the price of this Charter.

The citizens by this Charter[10] were empowered, in the

Edward I's Charter of Confirmation.

---
[1] P. 190; translated into English, p. 565.
[2] P. 191; translated into English, p. 566.
[3] P. 179.   [4] P. 183.   [5] P. 181.
[6] P. 214.   [7] P. 151.   [8] P. 155.
[9] *J. E.*, p. 27; certified to the Exchequer 28 May following. See MS. Cotton Appendix xl, ff. 4,*b*; 18: Vespasian D. XVI, f. 76,*b* (*Lat.*)
[10] Luffman, p. 67; *cf.* Riley *Lib. Cust.*, p. 266, where the date is 17 April, 27 Edward I, A.D. 1299.

absence of the king and the Barons of the Exchequer from London, to present their Mayor to the Constable of the Tower.

The Constitutions granted by Edward II. No. XXII of the series consists of the Constitution for the regular government of the City of London granted by King Edward II, in June, A.D. 1319. The editor of the *Liber Custumarum* has suggested, by a note on p. 273, that the true date of 8th June may have been the 18th June. It certainly happens that the king was at York both on the former and the latter day, as is shown by Mr. Hartshorne's *Itinerary of King Edward II*, published in the *Collectanea Archæologica*[1] of the British Archæological Association, but apart from the fact that the document which precedes this in the *Liber Custumarum* is dated on the 18th June, there is nothing to cause us to doubt the correctness of the Latin text, in which the earlier date of the two mentioned is attributed to this deed. Another passage tends to prove that the 8th of June is the correct date.[2]

The articles[3] were, in the seventh year of Richard II, A.D. 1384, confirmed by that king in Parliament, and added to the City Charters.

Miscellaneous Charters of Edward II. The *Liber Custumarum* contains the texts of several documents which are not included in this series, as not being of a general or constitutional nature. They may be examined by those who desire to study them in the following chronological order:—

1. Writ[4] to the bailiffs of John of Britanny, confirmatory of the Privileges of the Citizens of London at the fair of St. Botulph's. 22nd June, 1st year, A.D. 1308. (*Lat.*)

2. Letter[5] to the City authorities enjoining that the "Ordainers" shall make their Ordinances without molestation in the City of London. 29th May, 3rd year, A.D. 1310. (*Lat.*)

3. Writ[6] enjoining that proclamation shall be made of the said Ordinances in the City of London. 5th October, 5th year, A.D. 1311. (*Lat.*)

[1] Vol. i, p. 134.
[2] *Lib. Cust.*, p. 438, "dicto *octavo* die Junii," in an inspeximus of Edward III. So also in Vespasian D. XVI, ff. 73-77. (*Lat.*)
[3] Noorthouck, p. 64; Luffman, p. 78; *cf.* Cott. App. XI; and Bodl. MS. Barlow 15.
[4] P. 182.   [5] P. 202.   [6] P. 203.

INTRODUCTION. xxiii

4. Writ[1] commanding the Treasurer to make inquiry as to the justice of certain demands against the citizens in respect of a house in Milk Street. 22nd October, 6th year, A.D. 1312. (*Lat.*)

5. Writ[2] to the Mayor and Sheriffs of the City of London, enjoining that the statute "*De conjunctim Feoffatis*" shall be duly observed. 22nd January, 8th year, A.D. 1315. (*Lat.*)

6. Mandate[3] to the Mayor and Sheriffs of London against forestalling victuals, and enjoining the appointment of inspectors of the butchers' markets. 17th April, 8th year, A.D. 1315. (*Lat.*)

7. Writ[4] to the Royal Treasurer and Chamberlain in reference to the practice of calling to warranty in the City; and directing that inquiry shall be made for written evidence in reference thereto. 12th April, 9th year, A.D. 1316. (*Lat.*)

8, 9. Writs[5] enjoining observance of an article in the Statute of Gloucester, in London. 2nd and 12th May, 9th year, A.D. 1316. (*Lat.*)

10. Charter[6] confirmatory to the citizens of London, inspecting the Charter of Edward I, dated 17th April, 27th year, A.D. 1299, inspecting:—

    (*a.*) The First Charter of Henry III, dated 18th February, 11th year, A.D. 1227. [See No. XII, p. 21.]

    (*b.*) The Third Charter of Henry III, same date. [See No. XIV, p. 26.]

    (*c.*) The Fourth Charter of Henry III, dated 16th March, 11th year, A.D. 1227. [See No. XV, p. 28.]

    (*d.*) The Fifth Charter of Henry III, dated 15th August, 11th year, A.D. 1227. [See No. XVI, p. 30.]

    (*e.*) The Sixth Charter of Henry III, dated 12th June, 37th year, A.D. 1253. [See No. XVIII, p. 34.]

    (*f.*) Certain articles in a Charter of Henry III, dated 26th May,[7] 52nd year, A.D. 1268.

Dated 18th June, 12th year of Edward II, A.D. 1319. (*Lat.*)

---

[1] P. 137. [2] P. 212. [3] P. 679.
[4] P. 171. [5] Pp. 174, 178. [6] P. 255.
[7] For March, *Riley*.

INTRODUCTION.

11. Writ[1] to the Mayor and Sheriffs in behalf of the fishmongers. 18th August, 14th year, A.D. 1320. (*Lat.*)

12. Further writ[2] in behalf of the fishmongers of Fishwharf. 9th November, 14th year, A.D. 1320. (*Lat.*)

13. Writ[3] enjoining attendance on the Justices holding the Pleas of the Crown at the Iter, held at the Tower of London. 20th November, 12th year, A.D. 1320. (*Lat.*)

14. Writ[4] to the Justices Itinerant respecting the weavers of London. 12th December, 14th year, A.D. 1320. (*Lat.*)

15. Writ[5] to the Constable of the Tower enjoining that the citizens, in conformity with alleged usage, be allowed to essoin. 4th January, 14th year, A.D. 1321. (*Lat.*)

16. Writ[6] to the Justices Itinerant, enjoining further inquiry into the fishmongers' grievances. 1st February, 14th year, A.D. 1321. (*Lat.*)

17. Writ[7] to the Justices Itinerant respecting the cappers of London. 20th February, 14th year, A.D. 1321. (*Lat.*)

18. Another writ[8] enjoining inquiry as to the legality of the Fishmongers' Hallmote. 24th February, 14th year, A.D. 1321. (*Lat.*)

19. Writ[9] to the Justices Itinerant respecting a petition to the King from the bakers of London to be relieved from the payment for pesage imposed on them by the Mayor. 1st April, 14th year, A.D. 1321. (*Lat.*)

20. Second[10] writ to the like effect. 12th May, 14th year, A.D. 1321. (*Lat.*)

21. Royal[11] Pardon granted to the City for neglecting to keep watch on those who flee for sanctuary to the City churches. 3rd June, 14th year, A.D. 1321. (*Lat.*)

22. Writ[12] respecting extortion made upon the butchers of Eastcheap. 3rd July, 14th year, A.D. 1321. (*Lat.*)

23, 24. Writs[13] to the Justices Itinerant relating to the times of holding market on Cornhill. 15th and 30th July, 15th year, A.D. 1321. (*Lat.*)

---

[1] P. 388.
[2] P. 390.
[3] P. 285, etc.
[4] P. 419.
[5] P. 288.
[6] P. 395.
[7] P. 430.
[8] P. 397.
[9] Pp. 380, 605 (*Engl. Transl.*).
[10] P. 380.
[11] P. 346.
[12] P. 414.
[13] Pp. 426, 427.

No. XXIII is an important although brief Charter of King Edward II, exempting the citizens of London from levies of men for carrying on war out of the City, granted in December, A.D. 1321. According to Luffman,[1] "this Charter exempts the citizens from being ordered out of the City in arms in time of war or tumult, notwithstanding any precedent to the contrary. It is probable that by King Edward granting this Charter to the citizens, they were induced to present him with the sum of two thousand marks towards defraying the expenses of the war in Scotland."

Charter of Edward II exempting from levies.

At this time[2] the king had so far lost the respect of his subjects that the Queen, not long after, was denied admittance into Leeds Castle by Lord Badlesmere, and some of her retinue were killed. To punish this unjustifiable indignity, the king assembled some forces, chiefly Londoners, and after reducing the castle, granted the Charter above mentioned.

King Edward III's reign contributes five important charters of liberties to the City of London. Of these the first, No. XXIV. of this collection, is dated in March, A.D. 1327, and owes its origin to the king's gratitude for the assistance[3] rendered to him by the citizens against those whose conspiracies to deprive him of his just title are too well known to need even recapitulation here.

First Charter of Edward III.

This Charter[4] grants to the citizens many invaluable privileges. It constitutes the Mayor to be one of the judges for the trial of prisoners confined in Newgate for criminal offences committed in the City. It gives to the citizens a right to *infang-thef* and *outfang-thef*:—the first the right to try a robber taken within the City, and the latter a privilege of bringing a citizen apprehended for a felony committed in any part of the kingdom into the City, in order to his being tried there for his offence. It gives, also, a right to the citizens to the goods and chattels of such persons as are convicted of felonies within the City. A right of devising in mortmain is likewise allowed by this Charter, which is an alienation of lands and tenements to any guild, corporate body or fraternity, and their successors. It remitted one hundred pounds per annum

---

[1] P. 79.   [2] Noorthouck, p. 65.
[3] Noorthouck, p. 67.   [4] Luffman, p. 92.

extorted from the citizens for the fee-farm of the City of London and County of Middlesex. Foreign merchants, by this Charter, were obliged to sell their merchandises within forty days from their landing them in the City. The citizens were exempt thereby from the charge of such persons as took sanctuary in churches. It went to deprive the King's Marshal, Steward, and Clerk of the Household of the exercise of any authority in the City. It gave to the Mayor the office of Escheator of the City in perpetuity. It gave to the citizens the privilege of holding a "Pye Powder Court", a court where all differences arising in fairs are determined, in all places whereto they resorted. It exempts the citizens from tallages, except such as were borne by the subjects at large. It points out that the City liberties shall not be taken away for the offences of its magistrates. It forbids the king's purveyors from rating any sort of goods belonging to the citizens; and lastly, ordains that no market be kept within seven miles of the City of London.

Second Charter of Edward III. No. XXV, the Second Charter of this king, confers the Bailiwick of Southwark—then a vill, now a borough—upon the citizens.[1] It was granted on the same day as the previous Great Charter of Liberties.

Third Charter of Edward III. Edward III's Third Charter, No. XXVI of this collection, was granted in March, A.D. 1337, with a view to quieting[2] the apprehensions of the citizens of London, who were jealous of the encouragement given to foreigners. It declared[3] that the Privileges allowed to Merchant-Strangers should in no way affect the rights or liberties secured to the City by the Great Charter.

Miscellaneous Charters of Edward III. The *Liber Custumarum* contains the Latin text of a Charter[4] of this king, dated at Westminster, 26th of May, 15th year, A.D. 1341, reciting at length and "inspecting" (*a*) the confirmation charter[5] of his predecessor, King Edward II (No. XXII of this collection); and (*b*) other articles granted to the citizens on the same occasion.

Luffman gives the following notice of a charter of Edward III, not included in the following series:—

[1] Noorthouck, p. 67; Luffman, p. 96.   [2] Noorthouck, p. 68.
[3] Luffman, p. 99.
[4] P. 438. See also MS. Cott. App. XI, f. 7, *b*. (*Lat.*)
[5] Given at length in the *Lib. Cust.*, pp. 255-68.

"Henry III's Charter concerning the Mayor and Sheriffs, and also King Edward II's Articles for the better government of the City, which Charter and Articles being literally copied in this Charter of Edward III, and being to be found in their proper places, I shall therefore only add the confirming clause:—

"'Moreover, we, being willing to show more abundant favour to the citizens of the City aforesaid, have granted to them, for us and for our heirs, and by this Charter have confirmed that, although they or their predecessors, citizens of the City aforesaid, have not hitherto fully used, upon any emergent occasion, any of the liberties, acquittals, articles, or free customs, contained in the said charters and letters; yet the same citizens and their heirs and successors, citizens of that City, may henceforth fully enjoy those liberties, acquittals, articles, and free customs, and any of them, for ever.'

"Dated the third day of June, within the Tower of London, in the fifteenth year of the reign of Edward III [A.D. 1341]."[1]

Edward III's Fourth Charter, No. XXVII of this series, dated in June, A.D. 1354, shortly after the raging of pestilence which decimated the inhabitants of London, grants the privileges[2] of having maces of gold or silver carried before the Chief Magistrate. "This distinction," says Noorthouck, "becomes important when we find that all other cities and towns were, by a royal precept, expressly commanded not to use maces of any other metal than copper. It was on this occasion, probably, that the Chief Magistrate began to be called Lord Mayor, as corresponding with the increase of dignity added to his public appearance." The City made the king a substantial return by raising, at the expense of the Corporation, five-and-twenty men-at-arms and five hundred archers, who were sent to the king's army, then acting against the French.

Fourth Charter of Edward III.

No. XXVIII of this collection of charters is the Fifth Charter granted (in November, A.D. 1366) by King Edward III to the City of London. This Charter relates merely to the settling of disputes[3] between the citizens, so far as the choice of aldermen is concerned; which, it is to be observed, was at

Fifth Charter of Edward III.

---

[1] See also Maitland, p. 126 (*Lat.* and *Eng.*).
[2] Luffman, p. 102.   [3] *Ibid.*, p. 105.

this time an annual election on the Feast of St. Gregory the Pope (13th January).

This was followed, after an interval of a very few days, by the Sixth and last Charter of this King—December, A.D. 1366. By[1] this Charter, No. XXIX, merchant strangers are allowed to lodge with freemen only, and merchant strangers are prohibited from keeping houses and selling goods by retail. Noorthouck reproduces the English translation of a letter from Edward III to the Mayor and Sheriffs of London, in favour of the merchants and others of Flanders and Lombardy, forbidding any injury to be done to them, upon pain of severe penalty; dated in A.D. 1369.

Sixth Charter of Edward III.

The extracts from the Charter of King Richard II (No. XXX) belong to the year 1377. This is, in fact, the Parliamentary confirmation of the legislative power given to the City by a Charter of May 26th, 1341, which has been already dealt with at p. xxvi. The clauses dealing with restraint of "foreign merchants" and legislation by Act of Common Council are given at p. 70. Noorthouck[2] states that though the City had failed in obtaining a Parliamentary confirmation of the late king's charter relating to merchant strangers, yet the House of Commons now joined in application to the Throne for that purpose; the suit was granted, and this charter was obtained, which ordered that no foreigner should buy of or sell to any other foreigner within the City liberties. Soon afterwards the widows of citizens were by royal mandate exempted from the payment of tallages or contributions to the Government. This Charter,[3] thus made known to the citizens by proclamation of the Mayor, was esteemed of no small consequence towards establishing those rights and privileges of the citizens which had been so frequently and so unwarrantably violated by regal tyranny.

Charter of Richard II.

"The citizens," says Luffman,[4] "having petitioned Parliament for a confirmation of their charters, the said Parliament now inspected the Charters of Confirmation passed in the reigns of King Edward II and King Edward III, and by King Henry III, and also the Charter of Confirmation passed

---

[1] Luffman, p. 109. [2] P. 75.
[3] P. 114. See also *Appendix*. [4] P. 110.

in this reign. King Richard, by the consent of his Parliament, having recapitulated the aforesaid charters, concludes thus:—

"'We in truth grant and confirm all the ordinances abovesaid, and also all articles and other things in all the charters and letters abovesaid, as well ours as of our progenitors aforesaid, whatsoever be contained, rehearsed or opened, having freed them all and singular, at the instance and request of the commonalty of our realm of England in our present Parliament, for the greater quiet and peace between our laws to be nourished, and for the public good, by the assent of the prelates, lords, and peers, by us, being in the same Parliament, for us and our heirs, as much as in us lies, to the citizens of the said city of our special grace by the tenour of these present letters we grant and confirm as the charters and letters abovesaid plainly witnessed: giving and granting at the instance and request aforesaid, with the assent aforesaid, and also by this Charter confirming for us and our heirs aforesaid, to the citizens, their heirs and successors, citizens of the said City, all the franchises and free usages as wholly and fully to be restored, as they or their predecessors in the time of our progenitors more freely and fully had them, and although the said citizens or their predecessors, citizens of the same City, any of the franchises, quittances, grants, ordinances, articles, or free usages or other in the same charters or letters as is aforesaid might have misused: nevertheless the said citizens, their heirs and successors, citizens of the aforesaid City, all and singular the franchises, quittances, grants, ordinances, articles, free usages, and all manner of other things in those aforesaid charters and letters contained or not used, or also misused, and each of them, from henceforth fully and freely may enjoy and use without occasion or letting of us, or of our heirs, or of our justices, sheriffs or others our bailiffs or ministers whatsoever: any statutes or ordinances made, or any of our charters, or of our progenitors aforesaid in times past made and granted to the contrary notwithstanding.

"'Moreover, at the instance and request aforesaid, we will, and by this our Charter confirm, that all manner of wines in the aforesaid City to be sold, and also victuallers, as well fishmongers as others, dwelling in the City and [coming] to the said City from this time to come with victuals, shall be under the regulation and government of the Mayor and Aldermen of the said City, as they were used to be in ancient time.

"'Furthermore,[1] we order that the Mayor of the City from henceforth shall take no other oath than was taken by them in the time of King Edward III, our grandfather, [which] was used to [be] made at the Exchequer or other places, in any manner be compelled to do or make, any statutes or ordinances to the contrary notwithstanding.

"'Witness the worshipful Father William [Courtenay], etc. Given by our hand at Westminster, the twenty-sixth day of November, in the seventh year of our reign [A.D. 1383].'"

On the 8th of March, in the seventh year of this king, A.D. 1384, a letter was directed by Richard II to the Mayor and Commonalty of London, allowing, under certain conditions, the re-election of Aldermen at the expiration of their year of office. The Latin text is contained in Mr. Riley's edition of the *Liber Custumarum*.[2]

In the seventh year, also, of Richard II, 1384, in accordance with a petition from the Commons to the Crown for another confirmation of the liberties of the City of London, a charter was passed reciting, by way of "Inspeximus", the several charters of confirmation, and others passed in previous reigns, as also the Charter of Confirmation of the City liberties passed by the King himself in the first year of his reign.[3] This important concession[4] produced a proclamation[5] in April, which forms No. XXXI of this collection, issued by the joint authority of the King and Sir Nicholas Brembre, Lord Mayor, in which is contained an exposition or definition of the generally understood sense of the above-mentioned Parliamentary charter.

Proclamation.

The anonymous editor, "J. E.", prints, in his text of the

[1] Luffman's translation of this sentence is very much confused. Cf. Maitland, p. 144.   [2] P. 436.
[3] Probably that from which No. XXX of this series is an extract.
[4] Noorthouck, p. 80.
[5] Carefully preserved among the City Records, Liber H, folio 169, and translated into English by Noorthouck, see p. 80.

Great Charter[1] of King Charles II, portion of a charter of King Henry IV, dated on the 25th of May, in the first year of his reign, A.D. 1400. The following clause is contained in it:—"And[2] moreover, of our ample grace we have granted for us and our heirs, as much as is, to the same citizens, their heirs and successors, as aforesaid, that they shall have the custody, as well of the gates of Newgate and Ludgate, as all the other gates and posterns of the same city; and also the office of gathering of the tolls and customs in Cheap and Billingsgate and Smithfield, there rightfully to be taken and accustomed, and also the tronage, that is to say, the weighing of lead, wax, pepper, alum, madder, and other like wares, within the said City for ever; as by the said charters, amongst other things, more plainly may appear."

Charter of Henry IV.

In the *Liber Custumarum*[3] is the Latin text of a grant by Henry IV to the Mayor and Commonalty of London of power to arrest felons and malefactors in Southwark, and of waifs and estrays, and assay and assize of bread, wine, beer, etc. This bears date the 23rd day of July, in the seventh year, A.D. 1406.

Noorthouck gives a remarkable instance, under the year 1438, of the means whereby the freedom of the City was shown to be gained by anyone who tarried within the walls for a year and a day without challenge.[4] To this, students of our laws may refer with advantage.

In November, A.D. 1462, Edward IV granted his First Charter to the City of London. Of this important document, confirmatory of past charters and privileges, Noorthouck[5] and Luffman[6] write as follows:—"This Charter confirms the rights and liberties heretofore granted to the citizens by other charters, and also bestows on them the following privileges:— The Mayor, Recorder, and Aldermen past the chair are constituted Justices within the City in perpetuity; they are also appointed Justices of Oyer and Terminer, for the trying of persons charged with committing felonies within the City.

First Charter of Edward IV.

[1] See p. 40.   [2] Noorthouck, p. 86; Luffman, p. 115.   [3] P. 433.
[4] Cf. "Item si quis nativus quiete per unum annum et unum diem in aliqua villa privilegiata manserit, ita quod in eorum communiam, scilicet gyldam, tanquam civis receptus fuerit, eo ipso a villenagio liberabitur." *Glanvile*, v. 5.   [5] P. 100.   [6] P. 133.

xxxii INTRODUCTION.

The Mayor and Aldermen are exempted by this Charter from serving in foreign assizes or juries, and from the offices of assessor, collector of taxes, or overseer or comptroller of all public duties without the City. The grant of the Borough of Southwark, with its appurtenances, is confirmed, with the right of waifs, strays, and treasure-trove, also to the goods and chattels of felons convicted within the same. It gives to the citizens the privilege of holding a Fair annually within the same, together with a "Pye Powder Court", at the ancient fee-farm rent of ten pounds per annum.

Second Charter of Edward IV. Another Charter, No. XXXIII, was obtained from this king in August, A.D. 1463, which granted the tronage, weighing, and measuring of wool at Leadenhall, in consequence of which certain persons were appointed to regulate the prices under this grant.

Third Charter of Edward IV. The Third Charter of King Edward IV to the City, granted in June A.D. 1478, conferred the power of acquiring lands, rents, etc., in mortmain to the annual value of two hundred marks. It appears[1] by this Charter (No. XXXIV of the present series) that the citizens of London gave to the king the sum of one thousand nine hundred and twenty-three pounds nine shillings and eight pence for this liberty.

Fourth Charter of Edward IV. By the Charter, known as the Fourth of King Edward IV (No. XXXV of this collection), granted also in June, A.D. 1478, the citizens[2] hold the offices of package, portage, garbling,[3] gauging, wine-drawing and coroner within the City, to be held by them and their successors for ever—privileges which cost them the sum of seven thousand pounds, a considerable amount of money in the days of Edward IV.

Charter of Henry VII. Henry VIIth's Charter, from which the extracts comprising No. XXXVI are derived, cost the citizens[4] no less a sum than five thousand marks. It is a confirmation of the charter of King Edward III, dated the 4th of December, in the fiftieth year of his reign (No. XXIX); as also of one of Richard II, dated the 23rd of July, in the twentieth year of his reign, A.D. 1396. The principal objects of this deed were to

---

[1] Luffman, p. 136.   [2] Luffman, p. 147.
[3] For explanation of terms, see Index.
[4] Noorthouck, p. 111; Luffman, p. 151.

restrain the encroachments of the foreign merchants upon the franchises and customs of the citizens, and to regulate the qualifications of brokers.

In June, A.D. 1518, the Charter forming No. XXXVII of the following collection was granted by King Henry VIII, for removing the sessions[1] from St. Martin's-le-Grand, which, being out of the liberty of the City, was found to be inconvenient, and thought detrimental to the honour of the City, to the Guildhall. At this point in his work, Noorthouck puts on record some reflections *apropos* of the growth of trade, both in the City and immediately outside the limits, which are well worthy of perusal on the present occasion:— *First Charter of Henry VIII.*

"Everything in this world is continually fluctuating; Corporations had now answered the first end of their creation; their exclusive privileges sheltered and protected artisans against the feudal claims; but that tyranny was now no more, and the limitations of these seminaries of traders began, under the increase of traffic, to operate to their disadvantage. Strangers shut out of corporations settled round the walls, hence the trade without, being clear from municipal restrictions and burdens, grew formidable to the trade carried on within. This now began to be the case with London; foreigners to their jurisdiction, whether natives or not, were always regarded with a jealous antipathy,[2] and were frequently sufferers by tumultuous violence. A remarkable instance of this nature happened in 1517, when the usual pastimes on May-day were converted, by the London servants and apprentices, watermen, and other working people into an outrageous insurrection against foreigners. Preparatory to this commotion, one John Lincoln, a broker, engaged Dr. Bell, who was to preach a Spital sermon in Easter week, to inflame the people by a representation of the grievances the London artificers suffered from the strangers who settled round the City, and from the commerce carried on by foreign merchants. The heart-burnings thus excited discovering many indications

---

[1] Noorthouck, p. 115; Luffman, p. 153.

[2] "No stranger can be a member of any of those associations which are the guarantee of the freeman."—Kemble, *Saxons in England*, i, 158; cf. ii, 88.

of an approaching tumult, some riotous persons were committed to prison, and instructions given to the citizens to take care of their servants. Whether they were unable or unwilling to restrain their dependants is uncertain; but on May eve the tumult began. The crowd gathered from all parts; their companions were forcibly taken from prison, and then running to the out parts, they plundered and destroyed the houses and warehouses of strangers and foreigners until the dawn of day. About three o'clock the mob began to disperse, and then the magistrates seized and committed about 300 of them to several prisons. Cardinal Wolsey, who was then Minister, sent some forces into the City; but the disorder being over, nothing remained but to punish those who had been secured for the parts they had acted in it."

Second Charter of Henry VIII.

In April, A.D. 1531, the Second Charter[1] of King Henry VIII, forming No. XXXVIII of this series, was granted, whereby the office of Keeper of the Great Beam, or Common Balance of Weight, recently surrendered by Sir William Sidney, Knt. (who had held the office since June, A.D. 1521, in succession to William Stafford) to the king, was restored to the Corporation of London, which had originally enjoyed the privilege of keeping the weights and beams under a Charter of King Edward II, in A.D. 1319; a Charter of Henry IV, in A.D. 1400; and a confirmation of the same by Henry VIII in A.D. 1509.

Act of Common Council, A.D. 1538.

No. XXXIX of this collection reproduces the text of the Act of Common Council in A.D. 1538 to enforce the Statute 27 Hen. VIII, c. 18 (A.D. 1535-6), for preserving the navigation of the river Thames by encouraging the removal of sand, gravel, and so forth lying in any shelf within the river, without charge to the removers; ordering the erection of iron gates along the waterside where any watercourse passes into the river, and prohibiting the casting of rubbish or refuse into the water. We learn from Noorthouck,[2] writing in 1773, that this statute still remained then unrepealed, and by the complaints of the state of the river, unexecuted.

Charter of Edward VI.

In April, A.D. 1550, King Edward VI gave a Charter—which forms No. XL of the following collections—whereby the Manor of Southwark, and certain specified lands in Southwark and Surrey, were conveyed to the City.

[1] Luffman, p. 164; Noorthouck, p. 117.   [2] P. 118.

This Charter[1] grants to the citizens of London certain parcels of land in the borough of Southwark, and also in Saint George's Field, Newington, and Lambeth, in the county of Surrey. It appoints them Lord of the Manor of Southwark; it gives them certain yearly rents in the said borough, with all waifs and strays, treasure found, deodands, etc., in the parishes of St. Saviour, St. George, St. Thomas, and in Kent Street, Blackman Street, and Newington. It further gives them the privilege of assize of bread, wine, beer, ale, and victuals intended for sale in the said borough. Likewise a fair for three days, also execution of writs, and arrest of felons. It authorises the citizens to impanel the men of Southwark on juries in the City, and to choose two coroners for the same. It appoints the Lord Mayor for the time being Escheator and Clerk of the Market. The City justices are hereby empowered to act therein, and the inhabitants of the before-mentioned parishes and districts are declared subject to the City laws. The importance of this Charter, long and comprehensive as it is, cannot be overrated. Its clauses should be carefully studied by all who desire to understand the exact manner of incorporation of the neighbouring borough of Southwark with the great City.

It is followed by a proclamation, No. XLI of this collection, made by Queen Elizabeth in July 1580, "against new buildings in and about London." It appears[2] that the Lord Mayor made representations respecting the increase of buildings as an affair from which bad consequences were to be apprehended, not only to the City, but to the nation; and it was thought expedient to prevent the laying of new foundations. The actual inconvenience of close dwellings, crowded with inmates, cannot be denied, and the contagious disorders which had so frequently arisen and raged were a fatal proof of it; but, as the people had not then found out that opening the streets would enable them to live more healthily and commodiously, which would have been the best motive for extending the City, so the apprehensions expressed in the

Queen Elizabeth's Proclamation

[1] Luffman, who, in error, attributes this to A.D. 1557. See p. 195.
[2] Noorthouck, pp. 135, 136.

proclamation proceeded also from narrow views, and had the observance of the proclamation been stringently enforced, it would have led to great disturbance between the supply and demand of labour of all kinds. Noorthouck also lays stress upon the preservation of life by inoculation for small-pox, and the rebuilding of houses on a larger scale, as causes indirectly tending to the gradual growth of the metropolis about this period. London, vast as it is, still grows, and is probably three times as large now as it was in the sixteenth century. If we take the City to be a square, with a side of ten miles, this gives an area of a hundred square miles of houses. How long this increment may continue, cannot, perhaps, be foreseen, but it may safely be predicted that when the growth becomes injurious it will, like all other natural evils, correct itself.

First Charter of James I. The First Charter of King James I, granted in August, A.D. 1605 (No. XLII of this series), effectually secures to the citizens of London their right of metage of coals, grain, and salt; also of apples, pears, and other fruits, which had been, previous to this grant, frequently a matter in dispute between the lieutenant of the Tower of London and the said citizens.[1]

Second Charter of James I. By the Second Charter, No. XLIII of the collection, King James I confirmed to the City of London, in September 1608, all the ancient rights, privileges, and immunities of the citizens in the fullest manner; and the precincts of the Duke's Place, St. Bartholomew the Great and the Less in West Smithfield, Black-Friars, White-Friars, and Cold Harbour or Herberge, in Thames Street, are added to the City's jurisdiction.[2]

Third Charter of James I. By the Third Charter,[3] dated in September A.D. 1614 (No. XLIV), the king grants to the citizens of London the measuring and weighing of coals from Yenland to Staines Bridge, comprehending the whole port of London, allowing them eightpence per ton for such service, and forbids the unloading of coal vessels until notice be given to the mayor.

The First Charter of King Charles I, No. XLV of this col-

---

[1] Noorthouck, p. 146; Luffman, p. 206.
[2] Noorthouck, p. 147; Luffman, p. 225.
[3] Noorthouck, p. 150; Luffman, p. 238.

lection, is of an important and comprehensive character,[1] for it embraces in its full form a large number of the previous Charters. Luffmann remarks that by this Charter the citizens received a ratification in part of several former grants, among others, the restoration of all liberties and jurisdictions on the payment of the ancient fees. It authorises the three senior aldermen next the chair to be justices of the peace, previous to which time none but those who had filled the chair of mayoralty were eligible to that office. It entitles the mayor and aldermen before mentioned, and recorder, to hold sessions of the peace, to inquire concerning felonies, and take cognisance of all weights and measures, and also of all fines, forfeitures, etc., in the different courts of conservancy, and of all fines imposed by the Commissioners of Sewers, and of all houses, etc., erected on waste ground within the City or its liberties. It grants to the citizens Moorfields and West Smithfield, in free and common burgage, on consideration that the former shall not be built upon, but kept for common and public uses; and that in the latter a fair and market shall be held. It gives also to the citizens the office of garbling of all merchandising:—the guaging of wines and oils:—the keeping of the great balance or weight:—and the office of Common Crier in London and Southwark, with all fees annexed to the offices. It empowers the widows of freemen, so long as they shall continue the widows of such, to use and occupy manual arts and trades within the said City, and prohibits any market or markets from being held within seven miles of its boundaries. It authorises the mayor to nominate one justice of the peace for the county of Middlesex and another for the county of Surrey; obliges merchants in the City and its vicinity to take up their freedom; confirms the establishment of the Court of Requests stipulates the fees to be taken by the clerk of that court, and points out his duty; establishes a register-office of all pawns and sales; appoints the mayor and commonalty to execute the office of register of retailing brokers, with an allowance of fees according to the annexed schedule; it gives licence to the citizens to hang out signs from their

First Charter of Charles I.

[1] Noorthouck p. 162; Luffman. p. 299.

xxxviii   INTRODUCTION.

houses; and it finally grants Bethlem and St. Bartholomew's Hospitals to the mayor and citizens, and appoints how the estates belonging thereto shall be applied.[1]

Second Charter of Charles I.
No. XLVI of the collection is the Second Charter of King Charles I, granted in the year 1640, confirming the former rights, and adding a variety of other privileges of considerable importance. The ample schedule at the end of the deed is of great value as containing a large number of terms used in the trading community of the time, many of which are now disused or altered, and in some cases difficult of interpretation. (*See* Index.)

Confirmation of the Charter by Charles II.
The confirmation of the City Charters by Charles II, which forms No. XLVII of this series, dated in June, A.D. 1663, was granted by the king as an acknowledgment of the assistance afforded by the Corporation of London towards his restoration, and other instances of loyalty.

Proclamation by Charles II.
No. XLVIII, dated in September, A.D. 1666, the Proclamation regulating the rebuilding of houses in the City after the great Fire of London, is of considerable interest, and indirectly throws great light upon the condition of the City before that catastrophe took place. This event, although it occasioned great temporary distress, yet afforded an opportunity of restoring the City with greater uniformity, convenience, and, as far as the lights of the period went, with greater regard to sanitary and hygienic principles than could have been expected in a city of progressive growth. Thus the narrow, tortuous, and difficult passages, the dark, close, and ill-contrived houses, the projecting upper stories, primitive but objectionable customs, unwholesome air, and predisposition to epidemics, gave way to regular arrangement of streets, better arrangements of houses and rooms, improvements in drainage and ventilation, and sweeter air, which undoubtedly bore good fruit in many ways.

Confirmation of the Order of Common Council.
The next document, No. XLIX, is the confirmation, in May, A.D. 1667, of the order of Common Council for laying new foundations and widening the streets after the fire, the disputes occasioned by the obliteration of many of the boundaries of property having been adjusted without much difficulty,

[1] Luffmann, p. 209 *et seq.*

and the limits of the various claims satisfactorily ascertained by a Court of Judicature appointed for the purpose.

The next document of this series, No. L, dated in October, A.D. 1671, resulted from a statute[1] by which the sole power of regulating, maintaining, "pitching", and paving the streets of London, and of making and clearing the drains and sewers, was vested in the mayor, commonalty, and citizens, to be executed by the appointment of the Corporation, who were empowered to levy a tax on houses for the charges thereof.[2] By virtue of these powers, the Court of Common Council collected, into the act of which this document gives the text, the several customs, rules, and orders relating to paving and cleansing the streets, and preventing nuisances in passages, subject to the jurisdiction of the Court. *Act of Common Council for Paving and Scavengering.*

No. LI is the text of the act of Common Council of 20th June, A.D. 1678, made with a view of supplying the defects of former laws and regulations for the sale of woollen goods at Blackwell Hall,[3] Leaden Hall, and Welsh Hall. *Act of Common Council, 1678.*

Notwithstanding[4] the strict and solemn engagement of King Charles II, as expressed in his Charters, to preserve the City of London in her rights and privileges, "it happened, when the City, in the years 1682-3, opposed the measures of the Duke of York, who, it was believed, had threatened, if ever he came to the throne of these kingdoms, to enthral it into slavery, which all the subjects of the kingdoms are in to the Pope, that the king, intending to be revenged on the magistracy of London for thus opposing the succession of his brother to the Crown of England, issued out a commission to try the authors of the disorder which attended the election of sheriffs the last year, which disorder in the commission was called a "riotous and unlawful assembly", and aggravated as much as a thing of such little moment could admit of ; for fourteen aldermen and substantial citizens, the leaders of the "Whigs", were all tried and condemned in great fines. The

---

[1] Noorthouck, p. 235. [2] 22 and 23 Car. II, c. 17.
[3] At the south end of Basing-Hall Street on the west side, originally Basing's Haugh at the time of this Act, and thus named after its quondam owner, Thomas Bakewell.   [4] *J. E.*, p. 175.

subsequent conciliatory attitude of the citizens did not prevent a *quo warranto* from being brought by the king against the City, which was urged at length (given in full in *J. E.*, p. 177), and adjudged Mich. Term, 33 Car. II, in Banco Regis, Rot. 137. Sir Robert Sawyer, Knt., Attorney-General, against the Lord Mayor and Commonalty and Citizens of London."

The arguments were taken in the Court of King's Bench, Mich. Term, 1682; Hil. and Easter, 1683. In Trinity Term next the judges Jones, Raymond, and Withers pronounced the judgment of that Court:—"That the franchises of the City of London should be seized into the king's hands."

Noorthouck's[1] account of the matter is as follows:—"A writ of *quo warranto*, that is an inquiry into the validity of its charter, was issued against the City, which was argued at Hilary and Easter terms; and in Trinity term, June 12th, the Charter of the City was declared forfeited; but after sentence, the Attorney-General moved, contrary to custom, that judgment might not be recorded. A Common Council was called to deliberate on this exigency, when a total submission to his majesty, and a petition abject in the terms of it, imploring his princely compassion, were agreed on by a great majority, and carried to Windsor, on the 18th, by the Lord Mayor, at the head of a deputation from the Council. North, the lord-keeper, by the king's order, after reproaching them for not having been more early in their application, told them that his majesty would not reject their suit on the following conditions:—

1. "That no Lord Mayor, Sheriff, Recorder, Common-Serjeant, Town Clerk, or Coroner of the City of London, or Steward of the Borough of Southwark, shall be capable of, or admitted to, the exercise of their respective offices, before his Majesty shall have approved them under his sign manual."

2. "That, if his Majesty shall disapprove the choice of any person to be Lord Mayor, and signify the same under his sign manual to the Lord Mayor, or in default of a Lord Mayor, to the Recorder, or Senior Alderman; the Citizens shall within

[1] Page 253.

one week proceed to a new choice; and if his Majesty shall in like manner disapprove the second choice, his Majesty may, if he please, nominate a person to be Lord Mayor for the ensuing year."

3. "If his Majesty shall, in like manner, disapprove the persons chosen to be Sheriffs, or either of them, his Majesty may appoint persons to be Sheriffs for the ensuing year, by his commission, if he so please."

4. "That the Lord Mayor and Court of Aldermen may also, with the leave of his Majesty, displace any Alderman, Recorder, etc., *ut supra.*"

5. "Upon the election of an Alderman, if the Court of Aldermen shall judge and declare the person presented to be unfit, the ward shall choose again; and upon a disapproval of a second choice, the Court may appoint another in his room."

6. "The Justices of the Peace are to be by the King's Commission; and the settling of these matters to be left to his Majesty's Attorney and Solicitor-General, and Council learned in law."

He told them withal that the Attorney-General had received orders to enter upon judgment on the next Saturday, unless the Common Council prevented it by an assent to all these particulars.

On the return of the Lord Mayor and his attendants, a Common Council met to determine on the acceptance of these stipulations, and violent debates ensued on the question; the friends of liberty declared they would sacrifice all that was dear to them rather than yield to such vile, slavish conditions; nevertheless, the acceptance of them was at length carried by a majority of eighteen. Odious as these conditions were, which divested the citizens of the appointment of their magistrates, their most valuable privilege, the security of all the rest, they remained under them until the revolution. Some few Corporations, terrified by the proceedings against London, the tendency of which was too notorious to be mistaken, had surrendered their Charters before this judgment; but after that event, they almost all did so, to the great triumph of the Court. Considerable sums were exacted for restoring them; but the Crown retained the disposal of all offices of trust, and had now established a precedent which overturned the security of all national liberty. The other historians of London write in similar terms.

"Thus," says Luffman,[1] "were the citizens deprived of their liberty by an arbitrary monarch through the means of his tyrannical brother. However, this triumph was of very short duration. King Charles dying in February, A.D. 1685, the bigoted and gloomy-minded James succeeded to the Crown; his strides to establish the Roman Catholic religion were made with such precipitation as to become the means of his overthrow." But the king no sooner heard that it was the intention of the Prince of Orange, his son-in-law, to come to England, than he promised the citizens a restoration of their Charter, and finding things hastening to a crisis, sent the Lord Chancellor, "the bloody Jefferies", with the City Charters and some grants under the Great Seal for restoring the same, which he delivered to the Court of Custos and Assistants then sitting in the Council Chamber of the Guildhall, on the 6th of October, A.D. 1688.

Statute vacating the Judgment on the *Quo Warranto*.

No. LII represents the text of the Statute of 2 William and Mary, cap. 8, A.D. 1690, vacating the judgments on the *quo warranto* against the City of London, and confirming all the privileges of the Corporation. By this[2] national act every judgment given and recorded for seizing the franchises of the City was reversed and made void, and *vacates* entered on the Rolls, and it was thereby formally declared that the mayor, commonalty, and citizens of the City of London did remain a body politic by the name of Mayor and Commonalty of the City of London, and to have and enjoy all their rights and charters, and that all charters, letters patent, and so forth, concerning any of the liberties, lands, and tenements, rights, titles, etc., made since the said judgments by the late Kings Charles and James, were thereby declared void. Also the officers, companies, and Corporations were restored. This statute is the last confirmation of the rights and privileges of the citizens of London included in the present collection.

The next and last documents, No. LIII, for regulating elections and preserving the peace; No. LIV, the Charter of

[1] P. 344. [2] Noorthouck, p. 275; Maitland, p. 491.

King George II, constituting the aldermen of the City of London, *ex officio* Justices of the Peace; No. LV, Act regulating the nominations and election of sheriffs of the City of London and the County of Middlesex; and No. LVI, the Act of Common Council, passed in 1750, for licensing foreigners to work in the City of London, are sufficiently clear to everyone, and need no further notice on this occasion. As regards the last-mentioned document, it has been stated by many writers that numerous disputes arose regarding the employment of foreigners or non-freemen in the City, consequently a committee of aldermen and others was appointed to examine into the merits of the complaints on both sides between masters and journeymen freemen, and this Act is based upon the reports of that body.

[side note: Act of 11 Geo. I for regulating Elections, etc.]

Most of the originals of these Charters are in the possession of the Corporation, and the early ones are carefully preserved in the Town Clerk's office, under glass and in cases ingeniously contrived with a view to ventilation and prevention from handling. The originals of some, however, are, unfortunately, not known to exist.

The early numbers are written in a very elegant handwriting, and are remarkable for the beautiful condition of their seals. It has been stated in a tract of the Liberties of the City, attributed to Sir Henry Calthorpe, Knt., written in A.D. 1642 (p. 15), that the *signature* of King John is on one of the Charters of the 17th June, A.D., 1199 (see Nos. VII and VIII). This does not appear to be the case, as far as may be observed by inspection of the Charter itself, unless it be under the flap folded over the lower margin of the document. If the signature or mark of the king should be found to be there, it will be a very remarkable fact, for, notwithstanding a few isolated examples of actual handwriting or marks, such as the crosses asserted to have been made[1] by William the Conqueror and Henry I,[2] and the genuine signature of

---

[1] See Cotton Charter, viii, 15; Sir Frederic Madden *On Anglo-Saxon Charters*, in *Arch. Journ.*; Cotton MS. Vespasian F. III, folio 1; Musée des Archives Départmentales, Paris, Impr. Nat. 1878, pl. xviii, a large number of signatures and crosses, A.D. 1080.

[2] Vespasian F. III, folio 2.

Richard Tocliffe, Bishop of Winchester, A.D. 1185, among the Harley Charters (43, I, 38) in the British Museum, the earliest genuine handwriting of a king is probably that of Richard II, in the British Museum, Cotton MS., Vespasian, F. III, fol. 3; Egerton MS., 616, fol. 1; and the Stowe Collection, lately acquired from the Earl of Ashburnham by the trustees of the British Museum, containing a few lines of writing by Henry IV, when he was Earl of Derby, during the lifetime of Richard II.

Charters, according to Luffman, are the great bond of society, conferring liberty and security. Charters have been the means of raising the arts and sciences in this country to a degree of perfection almost unequalled on the face of the earth. Charters have been in an eminent degree the cause of that wonderful extension of commerce for which Britain stands unrivalled. Charters, finally, in this island at least, do not militate against the general good or favour oppressive monopoly—evils which some men have ascribed to them.

LIST OF CHARTERS AND DOCUMENTS.

	PAGE
I. The First Charter of William the Conqueror	1
II. Second Charter of William the Conqueror	2
III. Charter of Henry I	3
IV. Charter of Henry II	5
V. The First Charter of Richard I, 23 April, A.D. 1194	7
VI. The Second Charter of Richard I, 14 July, A.D. 1197	9
VII. The First Charter of King John, 17 June, A.D. 1199	11
VIII. Second Charter of King John, 17 June, A.D. 1199	13
IX. Third Charter of King John, 5 July, A.D. 1199	15
X. Fourth Charter of King John, 20 March, A.D. 1202	18
XI. Fifth Charter of King John, 9 May, A.D. 1215	19
XII. First Charter of Henry III, 18 Feb., A.D. 1227	21
XIII. Second Charter of Henry III, 18 Feb., A.D. 1227	24
XIV. Third Charter of Henry III, 18 Feb., A.D. 1227	26
XV. Fourth Charter of Henry III, 16 March, A.D. 1227	28
XVI. Fifth Charter of Henry III, 18 Aug., A.D. 1227	30
XVII. Charter of Henry III, confirming the Fee-Farm of Queenhithe to the Corporation of London, 26 Feb., A.D. 1247	32
XVIII. Sixth Charter of Henry III, 12 June, A.D. 1253	34
XIX. Charter of Remission granted to the Citizens by Henry III, 10 Jan., A.D. 1266	36
XX. Eighth Charter of Henry III, 26 March, A.D. 1268	38
XXI. Charter of Confirmation of the City Privileges by Edward I, 28 May, A.D. 1298	43

XXII. Constitutions for the Regular Government of the City, granted by Edward II, for the Citizens of London, concerning New Articles then made to be observed, 8 June, A.D. 1319 45

XXIII. Charter of Edward II, exempting the Citizens of London from Levies of Men for carrying on War out of the City, 12 Dec., A.D. 1321 51

XXIV. First Charter of Edward III, granted by consent of Parliament, 6 March, A.D. 1327 52

XXV. Second Charter of Edward III, granting the Bailiwick of Southwark to the Citizens of London, 6 March, A.D. 1327 59

XXVI. Third Charter of Edward III, 26 March, A.D. 1337 . 61

XXVII. Fourth Charter of Edward III, 10 June, A.D. 1354 . 63

XXVIII. Fifth Charter of Edward III, 12 Nov., A.D. 1376 . 65

XXIX. Sixth Charter of Edward III, 4 Dec., A.D. 1376 . . 67

XXX. Charter of Richard II . . 70

XXXI. A Proclamation made in the Mayoralty of Nicholas Brembre, Knight, Mayor, on Friday after the Feast of the B. V. Mary, and in the 7th year of Richard II, concerning the Liberties lately granted to the Citizens of London by the Lord King in his Parliament; and also concerning certain ancient Liberties renewed by the Lord King, and newly confirmed to the said citizens by his Royal Charter, 11 Sept., A.D. 1383 . . 71

XXXII. First Charter of Edward IV, 9 Nov., A.D. 1462 . . 74

XXXIII. Second Charter of Edward IV, 27 Aug., A.D. 1463 . 85

XXXIV. Third Charter of Edward IV, 20 June, A.D. 1478 . 87

XXXV. Fourth Charter of Edward IV, 20 June, A.D. 1478 . 90

XXXVI. Regulations concerning Strangers Buying and Selling within the City. From Henry VII's Charter, 22 Aug., A.D. 1485 94

XXXVII. Charter of Henry VIII, for removing the Sessions from St. Martin's-le-Grand to the Guildhall, 16 June, A.D. 1518 97

XXXVIII. Charter of Henry VIII, restoring the Office of Keeper of the Great Beam or Common Balance of Weight to the Corporation of London, 13 April, A.D. 1531 . 99

XXXIX. Act of Common Council in A.D. 1538, to enforce the Statute 27 Henry VIII, c. 18, for preserving the Navigation of the River Thames . . . 106

XL. Charter of King Edward VI, granting the Manor of Southwark to the City of London, 23 April, A.D. 1550 110

XLI. Proclamation of Queen Elizabeth against New Buildings in and about London, 7 July, A.D. 1580 . . 128

XLII. The First Charter of King James I, 20 Aug., A.D. 1605 132

XLIII. The Second Chapter of King James I, 20 Sept., A.D. 1608 139

XLIV. The Third Charter of King James I, 15 Sept., A.D. 1614 151

XLV. The First Charter of King Charles I, 18 Oct., A.D. 1638 159

XLVI. The Second Charter of King Charles I, 5 Sept., A.D. 1640 201

XLVII. The Confirmation Charter of King Charles II, 24 June, A.D. 1663 221

XLVIII. Proclamation issued by King Charles II to Prohibit the Rebuilding of Houses after the Great Fire of London, without conforming to the General Regulations therein premised, 13 Sept., A.D. 1666 224

XLIX. Confirmation of the Order of Common Council, for the Laying new Foundations, and for Widening the Streets of London, after the Great Fire, 8 May, A.D. 1667 . 231

L. Act of Common Council, for Paving, Cleansing, and for preventing Nuisances in the Streets of London and the Liberties thereof, 27 Oct., A.D. 1671 . . . 235

LI. Act of Common Council, for regulating the Markets for Woollen Goods at Blackwell Hall, Leaden Hall, and Welch Hall 251

LII. The Statute 2 W. & M. c. 8, vacating the Judgments on the Quo Warranto, against the City of London, and confirming all the Privileges of the Corporation, A.D. 1690 266

LIII. The Act 11 George I, c. 18, for regulating Elections within the City of London, and for preserving the Peace, good Order, and Government, A.D. 1725 . . 275

LIV. Charter of George II, constituting all the Aldermen of the City of London Justices of the Peace, 25 Aug., A D. 1741 290

LV. An Act for repealing all former Acts, Orders, and Ordinances, touching the Nomination and Election of Sheriffs of the City of London and County of Middlesex, and for regulating and enforcing such Nominations and Elections for the future, 7 April, A.D. 1748. . 295

LVI. Substance of the Act of Common Council for licensing Foreigners to Work in the City of London, 22 Nov., A.D. 1750 305

The Historical Charters

AND

CONSTITUTIONAL DOCUMENTS

OF THE

CITY OF LONDON.

No. I.

The First Charter of William the Conqueror.

WILLIAM the king friendly salutes William the bishop, and Godfrey the portreve, and all the burgesses within London, both French and English. And I declare, that I grant you to be all law-worthy, as you were in the days of king Edward; and I grant that every child shall be his father's heir, after his father's days; and I will not suffer any person to do you wrong. God keep you.

William the Norman, Bishop of London, A.D. 1051-1075.

No. II.

Second Charter of William the Conqueror.

WILLIAM the king friendly salutes William the bishop, and Swegn the sheriff, and all my thanes in Essex; whom I hereby acquaint, that I have granted to Deorman, my man, the hide of land at Gyddesdunc, of which he was deprived, and I will not suffer either the French or the English to hurt him in anything.

No. III.

Charter of Henry I.

HENRY, by the grace of God, king of England, to the archbishop of Canterbury, and to the bishops and abbots, earls and barons, justices and sheriffs, and to all his faithful subjects of England, French and English, greeting.

Know ye, that I have granted to my citizens of London, to hold Middlesex to farm for three hundred pounds, upon accompt to them and their heirs; so that the said citizens shall place as sheriff whom they will of themselves; and shall place whomsoever, or such a one as they will of themselves, for keeping of the pleas of the crown, and of the pleadings of the same, and none other shall be justice over the same men of London; and the citizens of London shall not plead without the walls of London for any plea. And be they free from scot and lot and danegeld, and of all murder; and none of them shall wage battle. And if any one of the citizens shall be impleaded concerning the pleas of the crown, the man of London shall discharge himself by his oath, which shall be adjudged within the city; and none shall lodge within the walls, neither of my household, nor any other, nor lodging delivered by force.

And all the men of London shall be quit and free, and all their goods, throughout England, and the ports of the sea, of and from all toll and passage and lestage, and all other customs; and the churches and barons and citizens shall and may peaceably and quietly have and hold their sokes with all their customs; so that the strangers that shall be lodged in the sokes shall give custom to none but to him to whom the soke appertains, or to his officer, whom he shall there put: And a man of London shall not be adjudged in amerciaments of money but of one hundred shillings (I speak of the pleas which appertain to money); and further there shall be no more miskenning in the hustings, nor in the folkmote, nor in any other pleas within the city; and the hustings may sit once in a week, that is to say, on Monday: And I will cause my citizens to have their lands, promises, bonds and debts, within the city and without; and I will do them right by the law of the city, of the lands of which they shall complain to me:

And if any shall take toll or custom of any citizen of London, the citizens of London in the city shall take of the borough or town, where toll or custom was so taken, so much as the man of London gave for toll, and as he received damage thereby; And all debtors, which do owe debts to the citizens of London, shall pay them in London, or else discharge themselves in London, that they owe none; but, if they will not pay the same, neither come to clear themselves that they owe none, the citizens of London, to whom the debts shall be due, may take their goods in the city of London, of the borough or town, or of the county wherein he remains who shall owe the debt: And the citizens of London may have their chaces to hunt, as well and fully as their ancestors have had, that is to say, in Chiltre, and in Middlesex and Surrey.

William Giffard, Bishop of Winchester, A.D. 1100-1129.

Witness the bishop of Winchester, and Robert son of Richier, and Hugh Bygot, and Alured of Toteneys, and William of Alba-spina and Hubert the king's Chamberlain, and William de Montfichet, and Hangulf de Taney, and John Bellet, and Robert son of Siward. At Westminster.

No. IV.

Charter of Henry II.

HENRY, king of England, duke of Normandy and Aquitaine, and earl of Anjou; to all archbishops bishops, abbots, earls, barons, justices, sheriffs, ministers, and all his faithful subjects, French and English, of all England, greeting.

Know ye, that I have granted to my citizens of London, that none of them plead without the walls of the city of London, upon any pleas, except only pleas of foreign tenures (my moneyers and officers excepted). Also I grant to them acquittal of murder within the city and portsoken thereof: And that none of them shall wage battle: And of the pleas of the crown they may discharge themselves, according to the old usage of the city. No man shall take lodging by force, or by delivery of the marshal.

And also I have granted to them, that all the citizens of London shall be quit from toll and lastage, throughout all England, and the ports of the sea; and that none shall be adjudged for amerciaments of money, but according to the law of the city, which they had in the time of king Henry my grandfather: And that there shall be no miskenning in any plea within the city: and that the hustings shall be kept once a week; and they justly have their lands and tenures and premises, and all their debts, whosoever do owe them: And that right be done to them, according to the custom of the city, of all their lands and tenures which be in the city, and of all their debts, which were lent at London.

Also I do grant to them, that they may have their huntings wheresoever they had the same in the time of king Henry my grandfather. And if any in all England shall take any custom or toll of or from the men of London, after he shall fail of right the sheriff of London may take goods thereof at London.

Furthermore also, for the advancement of the said city, I have granted to them, that they shall be free and quit of bridtoll, childwite, jeresgive, and scotale; so as the sheriff of London, or any other bailiff, may take no scotale.

These aforesaid customs I do grant unto them, and all their liberties and free customs which they had in the time of Henry my grandfather, wheresoever they had them more, better, and freely. Wherefore I will and steadfastly command that they and their heirs may have and hold all these things aforesaid, by inheritance, of me and my heirs.

Theobald, A.D. 1138-1161.
Philip, A.D. 1141-1163.
Rich. de Belmeis, Bp. London, A.D. 1152-1162.

Witness the archbishop of Canterbury, Richard bishop of London, Philip bishop of Bayeux, Arnulph bishop of Lisieux, Thomas the chancellor, Richard de Newburgh, R. de St. Walery, R. de Warren, Walkeline Maminot, Richard de Luci, Guarine son of Gerold, Manasser Biset, Goceline de Balliol. At Westminster.

No. V.

The First Charter of Richard I.

23 April, a.d. 1194.

RICHARD, by the grace of God, king of England, duke of Normandy, and earl of Anjou; To his archbishops, bishops, abbots, earls, barons, justices, sheriffs, ministers, and all others his faithful French and English people, greeting.

Know ye, that we have granted to our citizens of London, that none of them may plead without the walls of the city of London, for any pleas, saving pleas of foreign tenures, except our moneyers and ministers: Also we have granted to them acquittal of murder within the city, and in portsoken; and that none of them may wage battle; and that they may discharge themselves of pleas belonging to the crown, according to the ancient custom of the city; and that none may take any lodgings within the walls of the city by force, or by delivery of the marshal.

This also we have granted to them: that all the citizens of London be free from toll and lestage, throughout all England and the sea-ports; and that none be adjudged of amerciaments of money, but according to the law of the city, which they had in the time of king Henry, grandfather to Henry our father; and that there be no miskenning in any place within the city; and that the hustings be kept only once a week; and they justly have all their lands and tenures and promises, and all other their debts, whosoever do owe them to them; and that right be done to them, according to the custom of the city, of all their lands and tenures, which they have within the city; and of all their debts which shall be lent at London, and of promises there made: The pleas shall be holden at London; and, if any in all England shall take toll or custom of the men of London, after he shall fail of right the sheriff of London may take goods thereof at London.

Also we have granted to them, that they may have their huntings wheresoever they had the same in the time of king Henry, grandfather to Henry our father. Furthermore also, for the advancement of the city, we have granted to them, that they all be acquit of all bridtoll, childwite, jeresgive, and scotale; so that no sheriff of London, or any other bailiff, shall make any scotale. The said customs we do grant to them, and all other liberties and free customs which they had in the time of king Henry, grandfather unto Henry our father, when as they more better and freely had the same. Wherefore we will and steadfastly command, that they and their heirs have and hold all their things aforesaid of us and our heirs.

> Witness; Hubert, archbishop of Canterbury; Richard, bishop of London; Hugh, bishop of Durham; Gilbert, bishop of Rochester; Hugh, bishop of Lincoln; Rannulph, earl of Chester; Richard, earl of Clare; Will. Marshall, Rog. Bigot, Geoffrey son of Peter; Hugh Bardolfe, William Briwere, and William de Warenne. Given by the hand of William, bishop of Ely, our chancellor, at Winchester, the twenty-third day of April, in the fifth year of our reign.

W. Longchamp.

No. VI.

The Second Charter of Richard I.

14 July, a.d. 1197.

RICHARD, by the grace of God, king of England, duke of Normandy, and earl of Anjou; To his archbishops, bishops, abbots, earls, barons, justices, sheriffs, stewards, castle-keepers, justices, constables, bailiffs, ministers, and all his faithful subjects, greeting.

Know ye all that we, for the health of our soul, and for the soul's health of our father, and all our ancestors' souls; and also for the common weal of our city of London, and of all our realm, have granted and steadfastly commanded, that all wears that are in the Thames be removed, wheresoever they shall be within the Thames: Also we have quit-claimed all that which the keeper of our Tower of London was wont yearly to receive of the said wears. Wherefore we will and steadfastly command, that no keeper of the said Tower, at any time hereafter, shall exact any thing of any one, neither molest nor burden, nor any demand make of any person, by reason of the said wears. For it is manifest to us, and by our right reverend father, Hubert, archbishop of Canterbury, and other our faithful subjects, it is sufficiently given us to understand, that great detriment and discommodity hath grown to our said city of London, and also to the whole realm, by occasion of the said wears. Which thing, to the intent it may continue

Wears in the Thames to be removed.

Hubert Walter.

for ever firm and stable, we do fortify by the inscription of this present page, and the putting to of our seal:

> These being witnesses. Hubert, archbishop of Canterbury; John of Worcester, Hugh of Coventry, bishops; John, earl of Moreton, Ralph, earl of Chester, Robert, earl of Leicester, William, earl of Arundel, earl William Marshall, William of St. Mary's Church, Peter son of Herbert, Matthew his brother, Simon de Kyma, Seher de Quincy. Given by the hand of Eustace, dean of Salisbury, vice-chancellor, at the isle of Andely, on the fourteenth day of July, in the eighth year of our reign.

No. VII.

The First Charter of King John.

17 June, a.d. 1199.

JOHN, by the grace of God, king of England, lord of Ireland, duke of Normandy, Aquitaine, and earl of Anjou; to all archbishops, bishops, abbots, earls, barons, justices, sheriffs, ministers, and all his majesty's faithful subjects, French and English, greeting.

Know ye, that we have granted to our citizens of London, that none of them shall plead without the walls of the city of London, any pleas, saving the pleas of foreign tenures, our moneyers and ministers excepted: Also we have granted to them acquittal of murder, within the city and portsoken; and none of them shall wage battle; and of the pleas belonging to the crown they may discharge themselves according to the antient custom of the city; and that within the walls of the city or portsoken, no man shall take lodging by force, or delivery of the marshal: And also we have granted to them, that all the citizens of London shall be quit from toll or lastage, and every other custom throughout all our lands, on this side and beyond the seas: And that none shall be adjudged for amerciaments of money but according to the law of the city, which they had in the time of king Henry, grandfather to Henry our father: And that there shall be no miskenning in any plea in the city: And that the hustings shall be kept once in every week; and they justly have their lands, and tenures, and promises, and all other debts, whosoever owe them: And that right be holden to them of their lands and tenures, which be within the city, according to the custom of the said city; and all of their debts which shall be lent at London; and that pleas of all promises there made be holden at London; and if any, in any of our lands on this side or beyond the seas, shall take any toll or any other custom from the men of London, after that he shall fail of right, may take goods therefore at London. And we do grant unto them, that they may have their huntings, wheresoever they had the same in time of king Henry, grandfather to our father.

Furthermore, for the advancement of the said city, we have granted unto them, that they shall be free and quit of all bridtoll and childwite, and of jeresgive and scotale, so as neither the sheriff of London, nor any other bailiff, may make any scotale. These aforesaid customs we do grant; and all other liberties and free customs, which they had in the time of king Henry, grandfather of Henry our father, when as more freely and better they had the same. Wherefore we will and steadfastly command, that they and their heirs may have and hold all these things aforesaid hereditarily and wholly of us and our heirs.

> Witness Hubert, archbishop of Canterbury, our chancellor; William of London, Eustace of Ely, Godfrey of Winchester, Gilbert of Rochester, bishops; Geoffrey son of Peter, earl of Essex; William Marshal, earl of Pembroke; Hameline, earl of Warren; Richard, earl of Clare; earl Roger de Bigot; William, earl of Arundel; William de Braose; Robert son of Roger, Hugh Bard[olf], William Briew[er], William de Warren, Stephen de Turneham, Simon de Pateshille: Given by the hands of Hubert, archbishop of Canterbury, our chancellor, at Shoreham, the seventeenth day of June, in the first year of our reign.

No. VIII.

Second Charter of King John.

17 June, a.d. 1199.

JOHN, by the grace of God, king of England, lord of Ireland, duke of Normandy and Aquitaine, and earl of Anjou; to his archbishops, bishops, abbots, earls, barons, justices, sheriffs, stewards, castle-keepers, constables, bailiffs, ministers, and all his faithful subjects, greeting.

Know ye all, that we for our soul's health, and for the soul's health of Henry our father, and all our predecessors; and also for the common weal of our city of London, and all our realm; have granted and steadfastly commanded, that all the wears which are in the Thames or in the Medway [Wears to be removed.] be amoved, wheresoever they shall be within the Thames and Medway; and that no wears from henceforth be put any where in the Thames or Medway, upon forfeiture of ten pounds sterling; also we have clearly quit-claimed all that which the keepers of the Tower of London were wont yearly to receive of the said wears: wherefore we will and steadfastly command, that no keeper of the said Tower, at any time hereafter, exact any thing from any body, nor trouble or molest any person, by reason of the said wears; for it is sufficiently manifest to us, by the right reverend Hubert, archbishop of Canterbury, and other our faithful subjects, it is given us sufficiently to understand, that very great detriment and discommodity hath grown to our said city of London, and also to our realm, by occasion of these wears; which to the intent it may continue both firm and stable for ever, we do fortify the same by inscription of this present page, and putting to our seal:

These being witnesses, William of London, Eustace of Ely, Godfrey of Winchester, bishops; Geoffrey son of Peter, earl of Essex; William Marshall, earl of Pembroke; H. earl of Warren; earl Roger le Bigot; Richard, earl of Clare; William de Braose; Robert son of Roger, Hugh Bard[olf], William Briewerre, Stephen de Turneham, William de Warren, Simon Pateshill: Given by the hands of Hubert, archbishop of Canterbury, our chancellor, at Shoreham, the seventeenth day of June, in the first year of our reign.

No. IX.

Third Charter of King John.

5 July, a.d. 1199.

JOHN, by the grace of God, king of England, lord of Ireland, duke of Normandy and Aquitaine, and earl of Anjou; to his archbishops, bishops, abbots, earls, barons, justices, sheriffs, rulers, and to all his bailiffs and loving subjects.

Know ye, that we have granted, and by this our present writing confirmed, to our citizens of London, the sheriffwicks of London and Middlesex, with all the customs and things to the sheriffwick belonging, within the city and without, by land and by water, to have and to hold, to them and their heirs, of us and our heirs, paying therefore three hundred pounds of blank sterling money, at two terms in the year; that is to say, at the Easter exchequer, one hundred and fifty pounds; and at the Michaelmas exchequer, one hundred and fifty pounds; saving to the citizens of London all their liberties and free customs. *Sheriffwicks of London and Middlesex granted.*

And further, we have granted to the citizens of London, that they amongst themselves make sheriffs whom they will; and may amove them when they will; and those whom they make sheriffs, they shall present to our justices of our exchequer, of these things which to the said sheriffwick appertain, whereof they ought to answer us; and unless they shall sufficiently answer and satisfy, the citizens may answer and satisfy us the amerciaments and farm, saving to the said citizens their liberties as is aforesaid; and saving to the said sheriffs the same liberties which other citizens have: so that, if they which shall be appointed sheriffs for the time being, shall commit any offence, whereby they ought to incur any amerciament of money, they shall not be condemned for any more than to the amerciament of twenty pounds, and that without the damage of other citizens, if the sheriffs be not sufficient for the payment of their amerciaments: but, if they do any offence, whereby they ought to incur the loss of their lives or members, they shall be adjudged, as they ought to be, according to the law of the city; and of these things, which to the said sheriffs belong, the sheriffs shall answer before our justices at our exchequer, saving to the said sheriffs the liberties which other citizens of London have.

Also this grant and confirmation we have made to the citizens of London for the amendment of the said city, and because it was in ancient times farmed for three hundred pounds: wherefore we will and steadfastly command, that the citizens of London and their heirs may have and hold the sheriffwick of London and Middlesex, with all things to the said sheriffwick belonging, of us and our heirs, to possess and enjoy hereditarily, freely and quietly, honourably and wholly, by fee-farm of three hundred pounds; and we forbid that none presume to do any damage, impediment or diminishment to the citizens of London of these things, which to the said sheriffwick do or were accustomed to appertain: Also we will and command, that if we or our heirs, or any of our justices, shall give or grant to any person any of those things which to the farm of the sheriffwick appertain, the same shall be accounted to the citizens of London, in the acquittal of the said farm at our exchequer.

Witness Eustace of Ely, Savaric of Bath, bishops; William Marshall, earl of Pembroke; Randulph, earl of Chester; William, earl of Arundel; Robert, son of Walter; William de Albeniaco: Given by the hand of Hubert, archbishop of Canterbury, our chancellor, at Bonneville-sur-Touque [in Normandy], the fifth day of July, in the first year of our reign.

No. X.

Fourth Charter of King John.

20 March, a.d. 1202.

JOHN, by the grace of God, king of England, lord of Ireland, duke of Normandy and Aquitaine, and earl of Anjou; To his archbishops, bishops, abbots, earls, barons, justices, sheriffs, and to all his bailiffs and faithful subjects, greeting.

Know ye, that we, at the request of our mayor and citizens of London, have granted, and by this our present writing confirmed, that the guild of weavers shall not from henceforth be in the city of London, neither shall be at all maintained: But, because we have been accustomed yearly to receive eighteen marks in money, every year, of the said guild, our said citizens shall pay unto us and our heirs twenty marks in money, for a gift, at the feast of St. Michael, at our exchequer.

Witness Hubert, archbishop of Canterbury; Eustace, of Ely; William, of Avranches, bishops; Hugh de Gournai; Robert de Harcourt; Thomas Basset; Peter de Stoke; R. de Ryuuers: Given by the hands of Hubert, archbishop of Canterbury, at Gournay [in Normandy], the twentieth day of March, in the third year of our reign.

No. XI.

Fifth Charter of King John.

9 MAY, A.D. 1215.

JOHN, by the grace of God, king of England, duke of Normandy, Aquitaine, and earl of Anjou; to his archbishops, bishops, abbots, earls, barons, justices, sheriffs, rulers, and to all his faithful subjects, greeting.

Know ye, that we have granted, and by this our present writing confirmed, to our barons of our city of London, that they may choose to themselves every year a mayor, who to us may be faithful, discreet, and fit for government of the city, so as, when he shall be chosen, to be presented unto us, or our justice (if we shall not be present); and he shall swear to be faithful to us; and that it shall be lawful to them, at the end of the year, to amove him, and substitute another, if they will, or the same to retain, so as he be presented unto us, or our justice, if we shall not be present. We have granted to the same our barons, and by this our present charter confirmed, that they well and in peace, freely, quietly, and wholly, have all their liberties, which hitherto they have used, as well in the city of London as without, and as well by water as by land, and in all other places, saving to us our chamberlainship: Wherefore we will and strictly command, that our aforesaid barons of our aforesaid city of London may choose unto themselves a mayor of themselves, in manner

Citizens may choose their mayor.

and form aforesaid; and that they may have all the aforesaid liberties well and in peace, wholly and fully, with all things to the same liberties appertaining, as is aforesaid.

> Witness, the Lords, Peter de Rupibus, bishop of Winchester; Walter de Gray, bishop of Worcester; William de Cornhull, bishop of Coventry; William Brigwerre; Peter, son of Herbert; Geoffrey de Lucy; John, son of Hugh: Given by the hands of Master Richard de Mariscis, our chancellor, at the New Temple, London, the ninth day of May, in the sixteenth year of our reign.

No. XII.

First Charter of Henry III.

18 February, a.d. 1227.

HENRY, by the grace of God, king of England, lord of Ireland, duke of Normandy and Aquitaine, earl of Anjou; to his archbishops, bishops, abbots, earls, barons, justices, sheriffs, rulers, and to all his faithful subjects, greeting.

Know ye, that we have granted, and by these presents do grant and confirm, unto the citizens of London, the sheriffwick of London and Middlesex, with all the customs and things to the same sheriffwick belonging, within the city and without, by land and by water, to have and to hold, to them and to their heirs, of us and our heirs, paying therefore yearly to us and our heirs, three hundred pounds of blank money sterling, at two times of the year; that is to say, at the Easter exchequer, one hundred and fifty pounds; and at Michaelmas exchequer, one hundred and fifty pounds; saving to the citizens of London all their liberties and free customs: And further, we have granted to the citizens of London, that they may among themselves make sheriffs whom they will, and may amove them when they will; and those whom they make sheriffs, they shall present to our justices, who may answer to us and our justices in our exchequer, of those things which to the sheriffwick appertain, whereof they ought to

For election of sheriffs.

answer us; and unless they shall well answer and satisfy us, the citizens of London shall answer and satisfy the amerciaments and the farm; saving to the same citizens their liberties as is aforesaid, and saving to the sheriffs the same liberties which other citizens have; so that, if they which shall be appointed sheriffs for the time being commit any thing whereby they ought to incur any amerciament in money, they shall not be condemned for any more than to the amerciament of twenty pounds, and this without damage of other citizens, if the sheriffs be not sufficient for the payment of their amerciament: But, if they do any offence, whereby they ought to incur the loss of their lives or members, they shall be judged as they ought to be adjudged, according to the law of the city: But of these things which to the sheriffs belong, the sheriffs shall answer before the justices of the exchequer; saving to the sheriffs the liberties which other citizens have: Also this grant and confirmation we have made to our citizens of London for the amendment of the said city, and because it was anciently to be at the farm of three hundred pounds: Therefore we will, and strictly command, that the citizens of London and their heirs aforesaid may have and hold the sheriffwick of London and Middlesex, with all that to the said sheriffwick belongeth, of us and our heirs, hereditarily, freely and quietly, honourably and wholly, by the farm of three hundred pounds by the year, as the charter of the lord John our father, famous king of England, which we have seen, doth witness; and we forbid, that no person do presume to do any hurt, impediment or diminution of our said citizens, of things which to the said sheriffwick belong, or were accustomed to appertain: Also, we do will and command, that if we or our heirs, or any of our justices, shall give or grant to any person any thing which to the farm of the said sheriffwick appertains, the same shall be accounted to the citizens of London, in the acquittal of the said farm in the exchequer yearly, as the charter of king John our father, which they have, concerning the same, doth reasonably testify.

Witness Lord Eustace, bishop of London, etc.

Given by the hands of the reverend Ralph, bishop of Chichester, the eighteenth day of February, in the eleventh year of our reign. Ralph Neville, A.D. 1223-1244.

No. XIII.

Second Charter of Henry III.

18 February, a.d. 1227.

HENRY, by the grace of God, king of England, lord of Ireland, duke of Normandy and Aquitaine, earl of Anjou; to his archbishops, bishops, abbots, earls, barons, justices, sheriffs, rulers, bailiffs, and his faithful subjects, greeting.

<small>For election of a mayor.</small> Know ye, that we have granted, and by this present charter confirmed, to our barons in our city of London, that they may choose to themselves a mayor of themselves, every year, who may be to us faithful, discreet, and fit for the government of the city, so as, when he is chosen, he may be presented unto us, or our justices, if we be not present, and shall swear to be faithful to us: And that it shall be lawful for them in the end of the year to amove him, and to substitute, or, if they will, to retain him still, so as always that he be presented to us, or to our justices, if we be not present.

Also we have granted to the said barons, and by this present charter confirmed, that they may have well, and in peace, freely, quietly and wholly, all their liberties, which hitherto they used, as well in the city of London as without, and as well on the water as on the land, and in all other places; saving to us our chamberlainship: Wherefore we will and strictly command, that our barons of our said city of London may choose to themselves a mayor of themselves every year in manner aforesaid; and that they have all their liberties well and in peace, wholly and fully, with all that to the said liberties belongeth, as the charter of the excellent lord John, king of England, which we have seen, doth reasonably testify.

Witness the lord Eustace of London, Peter de Rupibus, of Winchester; Joceline, of Bath, Robert, of Salisbury, bishops; Hubert de Burgh, earl of Kent, and our Justice; Gilbert de Clare, earl of Gloucester and Hertford; Ralph, son of Nicholas; Richard de Argentein, our steward: Given by the hand of the reverend father Ralph bishop of Chichester, at Westminster, the eighteenth day of February, in the eleventh year of our reign.

No. XIV.

Third Charter of Henry III.

18 February, a.d. 1227.

HENRY, by the grace of God, king of England, lord of Ireland, Duke of Normandy, Aquitaine, earl of Anjou; to the archbishops, bishops, abbots, earls, barons, justices, sheriffs, stewards, castle-keepers, constables, bailiffs, ministers, and all his faithful subjects, greeting.

Ye shall know, that we, for our soul's health, and for the soul's health of king John our father, and for the souls' health of all our ancestors, and also for the commonweal of our city of London, and of all our realm, have granted and strictly commanded, Concerning wears in the Thames and Medway. that all the wears which are in the Thames or in the Medway shall be amoved; and that no wears from henceforth be put anywhere in the Thames, or the Medway, upon forfeiture of ten pounds sterling. We have also quit-claimed all that which the keepers of our Tower of London were wont yearly to receive of the aforesaid wears:

Wherefore we will and steadfastly command, that no Keeper of the said Tower, at any time hereafter, exact any thing from any, or bring any demand, burden or trouble to any person, by reason of the aforesaid wears; for it fully appears to us, and it is sufficiently given us to understand by the right reverend father Hubert, archbishop of Canterbury, and by others our faithful subjects, that very great hurt and discommodity hath grown to the aforesaid city, and also to our said whole realm, by occasion of the aforesaid wears; which same thing, that it may continue firm and stable for ever, we have fortified by the inscription of this page, and putting to our seal, as that charter of the lord king John our father, which the barons of London have, thereof doth reasonably testify.

Witness the lord Eustace of London, Peter de Rupibus, of Winchester; Joceline, of Bath; Robert, of Salisbury, bishops; Hubert de Burgh, earl of Kent, and our Justice; Gilbert de Clare, earl of Gloucester and Hertford; Ralph, son of Nicholas; and Richard de Argentein, our steward. Given by the hands of the reverend father Ralph, bishop of Chichester, our chancellor, at Westminster, the eighteenth day of February, in the eleventh year of our reign.

No. XV.

Fourth Charter of Henry III.

16 March, a.d. 1227.

HENRY, by the grace of God, king of England, lord of Ireland, duke of Normandy and Aquitaine, earl of Anjou; to all archbishops, bishops, abbots, priors, earls, barons, justices, ministers, and all our faithful subjects, French and English, greeting.

None to plead out of the city. Know ye, that we have granted to our citizens of London, that none of them shall plead without the walls of the city of London, saving the pleas of foreign tenures, our moneyers and ministers excepted: And we have granted to them acquittal of all murder within the city and portsoken, and that none of them shall wage battle; and that they may discharge themselves of the pleas belonging to the Crown according to the ancient custom of the city; and that within the walls of the city and portsoken, no man may take any lodging by force, or by delivery of the marshal: This also *Free from toll in all the king's dominions.* we have granted to them, that all the citizens of London be quit of toll and lastage, and of all other customs throughout all our lands, on this side, or beyond the seas: And that none be condemned of any amerciaments of money, but according to the law of the city, which they had in the time of king Henry, grandfather to king Henry our grandfather; and that no miskenning be in any pleading in the city; and that the hustings be kept only once a week; and that they may justly have all their lands and promises, and debts, whosoever owe them to them; and that right be holden to them of all their lands and tenures, which be in the city, according to the custom of the city; and that pleas be there holden of all debts which be lent at London, of all promises there made; and that, if any shall take any toll or any other custom of our men of London, in any our lands on this side, or beyond the seas, or in the ports of the seas on this side, or beyond the seas, after he shall fail of right, the sheriffs of London may take goods for the same: Also we do grant to them, that they may have hunting wheresoever they had in the time of king Henry, grandfather to king Henry our grandfather: Furthermore also, for the amendment of the said city, we have granted to them, that they be all quit from bridtoll, childwite, jeresgive, and of all scotale, so that our sheriff of London, or any other bailiff, shall not make any scotale. These customs aforesaid we do grant to them, and all other liberties and free customs which they had in the time of king Henry, grandfather to king Henry our grandfather, whenas they had the same better and more freely, as the charter of the Lord John our father, which they have, of the same doth reasonably testify: Wherefore we will and steadfastly command, that they and their heirs may have and hold all these things aforesaid hereditarily of us and our heirs.

How to recover debts.

Right of hunting.

Quit of certain old impositions.

These being witness, the lord Eustace, of London; Joceline, of Bath; Richard, of Salisbury; Peter de Rupibus, of Winchester, bishops, etc. Given by the hands of the reverend father in God Ralph, bishop of Chichester, our chancellor, at Westminster, the sixteenth day of March, in the eleventh year of our reign.

No. XVI.

Fifth Charter of Henry III.

18 August, A.D. 1227.

HENRY, by the grace of God, king of England, lord of Ireland, duke of Normandy and Aquitaine, earl of Anjou; to his archbishops, bishops, abbots, priors, earls, barons, justices, sheriffs, rulers, ministers, foresters, and all bailiffs, and faithful subjects, greeting.

Know ye, that we have granted, and by this present charter confirmed, for us and our heirs, unto our archbishops, bishops, abbots, priors, earls, barons, knights, freeholders, and to all of the county of Middlesex, that all the Warren of Staines, with the appurtenances, be unwarrened and disforested for ever, so that all they aforesaid, and their heirs and successors, may have all liberties and benefit of warren and forest, in the aforesaid warren, wherein they may till or plough all their lands, and cut all their woods, and dispose of the same at their will, without the view or contradiction of our warreners or foresters, and all their ministers, and within the which no warrener or forester, or justice of our forest, shall or may in any wise meddle with their lands or woods; neither with their herbage, or hunting, or corn; neither, by any summons or distress, shall cause them, their heirs or successors, to come before our justices of the forest, or warreners, by occasion of the lands and tenements situate in those

To have liberty in the Warren of Staines.

parts where the said warren was wont to be; but that they, and their heirs and successors, and their lands and tenements contained in the parts, be quit and free from all exactions, occasions, demands and attachments, and of all things which belong to warrens or forests: Wherefore we will and steadfastly command, that all they aforesaid, holding lands and tenements within the said parts, and their heirs and successors for ever, have the aforesaid liberties and freedoms: and that their lands and tenements aforesaid be unwarrened and disforested for ever, and quit from all things, which either to warren or forest, warreners or foresters, pertain, as is aforesaid.

> These being witness, Hubert de Burgh, earl of Kent, Justice of England; Gilbert, earl of Gloucester and Hertford; William Marshall, earl of Pembroke; Philip de Albeniaco; Walter de Evermue; Osbert Giffard; Richard de Argentein; John, son of Philip; Richard, son of Hugh, and others. Given by the hand of the reverend father Ralph, bishop of Chichester, our chancellor, at Woodstock, the eighteenth day of August, in the eleventh year of our reign.

No. XVII.

Charter of King Henry III.

26 February, a.d. 1247.

Confirming the Fee Farm of Queenhithe to the Corporation of London.

HENRY, by the grace of God, king of England, lord of Ireland, duke of Normandy and Aquitaine, and earl of Anjou; to all archbishops, bishops, priors, earls, barons, justices, sheriffs, rulers, ministers, and all bailiffs, and his faithful subjects, greeting.

Know ye, that we have seen a covenant made between Richard earl of Cornwall, our brother, on the one part, and the mayor and commonalty of the city of London, on the other part, in these words:

13 Oct., a.d. 1246.

In the thirtieth year of the reign of Henry, the son of king John, in the day of the translation of saint Edward, this covenant was made at Westminster, between the right honourable man, Richard earl of Cornwall, on the one part, and John Gisors, then mayor of the city of London, and the commonalty of the same city of London, on the other part, for and concerning certain exactions and demands belonging

Queenhithe.

to Queenhithe, of the city of London; that is to say, that the said earl hath granted for him and his heirs that the said mayor, and all the mayors after him, and all the commonalty of the said city, may have and hold the said Queenhithe, with all their liberties, customs, and other things to the same belonging, in fee-farm, paying therefore yearly to the said earl, his heirs and assigns, fifty pounds, at two terms in the year, at Clerkenwell; that is to say, at the close of Easter twenty-five pounds; and on the Octave of Saint Michael twenty-five pounds; and for the greater surety thereof, to the part of the chirograph remaining with the mayor and commonalty of London, the said earl hath put his seal; and to the writing thereof remaining with the said earl, the foresaid mayor and commonalty have set their common seal. We, therefore, allowing and approving the said covenant, do, for us and our heirs, grant and confirm the same.

> These same being witnesses, Ralph son of Nicholas, Richard de Grey, John and William his brothers, Paulinus Peyvre, Ralph de Wauncy, and John Gumbaud. Given by our hand at Windsor, the twenty-sixth day of February, in the twenty-first year of our reign.

No. XVIII.

Sixth Charter of Henry III.

12 June, a.d. 1253.

HENRY, by the grace of God, king of England, lord of Ireland, duke of Normandy and Aquitaine, and earl of Anjou; to his archbishops, abbots, priors, earls, barons, justices, sheriffs, rulers, ministers, and all his bailiffs, and faithful people, greeting.

Know ye, that we have granted, for us and our heirs, and confirmed it by this our present charter, that our mayor and citizens of London may have and hold all their liberties and free customs, which they had in the time of king Henry our grandfather, and which they had by charters of our ancestors, kings of England, as they more freely and better had the same, and they most freely and fully have and use the same for ever.

Mayor to be presented to the barons of the exchequer. Also we have granted to the said citizens, that every mayor whom they shall choose in our city of London, (we being not at Westminster) they may yearly present to the barons of our exchequer, that he may be admitted by them as mayor; so notwithstanding, at the next coming of us or our heirs to Westminster or London, he be presented to us or our heirs, and so admitted mayor. And we will and command, for us and our heirs, that, out of the farm of our city of London, there be allowed to our sheriff of the said city yearly, in his said account, seven pounds, at our exchequer, for the liberty of St. Paul's, London: and that our said citizens throughout all our dominions, as well on this side the sea as beyond, be quit of all toll and custom for ever, as in the charters of the aforesaid kings is granted. And we forbid, upon our forfeiture, that none presume henceforth to vex or disquiet the said citizens, contrary to this liberty, and our grant.

£7 to be paid yearly to the sheriffs at the exchequer.

Acquittal from all toll and custom.

> These being witnesses, the reverend father Peter, bishop of Hereford; Richard, earl of Cornwall, our brother; Peter de Sabaudia; John Maunsel, provost of Beverley; Master William Kilkenni, archdeacon of Coventry; Bertram de Kyriolle, John de Lexingtone; John de Grey; Henry de Wyngham; Robert Walravensis, William de Grey; Nicholas de St. Mauro; William Gernoun, and others. Given by our hand at Windsor, the twelfth day of June, in the thirty-seventh year of our reign.

No. XIX

Charter of Remission granted to the Citizens by Henry III.

10 January, a.d. 1266.

HENRY, by the grace of God, king of England, lord of Ireland, and duke of Guienne; to all men, greeting.

Know ye, that in consideration of twenty thousand marks, paid to us by our citizens of London, as an atonement for their great crimes and misdemeanours committed against us, our royal consort, our royal brother Richard, king of the Romans, and our dear son Edward: that we have and do by these presents remit, forgive, and acquit, for us and our heirs, the citizens of London, and their heirs, of all crimes and trespasses whatsoever; and that the said citizens, as formerly, shall enjoy all their rights and liberties; and that from Christmas last they shall and may receive the rents and profits of all their lands and tenements whatsoever: and also, that the said citizens shall have all the goods and chattels of such criminals as have or shall be indicted on account of the late rebellion; except the goods and chattels of the persons already mentioned, which we have given to our son Edward; and also, all the lands and tenements that shall escheat to us, by reason of the foresaid rebellion. And we likewise grant, that all the citizens confined in our several prisons shall be discharged;

except those given as pledges to our son Edward for his prisoners, and those for citizens that are fled.

In witness whereof we have made these letters patent.

Witness myself at Northampton, the tenth day of January, in the fiftieth year of our reign.

No. XX.

Eighth Charter of Henry III.

26 March, a.d. 1268.

HENRY, by the grace of God, king of England, lord of Ireland, duke of Aquitaine; to his archbishops, bishops, abbots, priors, earls, barons, sheriffs, justices, rulers, ministers, and all bailiffs, and his faithful subjects, greeting.

Know ye, that we have granted to our citizens of London, for us and our heirs, whom of late we have received again into our grace and favour, after divers trespasses and forfeitures of them and their commonalty to us made, for the which, both for life and member, and all other things belonging to the said city, they have submitted themselves to our will, that none of them be compelled to plead out of the walls of the said city, for any thing except foreign tenures, and except our moneyers and officers, and except those things which shall happen to be done against our peace, which according to the common law of our realm, are wont to be determined in the parts where those trespasses were done; and except pleas concerning merchandises, which are wont to be determined according to the law-merchant in boroughs and fairs, so yet notwithstanding that those plaints be determined in the boroughs and fairs, by four or five of the said citizens of London, who shall be there present; saving to us the amer-

None compelled to plead out of the city.

Law-merchant.

ciaments in any wise coming, which they shall faithfully answer us and our heirs, upon pain of grievous forfeitures.

We have also granted to our same citizens acquittal of murder in the said city and in portsoken; and that none of the said citizens may wage battle; and that for the pleas belonging to the crown, chiefly those which may chance within the said city and suburbs thereof, they may discharge themselves according to the ancient custom of the said city; this notwithstanding except, that upon the graves of the dead, for that which they should have said, if they had lived, it shall not be lawful precisely to swear; but in place of those deceased, who before their death had been elected to discharge those who for the things belonging to the crown, were appealed or accased, other free and lawful men may be chosen, who may do and accomplish the same without delay, which by the deceased should have been done, if they had lived; and that within the walls of the city and in portsoken none may take lodgings by force, or delivery of the marshal. Acquittal of murder, etc. Graves of the dead.

We have also granted to our said citizens throughout all our dominions, wheresoever they come to dwell with their merchandizes and things, and also throughout all the sea-ports, as well on this side as beyond the seas, they shall be free of all toll and lastage, and of all customs, except everywhere our due and ancient custom and prices of wines; that is to say, one tun before the mast, and of one other behind the mast, at twenty shillings the tun, to be paid in such form as we and our ancestors have been accustomed to have the said prices; and if any in any of our lands, on this side or beyond the seas, or in the ports of the said sea, on this side or beyond the seas, shall take of the men of London toll, or any custom, con- Free of toll and lastage, etc. What is due to the king.

trary to this our grant (except the aforesaid prices) after he shall fail of right, the sheriff may take goods therefor at London.

Husting once a week.

(We have also granted to them, that the hustings might be kept in every week once the week, and that only for one day; or as notwithstanding that those things within the same day cannot be determined, may continue till next morning, and no longer;) and that right be holden to them for their lands and tenures within the same city, according to the custom of the said city; so as nevertheless, that as well foreigners as others may make their attorneys, as well in pleading as defending, as elsewhere in our courts; and they may not be questioned as miskenning in any their pleas; that is to say, if they have not declared altogether well; and of all their debts which were lent at London, and promises there made, pleas be there holden, according to the just and ancient custom.

Acquittal of childwite, jeresgive, and scotale.

[Furthermore, we do also grant, toward the amendment of the aforesaid city, that all be quit of childwite and jeresgive, and from scotale; so that our sheriffs of London, nor any other bailiff, shall not make any scotale: and also, that the said citizens may justly have and hold their lands, tenures or promises; and also their debts, whosoever do owe

Against forestalling.

them; and that no merchant or other do meet any merchants coming by land or by water, with their merchandises or victuals, towards the city, to buy or sell again, till they come to the said city, and there have put the same to sale, upon the forfeiture of the things brought, and pain of imprisonment; from whence he shall not escape without great punishment: and that none shew out their wares to sell,

Custom to be paid.

who owe any custom, until the custom thereof be levied, without great punishment, and upon pain or forfeiture of all that commodity of him that happens to do otherwise: and that no merchant stranger or other, may buy or sell any wares, which ought to be weighed or troned, unless by our beams or trone, upon forfeiture of the said wares. *Goods to be weighed at the king's beam.*

Moreover, those debts, which of their contracts or loans shall be due unto them, they may cause to be enrolled in our exchequer, for the more surety of them, upon the recognizance of those who shall stand bound unto them in the said debts; so as nevertheless that no debts be enrolled upon the recognizance of any person who is not there known; or unless it be manifested concerning his person by the testimony of six or four lawful men, who be sufficient to answer as well for the debt as for the damages which any may have of such recognizances, if the same happen to be falsely done under their names: and for every pound to be enrolled in the exchequer, one penny to be paid to our use, for the charge of sustentation of those who must attend to such enrolling. *Debts to be enrolled in the exchequer. A penny to be paid for enrolment.*

These liberties and free customs we grant to them, to hold to them and their heirs, so long as they shall well and faithfully behave themselves to us and our heirs, together with all their just and reasonable customs, which in time of us and our predecessors heretofore they have had, as well for manner of pleading of their tenures, debts, and promises, as for all other causes whatsoever, concerning both them and the same city: so long as the customs be not contrary to right, law and justice; saving in all things the liberty of the church of Westminster to the abbots and monks of the same place, to them granted by the charters of us and our predecessors, kings of England: but, as touching our Jews and merchant strangers, and other things out of our foresaid grant touching us or our said city, we and our heirs shall provide as to us shall seem expedient.

    These being witnesses; Richard, king of Germany, our brother; Edward our first-born son; Roger de Mortimer; Roger de Clifforde; Roger de Leyburne; Robert Waleraunde; Robert Aguillum, Master Godfrey Gyffarde, our chancellor; Walter de Mertone; John de Cheshulle, archdeacon of London; John de la Lynde; William de Aette, and others. Given by our hand at Westminster, the twenty-sixth day of March, in the two and fiftieth year of our reign

No. XXI.

Charter of Confirmation of the City Privileges, by Edward I.

28 MAY, A.D. 1298.

* * * * *

WHEREAS our said citizens, by the charters of our said progenitors, have been accustomed hitherto to present every mayor, whom they have chosen in the said city yearly, before the barons of the exchequer, (our progenitor or we not being at Westminster) that he may be admitted by the said barons as mayor for us, notwithstanding that, at the next coming of our progenitor or of us unto Westminster or London, he may be presented to our progenitor, or to us, and so admitted mayor: We, willing to shew more ample favour to the said citizens in that behalf, do grant to them, for us and our heirs, the mayor of the said city, when he shall be chosen by the said citizens, (we, and our heirs, and our barons, not being at Westminster or London), they may or shall be presented or admitted to and by the constable of our Tower of London yearly, in such sort as before they were wont to be presented and admitted; so as nevertheless, that, at the next coming of us or our heirs to Westminster or London, the said mayor be presented to us or our heirs, and admitted for mayor. *Permission to present the mayor to the constable of the Tower, in absence of the king and barons.*

And also, we have granted for us and our heirs, to our said citizens, that they and their successors, citizens of the said city, be for ever free and quit of

Citizens acquitted of pannage, pontage, and murage. Sheriffs, how to be amerced.

pannage, pontage and murage throughout all the realm, and all our dominions: and that the sheriffs of the said city, as often as it shall happen them to be amerced in our court for any offence, shall be amerced according to the measure and quantity of the offence, as other the sheriffs of our said realm have been amerced for the like offence.

Citizens to enjoy their liberties and customs.

Wherefore we will, and strictly charge and command, for us and our heirs, that the said citizens and their successors have all the liberties, freedoms, quittals and free customs aforesaid, and may or shall use them according to our confirmation, renovation, and grants aforesaid, for ever, as by the aforesaid charter (amongst other things) more fully appeareth.

All which the king certified by the following brief to his officers of the exchequer:

Brief to the exchequer, for restoration of liberties.

Edward, by the grace of God, etc., to his treasurers and barons of the exchequer, greeting. Whereas, for the good service that our beloved citizens of London have hitherto done us, by our letters patent we have rendered and restored to the same our foresaid city, together with the mayoralty, all their liberties (which city mayoralty and liberties we have long since caused to be taken in our hands), to be had and held to the same citizens, according to their will, as freely and entirely as they had and held them on the day of the said taking them away, as is contained more fully in our said letters: we command you, that ye permit the same citizens to use and enjoy the liberties which they have reasonably used on the day of the foresaid taking, before you in the exchequer beforesaid, according to the tenor of our foresaid letters.

Witness myself at York, the eight-and-twentieth day of May, in the six-and-twentieth year of our reign.

No. XXII.

Constitutions for the regular Government of the City; granted by Edward II.

For the citizens of London, concerning new articles then made to be observed.

8 June, a.d. 1319.

EDWARD, by the grace of God, king of England, lord of Ireland, and duke of Aquitaine, to all to whom the present letters shall have come, greeting. Articles of agreement for the composing differences in the city.

Know ye, that whereas our beloved and faithful the mayor and aldermen, and the other citizens of our city of London, had lately ordained and appointed among themselves, for the bettering of the same city, and for the common benefit of such as dwell in that city, and resort to the same, certain things to be in the same city perpetually observed, and had instantly besought us that we would take care to accept and confirm the same.

We having seen certain letters, patentwise, signed with the common seal of that city, and the seal of the office of the mayoralty of that city, upon the premises, and to us exhibited, have caused certain articles to be chosen out of the foresaid letters, and caused them in some things to be corrected, as they are underneath inserted, viz.

1. That the mayor and sheriffs of the same city be elected by the citizens of the said city, according Mayor to be elected annually.

to the tenor of the charters of our progenitors, heretofore kings of England, made to them thereby, and no otherwise.

2. That the mayor remain only one year together in his mayoralty.

Sheriffs' officers.

3. That sheriffs have but two clerks and two serjeants; and that they take such for whom they will answer.

Mayor's office.

4. That the mayor have no other office belonging to the city, but the office of mayoralty; nor draw to himself the sheriffs' plea in the chamber of London, nor hold other pleas than those the mayor, according to ancient custom, ought to hold.

Aldermen to be annually elected, and not re-elected.

5. That the aldermen be removed from year to year, on the day of St. Gregory the Pope, and not re-elected; and others chosen by the same wards.

Tallages.

6. That tallages or aids henceforth to be assessed for the king's business, or for the state and benefit of the city, after they shall be assessed by the men of the wards elected and deputed for this, be not increased or heightened but by the common consent of the mayor and commonalty. And that the money coming from these tallages and aids be delivered into the custody of four honest men, commoners of the city, to be chosen by the commonalty, to be further delivered by the testimony of the said four men; so that they may inform the commonalty to what profit, and for what uses, those moneys go.

Strangers, how to be admitted.

7. That no stranger be admitted into the freedom of the city in the husting; and that no inhabitant, and especially English merchant, of any mystery or trade, be admitted into the freedom of the city, unless by surety of six honest and sufficient men of the mystery or trade that he shall be of, who is so to be admitted into the freedom; which six men may undertake for him, of keeping the city indemnified in

that behalf. And that the same form of surety be observed of strangers to be admitted into the freedom in the husting, if they be of any certain mystery or trade. And if they are not of some certain mystery, then that they be not admitted into the freedom without the assent of the commonalty. And that they who have been taken into the freedom of the city (since we undertook the government of the realm) contrary to the forms prescribed, and they who have gone contrary to their oath in this behalf, or contrary to the state of the city, and are thereof lawfully convicted, lose the freedom of the said city.

Saving always, that concerning apprentices the ancient manner and form of the said city be observed.

8. That each year in the same city, as often as need shall be, inquiry be made, if any of the freedom of the same city exercise merchandises in the city, of the goods of others not of the same freedom, by calling those goods their own, contrary to their oath, and contrary to the freedom of the said city; and they that are lawfully convicted thereof to lose the freedom of the said city. *Freemen.*

9. That all and every one being in the liberty of the said city, and that would enjoy the liberties and free customs of the said city, be in lot and scot, and partake of all burthens for maintaining the state of the said city, and the freedom thereof, according to the oath they have taken, when they were admitted into their freedom; and whoso will not, to lose his freedom. *Scot and lot to be paid by all freemen.*

10. And that all and every one, being of the freedom of the city, and living without the city, and that either by themselves, or by their servants, exercise their merchandises within the city, be in lot and scot with the commoners of the said city, for their merchandises, or else to be removed from their freedom. *Non-resident freemen to pay scot and lot for their goods.*

Common seal, how to be kept and used.

11. And that the common seal of the city remain in the custody of two aldermen and two others, commoners, to be chosen for this purpose by the commoners; and that that seal be not denied, neither to poor nor rich commoners, when they shall need it; yet so that they reasonably prove the cause of their demand: and that for the putting to of the seal nothing be taken. And that the giving of judgments in the courts of the city, and especially after the verdicts of inquisition taken, in cases where inquisitions have been taken, be not deferred, unless difficulty intervene. And if difficulty intervene by reason of this, giving judgment shall not be put off beyond the third court.

Weights and scales.

12. That weights and scales of merchandises to be weighed between merchants and merchants, the issues coming of which belong to the commonalty of the said city, remain in the custody of honest and sufficient men of the same city, expert in that office, and as yet to be chosen by the commonalty, to be kept at the will of the same commonalty; and that they be by no means committed to others than those so to be chosen.

Sheriffs' deputies.

13. That the sheriffs for the time being commit toll, and other customs belonging to their farm, and other public offices belonging to them, and to be exercised by others, to sufficient men, for whom they will answer, and not commit them to others. And if any deputed by the said sheriffs to any of the aforesaid offices, take undue cusotm, or carry himself otherwise in that office than he ought, and is thereupon convicted at the suit of the complainant, let him be removed from that office, and punished according to his demerits.

Non-freemen not to sell by retail.

14. Merchants who are not of the freedom of the city, not to sell, by retail, wines or other wares, with'n the city or suburbs.

15. That there be no brokers hereafter in the city of any merchandises, unless elected to this by merchants of the mysteries in which the brokers themselves may have to exercise their offices; and at least of this to make oath before the mayor. *Brokers.*

16. That the common harbourers in the city and suburbs, although they are not of the freedom of the same, be partakers of the contingent burdens for maintaining the said city, according to the state of it, as long as they shall be so common harbourers, as other like dwellers in the city and suburbs shall partake, on account of those dwellings. Saving always, that the merchants of Gascony, and other foreigners, may, one with another, inhabit and be harboured in the said city, as hitherto they have accustomed to do. *Non-freemen to pay taxes.*

17. That the keeping the bridge of the said city, and the rents and profits belonging to that bridge, be committed to be kept to two honest and sufficient men of the city, other than the aldermen, to be chosen to this by the commonalty, at the will of the said commonalty, and not to others; and who may answer thereupon to the said commonalty. *Bridge-masters.*

18. That no serjeant of the chamber of Guyhald take fee of the commonalty of the city, or do execution, unless one chosen for this by the commonalty of the city; and that the chamberlain, common clerk and common serjeant be chosen by the commonalty of the city, and be removed according to the will of the same city. *Common serjeant and common clerk.*

19. And that the mayor and recorder, and the foresaid chamberlain and common clerk, be content with their fees anciently appointed and paid on account of their offices, and take not other fees for the abovesaid offices. *Fees.*

20. That the goods of the aldermen, in aids, tallages, and other contributions, concerning the said city, be *Aldermen to be taxed as other citizens.*

taxed by the men of the wards in which those aldermen abide, as the goods of other citizens, by the said wards.

Which articles, as they are above expressed, and the matters contained in the same, we accept, approve and ratify; and we yield and grant them, for us and our heirs, as much as in us is, to the aforesaid citizens, their heirs and successors, in the aforesaid city and suburbs, for the common profit of those that inhabit therein, and resort thither, to obtain the same, and to be observed perpetually.

Moreover, we, willing to show ampler grace to the mayor, aldermen and citizens, at their request have granted to them, for us and our heirs, that the mayor, aldermen, citizens and commonalty of the commoners of the city, and their heirs and successors, for the necessities and profits of the same city, may, among themselves of their common assent assess tallages upon their own goods within that city, as well upon the rents as other things, and as well upon the mysteries as any other way, as they shall see expedient, and levy them, without incurring the danger of us or our heirs, or our ministers whomsoever. And that the money coming from such tallages remain in the custody of four honest and lawful men of the said city, to be chosen to this by the commonalty, and be laid out, of their custody, for the necessities and profits of the said city, and not otherwise. In witness whereof, etc.

Witness the king, at York, the eighth day of June, in the twelfth year of our reign.

No. XXIII.

Charter of Edward II,

Exempting the Citizens of London from Levies of Men for carrying on War out of the City.

12 December, a.d. 1321.

EDWARD, by the grace of God, king of England, lord of Ireland, and duke of Aquitaine; to all to whom these present letters shall come, greeting.

Know ye, that whereas the mayor and the good men of the city of London have of late thankfully done us aid of armed footmen at our castle of Leeds, in our county of Kent; and also aid of like armed men now going with us through divers parts of our realm for divers causes: we, willing to provide for the indemnity of the said mayor and men of our city of London in this behalf, have granted to them for us and our heirs, that the said aids, to us so thankfully done, shall not be prejudicial to the said mayor and good men, their heirs and successors, nor shall they be drawn into consequent for time to come. In witness whereof we have caused these our letters to be made patent.

Witness myself at Aldermanston, the twelfth day of December, in the fifteenth year of our reign.

No. XXIV.

First Charter of Edward III,

Granted by consent of Parliament.

6 March, a.d. 1327.

EDWARD, by the grace of God, king of England, lord of Ireland, and duke of Aquitaine; to his archbishops, bishops, abbots, priors, earls, barons, justices, sheriffs, rulers, ministers, and other his bailiffs and faithful subjects, greeting.

Know ye, that we for the bettering of our city of London, and for the good and laudable service which our beloved mayor, aldermen and commonalty of the said city heretofore have often done to us and our progenitors, with the assent of the aforesaid earls, barons, and all the commonalty of our realm, being called to this our present parliament at Westminster, have granted, and by this our charter, for us and our heirs, confirmed to the citizens of the aforesaid city, the liberties here underwritten, to have and to hold to them and their heirs and successors for ever.

<small>Liberties granted by former charters confirmed.</small> First, whereas in the great charter of the liberties of England it is contained, that the city of London have all their ancient liberties and customs; and the same citizens, at the time of the making of the charter, from the time of St. Edward the king and Confessor, and William the Conqueror, and of other our progenitors, had divers liberties and customs, as well by the charters of those our progenitors, as

without charter by ancient custom, whereupon in divers the circuits, and other the courts of our said progenitors, as well by judgments as by statutes, they were invaded, and some of them adjudged; we will and grant, for us and our heirs, that they may have the liberties according to the form of the above-said great charter; and that impediments and usurpations to them in that behalf made shall be revoked and annulled.

We have further granted, for us and our heirs, to the said citizens, their heirs and successors aforesaid, that the mayor of the aforesaid city, which for time shall be one of the justices to be assigned of the gaol-delivery of Newgate, and be named in every commission thereof to be made; and that the said citizens may have infangthef and outfangthef, and chattels of felons, of all those which shall be adjudged before them within the liberties of the same city, and of all being of the liberty aforesaid, at the aforesaid gaol to be adjudged. *Mayor made one of the justices of gaol delivery.*

And whereas also, by the charters of our progenitors, it was granted to the same citizens, that they should hold the sheriffwicks of London and Middlesex, for three hundred pounds yearly, to be paid at our exchequer, and they are charged with the payment of four hundred pounds yearly, every year to be paid at our exchequer, for the sheriffwicks, contrary to the form of the said charters: We will and grant, for us and our heirs, that the said citizens, their heirs and successors, may henceforth hold the aforesaid sheriffwicks for three hundred pounds yearly, to be yearly paid at our exchequer, according to the tenor of the aforesaid charters; and that they may be from henceforth acquitted of the said one hundred pounds. *To hold the sheriffwicks of London and Middlesex at £300 yearly.*

Furthermore, we have granted, for us and our *To bequeath in mortmain.*

heirs, to the said citizens, that they, their heirs and successors, may bequeath their tenements within the liberties of the aforesaid city, as well in mortmain as in other manner, as of ancient time they have been accustomed so to do.

Sheriffs to be amerced as other sheriffs on this side Trent.

And whereas in a certain charter of the lord Edward, late king of England, our father, to the said citizens made, (amongst other things) it is contained, that the sheriffs of the said city, as often as they shall happen to be amerced for any offence in the court, shall be amerced according to the measure and quantity of their offence, as other the sheriffs of our realm were wont to be amerced for like offences; and the sheriffs of the aforesaid city, after the making of that charter, were otherwise amerced for the escape of thieves, than other sheriffs were on this side Trent; who, for such-like escapes, were amerced only, as it is said, one hundred shillings.

We will and grant, for us and our heirs, that the sheriffs of the same city, for the time being, shall be in no wise amerced or charged for the escape of thieves, in any otherwise than as other the sheriffs on this side Trent; and that the aforesaid citizens shall not be charged for the custody of those that fly to the churches within the aforesaid liberty, for to have immunities, otherwise than of old hath been accustomed to be charged; any thing in the last circuit at the Tower of London made or adjudged notwithstanding.

May take away all wears.

And that the said citizens may remove and take away all the wears in the waters of Thames and Medway, and may have the punishments thereof to us belonging.

Merchant strangers to sell their wares within forty days.

Also we will and strictly command, that all merchant strangers, coming to England, shall sell their wares and merchandises within forty days after their coming thither; and shall continue and board with free hosts of the said city, and other cities and towns in England, without any households or societies by them to be kept.

And also we will and grant, for us and our heirs, that the marshal, steward or clerk of the market of our household, may not sit from henceforth within the liberty of the aforesaid city, nor exercise any office there, nor any way draw any citizen of the said city to plead without the liberties of the said city, of any thing that happen within the liberties of the same; and that no escheator, or other officers, may, from henceforth, exercise the office of escheator within the liberties of the said city: but that the mayor of the said city for the time being may do the office of the escheator within the said liberty; so as always he take his oath that he exercise the said office, and that he answer thereof to us and our heirs, as he ought to do. And that the said citizens, from henceforth shall not be compelled to go or send to war out of the said city. And that the constable of the Tower of London for the time being shall not make any prizes, by land or by water, of victual or other thing whatsoever, of the men of the said city, nor of any other coming towards the said city, or going thence; neither shall or may arrest, or cause to be arrested, the ships or boats bringing victuals, or other such-like goods, to or from the said city. *No citizen obliged to plead without the city. Mayor to be escheator. No citizen to be compelled to war out of the city. Constable of the Tower not to arrest ships, etc.*

And forasmuch as the citizens, in all good fairs of England, were wont to have among themselves keepers to hold the pleas touching the citizens of the said city assembling at the said fairs: We will and grant, as much as in us is, that the same citizens may have such-like keepers, to hold such pleas of their covenants, as of ancient time they had, except the pleas of land and of the crown. *May hold a court of pie-powder in all fairs.*

Sheriffs not compelled to take an oath, except when yielding up their account.

Furthermore, we grant for us and our heirs, that the sheriffs of the said city for the time being shall not be compelled to take any oath at our exchequer, but upon the yielding up of their accounts. Also, whereas the said citizens, in the circuit of Hervey de Stantone, and his fellow-justices of the lord Edward, late king of England, our father's last circuit at the Tower of London, were compelled, contrary to their ancient customs, to claim their liberties and free customs, and thereupon did claim divers liberties, by the charters of our said progenitors, and of other their liberties and free customs, of old use and custom; which said claims do as yet hang before us undecided:

Old liberties allowed to be recorded.

We will and grant, for us and our heirs, that the same citizens, their heirs and successors, may have the liberties and free customs, and may use them, as of old time they were wont; and that they may record their said liberties and free customs before us, our justices, and other ministers whatsoever, in such sort as they were wont to do before the said circuit; notwithstanding that the said citizens in the said circuit were impeached upon some like record and liberties and free customs aforesaid; and also notwithstanding any statutes or judgments made or published to the contrary. And that to the allowance of their charters to be had before us in our exchequer, and other pleas whatsoever, one writ shall suffice in all pleas for every king's time. And that

No summons, etc. but by city officers.

no summons, attachments, or executions be made by any of the officers whatsoever of us or our heirs, by writ, or without writ, within the liberty of the said city; but only by the ministers of the said city. And

Sheriffs to have forfeiture of victuals, etc.

that the sheriffs of the same city (which shall be towards the aid of the fame of that city) may lawfully have the forfeitures of victuals, and other things and merchandises, according to the tenor of the charter thereof made to the said citizens, and shall not be debarred thereof hereafter, contrary to the tenor of the same charter.

And that the same citizens, in the circuits of the justices, from henceforth sitting at the Tower of London, shall be guided by the same laws and customs whereby they were guided in the circuits holden in the time of lord John and Henry, sometime kings of England, and other our progenitors; and if any thing in the last circuit was done or attempted, contrary to their liberties and free customs, we will not that they be prejudicial to them, but that they may be guided as of old time they were. *To be guided by the laws of king John and king Henry.*

We have also granted, for us and our heirs, that the same citizens, from henceforth, in and towards subsidies, grants and contributions whatsoever, to be made to the use of us or our heirs, shall be taxed and contributory with the commonalty of our realm, as common persons, and not as men of the city. And that they be quit of all other tallages. And that the liberties of the said city shall not be taken into the hands of us or our heirs, for any personal trespass, or judgment of any minister of the said city. Neither shall a keeper in the said city for that occasion be deputed; but the same minister shall be punished according to the quality of his offence. *To be taxed as other commoners. Liberties not to be forfeited for personal trespass.*

And that no purveyor and taker, officer and other minister of us and our heirs, or of any other, shall make any prices in the said city, or without, of the goods of the citizens of the said city, contrary to their will and pleasure, unless immediately they make due payment for the same, or else may have respite thereof, with the good-will of the seller. And that no price be made of the wines of those *King's purveyors not to interrupt the sale of citizens' goods, etc.*

citizens, by any the officers of us or our heirs, or otherwise against their wills; that is to say, of one tun before the mast, and another behind it, nor by any other means; but shall be quit thereof for ever.

Furthermore, we forbid, that any officer of us or our heirs shall merchandise by himself or others within the said city, or without, of any thing touching their offices

Also we grant, that the lands and tenements (lying without) of the said citizens, which have been, or hereafter shall be ministers of the said city, be bound to keep the said city harmless against us and our heirs, of those things which concern their offices, as their tenements be within the said city; and that no market from henceforth shall be granted by us or our heirs, to any within seven miles in circuit of the said city. And that all inquisitions from henceforth to be taken by our justices or ministers of the said city, shall be taken in St. Martin's-le-Grand, in London, and not elsewhere; except the inquisitions to be taken in the circuits at the Tower of London, and for the gaol-delivery at Newgate; and that none of the freemen of the said city shall be impleaded or troubled at our exchequer, or elsewhere by bill, except it be by those things which touch us or our heirs.

No market to be kept within seven miles of London.

Wherefore we will and strictly command, for us and our heirs, that the said citizens, their heirs and successors, have all their liberties and free customs, and the same may use and enjoy for ever, in form aforesaid.

> These being witnesses, Walter Reynolds, archbishop of Canterbury, John Hotham, bishop of Ely, our chancellor, and others. Given at Westminster the sixth of March, in the first year of our reign.

No. XXV.

Second Charter of Edward III.

Granting the Bailiwick of Southwark to the Citizens of London.

6 MARCH, A.D. 1327.

EDWARD, by the grace of God, king of England, lord of Ireland, and duke of Aquitaine; to all to whom these present letters shall come, greeting.

Know ye, that whereas our well-beloved, the citizens of the city of London, by their petition exhibited before us and our council, in our present parliament at Westminster assembled, have given us to understand that felons, thieves, and other malefactors, and disturbers of the peace, who, in the said city and elsewhere, have committed manslaughters, robberies, and divers other felonies, privily departing from the said city, after those felonies committed, into the village of Southwark, where they cannot be attached by the ministers of the said city, and there are openly received: and so for default of due punishment are more bold to commit such felonies; and they have besought us, that, for the confirmation of our peace within the said city, bridling the wickedness of the said malefactors, we would grant unto them the said village, to have to them, their heirs and successors, for ever, for the farm and rent therefor yearly due to us, to be yearly paid at our exchequer: We, having consideration to the premises, with the assent of the prelates, earls, barons, and commonalty, being in our present parliament aforesaid, have granted, for us and our heirs, to the said citizens, the said village of Southwark, with the appurtenances, to have and to hold, to them and their heirs and successors, citizens of the same city, of us and our heirs for ever, to pay to us by the year, at the exchequer of us and our heirs for ever, at the accustomed times, the farms therefor due and accustomed. In witness whereof we have caused these our letters to be made patent.

Witness myself at Westminster, the sixth day of March, in the first year of our reign.

No. XXVI.

Third Charter of Edward III.

26 March, a.d. 1337.

EDWARD, by the grace of God, king of England, lord of Ireland, and duke of Aquitaine; to all to whom these present letters shall come, greeting.

Know ye, whereas in our parliament at York, holden the morrow after the ascension of our Lord, in the ninth year of our reign, it was enacted, That all merchant strangers and English-born, and every of them, of what estate or condition soever, who would buy or sell corn, wine, ponderable[1] wares, fish or other victuals, wool, cloth, wares, or other vendible things whatsoever, wheresoever they were, either in cities, towns, boroughs, ports of the sea, fairs, markets, or other places in the realm, whether within liberties or without, might without impediment freely sell the same victuals or wares, to whom they would, as well to foreigners as English-born, the enemies to us and our realm only excepted; notwithstanding of the charters of liberties to any cities or places aforesaid, granted to the contrary, or custom or judgment upon the said charters, as in the foresaid state is more plainly contained; yet nevertheless, because in the statutes, as well in our said

[1] "Aver de pois", or "haberdash ware". See *Statutes of the Realm*, Record Edition, vol. i, pp. 269, 270. Luffman, Noorthouck, and others, read "powderable", by error.

parliament, as in other parliaments of our progenitors, sometimes king of England, made by us and our progenitors, with the common consent of the prelates, earls, barons, and commonalty of our realm, it was granted and established, that the great charter of the liberty of England, in all and singular its articles, should be maintained and firmly observed.

And in the same charter, among other things, it is contained, the city of London may have its ancient liberties and free customs unhurt; and it hath been the intent and meaning, as well of us as our progenitors, and yet is, that the said great charter, in all the articles thereof, may be still observed; and that by pretext of the said statute, or any other, nothing shall be done to the prejudice or infringement of the said charter, or of any article therein contained, or of the ancient liberties or customs of the said city may be unjustly burthened, touching their said liberties and free customs, contrary to such intent, with the consent of the prelates, earls, and barons, assistant with us in this our parliament: We have granted, for us and our heirs, that the citizens of the said city, their heirs and successors, may have all their liberties and free customs unhurt and whole, as before these times they more fully had the same; the foresaid statute for the said merchants, made to the hurt of the liberties and customs of the said city, notwithstanding. In witness whereof we have caused these our letters to be made patent.

Witness myself at Westminster, the twenty-sixth day of March, in the eleventh year of our reign.

No. XXVII.

Fourth Charter of Edward III.

10 June, a.d. 1354.

EDWARD, by the grace of God, king of England and France, and lord of Ireland, to all to whom these our letters shall come, greeting.

Know ye, that we being worthily careful of the conservation and increase of the name and honour of our city of London, and at the supplication of the mayor, sheriffs, and commonalty of the said city to us humbly made, will and grant for us and our heirs, that the serjeants appointed to bear the maces in our said city may lawfully carry them of gold or silver, or silvered or garnished with the sign of our arms, or others, everywhere in the said city, and in the suburbs of the same, and in the county of Middlesex, and other places to the liberties of the said city appertaining; and also without the said city to meet with us, our mother, consort, or the children of us or our heirs, or other royal persons, when we or any of us shall come to the said city, and also in going forth with us, or any of us, when we shall depart from the said city; as also in the presence of us, our mother, or consort, or our children, when the said mayor, or sheriffs, or aldermen of the said city, or any of them, shall come to us or our heirs, at or without the command or warning of us, or of any of us; and as often as it shall happen any of the said

[margin: Mayor's serjeants to carry maces of gold or silver.]

serjeants to be sent to foreign places, and without the city, to do their offices at the command of us, or of the mayor and sheriffs aforesaid, they may lawfully carry, going and coming publicly, as our own serjeants at arms, attending our presence, do carry their maces; any ordinance or commandment made to the contrary notwithstanding. In witness whereof we have caused these our letters to be made patent.

Witness myself at Westminster, the tenth day of June, in the twenty-eighth year of our reign of England, and of France the fifteenth.

No. XXVIII.

Fifth Charter of Edward III.

12 NOVEMBER, A.D. 1376.

EDWARD, by the grace of God, king of England and France, and lord of Ireland, to all men to whom, etc., greeting.

Among other articles which our lord Edward, sometime king of England, our father, in the twelfth year of his reign, by his letters patent hath granted and confirmed to the citizens of the said city of London, for the amendment and common profit of them that dwell in the same city, and of them that repair thereto: In the same letters it is contained, that the aldermen of the aforesaid city every year be removed on the day of St. Gregory, by the commonalty of the said city, and that they so removed be not chosen again the next year ensuing; but, instead of them that have been removed, others be chosen by the same wards from which such aldermen were removed, as in the same letters plainly it is contained. Concerning which, on the part of the commonalty of the aforesaid city, by their petition before us in our great council, now again asked, of us meekly it is besought, that since divers opinions and divers strifes have sprung up between the aldermen and the commonalty of the said city upon the removing of aldermen, for the wrong interpretation of words in the aforesaid articles contained, that is to say, that the aforesaid aldermen affirm, that by the words, viz., *sint amobiles per communitatem,* etc. *i.e.,* "let them be removed by the commonalty", they ought not to be removed from the office of aldermanship without sufficient reason, or some notorious offence to be found in them: But others of the said citizens being of a contrary opinion, and willing to abolish this article, they have besought us to explain the said article, so as to remove all doubt about the premises: We being willing, as much as lieth in us, to contribute to the peace and tranquillity of the said mayor, aldermen, and commonalty, and their successors henceforward, concerning the interpretation of the said article, do, by and with the advice of our said council, declare that all and every alderman of the said city, every year, for ever, on the feast of St. Gregory the Pope, from the office of an alderman utterly and precisely shall cease, and shall not be chosen again; but that, instead of those removed, other aldermen shall be chosen every year, for ever, out of the discreet citizens of good fame, by the said wards from which the said aldermen were removed. In witness whereof we have caused these our letters to be made patent.

Aldermen to be chosen yearly, and not to be re-eligible.

 Witness myself at Westminster, the twelfth day of November, the fiftieth year of our reign in England, and the thirty-seventh over France.

No. XXIX.

Sixth Charter of Edward III.

4 December, a.d. 1376.

EDWARD, king of England and France, and lord of Ireland, to all to whom these letters shall come, greeting.

Know ye, that whereas among other liberties granted to the citizens of our city of London, by the charters of our progenitors, sometime kings of England, which we have confirmed, and by ours, it hath been granted unto them, that all merchant strangers coming into England shall remain at board with the free hosts of the city aforesaid, and of other cities and towns in England, without keeping any houses or societies by themselves; and that there shall be no brokers of any merchandises from henceforth, unless they were chosen thereunto by the merchants in the mysteries in which the said brokers exercise their offices, and thereupon at the least do take their oaths before the mayor of the said city: And also, that the merchants who are not of the freedom of the said city, should not sell by retail any wines or other wares within the said city, or the suburbs thereof. And now our well-beloved subjects, the mayor, aldermen and other citizens of the said city, have humbly besought us and our council in the last parliament by their petition exhibited in these words:

Merchant strangers to board with freemen.

What brokers should act for merchants.

No foreigners to sell by retail.

City petition to king and parliament. "To our lord the king and his good council, your liege subjects the mayor, aldermen, and commonalty of the city of London shew, That whereas they have often sued in divers parliaments to have consideration how that they are impoverished and undone, by reason that their liberties by him and his progenitors to them granted are restrained, and great part taken away; and now at the last parliament held at Westminster, it was answered to them, that they should declare their griefs specially, and they should have good remedy therefor: of which griefs (among divers others) these be: that every stranger might dwell in the said city, and keep a house, and be a broker, and sell and buy all manner of merchandises by retail; and one stranger to sell to another to sell again, to the great enhancing the prices of merchandises, and a cause to make them remain there more than forty days; whereas, in time past, no merchant stranger might use any of these points, contrary to the franchises of the said city before these times had and used; By which grievance the merchants of the said city are greatly impoverished, and the navy impaired, and the secrets of the land by the said strangers discovered to our enemies by spies and other strangers into these houses received.

"May it therefore please your majesty and council to ordain in this parliament, that the merchant strangers may be restrained in the points aforesaid, and the mayor, aldermen, and commons in the said city may enjoy the said franchises."

Confirmation of the foresaid liberties concerning buying and selling, and the qualifications of brokers. We, for the special affection we bear to the said citizens, willing to provide for the tranquillity and profit of the said citizens in that behalf, with the assents of our prelates, nobles, etc., have granted for us, and our heirs, to the said mayor and aldermen, and citizens of the said city, and their successors, upon condition that they put the said city under good government, to our honour, and the profit of our realm of England, and rightly govern the same, that no strangers shall from henceforth sell any wares in the same city, or suburbs thereof, by retail, nor shall keep any house, nor be any broker in the said city or suburbs thereof; any statute or ordinance made to the contrary notwithstanding. Saving always to the merchants of High Almaine, their liberties by us and our progenitors to them granted and confirmed. In witness whereof we have caused these our letters to be made patent.

> Witness myself at Westminster the fourth day of December, in the fiftieth year of our reign over England, and of our kingdom of France the thirty-seventh.

No. XXX.

Extracts from the Inspeximus Charter of Richard II.

4 December, a.d. 1377.

* * * * *

WHEREAS the said citizens, by their petition exhibited to us in parliament, did set forth, that although they, for a long time past, have used and enjoyed certain free customs, until of late years they have been unjustly molested; which customs are as followeth, viz., that no foreigner do sell or buy

Foreign merchants not to trade in London among themselves.

of another foreigner any merchandises within the liberties of the said city, upon pain of forfeiting the same. Nevertheless, being desirous for the future, to take away all controversies about the same, we do by these presents, with the assent aforesaid, will and grant, and by these presents, for us and our heirs, do confirm unto the said citizens, and their successors, that, for the future, no foreigner sell to another foreigner any merchandises within the liberties of the said city; nor that any foreigner do buy of another foreigner any merchandise, upon pain of forfeiting the same; the privileges of our subjects of Aquitaine in all things excepted, so that such buying and selling be made betwixt merchant and merchant.

* * * * *

Legislation by Act of Common Council.

We have granted to the mayor and aldermen that if any customs in the said city hitherto held and used shall be in any part difficult or defective, or any matters in the same city newly arising shall need amendment for which a remedy was not before ordained, the same mayor and aldermen, and their heirs and successors, with the assent of the commonalty of the same city, may appoint and ordain, so often as, and when, to them it shall seem expedient, a suitable remedy, consonant with good faith and reason, for the common profit of the citizens of the said city and other our liege people resorting thereto; provided, however, that such ordinance shall be profitable to us and our people, and consonant with good faith and reason as aforesaid.

* * * * *

71

No. XXXI.

A Proclamation

Made in the Mayoralty of Nicholas Brembre, Knight, Mayor, on Friday after the Feast of the B. V. Mary, and in the seventh Year of the Reign of Richard II, concerning the Liberties lately granted to the Citizens of London, by the Lord King in his Parliament; and also concerning certain ancient Liberties renewed by the Lord King, and newly confirmed to the said Citizens by his Royal Charter.

11 SEPTEMBER, A.D. 1383.

IT is proclaimed, on the part of the lord our king, and of the mayor of the city of London, by virtue of the confirmation and concession made by the said lord king, concerning the liberties and ancient customs of the said city, as well by charters of the kings of England granted unto them, as without charters, that it may be made known to all foreigners concerning the following liberties of the said citizens, especially touching as well the said foreigners as the citizens of the city aforesaid:

So that no summons, attachment, or execution be made by any ministers or officers of the lord the king, or of his heirs, either with or without a warrant, within the liberties of the city aforesaid, but by the officers of the city only.

Also the same lord our king has, out of his special grace, by his charter granted and confirmed, as will fully appear by having recourse to the said charters and letters, the gifts, grants, confirmations, innovations, and the ordinances aforesaid; and also all the articles, and all other and every thing contained, recited, explained in all the charters and letters as well of him the lord the king, as any of his progenitors; ratifying and granting all and each thereof, at the instance and request of the Commons of the realm of England, in his last parliament, for the nourishing greater quiet and peace among his liege subjects, and for the public good, and by and with the assent of the prelates, lords, nobility, and great men, assisting him in the same parliament, for himself and his heirs, as much as in him lies, to the citizens of the aforesaid city, and to their heirs and successors, citizens of the same city.

Also the same our lord the king has further granted, at the instance and request as aforesaid, and by the assent aforesaid, and also by his own charters confirmed, for himself and his heirs aforesaid, that the aforesaid citizens, and their successors, citizens of the city aforesaid, shall be as entirely and fully restored to all their liberties and free customs as ever they or their predecessors have at any time more freely and fully enjoyed the same under the predecessors of him the lord king.

Also the same the lord our king willeth, that, although the same citizens, or their predecessors, citizens of the city aforesaid, have not, on any occasion whatsoever, hitherto fully used any or either of the liberties, acquittances, grants, ordinances, articles, or free customs, or other things granted in the said charters or letters, or perhaps have abused any or all of the acquittances, grants, ordinances, articles, or free customs, or any other things, in the same charters or letters, as aforesaid, contained; nevertheless, the same citizens and their heirs and successors, citizens of the city aforesaid, may for the future fully enjoy and use all and singular the liberties, acquittances, grants, ordinances, articles, free customs, and whatsoever else is contained in the charters and letters aforesaid, whether the same were not used, or perhaps abused, and every one of them, without let or impediment of the same the lord the king, or of his heirs, justices, escheators, sheriffs, or any other his bailiffs or ministers whomsoever, any statutes or ordinances published, or judgments given, or any charters of the same the lord the king, or of his progenitors aforesaid, in times past made and granted, to the contrary notwithstanding.

No. XXXII.

First Charter of Edward IV.

9 November, A.D. 1462.

EDWARD, by the grace of God, king of England and France, and lord of Ireland; to all archbishops, etc., greeting.

Although, as we understand, such things all together as ought to be holden and determined by conservators of the peace, and justices assigned for hearing and determining divers felonies, trespasses, and misdemeanours in all the counties of our realm of England by the king's authority, by virtue of the ordinances and statutes of our realm aforesaid, made for the good of the peace and rule of our people, have always, time out of mind, been used and well affirmed, and yet be in our city of London: Nevertheless, to the end that from henceforth one good, certain, and undoubted manner may be continually had in our said city, for the conservation of the peace, and governing our people of the same, and that the same may always be and remain a city of peace and quietness; we will, of our mere motion, and, by tenor of these presents, do grant, for us, and as much as in us is, to the mayor and commonalty of the city aforesaid, and to the citizens of the same, and to their successors for ever, that they may have and hold all and singular their liberties

Confirmation of former liberties and free customs.

and authorities, acquittals and franchises underwritten; that is to say, that from henceforth the mayor and recorder of the said city who now be, and their successors, and the mayors and recorders which for the time shall be, as well those aldermen which before this time have been mayors of the same city, as other aldermen who shall hereafter sustain the charge of mayoralty, and shall be thereof dismissed, as long as they shall there remain aldermen for ever, shall be conservators of the present peace of our city, and the peace of our successors of the said city, and liberties thereof, as well by land as by water; both to keep or cause to be kept all ordinances and statutes, made and to be made for the good of our peace, and for the quietness, rule, and government of our people in all their articles, as well within the city aforesaid as the liberty and suburbs of the same, as well by land as by water, according to all the force, form, and effect of the same, and to chastise and punish whom they shall find offending, contrary to the form and effect of the said ordinances and statutes, as according to the form of the ordinances and statutes aforesaid should be done. *The mayor, recorder, and aldermen past the chair made perpetual justices.*

We will also, and grant to the said mayor and commonalty, and citizens, and their successors, that the now mayor and his successors aforesaid, and the recorder of the said city, which for the time shall be, and such aldermen as aforesaid, or four of the same, mayor, recorder, and aldermen, of whom we will that such mayor for the time being and his successors, be one, be justices, and have so assigned them justices for us and our successors for ever; to enquire, hear, and determine, as often and at such times as to them shall seem meet, of all manner of felonies, *And they, or any four of them, to be justices of Oyer and Terminer, to enquire, hear, and determine of all felonies, trespasses, etc.*

trespasses, forestalling and regratings, extortions, and other misdemeanours within the said city, or the liberties or suburbs thereof, as well by land as by water, by whomsoever, or after what manner soever, done or committed, and which from henceforth shall happen to be done; and also to hear, and determine, and execute all and singular other things, which shall pertain to our justices of the peace within our realm of England; so always that the said mayor and citizens, and their successors, may have and hold all and singular their ancient liberties and customs, whole, free, and sound, the premises in any thing notwithstanding; Given to our sheriffs of the city aforesaid for the time being, and to their successors, and to all whatsoever, citizens of the said city, which now be, and which hereafter for the time shall be, by tenor of these presents, strictly in commandment, that they be attendant, counselling, answering, and aiding the said keepers of the peace aforesaid, the now mayor, recorder, and their successors, and such aldermen as aforesaid, in all things they do, or may pertain to the office of conservator of the peace, and of such justices within the said city and liberties thereof, according to the form aforesaid, as often and at such times as shall be by them or any of them on our behalf duly required: saving always to the mayor and commonalty, and citizens of the same city, and to their successors, their customs, liberties, and franchises, which we will and strictly command inviolably to be observed in all things, as they and their predecessors, before the making of these presents, have observed the same.

Disputes concerning city custom to be determined in court, upon

And because we understand, that by the most ancient custom of the said city, it is there had, and in the circuits of the justices of our progenitors, sometime kings of England, it is allowed to the said citizens,

FIRST CHARTER OF EDWARD IV. 77

that the mayor and aldermen of the said city, for the time being, ought to record all their ancient customs by word of mouth, as often and at such time as any thing shall be moved in act or question before any judges or justices touching their customs aforesaid, as in their claims in the last circuit of justices holden at our Tower of London it is more fully contained: We, considering the same thing, being willing rather to enlarge than diminish the customs of the said city, of our special grace have granted, for us and our heirs and successors, unto the said mayor and commonalty and citizens, and their successors, that whensoever any issue shall be taken in any plea of or upon the customs of the city of London between any parties in pleading (yea, though they themselves be parties) or if any thing in plea, act, and question, touching the said customs, be moved or happen before us, or our heirs, to be holden, the justices of the common bench, the treasurer and barons of our exchequer, or of our heirs, or before the barons of such-like exchequer, or any other the justices of us, or of our heirs, which shall exact or require inquisition, recognizance, certificate, or trial; the same mayor and aldermen of the said city for the time being, and their successors, shall record, testify and declare, whether such be a custom, or not, by the recorder of the same city for the time being, by word of mouth; and that there may be speedy process by that record, certificate, and declaration, such custom so alleged shall be allowed for a custom, or accounted not for a custom, without any jury therefore to be taken, or further process thereupon to be made. *[hearing the recorder's report thereof.]*

And furthermore, we have granted to them, the mayor and commonalty and citizens, that though they and their successors, or the said mayor and aldermen, and their predecessors in times past, or *[No forfeiture to be taken for any crime or default in the mayor, etc.]*

their successors hereafter, have, for some cause, perchance fully not used, or abused any of the liberties, acquittals, grants, ordinances, articles, or free customs, or other thing contained in these our writings, or in other our writings, or of our progenitors sometime kings of England, to the same mayor and commonalty granted; notwithstanding we will not, that the same mayor and commonalty, aldermen and citizens, or their successors, shall therefore incur the forfeiture of any of the premises; but that they and their successors may, from henceforth, fully enjoy, and use all and singular the liberties, grants, acquittals, ordinances, articles, free customs, and other things whatsoever, so not used or abused, in the charters aforesaid contained, and every of them, without impeachment or let of us or our heirs, justices, escheators, sheriffs, or other our bailiffs and ministers, or of any other whatsoever ally, statutes or ordinances made, or judgments given, or any other charters, or any the charters of our progenitors whatsoever in times past granted to the contrary notwithstanding.

<small>All inhabitants of the city liable to be assessed in all taxes.</small> And we, being willing further to do the same mayor and commonalty a greater pleasure, and also for the bettering and common profit of our said city, will and grant to the same mayor and commonalty, and their successors, that from henceforth all and singular merchants, as well denizens and aliens, abiding within the said city, and the liberties and suburbs of the same, and exercising merchandising or occupations there by any means, by themselves or others, though they be not of the liberty of the same city, shall be partakers, shall be taxed and contribute according to their faculties in subsidies, tallages, grants, and other contributions whatsoever by any means to be assessed for the need of us, or

of our heirs, or of the said city, for the maintenance of the state, and profit of the same, with the citizens of the same city; Yet notwithstanding that this our present grant be not be in prejudice or derogation of any grants by us, or any of our progenitors, made or granted to those merchants of Almaine, which have a house in the city of London, which is commonly called the Guildhall of the Almaines, or their successors. *But not in prejudice to the grants to the merchants of Almaine.*

And further, because it is well known and manifest, that those of the said city which are called, elected, and taken to the degree of aldermen, proper for the conditions and merits requiring the same, have sustained and supported great charges, cost, and pains for the time they make their abode and residence in the same city, being vigilant for the common good, rule, and government of the same, and for that cause oftentimes do leave their possessions and places in the counties there, that therefore they, and every of them may, without all fear of unquietness or molestation, peaceably abide and tarry in such their houses, places, and possessions, when they shall return thither for comfort and recreation's sake: We have, of our special grace, granted to the said mayor and commonalty, and to their successors aforesaid, that all and every of these, which be aldermen of the said city, and their successors, which for the time shall be aldermen there for the term of their lives, shall have this liberty; that is to say, that as long as they shall continue aldermen there, and shall bear the charge of aldermen proper; and also those which before had been aldermen, and have also with their great costs and expenses borne the office of mayoralty, shall not be put in any assizes, juries, or attaints, recognisances, or inquisitions, out of the said city; and that they, nor any of them, shall *Aldermen not to be put upon assizes, attaints, or juries, nor to be appointed collectors or taxers out of the city.*

be trier or triers of the same, although they touch us, or our heirs or our successors, or other whomsoever: And that, without that city, neither they, nor any of them, be made collectors or collector, assessor, taxer, overseer, or comptroller of the tenths, fifteenths, taxes, tallages, subsidies, or other charges or impositions whatsoever, to us, our heirs or successors hereafter to be granted or given; and if they or any of them be elected to any of the offices or charges aforesaid, and the same mayor or aldermen do deny, refuse, or not do the offices or charges aforesaid, then they or any of them shall not, by any means, incur any contempt, loss, fine, imprisonment, or forfeiture, by occasion of their so refusing or not doing, nor shall, for that cause, forfeit any issues by any means.

Southwark, with the waifs, etc., granted to the city.

A.D. 1327.

And further, as we understand, the lord Edward, sometime king of England, the third after the Conquest, our progenitor, with the assent of the prelates, earls, barons, and commonalty of the realm of England assembled in parliament holden at Westminster, in the first year of his reign, at the petition of the then citizens of the said city, by his letters patent granted for him and his heirs to the same citizens the town of Southwark, with the appurtenances, to have and hold to them and their successors, citizens of the same city, of the same our progenitors and their heirs for ever, paying unto him by the year, at the exchequer of him and his heirs, at the terms accustomed, the farm therefor due and accustomed, as in the said letters patent more fully is contained: And now the mayor and commonalty of the same city, and their predecessors, have and hold certain liberties and franchises in the town aforesaid, by virtue of those letters patent, and do use the same as their predecessors have had and held them, and have used and enjoyed them ; and they now fear that divers doubts, opinions, varieties, and ambiguities, controversies, and dissensions may light, and be likely to spring, grow, be imagined, holden and had in time to come, in and about the use and exercise of such liberties and franchises, for want of more clear and full declaration and expressing of the same, for that divers diversely interpret, judge, and understand: We therefore, to the end to take away from henceforth and utterly to abolish all and all manner of causes, occasions, and matters, whereupon such opinions, ambiguities, varieties, controversies, and dissensions may spring, be holden, and moved in this behalf, have, of our special grace, and from our mere notion, granted to the said mayor and commonalty of the said city which now be, and their successors, mayor and commonalty and citizens of that city, which for the time being shall be for ever, the town of Southwark, with the appurtenances, with all chattels called waif and estray, and also treasure found in the town aforesaid, and all manner of handiwork, goods and chattels of traitors, felons, fugitives outlawed, condemned, convicted, and of felons defamed and denying the laws of our land, wheresoever, or before whomsoever, justice shall be done upon them ; and also goods disclaimed, found, or being within the town aforesaid ; and also all manner of escheats and forfeitures which may there pertain unto us, as fully and wholly as we should have them, if the same town were in our hands : And that it shall be lawful to the same mayor and commonalty, and to their successors, by their deputy and ministers of the same town, to put themselves in possession of and in all the handiworks and chattels of all manner of traitors, felons, fugitives, outlaws condemned, convicted, and

G

of felons defamed and denying the laws of our land; and also of and in all the goods disclaimed, found, and being within the same; and also of and in all the escheats and forfeitures to us and our heirs there pertaining: And that the same mayor and commonalty and citizens, and their successors, by themselves, or their deputy or ministers, may have in the town aforesaid assay, and assize of bread, wine, beer and ale, and all other victuals and things whatsoever saleable in the said town; and also all and whatsoever doth and may pertain to the office of clerk of the market of our house or of our heirs, together with the correction and punishment of all persons there selling wine, bread, beer, ale, and other victuals, and all other inhabiting and exercising any arts whatsoever; and with all manner of forfeitures, fines, and amerciaments to be forfeited, and all other which there do, and in any time to come may there pertain to us, our heirs or successors: And that they shall have in the said town the execution of all manner of writs of ours, or of our heirs or successors, and of all other writs, commandments, precepts, extracts, and warrants, with the return of the same by such their ministers or deputy whom they shall thereunto choose; so always that the clerk of the market of our house, or of the house of our heirs, or the sheriff or escheator of the county of Surrey, which now is, or hereafter shall be, do not, by any means, intermeddle, enter, or do any execution.

Assize of bread, etc., there.

Execution of writs.

To hold a fair and court of pie-powder for three days. We have also granted to the same mayor and commonalty and citizens, and their successors for ever, that they shall and may have yearly one fair in the town aforesaid for three days; that is to say, the seventh, eighth, and ninth days of September, to be holden, together with a court of pie-powder, and with all liberties and free customs to such fair appertaining; and that they may have and hold there at their said courts, before their said ministers or deputy, the said three days, from day to day, and hour to hour, from time to time, all occasions, plaints, and pleas of a court of pie-powder, together with all summons, attachments, arrests, issues, fines, redemptions and commodities, and other rights whatsoever, to the same court of pie-powder any way pertaining, without any impediment, let, or hindrance of us, our heirs, or successors, or other our officers and ministers whatsoever; and also that they may have there a view of frankpledge, and whatsoever thereto pertaineth, together with all summons, attachments, arrests, issues, amerciaments, fines, redemptions, profits, commodities, and other things whatsoever, which there may or ought therefore to pertain to us, our heirs or successors.

And furthermore, the aforesaid mayor and commonalty and citizens, and their successors, may, by themselves, or by their minister or deputy in the said town appointed, take and arrest all manner of felons, thieves, and other malefactors found within the said town, and may lead them to our gaol of Newgate, safely to be kept, until they shall be by process of law delivered. *To carry thieves thence to Newgate.*

And further, the said mayor and commonalty and citizens, and their successors, may, for ever, have in the town aforesaid all manner of liberties, privileges, franchises, acquittals, customs, and rights, which we should or might there have, if the said town were and remained in our hands, without any thing to be by any means given or paid to us or our heirs, beside only ten pounds for the ancient farm therefor due, and without impeachment, let, molestation, or disturbance of us, or our heirs or successors, justices, escheators,

<small>Archbishop of Canterbury's right reserved.</small> sheriffs, officers, or ministers of ours, or of our heirs or successors whatsoever; the rights, liberties, and franchises of right belonging to the most reverend father and lord in Christ, Thomas, lord archbishop of Canterbury, and of other persons there, always saved; although express mention be not here made of the true yearly value of the premises, or of any other gifts or grants to the mayor or aldermen, sheriffs and citizens, or to their successors, or any of them made, according to the form of the statute thereof had, made, and provided, or any other statute, ordinance, act, thing, cause, or matter whatsoever notwithstanding.

> These being witness, the reverend father Thomas archbishop of Canterbury, William archbishop of York, George bishop of Exeter, chancellor, and William bishop of Ely, and our dear brothers George of Clarence, and Richard of Gloucester, dukes, etc. Given by our hand at Westminster, the ninth day of November, in the second year of our reign.

No. XXXIII.

Second Charter of Edward IV.

27 August, a.d. 1463.

EDWARD, by the grace of God, king of England and France, and lord of Ireland, to all to whom these present letters shall come, greeting.

Know ye, that for certain and notable causes us specially moving, of our special grace and certain knowledge, we have granted to the mayor and commonalty, and citizens of our city of London, that the tronage and weighing, and measuring, laying-up, and placing, and housing of whatsoever wools, by whomsoever, from whatsoever parts, brought or to be brought to the city aforesaid, or which have before time been accustomed to be brought to the staple at Westminster, shall from henceforth be, and be made in the place called Leadenhall, within our city aforesaid, and in no other place within three miles of the said city, to have the laying-up, placing, and housing aforesaid, together with all fees, profits, and emoluments to the same laying-up, placing, and housing or any of them due, used, or accustomed to the aforesaid mayor and commonalty, and citizens of the same city, and their successors, for ever, without any account to be made, or any other thing therefor to us to be paid, although express mention be not in these presents made of the clear yearly value or certainty of the premises, or of any other gifts or

Weighing of wool confined to Leadenhall.

grants by us or our progenitors to the said mayor and commonalty and citizens, and their successors, by any means made, or any other statute, act, ordinance, or any other thing whatsoever made to the contrary notwithstanding. In witness whereof, we have caused these our letters to be made patent:

> Witness myself at Westminster, the twenty-seventh day of August, in the third year of our reign.

No. XXXIV.

Third Charter of Edward IV.

20 June, a.d. 1478.

EDWARD, by the grace of God, king of England and France, and lord of Ireland, to all to whom these presents shall come, greeting.

Know ye, that whereas the sum of twelve thousand nine hundred and twenty-three pounds nine shillings and eightpence is by us, amongst other things, due to our beloved and faithful subjects, the mayor, commonalty and citizens of our city of London, as in the receipt of our exchequer more plainly appeareth; of which sum the said mayor and commonalty are willing to remit and release unto us nineteen hundred and twenty-three pounds nine shillings and eight-pence, to the intent we should vouchsafe to grant them licence, that they and their successors might purchase lands, rents and services, and other possessions whatsoever, to the value of two hundred marks by the year, over all charges and reprises, although they should be holden of us or of others by any manner of service, of whatsoever person or persons willing to give, bequeath, or assign the same to them; to have and to hold to the same mayor and commonalty, and to their successors aforesaid, for ever, in form following: *On condition of £1923 9s. 8d. released to the king, gives liberty to purchase lands in mortmain to the value of 200 marks per annum.*

We inwardly pondering, not only the premises, but also the manifold pleasures to us by the mayor and commonalty of the said city before this time acceptably done, and willing (as we are bound) before all other things wholly to pay and recompense our debts, have of our special grace, and for that the said mayor and commonalty, for them and their successors, have remitted and altogether released unto us the said sum of nineteen hundred and twenty-three pounds nine shillings and eight pence, granted and given licence, and by these presents do grant and give licence, for us and our heirs (as much as in us is) to the said mayor and commonalty, that they and their successors may purchase lands, revenues, rents, services, and other possessions whatsoever, to the value of two hundred marks, by the year, over all charges and reprises, of any person or persons willing to give, grant, bequeath or assign the same unto them, although they be holden of us or others by any manner of service, in full satisfaction and contentment of the said sum of nineteen hundred and twenty-three pounds nine shillings and eight pence, to them by us due, without any fine or fee to be paid to the use of us or our heirs, to have and to hold to the same mayor and commonalty and their successors for ever.

And we have by tenor of these presents given special licence to the same person and persons, that he or she may give, grant, bequeath or assign lands, tenements, rents, possessions and services, to the yearly value aforesaid, over and above all reprises and charges as aforesaid, unto the said mayor and commonalty, and to their successors as aforesaid, for ever, without hindrance of us or our heirs, our justices, escheators, sheriffs, coroners, bailiffs, or other the ministers of us or our heirs whatsoever; and this without any other the king's letters patent, or inquisitions upon any writ of *Ad quod damnum*, or any other the king's commandments in this behalf, by any means to be had, prosecuted and taken; the statute concerning lands and tenements not to be put in mortmain, or any other statute, act, or ordinance made to the contrary notwithstanding.

And we also will and grant to the said mayor and commonalty, that they and their successors may have so many and such writs *Ad quod damnum*, and other royal letters patent executory, from time to time, upon the licence aforesaid, in full satisfaction and contentment of the said sum of nineteen hundred and twenty-three pounds nine shillings and eight pence. In witness whereof we have caused these our letters to be made patent.

Witness myself at Westminster, the twentieth day of June, in the eighteenth year of our reign.

No. XXXV.

Fourth Charter of Edward IV.

20 JUNE, A.D. 1478.

EDWARD, by the grace of God, king of England and France, and lord of Ireland, to all to whom the present letters patent shall come, greeting.

Know ye, that whereas the sum of twelve thousand nine hundred and twenty-three pounds nine shillings and eight pence, is, amongst other things, due by us to our well-beloved the mayor and commonalty of our city of London, as in the receipt of our exchequer more fully appeareth; of which sum the mayor and commonalty are willing to remit and release unto us

On condition of £7,000 released and remitted to the king.

the sum of seven thousand pounds, to the intent we should vouchsafe to grant to the said mayor and commonalty, and their successors, the offices and occupations under-written, to be had in form following:

We inwardly pondering, not only the premises, but also the manifold pleasures to us by the mayor and commonalty of the said city before-time acceptably done, and willing, as we are bound, before all other things, to pay or recompense our debts, have, of our special grace, and for that the said mayor and commonalty have, for them and their successors, remitted and released unto us seven thousand pounds, parcel of the twelve thousand nine hundred and twenty-three pounds nine shillings and eight pence, granted and by these presents do grant, to the said mayor and commonalty, and their successors, in full satisfaction and contentment of the said sum of seven thousand pounds, to them by us due: the offices of packing of all manner of woollen cloths, sheep skins, calves-skins, goat-skins, vessels of amber, and of all other merchandises whatsoever, to be packed, tunned, piped, barrelled, or anywise to be included, with the oversight of opening all manner of customable merchandises arriving at the port of safety, as well by land as by water, within the liberties and franchises of the said city and suburbs of the same, as well of the goods of denizens as of aliens, wheresoever they shall be accustomed; and also the office of packing all woollen cloths, sheep-skins, lamb-skins, goat-skins, and calves-skins, with picking and poundering of the same, and all amber vessels, and of all other merchandises to be packed, picked, and poundered in London, or the suburbs of the same, or to be carried by land, or to be accustomed, as well concerning the goods of merchants denizens, as of aliens; and also of the office of carriage and portage of all wools, sheep-skins, tynn-bails, and other merchandises whatsoever, which shall be carried in London from the water of Thames unto the houses of strangers, and contrarywise from the same houses to the said water, or of other merchandises which ought to be carried, being in any house for a time.

And also the office of occupation of garbling of all manner of spices, and other merchandises coming to the said city at any time, which ought to be garbled; and the office of gauger within the said city; and also the office of wine-drawers, to provide for the carrying of wines brought to the port of the said city, and laid on land wheresoever it be, and elsewhere to be carried, to have the occupations and offices

Grants the office of package,

Carriage, portage,

Garbling, gauging, wine-drawers.

aforesaid, and every of them, and the dispositions, ordinances, oversights, and corrections of the same, together with all fees, profits and emoluments to the same offices or occupations, and other the premises, and every of them due, used and accustomed to the said mayor and commonalty, and citizens of the same city, and their successors for ever; and also the exercising of the same offices by themselves, or by their sufficient deputies, without any account or any other thing to us or our heirs therefore to be given or made, in full satisfaction and contentment of the said sum of seven thousand pounds.

<small>Anthony Widvile, 2nd Earl Rivers.</small> And further, whereas our most dear cousin, Anthony earl Rivers, hath of our grant, by our letters patent, the office of our chief butler of England, under a certain form in the said letters patent specified; by reason of which office, the earl hath granted, <small>Office of coroner.</small> and pretendeth to grant, the office of coroner within the said city and suburbs of the same; we likewise, in satisfaction and contentment of the said sum of seven thousand pounds, to the said mayor and commonalty, as is aforesaid, due, have of our special grace granted that the same mayor and commonalty, and their successors, may lawfully and safely grant the said office of coroner to any person who shall please the said mayor and commonalty and their successors, and may make a coroner there whom shall please them immediately, and as soon as the said office of chief butler of England, or the office of coroner aforesaid, shall happen to be void, or to come to our gift, by the surrender of the said earl, or by any other cause whatsoever.

And we will, by these presents, that the same office of coroner be from henceforth severally and distinctly and altogether separated from the coroner so made by the said mayor and commonalty, or their successors,

[who] may have full power and authority to exercise and do all and singular things, which to the office of coroner within the said city, and suburbs of the same, do pertain to be exercised and done; so that none other our coroner, nor of our heirs or successors, shall by any means intermeddle within the said city or suburbs of the same; although express mention of the true yearly value or certainty of the premises, or any of them, or if any other gift or grants, by us or our progenitors to the said mayor and commonalty, and citizens, or to their predecessors before this time by any means made, be not in these presents made, or any statute, act, ordinance or provision thereof made, published or ordained to the contrary, or any other thing whatsoever notwithstanding. In witness whereof we have caused these our letters to be made patent.

Witness myself at Westminster, the twentieth day of June, in the eighteenth year of our reign.

No. XXXVI.

Regulations concerning strangers buying and selling within the City.

From Henry VIIth's Charter.

22 August, a.d. 1485.

* * * * *

OF all time, of which the memory of man is not to the contrary, for the commonweal of the realm and city aforesaid, it hath been used, and by authority of parliament approved and confirmed, that no stranger from the liberty of the city may buy or sell, from any stranger from the liberties of the same city, any merchandise or wares within the liberties of the same city, upon forfeiture of the same. The said mayor and commonalty, and citizens, and their predecessors by all the time aforesaid, have had and received, and have been accustomed to receive, perceive, and have, to the use of the said mayor, commonalty, and citizens, all and all manner of merchandises and wares bought and sold within the liberties of the same city as aforesaid, and forfeitures of the same merchandises and wares, until of late past time they were troubled or molested.

The same lord Henry the seventh, by his letters patent as aforesaid, for pacifying and taking away from henceforth controversies and ambiguities in that behalf, and to fortify and by express words to explain and declare the liberty and custom aforesaid to them the said mayor and commonalty and citizens, and their heirs and successors, and willing the said liberties to be peaceably and quietly had, possessed, and enjoyed to the said mayor and commonalty and citizens, and their successors, with the forfeitures aforesaid, against the said late lord king Henry, his heirs and successors granted, and by his said charter confirmed to the same mayor and commonalty and citizens, and their successors, that no stranger from the liberties of the same city may buy or sell from any other stranger to the liberty of the same city, any merchandises or wares within the liberties of the same city; and if any stranger to the liberty of the same city shall sell or buy any merchandises or wares within the liberty of the same city of any other stranger to the liberty of the same city, that the same mayor, commonalty and citizens, and their successors, may have, hold, and receive all and all manner of such-like merchandises and wares, so bought and to be bought, sold or to be sold, within the liberty of the said city, between whatsoever strangers to the liberty of the same city, as forfeited; and all the forfeitures of the same, and also the penalties, fines, and redemptions whatsoever any ways forfeited, lost or to be lost, or to be forfeited or due thereon, to the use and profit of the same mayor and commonalty and citizens, and their heirs and successors, without hindrance of the same late king, his heirs or successors, and without any account or any other thing to be rendered or paid thereof to the late king, his heirs and successors, any statute, act, or ordinance of us or our progenitors made to the contrary notwithstanding; although the same mayor and commonalty, and citizens of the said city, or their predecessors, have before that time used, abused, or not used those customs and liberties: Saving always, that the great

Strangers not to buy and sell to other strangers within the city.

Forfeitures, etc., to the use of the city.

men, lords and nobles, and other English and strangers, of what condition they shall be, may freely buy whatsoever merchandises in gross for their families and proper uses within the liberties of the said city, without any forfeiture, loss, or hindrance whatsoever, so that they do not sell again the said merchandises to any other.

<small>Office of gauger.</small>

And further, the same late king, of his ample grace, by his said letters patent, amongst other things, did give and grant to the mayor, commonalty, and citizens of the same city of London, and their successors, the office of gauger within the said city, and the disposing, ordering, surveying, and correcting of the same, to have, hold, exercise, and occupy the said office, and other premises, with all fees, profits, and emoluments to the said office in any manner belonging or appertaining, to the same mayor and commonalty, and citizens, by themselves, or by their sufficient deputy or deputies, from the twenty-second day of August, in the first year of his reign, for ever, without any account to be made thereof, or any other thing rendering or paying to the said lord Henry the seventh, his heirs or successors, as by the said letters patent doth more plainly appear.

No. XXXVII.

Charter of Henry VIII,

For removing the Sessions from St. Martin's le Grand to the Guildhall.

16 JUNE, A.D. 1518.

HENRY, by the grace of God, king of England and France, and lord of Ireland, to all to whom these presents shall come, greeting.
Whereas Edward the third, sometime king of England, our progenitor, by his letters patent, amongst other things, has granted to the citizens of the city of London, that all inquisitions from henceforth to be taken by the justices, and other the ministers of the men of the said city, should be taken at Great St. Martin's in London, and not elsewhere, except inquisitions to be taken in circuits in the Tower of London, and for the gaol-delivery of Newgate.
Know ye, that we, for some urgent causes reasonable us moving, at the petition of the mayor and commonalty aforesaid, and of the citizens of the same city, have, of our special grace, and from our certain knowledge and mere motion, granted, and by these presents do grant, for us and our heirs (as much as in us is) to the said mayor and commonalty, and unto their successors, and unto the same citizens of the same city, that all inquisitions by the justices, or other our ministers, or of our heirs, to be from henceforth taken of the men of our city aforesaid, shall be taken at the Guildhall, within the city afore-

H

said, or at any other place within the same city, where it shall from time to time be thought to our justices for the time being, before whom those inquisitions ought hereafter to be taken, most expedient and most convenient, and not elsewhere, except inquisitions be taken at the circuits of the Tower of London, and for the gaol-delivery of Newgate. In witness whereof, we have caused these our letters to be made patent:

Witness myself at Westminster, the sixteenth day of June, in the tenth year of our reign.

No. XXXVIII.

The Charter of King Henry VIII,

Restoring the Office of Keeper of the Great Beam or Common Balance of Weight, to the Corporation of London.

13 APRIL, A.D. 1531.

HENRY the eighth, by the grace of God, king of England and France, defender of the faith, and lord of Ireland, to all to whom these present letters shall come, greeting.

Whereas we, by our letters patent, the date whereof is the eighteenth day of June, in the thirteenth year of our reign, have, of our special grace, and from our certain knowledge and mere motion, given and granted for us and our heirs, forasmuch as in us then was, to Sir William Sidney, knight, the office of keeper of the great beam and common balance or weight within our city of London, for weighing all merchandises of avoirdupois, and also all weights whatsoever within the same city; which office one William Stafford, deceased, lately exercised and occupied, by what name soever the same office was named or known; and have ordained, made, and constituted the said Sir William Sidney keeper of the great beam, balance and weight, and of all other weights whatsoever; and also of the weights of all spices, wares, commodities, merchandises and things in the city aforesaid, there to be weighed and accustomed, and used to be bought and sold by weight: *Right of weighing at the beam formerly granted to Sir William Sidney, kt., 18 June, A.D. 1521.*

And have granted also, by our said letters patent, to the said Sir William, authority and power to make, name and assign, from time to time, all manner of clerks, porters, servants and ministers of the great beam and balance, and of the iron beam, and of the beam of the Stillyard, and of the weights aforesaid: and also all other clerks, porters, servants and ministers to the same office belonging; and also to remove the same or any of them, and other or others to make, put and constitute in his or their place, as often as to him shall seem expedient, to have, occupy, and exercise the office and offices aforesaid, together with the authority aforesaid, to the said Sir William Sidney, by himself, or by his deputy or deputies, during our pleasure, to his proper use and behoof, with all and singular commodities, houses, advantages, profits, fees and emoluments to the said office in our time, or in the times of any of our progenitors, kings of England, due and accustomed, pertaining or belonging, in as ample manner and form as any person, having or occupying such office before this time, had received and enjoyed the same: And have given and granted the same commodities, houses, advantages, profits, fees and emoluments, and all and singular the premises, for the exercise and occupation of the office aforesaid, in manner and form aforesaid, to the said Sir William, during our pleasure, to the use and behoof of the said Sir William, without account, or any other thing to us or our heirs, in this behalf, for the premises to be made, given, or paid; although express mention be not made of the true yearly value, or of any certainty of the premises, or any grant or grants by us or any of our progenitors to the said Sir William before this time made, contained in the said letters patent above specified, or any statute, act, ordinance, restraint or provision before this time made or provided to the contrary, or any other thing, cause, or matter whatsoever in any thing notwithstanding, as by the same our letters patent fully appeareth; which our pleasure in that behalf we will by these shall be determined; and which letters patent the same Sir William Sidney hath surrendered into our chancery to be cancelled, to the intent we would vouchsafe to grant our letters patent to the mayor, commonalty, and citizens of our city of London. Now surrendered.

And because now of late we understand of the grievous complaint of our well-beloved the mayor, commonalty, and citizens of our said city of London, that the said lord Edward, some time king of England, the second, our progenitor, by his charter, dated the eighteenth day of June, in the twelfth year of his reign, amongst other things, granted to the then citizens of the said city, predecessors to the now mayor, commonalty, and citizens aforesaid, that the weights and beams for the weighing of merchandises between merchants and merchants, of which the profits growing and knowledge of the same pertain to the commonalty of the said city, should remain to be kept, at the will of the said commonalty, in the custody of two sufficient men of the same city expert in that office, to be thereunto chosen by the commonalty of the said city; and that they should in no wise be committed to any others, than to such as should be so chosen, as by the same his letters patent, which we have seen, more fully appeareth. A.D. 1319.

And because also the lord Henry, sometime king of England, the fourth, our progenitor, by his letters patent dated the twenty-fifth day of May, in the first year of his reign, of his favourable grace, amongst other things, granted to the said citizens of the said city tronage; that is to say, the weighing of lead, wax, pepper, alum, madder, and all other such-like wares A.D. 1400.

within the said city for ever: which letters patent we, of our special grace, by our charter dated the twelfth day of July, in the first year of our reign, ratified and confirmed to the same then citizens, and to their successors, as by the same our letters patent more fully appeareth: by which letters patent, and by the continual keeping of the office of beam, balance, weights, and of other the premises time out of mind, by the said citizens and their predecessors, and by the exercise and occupation of the same within the said city, without any challenging, it is manifest, and without any difficulty evident and apparent unto us, that the said office of the great beam and common balance, ordained for weighing between merchants and merchants, and the office of keeping of the great balance or weight within our city of London, for the weighing of all merchandises of avoirdupois, and also of all weights whatsoever, within the said city; and also of all spices, wares, merchandises, and things in the city aforesaid, there to be weighed; and also the authority and power to make, name, and assign all and all manner of clerks, porters, servants, and ministers of the said great beam and balance, and of the iron beam, and of the beam of the Stillyard; and also all other clerks, porters, servants, and ministers to the said office pertaining, and the issues and revenues thereof coming, and all and singular the premises pertaining and of ancient right belonging to the mayor, commonalty and citizens, we will in no wise be wronged.

And to the end that from henceforth all ambiguities in such case might be taken away, and that the said mayor and commonalty, and citizens, and their successors, may not in time to come be impeached, impleaded, or grieved, by us, our heirs or successors, or any of our justices or ministers, of or for the premises, or any of them, we will and grant to the now mayor, commonalty, and citizens, and to their successors, that the weights and beams for weighing of merchandises between merchant and merchant, whereof the profits growing, and the knowledge of them, to pertain to the commonalty of the city aforesaid, shall remain at the will of the commonalty of the same city, to be kept in the custody of good sufficient men of the same city, expert in that office, and to be thereunto chosen by the commonalty aforesaid, and that to others than so to be chosen in no wise they be committed; and that they shall have tronage that is to say, the weighing of wax, lead, pepper alum, madder, and all other such-like wares within the said city for ever. *Hereby granted to the city.*

Willing also to do the said mayor and commonalty a more ample pleasure in this behalf, we have, of our favourable grace, and from our certain knowledge and mere motion, given and granted, and by these presents do give and grant to the same mayor, commonalty, and citizens of the city of London, the aforesaid office of keeper of the great beam and common balance, ordained for weighing between merchant and merchant; and also the office of the great beam and weights within the said city, for weighing of merchandises of avoirdupois; and also of all weights whatsoever within our said city, and of all spices, wares, merchandises, and things in our said city, there to be weighed, by whatsoever name the said office is named or known; and do by these presents make, ordain, and constitute the same mayor, commonalty, and citizens, and their successors, keepers of the great beam, balance, and weights aforesaid, and other weights whatsoever; and also the weighing of all spices, wares, merchandises, and things in the city aforesaid, there to be weighed, and accustomed to be bought and sold by weight within our said city.

And also we do give and grant to the mayor, commonalty, and citizens of our city aforesaid, authority and power to make, name, and assign from time to time all and all manner of clerks, porters, servants, and ministers of the great beam and balance, and of the iron beam, and of the beam of the Stillyard, and weights aforesaid; and also all other clerks, servants, and ministers to the same office pertaining; and also to remove them or any of them, and to make, constitute, and place other in his or their place, as often as to them shall seem expedient, to have, occupy, and exercise the office aforesaid, together with the authority and power aforesaid, to the said mayor and commonalty and citizens, and their successors, by themselves, their deputy or deputies, for ever, to their own proper use and behoof, together with all and singular commodities, houses, advantages, profits, wages, fees, and emoluments in our time, or in the times of any of our progenitors kings of England, due and accustomed, pertaining or belonging to the same office, in as ample manner and form as the same citizens and their predecessors, or any other person or persons having or occupying the same office before this time, had and received or enjoyed the same.

And also we give and grant by these presents to the said mayor, commonalty, and citizens, and their successors, the commodities, houses, advantages, profits, fees, and emoluments, and all and singular the premises, for the exercise and occupation of the said office, to the proper use and behoof of the said mayor, commonalty, and citizens, and their successors, without account, or any other thing to us or our heirs to be delivered, made, given, or paid in this behalf for the premises, or any of them, in these letters patent specified and contained; although express mention be not in these presents made of the true value or certainty of the premises, or of their gifts or grants by us to the said mayor, commonalty, and citizens of the said city before this time made, or any statute, act, ordinance, provision, or restraint thereof made, ordained, or provided to the contrary, or any other thing, cause, or matter whatsoever in any wise notwithstanding. In witness whereof we have caused these our letters to be made patent.

Witness myself at Westminster, the thirteenth day of April, in the twenty-second year of our reign.

No. XXXIX.

Act of Common Council in 1538,

To enforce the Statute 27 Hen. VIII, c. 18, for preserving the Navigation of the River Thames.

A.D. 1535-6.

WHEREAS, by a statute made in the twenty-seventh year of the reign of our sovereign lord king Henry the eighth, for reformation of the river of Thames, among other abuses, by casting in dung and other filth, many great shelves, and other risings, have of late grown and been made within the said river; by reason whereof many great breaches have ensued by occasion thereof, which of like shall be the occasion of the utter destruction of the said river, unless that the same law be put in due execution, according to the true intent and meaning thereof:

Wherefore, for a future reformation of the same, and to the intent that the said good and wholesome statute may be put in more execution, and better knowledge of the people:

Permission to remove sand, etc.

It is enacted, by the authority of this common council, that proclamation may be made within this city, and the same to be put in writing, and tables thereof made, and set up in divers places of this city, that it shall be lawful to every person or persons, to dig, carry away, and take away sand, gravel, or any rubbish, earth, or anything lying and being in any shelf or shelves, within the said river of Thames, without let or interruption of any person or persons,

ACT OF COMMON COUNCIL IN 1538.

and without paying anything for the same; and after that to sell the same away, or otherwise occupy or dispose of the said gravel, sand, or other thing, at their free liberty and pleasure.

And that all paviours, bricklayers, tilers, masons, and all others that occupy sand or gravel, shall endeavour themselves, with all diligence, to occupy the said sand or gravel, and none other, paying for the same reasonably, as they should or ought to pay for other sand or gravel digged out of other men's grounds about the said city, which after is filled again with many filthy things, to the great infection of the inhabitants of the said city, and all others repairing unto the same: and further that humble suit be made to the king's highness, that all persons, having lands or tenements along the river side, upon certain pain, by his highness and the lords of his honourable council to be limited, shall well and sufficiently repair and maintain all the walls and banks adjoining unto their said lands, that so the water may not, nor shall break in upon the same; and the same to be continued till the time the said noble river be brought again to its old course and former state.

And that strong gates of iron, along the waterside, and also by the street-side, where any watercourse is had into the said Thames, be made by the inhabitants of every ward, so along the said water, as of old times has been accustomed; and that every grate be in height twenty-four inches at the least, as the place shall need; and, in breadth, one from another one inch; and the same to be done with all expedition and speed. *Iron gates to be erected.*

And, if the occupiers of the said lands and tenements make default contrary to the ordinance aforesaid, or else if any person or persons in great rains, or other times, sweep their soilage or filth off their houses

Those who pollute the river to be fined.

into the channel, and the same afterwards is conveyed into the Thames, every person so offending shall forfeit for every such default one shilling and eight pence; and that, upon complaint to be made to any constable next adjoining to the said place where any such default shall be found, it shall be lawful for the said constable, or his sufficient deputy, for the time being, from time to time, to distrain for the said offence, and to retain the same irreplagiable. And a like law to be observed and kept, and like penalty to be paid, by every person that burns rushes and straw in their houses, or washes in the common streets or lanes, and to be recovered as aforesaid; and the one moiety thereof to be to the mayor and commonalty, and the other moiety to be divided betwixt the said constable that taketh pain and the party finder of the said default. And if the constable, or his deputy, refuse to do his duty, according to the true meaning of this act, that then the constable, or his deputy, which shall so refuse to do his duty, as aforesaid, shall forfeit and pay for every time so offending three shillings and four pence; and the same penalty of the constable, to be recovered and obtained by distress irreplagiable, to be taken by any of the officers of the chamber of London, to the use of the mayor and commonalty of London. And further, that no person or persons, having any wharf or house by the waterside, make their lay-stalls where the common rakers of this city use to repose and lay all their soilage, to be carried away by them with their dung boats; and that the said rakers shall lay their said dung, carried in their said dung boats, at such convenient place or places, as shall be appointed by the lord mayor of London, for the time being, with the advice of his brethren, the aldermen of the same, and at no other place or places, upon pain to forfeit for every such default five pounds, to be recovered in any of the king's courts within the city of London, by bill, plaint, moiety of debt, or information, by any person that will or shall sue for the same; the one moiety thereof to be unto the mayor and commonalty of London, and the other moiety to him or them that will or shall sue for the same; in which actions or suits, no wager of law or essoign shall be allowed.

No. XL.

Charter of King Edward VI,

Granting the Manor of Southwark, etc., to the City of London.

23 April, a.d. 1550.

<small>Certain parcels of land, etc., in Southwark and Surrey granted.</small>

EDWARD the sixth, by the grace of God, king of England, France, and Ireland, defender of the faith, and on earth supreme head of the church of England and Ireland; to all to whom these present letters shall come, greeting.

Know ye, that for the sum of six hundred and forty-seven pounds two shillings and a penny, of lawful money of England, paid to the hands of the treasurer of our Court of Augmentation and Revenues of our crown, to our use, by our well-beloved the mayor and commonalty and citizens of the city of London, whereof we acknowledge ourselves to be fully satisfied and paid, and the mayor and commonalty and citizens and their successors to be thereof acquitted and discharged by these presents; and for other causes and considerations, us thereunto especially moving; we have of our special grace, and of our certain knowledge and mere motion, and also with the advice of our council, given and granted, and by these presents do give and grant, to the said mayor and commonalty and citizens of the city of London, all that our messuage or tenement, with the appurtenances, now or late in the tenure of Simon Sebatson, situate and being next our mansion, late that of Charles, late duke of Suffolk, in Southwark, in the county of Surrey; and all that our messuage or tenement, with the appurtenances, next the broad gate of the same our mansion in Southwark aforesaid; and all that our close of ground called "Moulter's Close", containing by estimation fifteen acres, lying in Newington, in our said county of Surrey; and all that our close of ground, containing by estimation two acres, now or late in the tenure of John Parrow, lying and being in St. George's dunghill, in the parish of St. George, in Southwark aforesaid; and also that one close of ground, late in the tenure of John Billington, lying in Lambeth marsh, in the parish of Lambeth, in the said county of Surrey; and also all those our thirty-nine acres and three rods of meadow, with the appurtenances, now or late in the tenure of William Basely, lying and being in divers parcels in the field called St. George's field, in the parish of St. George in Southwark, in our said county of Surrey; and one messuage or tenement of ours, situate near "Broad Gates", in Southwark aforesaid; and all those our two messuages or tenements and one chamber, and three stables, and one garden of ours, with all their appurtenances, situate and being in Southwark aforesaid; all and singular which premises were some time parcel of the possessions and hereditaments of Charles duke of Suffolk; and all other the messuages, lands, tenements, rents, reversions, and hereditaments whatsoever, with their appurtenances, in Southwark, in the said county of Surrey, which belonged to the aforesaid Charles duke of Suffolk, and which were late purchased by our dear father Henry the eighth, late king of England, of the same Charles, late duke of Suffolk; except nevertheless always to us and our heirs and successors, all that our capital messuage and mansion house called "Southwark Place", in Southwark afore-

Charles Brandon, D. of Suffolk.

Parts reserved.

said, late the said duke of Suffolk's, and all gardens and grounds to the same adjoining or appertaining; and all our park in Southwark aforesaid, and all the messuages, and all the buildings and grounds called the "Antelope" there.

<small>The lordship and manor of Southwark also granted to the city.</small>

Furthermore, we give, and for the consideration aforesaid, with the advice aforesaid, do by these presents grant to the aforesaid mayor and commonalty and citizens of the said city of London, all that our lordship and manor of Southwark, with their rights, members and appurtenances in the said county of Surrey, late pertaining to the late monastery of Bermondsey in the said county; and all messuages, houses, buildings, barns, stables, dove-houses, ponds, pools, springs, orchards, gardens, lands, tenements, meadows, feedings, pastures, commons, waste-street, void ground-rents, reversions, services, court-leet, view of frankpledge, chattels, waifs, estrays, free warren, and all other rights, profits, commodities, emoluments, and hereditaments whatsoever in Southwark aforesaid, to the said lordship and manor of Southwark by any means belonging, or being before this time accounted, known, or taken as member or parcel of the said lordship and manor, except the things before excepted.

<small>And certain yearly rents, services, etc.</small>

Furthermore, we give, and for the consideration aforesaid, and with the assent aforesaid, by these presents do grant unto the said mayor and commonalty and citizens, all our manor and borough of Southwark, with all their rights, members, and appurtenances, in the said county of Surrey, late parcel of the possessions of the archbishop and archbishopric of Canterbury; and all our annual rent of three shillings and twopence halfpenny, and the services going out of the lands and tenements some time of John Burcetor, knight, and now or late in the tenure of William Glassock, esquire, in Southwark aforesaid;

and all that our yearly rent of three shillings, and
service going out of the house or tenement called the
"Swan", in Southwark aforesaid; and all that our
yearly rent of four shillings and tenpence, and the
service going out of the messuage or tenement called
the "Mermaid", in Southwark aforesaid; and all that
the yearly rent of twentypence a quarter, and the
service going out of the messuage or tenement called
the "Helmet", in the borough of Southwark aforesaid;
and all that our annual rent of sixteen shillings, and
the services going out of the messuage or tenement
called the "Horsehead", in the borough of Southwark
aforesaid; and also all that our annual rent of six
shillings and fourpence, and the service going out of
the messuage or tenement called the "Gleyne", in
Southwark aforesaid; and all that our annual rent of
two shillings a quarter, and the services going out of
the messuage or tenement called the "Rose"; and one
acre of ground lying in the Lock in Southwark;
and all that our annual rent of twentypence a
quarter, and the service going out of one messuage or
tenement called the "Lamb", in Southwark aforesaid,
pertaining to the Company of Fishmongers of London;
and also that our annual rent of twentypence a
quarter, and the service going out of one messuage
or tenement pertaining to the said society of Fishmongers in London, called the "Bale", in Southwark
aforesaid; and all that annual rate of twentypence a
quarter, going out of one messuage or tenement pertaining to the said society of Fishmongers, commonly
called the "Flower de Luce", in Southwark aforesaid;
and also that our annual rent of four shillings, and
the service going out of the twelve acres of land lying
at the Lock of Southwark aforesaid, some time the
Lord Wilford's, and now or late pertaining to the said
society of Fishmongers; and all that our annual rent

I

of eightpence, and the service going out of two acres of land of Giles Athorn, called "Tipping in the Hole", in Southwark aforesaid; and also that our annual rent of three shillings, and the service going out of one messuage or tenement, late Thomas lord Poynings', in Southwark aforesaid; and all that our annual rent of twelvepence halfpenny, and the service going out of the messuage or tenement now or late of William Malton, in Southwark aforesaid; and all that our annual rent of twentypence halfpenny, and the service going out of the messuage or tenement called the "White Hart", in Southwark aforesaid; and also all that our annual rent of seven shillings and fourpence, and the service going out of a messuage or tenement called the "Crown", in Southwark aforesaid, now or late of the Masters of the Bridge House, London; and also all that our annual rent of two shillings, and the service going out of the messuage or tenement of the same Masters of the Bridge House called the "Christopher", in Southwark aforesaid; and all that our annual rent of twelvepence, and the service going out of the lands and meadows of the Masters of the Bridge House of London, lying and being at the Lock, called "Carpenter's Hall", in Southwark aforesaid; and all that our annual rent of tenpence halfpenny, and the service going out of the messuage or tenement called the "Blue Mead", in Southwark aforesaid; and all that our annual rent of two shillings, and the service going out of one messuage or tenement now or late of William Salisbury, in Southwark aforesaid; and also all that our annual rent of sixteenpence, and the service going out of a certain field of ground of four acres of land, now or late belonging to the heirs of Robert Linled, lying and being in the Lock, and abutting upon the lands of the late duke of Suffolk, in Southwark aforesaid; and in Newington, or in either of them, in the said county of Surrey; and all our annual rent of two shillings, and the service going out of a certain field of ground, some time John Solas's field, and now or late belonging to the heirs of Robert Linled, in Southwark and Newington aforesaid, or either of them; and all our annual rent of twentypence, and the services going out of five acres of ground, now or late Stephen Middleton's, lying and being at the Lock of Southwark and Newington aforesaid, or in either of them; and all that our annual rent of fourpence, and the service going out of four acres of land, now or late William Champion's, lying and being in Southmead, in Walworth's field, in the parish of Newington, in our said county of Surrey; and all that our annual rent of twentypence farthing, and the service going out of the messuage or tenement called "Circot", in Southwark and Newington aforesaid, and either of them; and all other our messuages, lands, tenements, rents, reversions, services, and hereditaments whatsoever, which were parcel of the possessions, rents, and revenues of the archbishopric and bishopric of Canterbury, in Southwark, in the said county of Surrey.

We furthermore give, and for the considerations aforesaid, and with the advice aforesaid, do grant by these presents to the said mayor and commonalty and citizens of the city of London, all and all manner of woods, underwoods, and trees whatsoever, growing and being of, in, and upon all and singular the premises, and the soil and ground of the same; and also whatsoever reversions of all and singular the premises, and every part thereof, and all the rents and yearly profits whatsoever, reserved upon whatsoever demises and grants made of the premises, or any part thereof, by any means.

And all woods, underwoods, etc.

We also give, and by these presents grant to the

said mayor and commonalty and citizens of the city of London, all and singular the premises, with the appurtenances, as fully, and in as ample manner and form, as the said Charles late duke of Suffolk, or any other abbot of the late monastery of Bermondsey, or any archbishop of Canterbury, or any of them, or others before this time, having or possessing the said manors and other premises, or any parcel thereof, or being thereof seized, ever had, held, or enjoyed, or ought to have or enjoy the same, or any parcel thereof, and as fully, freely and wholly, and in as large manner and form, as all and singular the same came or ought to have come to our hands, or to the hands of our most dear father Henry the eighth, late king of England, by reason or pretence of any charter, gift, grant, or confirmation, or by reason or pretence of the dissolution of the said late monastery, or by whatever other means or right they came or ought to have come, or as the same now be, or ought to be in our hands.

Know ye, moreover, that we, as well of our grace, knowledge, and motion aforesaid, and with the advice aforesaid, as for the sum of five hundred marks of lawful money of England, paid into the hands of our treasurer of our court aforesaid, to our use, by the said mayor and commonalty, and citizens of the said city of London, whereof we confess ourselves fully satisfied, and the said mayor and commonalty and citizens, and their successors, thereof acquitted and discharged by these presents, have given and granted, and by these presents do give and grant, for us and our heirs, to the same mayor and commonalty and citizens of the city aforesaid, and to their successors, in and through all the borough and town of Southwark aforesaid, and in and through all the parishes of St. Saviour's, St. Olave's, and St.

<small>And all waifs and estrays, treasure found, deodands, etc., in the borough of Southwark, parishes of St. Saviour, St. Olave, St. George, St. Thomas's Hospital, etc., and in Kent Street, Blackman</small>

George's in Southwark, and in the parish, and through all the parishes late called St. Thomas's Hospital, and now called the King's Hospital, in Southwark aforesaid, and elsewhere soever in the said town and borough of Southwark aforesaid, and in Kentish Street and in Blackman Street aforesaid, and the parish of Newington, and elsewhere in the said town and borough of Southwark, all goods and chattels waifed, estrays, and all treasure found in the town and precinct aforesaid, and all manner of handiwork, goods and chattels of all manner of traitors, felons, fugitives, outlawed, condemned, convicted, and of felons defamed and put in exigent, felons of themselves, and deodands, and denying the law of our land, wheresoever or before whomsoever justice ought to be done of them, and all goods disclaimed, found, and being within the borough, town, parishes, and precincts aforesaid, and also all manner of escheats and forfeitures which to us and our heirs may there pertain, as fully and wholly as we should have them, if the said town and borough were in the hands of us or of our heirs; and that it shall be lawful to the same mayor and commonalty and citizens, and their successors, by their deputy or ministers of the same town and borough, to put themselves in seizin of and in all the handiworks and chattels of all manner of traitors, felons, fugitives, outlawed, condemned, convicted, and of felons defamed, and denying our law of the land, and of other premises; and also of and in all goods disclaimed, found or being within the same borough, town, parishes or precincts aforesaid; and also of and in all escheats and forfeitures to us and our heirs there pertaining.

And that the same mayor and commonalty and citizens, and their successors, by themselves, or their deputy, or minister or ministers, shall have in the

Street, and Newington.

The assize of bread, wine, etc., in the said places.

borough, town, parishes and precincts aforesaid, the assize and essay of bread, wine, beer, and ale, and of all other victuals and things whatsoever set to sale in the town aforesaid; and also all and whatsoever doth or may pertain to the clerk of the market of our house, or of the house of our heirs, together with the correction and punishment of all persons selling wine, bread, beer, ale, and other victuals there to be sold, and of others there dwelling, or exercising arts howsoever, and with all manner of forfeitures, fines and amerciaments to be forfeited, with all other things which therefore do or may there pertain to us, our heirs or successors in time to come; and that they shall have there the execution of all manner of writs of ours, or of our heirs and successors, and of all other writs, commands, extracts and warrants, with the returns of the same, by such their ministers and deputies, whom they shall thereunto choose; and that the same mayor and commonalty and citizens, and their successors, shall every year have there, and through all the town, borough, parishes and precincts aforesaid, one fair or mart, to endure three days; that is to say, the seventh, eighth, and ninth days of the month of September, to be holden together with a court of pie-powder, and with all liberties and free customs to such fair pertaining; and that they may have and hold therein, and at the said court, before their minister or deputy, through the said three days, from day to day, and hour to hour, and from time to time, all the actions, plaints and pleas of the said court of pie-powder, together with all summons, attachments, arrests, issues, fines, redemptions and commodities, and other rights whatsoever to the same court of pie-powder by any means belonging, without any impediment, let, or disturbance of us, our heirs or successors, or of other our officers or

Execution of writs.

A fair and pie-powder in September.

ministers whatsoever; and also that they may have in and through all the precinct aforesaid, view of frankpledge, together with all summons, attachments, arrests, issues and amerciaments, fines, redemptions, profits, commodities, and other things whatsoever, which therefore may or ought there to pertain to us, our heirs and successors, by any means.

And further, that the said mayor and commonalty and citizens, and their successors, may, by themselves, or by their minister or deputy, in the borough, town, parishes or precincts aforesaid constituted and to be constituted, take and arrest all manner of felons, thieves and other malefactors found within the borough, town, parishes and precincts aforesaid, and may bring them to our gaol of Newgate, there to be safely kept, until by due process of law they may be delivered. *The arrest of felons, etc. to be brought to Newgate.*

And furthermore, that the said mayor and commonalty and citizens, and their successors, may have in the borough, town, parishes and precincts aforesaid for ever, all and all manner of liberties, privileges, franchises, acquittals, customs and rights, which we or our heirs should or might there have, if the same borough or town were or remained in the hands of us or our heirs. *All and all manner of royal liberties, etc.*

And further, we have of our grace, knowledge and motion aforesaid, and by the advice aforesaid, granted, and by these presents do grant, for us, our heirs and successors, to the said mayor and commonalty and citizens, and their successors, that the said mayor and commonalty and citizens, from henceforth for ever, shall and may hold all and all manner of contracts and demands whatsoever, within the town, borough, parishes and precincts aforesaid, chancing, happening and growing, before the mayor and aldermen, and sheriffs of the said city, and the sheriffs of the said city for the time being, or any of them, in the Guildhall of the chamber of the Guildhall and hustings of the said city, or any of them, to be holden, by like actions, bills, plaints, process, arrests, judgments, executions, and other things whatsoever, and at the same days and times, and in such-like manner and form, as such happening in the said city have, time out of mind, been taken, held, levied, prosecuted and executed in the court before the mayor and aldermen, and sheriffs of the said city, or in any of them.

Trials at Guildhall for debts.

And that the serjeants at mace of the city of London, for the time being, which have used to execute and serve any process, or any other things in the said city, may hereafter make, do and execute any manner of process, and do whatsoever things in the said borough, town, parishes and precincts concerning all and singular things arising and happening about such pleas and executions of the same within the precincts aforesaid, as by all the time aforesaid it hath been used in the said city of London.

Serjeants at mace to serve processes.

And that the inhabitants of the town and borough, parishes and precincts aforesaid, as concerning the causes and matters there arising, may be impleaded and plead in the same city in form aforesaid, and in the courts aforesaid. And, if the men impannelled and summoned in juries for trials of such issues, have not appeared before the said mayor, aldermen and sheriffs in the said courts of the said city, that then such men impannelled and summoned as aforesaid, making default, shall be amerced by the said mayor or sheriffs, and shall forfeit such issues upon them returned and to be returned, after the same, or in like manner and form, as the men impannelled and summoned in the said city for the like issues in the courts of the said city to be tried, have before this time forfeited, and have accustomed to forfeit; and

In all pleas to observe the city forms.

To fine defaulters on juries.

also that such amerciaments and issues forfeited should be levied by the ministers of the said city, to the use of the mayor and commonalty and citizens, and their successors, for ever.

And also, that the same mayor and commonalty and citizens, and their successors, shall and may, from henceforth for ever have cognizance of all manner of pleas, actions, plaints, and suits personal, happening or growing out of any court of ours, or of our heirs, before us or our heirs, or before any of the justices, for or concerning any thing, cause or matter within the town, borough, parishes and precincts aforesaid, before the mayor, aldermen, and sheriffs, or any of them, in the said courts of the said city, or any of them; and that the issues happening upon the said pleas and suits shall be tried in the same courts, before the mayor and aldermen and sheriffs, or any of them, by the men of the same borough or town, in such sort as issues in the same city are tried; and that the said mayor and commonalty and citizens, and their successors, may for ever choose, according to the form of law, and may constitute every year, or as often as, and in what times soever shall seem to them expedient, two coroners in the borough or town aforesaid; and that the said coroners, or either of them, being duly elected and constituted, may and shall have full power and authority to do and execute in the said borough, town, parishes and precincts aforesaid, all and singular things, which to the office of coroner in any county of our realm of England do, or ought to pertain to be done and executed; and that none other coroners of us, our heirs or successors, shall enter into anything which to the office of such coroner pertaineth to be done within the said borough, parishes or precincts, neither shall at all intermeddle about anything belonging to the office

To choose two coroners. Their power.

Lord Mayor to be escheator.
His power in this office.

of coroner, happening within the borough, town, parishes and precincts abovesaid; and that the mayor of the said city for the time being shall be our escheator, and escheators of our heirs, in the borough, parishes and precincts aforesaid; and that he shall have full power and authority to make his precept and commandment to the sheriff of the county of Surrey for the time being, and do, execute, and finish there all and singular things which appertain to the office of escheator in any county of our realm; and that none other escheator of ours, or of our heirs, shall enter there into anything, which to the office of escheator appertaineth to be done, neither shall at all intermeddle with anything to the office of escheator there belonging.

And clerk of the market.

And that the mayor of the said city for the time being shall be clerk of the market, and of the market of our heirs, within the borough, town, parishes and precincts aforesaid, and shall do and execute therein all such things which to the clerk of the market appertain; and that the clerk of the market of our houses, or of the house of our heirs, or any other clerk of the market, intermeddle not there.

And that the said mayor and commonalty and citizens, and their successors, shall and may, from henceforth for ever have, hold, enjoy and use, as well within the said manor, as in the town, borough, parishes and precincts aforesaid, as well all and sin-

To have tolls, stallage, etc.

gular liberties and franchises aforesaid, as tolls, stallages, pickages, and other our jurisdictions, liberties, franchises and privileges whatsoever, which any archbishop of Canterbury, and which the said Charles, late duke of Suffolk, or any master, brethren or sisters of the late hospital of St. Thomas, in Southwark aforesaid, or any abbot of the said late monastery of St. Saviour's at Bermondsey next Southwark aforesaid, in the county aforesaid, or any prior and convent of the late priory of St. Mary Overy, in the said county of Surrey, or any of them ever had, held or enjoyed in the said manors, lands, tenements, and other the premises or places aforesaid, or any of them, or which we have, hold or enjoy by any ways or means whatsoever, as fully, freely, and in as ample manner as we, or our most dear father Henry the eighth, late king of England, had, held and enjoyed, or ought to have, hold and enjoy the same; and that none of our sheriffs, or any other officer or minister of ours, or of our heirs or successors, shall any way intermeddle in the town, borough-town, parishes and precincts aforesaid, or in any of them, contrary to this our grant.

And we, with the advice aforesaid, do further, by these presents, grant to the said mayor, commonalty, and citizens of the said city of London, and to their successors, that all and singular persons, from time to time inhabiting or resident within the town, borough, parishes and places aforesaid, shall from henceforth be in the order, government and correction of the mayor and officers of the city of London, and their deputies, for the time being, as the citizens and inhabitants of the said city of London be and ought to be, by virtue of the charters before this time by any means made, granted and confirmed by any of our progenitors to the said mayor and commonalty and citizens of the said city; and their successors shall and may, from henceforth, have, hold, and enjoy so many, so great, the same, such and the like rights, jurisdictions, liberties, franchises and privileges whatsoever, in the towns, parishes and places aforesaid, and in every parcel thereof, as fully, freely and wholly, as the said mayor and commonalty and citizens of the said city enjoy and use, or may have,

That the inhabitants of the town, borough, parishes, etc., aforesaid, shall be subject to the city laws.

enjoy and use in the said city, by virtue of any of the charters and grants made, granted and confirmed by any of our progenitors kings of England, to any mayor, commonalty and citizens of the said city.

<small>City justices to act in the places aforesaid.</small>

And that the mayor of the same city for the time being, and the recorder thereof for the time being, after the said aldermen have exercised and borne the charge of mayor of the said city, shall be justices of our peace, and of our heirs, in the town, borough, parishes and limits aforesaid, so long as the same aldermen shall be and remain aldermen of the said city; and every of them shall there do and execute all and singular things, which other justices of our peace, and our heirs, may do and execute within the said county of Surrey, according to the laws and statutes of our realm of England.

<small>A market on Monday, Wednesday, Friday, and Saturday. What parts are excepted.</small>

And that the said mayor and commonalty and citizens, and their successors, shall have, in every week, on Monday, Wednesday, Friday and Saturday, within the borough and town aforesaid, one market or markets to be there holden, and all things which to a market do appertain, or may appertain, for ever; except always, and reserved to us, our heirs and successors, out of these our letters patent, all, and all manner of rights, jurisdictions, liberties and franchises whatsoever, within the walk, circuit and precinct over the capital messuage, gardens and park in Southwark aforesaid, and in all gardens, curtilages and lands, to the same mansion, gardens and park appertaining; and except and always reserved the house, messuage or lodging there, called the "King's Bench", and the garden or gardens to the same pertaining, with the appurtenances, so long as it shall be used for a prison for the imprisoned, as it now is; and except the messuage and lodging there, called the "Marshalsea", and the gardens to the same belonging, with the appurtenances, so long as it shall be used for a prison, as now it is.

Provided also, that [neither] these our letters patent, nor anything therein contained, shall extend to the prejudice of the officers of the great master, steward, and marshal of our house, or of the house of our heirs and successors, to be exercised within the town, borough, parishes and limits aforesaid, [that] be within the verge; nor of Sir John Gate, knight, one of the gentlemen of our privy chamber, of or for lands, tenements, offices, franchises, or liberties, by us or our father to the said [Sir] John Gate granted during his life; which manors, lands, tenements, rents, privileges, and all other the premises, are now extended to the yearly value of thirty-five pounds fourteen shillings and fourpence, to have, hold and enjoy the said manors, messuages, lands, tenements, meadows, feedings, pastures, commons, woods, underwoods, rents, services, reversions, court-leets, views of frankpledge, chattels, waived, strays, free-warrens, and all and singular the said premises, with the appurtenances (except as before excepted) to the said mayor and commonalty and citizens of the said city of London, and to their successors, for ever, to be holden of us, and our heirs and successors, as of our manor of East Greenwich, in our county of Kent, by fealty only, in free soccage, and not in chief, for all services and demands whatsoever. *Proviso for the Lord Marshal.* *And Sir John Gate.*

We give also, and for the consideration aforesaid, do, by these presents, grant to the said mayor and commonalty and citizens of the said city of London, all the issues, rents, revenues and profits of the said manors, messuages, lands, tenements, and all other the premises, with their appurtenances, coming and growing from the feast of St. Michael the archangel last past hitherto, to have the same to the said mayor and commonalty and citizens, of our gift, without account, or any other thing to us, our heirs or successors, by any means, therefore to be given, paid or made.

And furthermore, of our ample grace, we will, and for us, our heirs and successors, do, by these presents, grant to the said mayor and commonalty and citizens, and their successors, that we, our heirs and successors, will yearly, for ever, discharge, acquit and save harmless, as well the said mayor and commonalty and citizens, and their successors, as the said manors, messuages, lands, tenements, and all other the premises, with their appurtenances, and every part thereof, against us, our heirs and successors, and against whatsoever persons, concerning all and all manner of corrodies, rents, fees, annuities, sums of money and charges whatsoever, by any means, going out, or to be paid out of the premises, or to be charged thereupon; saving the services above by these presents reserved, and the demises and grants by any means made for terms of life, or years of the premises, or any parcel, whereupon the old rent and more is reserved, and shall be due yearly, during the terms aforesaid, and besides the covenants in those demises and grants being; and saving ten pounds by the year, of the ancient farm, for the town of Southwark aforesaid, by the said mayor and commonalty and citizens due, in our exchequer yearly to be paid and payable; willing, and by these presents, by strict injunction, commanding, as well our chancellor and general overseers, and council of our said court of augmentations and revenues of our crown, and all receivers, auditors, and other our officers of ours, or of our heirs, whatsoever, for the time being, that they and every of them, upon the only showing of these our letters patent, or of the enrolments of the same, without any other writ or warrant from us or our heirs by any means to be obtained and prosecuted, shall make and cause to be made unto the said mayor and commonalty and citizens of the said city of London, and their successors, full power and due allowance, and manifest discharge of all such corrodies, rents, fees, annuities and sums of money whatsoever, going out, or to be paid out of the premises, or thereupon charged or to be charged, except as before excepted; and these our letters patent, and the enrolment of the same, shall be yearly, and from time to time, a sufficient warrant and discharge, as well to the said chancellor and general overseers, and to our council of our said court of augmentations and revenues of our crown, as to all receivers, auditors, and other officers and ministers of ours, our heirs and successors whatsoever, for the time being, in this behalf.

We will also, and by these presents, do grant to the said mayor and commonalty and citizens of the said city of London, that they may and shall have these our letters patent in due manner made and sealed under our great seal of England, without fine or fee, great or small, to us, in our hamper, or elsewhere to our use, to be by any means given, paid or made, although express mention be not made in these presents of the true yearly value, or of the certainty of the premises, or of other gifts or grants of us, or by any of our progenitors, to the said mayor and commonalty and citizens before this time made; any statute, act, ordinance, provision or restraint thereof made, ordained or provided to the contrary, or any thing, cause or matter whatsoever in any thing notwithstanding. In witness whereof we have caused these our letters to be made patent. *To be sealed without fine or fee.*

Witness myself at Westminster, the twenty-third day of April, in the fourth year of our reign.

No. XLI.

Proclamation of Queen Elizabeth against New Buildings in and about London.

7 July, a.d. 1580.

THE Queen's Majesty perceiving the state of the city of London (being anciently termed her chamber) and the suburbs and confines thereof to increase daily, by access of people to inhabit in the same, in such ample sort, as thereby many inconveniencies are seen already, but many greater of necessity like to follow, being such as her majesty cannot neglect to remedy, having the principal care, under Almighty God, to foresee aforehand, to have her people in such a city and confines not only well governed by ordinary justice, to serve God and obey her majesty (which by reason of such multitudes lately increased, can hardly be done without devise of more new jurisdictions and officers for that purpose), but to be also provided of sustentation of victual, food, and other like necessaries for man's life, upon reasonable prices, without which no city can long continue.

And finally, to the preservation of her people in health, which may seem impossible to continue, though presently, by God's goodness, the same is perceived to be in better estate universally, than hath been in man's memory; yet where there are such great multitudes of people brought to inhabit in small rooms, whereof a great part are seen very poor, yea, such as must live of begging, or by worse means, and they heaped up together, and in a sort smothered with many families of children and servants in one house or small tenement; it must needs follow, if any plague or popular sickness should, by God's permission, enter amongst those multitudes, that the same would not only spread itself, and invade the whole city and confines, but that a great mortality would ensue the same, where her majesty's personal presence is many times required: besides [by] the great confluence of people from all parts of the realm, by reason of the ordinary terms of justice there holden, the infection would be also dispersed through all other parts of the realm, to the manifest danger of the whole body thereof; out of the which neither her majesty's own person can be (but by God's special ordinance) exempted, nor any other, whatsoever they be.

For remedy whereof, as time may now serve, until by some further good order [to] be had in parliament or otherwise the same may be remedied; her majesty, by good and deliberate advice of her council, and being also thereto moved by the considerate opinions of the lord mayor, aldermen, and other the grave wise men in and about the city, doth charge and strictly command all manner of persons, of what quality soever they be, to desist and forbear from any new buildings of any house or tenement within three miles from any of the gates of the said city of London, to serve for habitation or lodging for any person, where no former house hath been known to have been in the memory of such as are now living; and also to forbear from letting or setting, or suffering any more families than one only to be placed, or to inhabit from henceforth in any one house that heretofore hath been inhabited.

And to the intent this her majesty's royal commandment and necessary provision may take place, and be duly observed, for so universal a benefit to the whole body of the realm, for whose respects all particular persons are bound, by God's law and man's to forbear from their particular and extraordinary lucre; her majesty strictly chargeth the lord mayor of the city of London, and all other officers having authority in the same, and also all justices of peace, lords and bailiffs of liberties not being within the jurisdiction of the said lord mayor of London, to foresee that no person do begin to prepare any foundation for any new house, tenement, or building, to serve to receive or hold any inhabitants to dwell or lodge, or to use any victualling therein, where no former habitation hath been in the memory of such as now do live; but that they be prohibited and restrained so to do. And both the persons that shall so attempt to the contrary, and all manner of workmen that shall (after warning given) continue in any such work tending to such new buildings, to be committed to close prison, and there to remain without bail, until they find good sureties, with bonds for reasonable sums of money (to be forfeitable and recoverable at her majesty's suit, for the use of the hospitals in and about the said city) that they will not at any time hereafter attempt the like.

And further the said officers shall seize all manner of stuff, so (after warning given) brought to the place where such new buildings shall be intended, and the same cause to be converted and employed in any public use for the city or parish where the same shall be attempted.

And for the avoiding of the multitudes of families heaped up in one dwelling-house, or for the converting of any one house into a multitude of such tenements for dwelling or victualling-places, the said lord mayor, and all other officers, in their several liberties within the limits of three miles, as above mentioned, shall commit any person giving cause of offence, from the day of the publication of this present proclamation, to close prison, as is afore limited.

And also for the offences in this part of increase of many indwellers, or, as they be commonly termed, inmates or undersitters, which have been suffered within these seven years, contrary to the good ancient laws or customs of the city, or of the boroughs and parishes within the aforesaid limit of three miles afore-mentioned, the said lord mayor, and the other officers above-mentioned, shall speedily cause to be redressed in their ordinary courts and law days, betwixt this and the feast of All Saints next coming; within which times such undersitters or inmates may provide themselves other places abroad in the realm, where many houses rest uninhabited, to the decay of divers ancient boroughs and towns. And, because her majesty intendeth to have this ordinance duly executed, her pleasure is, that the said lord mayor of London, and other the officers, having jurisdiction within the said space of three miles above-mentioned, shall, after the proclamation hereof, as speedily as they may, meet in some convenient place near to the said city, and there (after conference had) accord among themselves how to proceed to the execution hereof; and, if any cause shall so require, to impart to her majesty's privy council any let or impediment that may arise, to the intent that remedy be given to any such impediment, according to her majesty's pleasure heretofore expressed.

> Given at Nonesuch, the seventh day of July 1580, in the two-and-twentieth year of her majesty's reign.

No. XLII.

The First Charter of King James I.

20 August, a.d. 1605.

Preamble.

JAMES, by the grace of God, of England, Scotland, France, and Ireland, king, defender of the faith, etc., to all to whom our present letters shall come, greeting.

Whereas our beloved the mayor and commonalty and citizens of our city of London, time out of mind, have had, exercised, and ought, and have accustomed themselves to have and exercise the office of bailiff, and conservation of the water of Thames, to be exercised and occupied by the mayor of the same city for the time being, during the time of his mayoralty, or by his sufficient deputies, in, upon, and about the water of Thames; that is to say, from the bridge of the town of Staines in the county of Middlesex, and toward the east, unto London Bridge, and from thence to a certain place called Kendall, otherwise Yenland, otherwise Yenleet, towards the sea, and east, and in Medway, and in the port of London aforesaid, and upon whatsoever bank, and upon every shore, and upon every wharf of the same water of Thames, within the limits and bounds aforesaid, and in, upon, and about all and every of them : And also, for all the time aforesaid, have had and taken, and ought and have accustomed to have and take to their own proper use, by the mayor of

Yantlet Creek.

the same city for the time being, during the time of his mayoralty, or his sufficient deputies, all wages, rewards, fees, and profits belonging to the same office of bailiff.

And whereas the said mayor and commonalty and citizens, from all the time aforesaid, have had and exercised the office of measurer, and measuring of all coals, and grain of whatsoever kind; and also of all kind of salt, and all kind of apples, pears, plums, and other fruit whatsoever, and also all kind of roots eatable of what kind soever, and of onions, and all other merchandises, wares, and things whatsoever measurable, and the measuring of every of them, in, or unto the said port of London, coming, carried, or brought upon the said water, in whatsoever ship, boat, barge, or vessel, floating, laden, and being on whatsoever part of the said water of Thames, or upon whatsoever bank, shore, or wharf of the same water of Thames, which shall come to, arrive, abide, be delivered or laid down, from the said bridge of the said town of Staines westward, to the said bridge of London, and from thence to the said place called Yendall, otherwise Yenleet, towards the sea, and east, and in Medway, and in the said port of the city of London aforesaid: to exercise and occupy the same office, by the mayor of the said city for the time, during the time of his mayoralty, or by his sufficient deputies; and also, for all the said time they have had and taken, and ought to have and take to their proper use, by the mayor of the said city for the time being, during his mayoralty, or by his sufficient deputies, all wages, rewards, fees, and profits to the same office belonging.

And, notwithstanding they, the mayor and commonalty and citizens, of late times thereof have been disquieted, and in some measuring aforesaid unjustly hindered, and especially in the said office of measuring coals, supposing that office to the mayor, commonalty, and citizens anciently not to appertain, neither by any lawful grant, nor prescription, as yet to appertain or belong; whereas in truth it doth manifestly and plainly appear, that the same offices, and all other premises to them of old time appertaining, do now of right appertain, and that they lawfully received and enjoyed, and ought to have, take, and enjoy the wages and rewards, fees and perquisites thereof. We therefore, to take away all controversies, and remove all doubt in this behalf, and to the intent that the said mayor and commonalty and citizens, may securely, freely, and quietly use, have, exercise and enjoy the offices aforesaid, and every of them, and the measuring aforesaid, and the fees, wages, rewards and profits to the said office and measuring belonging, and all and singular other the premises, to them and their successors for ever, without the contradiction, molestation, or hindrance any way of us, our heirs or successors, admiral of England, justices, escheators, sheriffs, bailiffs, or other our officers or ministers whatsoever. And because it is well-pleasing to us to show favour in this behalf to the same mayor, commonalty, and citizens, and rather increase, strengthen, and enlarge, than diminish the liberties, franchises, jurisdictions, privileges, and free customs of the city of London aforesaid; of our special grace, and from our certain knowledge and mere motion, we do by these presents approve, allow, ratify and confirm, for us, our heirs and successors, all and singular the offices and measuring aforesaid, and other recited premises, and the wages, rewards, fees, and profits belonging or appertaining thereto, and the uses and customs aforesaid, to the said mayor and commonalty and citizens of the said city aforesaid, and their successors.

And further, of our special grace and certain Granting the conservancy of the Thames from Staines to Yantlet to the mayor.
knowledge, and mere motion, we have granted, and
by these presents, for us, our heirs, and successors,
do grant to the said mayor and commonalty and
citizens, and their successors, that they may exercise
and execute the said office of bailiff and conservation
of the water of Thames, by the mayor of the same
city for the time being, during the time of his
mayoralty, or his sufficient deputies, from time to
time, for ever, in, upon, or about the same water of
Thames; (that is to say) from the bridge of Staines
to the bridge of London, and from thence to a certain
place called Yenland, otherwise Yenleet, towards
the sea, and towards the east, and Medway, and in
the port of the city of London aforesaid, and upon
whatsoever bank, shore, and wharf of the same water
of Thames, within the limits and bounds aforesaid, in,
upon, and about every one of the same, and to have,
receive, and collect and enjoy all and singular wages,
rewards, fees and profits to the same office of bailiff
pertaining, to the proper use of the said mayor and
commonalty and citizens, by the mayor of the same
city, for the time being, during the time of his
mayoralty, or by his sufficient deputies.

And also, of our more ample grace, and from our
certain knowledge and mere motion, we have given
and by these presents for us, our heirs and successors,
do grant to the said mayor and commonalty and
citizens, and their successors, that they may peaceably
and quietly, from time to time, for ever, execute and
exercise the aforesaid office of measurer of all and The office of measurer of coals, grain, salt, fruits.
singular coals, and grain of what sort soever, and all
kind of apples, pears, plums, and other fruit whatsoever, and all roots to be eaten of what sort soever:
And also of onions, and other merchandises, wares,
and things measurable, and the measuring of them

whatsoever, in or to the port of the city of London, coming, carried, or brought, in whatsoever ship, boat, barge, or other vessel, floating, laden, remaining or being in any part of the same river of Thames, and upon any bank, or shore, or wharf of the same water of Thames, happening to unlade, stay, remain, be delivered, or laid down, from the said bridge of the town of Staines in the county of Middlesex, and towards the east, unto London Bridge aforesaid, and from thence to the said place called Yendall, alias Yenleet, towards the sea, and east, and in Medway, and in the said port of the city of London, by the mayor of the aforesaid city for the time being, during the time of his mayoralty, or by his sufficient deputies. And to have, receive, collect, and enjoy all and singular the wages, rewards, fees and profits whatsoever, to the same office of measuring belonging or appertaining, to the use of the said mayor and commonalty and citizens, and their successors, to be received and taken up by the mayor of the aforesaid city for the time being, during the time of his mayoralty or his sufficient deputies, without the hindrance of us, our heirs or successors, or any of our officers, bailiffs, or ministers, or of our admiral of England, or of our successors, or any others of our subjects, or of our heirs or successors to be made to the contrary: To have, hold, and enjoy the said office, and all and singular the premises, with all and singular wages, rewards, fees, profits and appurtenances whatsoever, to the said offices, and every or any of them, belonging or appertaining, to the aforesaid mayor, and commonalty, and citizens, and their successors for ever, by the mayor of the aforesaid city for the time being, during the time of his mayoralty, or his sufficient deputies, to be exercised and executed without any account, or any other thing to be rendered, or made thereof to us, our heirs or successors; so as no other bailiff or conservator of the aforesaid water, or measurer of coals, grain, salt, apples, plums, roots to be eaten, onions, or other merchandises, or commodities, or of any thing or things above-mentioned, shall be, or shall in any ways intermeddle in the premises, or any of them.

And we, willing to show our said mayor and commonalty and citizens more ample favour, of our special grace, and from our certain knowledge, and mere motion, for us, our heirs and successors, grant, and by this our present charter confirm, that although the said mayor, and commonalty, and citizens, and their successors, hitherto in some case happening, have not used, or peradventure have abused the offices aforesaid, or any or some of the offices or the measuring abovesaid, or any thing or things, to any or some of them appertaining or belonging: Notwithstanding they, the mayor and commonalty and citizens, and their successors, from henceforth freely and peaceably shall use and enjoy the said offices, so not without hindrance used or abused, and every of them, without the let or impediment of us, our heirs or successors, or of our justices, escheators, sheriffs, or other bailiffs, officers or ministers of us, our heirs or successors; any statute or ordinance made, or judgment rendered, or any charter of us, our progenitors or predecessors, in times past made or granted notwithstanding: Although there be no express mention in these presents of the true yearly value or certainty of the premises, or of any of them, or of other gifts or grants by us, or by any of our progenitors or predecessors to the said mayor and commonalty and citizens of the city of London aforesaid, before these times made, or any statute, act, ordinance, provision, proclamation, or restraint to the contrary thereof therefore had, made, published, ordained or provided, or any other thing, cause, or matter whatsoever notwithstanding. In witness whereof, these our letters we have caused to be made patent.

 Witness myself, at Westminster, the twentieth day of August, in the third year of our reign of England, France and Ireland, and of Scotland the thirty-ninth.

No. XLIII.

The Second Charter of King James I.

20 SEPTEMBER A.D. 1608.

JAMES, by the grace of God, of England, Scotland, France, and Ireland, king, defender of the faith, etc. To all to whom these present letters shall come, greeting.

Whereas very many of our progenitors, sometime kings of England, of their special grace, and for free, laudable, multiplied and continued service done and expended in times past by the mayor, commonalty, and citizens of the city of London, and their predecessors; and also for divers other urgent causes and considerations them thereunto especially moving, have given, granted, and confirmed to the mayor and commonalty and citizens of the said city of London, and their successors, divers liberties, jurisdictions, privileges, franchises, immunities, authorities, ordinances, customs, and quittances, as by the several letters patent of our progenitors and predecessors, sometime kings of England, more fully and manifestly is and appeareth.

We also, for and in consideration of the high fidelity, constancy, and ready and laudable service, by the said mayor and commonalty and citizens of our said city of London, to us in the beginning of our reign, and continually ever since manifested, faithfully done, and expended, have ratified and

140 THE SECOND CHARTER OF KING JAMES I.

Confirms all former charters and customs.

allowed, and for us, our heirs and successors, as much as in us is, do accept of and approve all and singular the letters patent, charters, and confirmations of our most famous progenitors and ancestors, to the same mayor and commonalty and citizens of the said city of London, and their predecessors, by whatsoever name of incorporation before these times made, granted, or confirmed; and all and singular gifts, grants, confirmations, restitutions, customs, ordinances, explanations, and all other things whatsoever, in whatsoever letters patent, or charters of our predecessors, progenitors or ancestors, kings of England; and also all and singular things in the said letters patent, charters, grants, confirmations, or any of them, contained, recited, confirmed or explained; and all and singular jurisdictions, authorities, privileges, acquittances, and free customs and hereditaments whatsoever, which the said mayor and commonalty, and citizens of the said city of London, or

Styles of incorporation.

their predecessors, by the name of the mayor and commonalty and citizens of the city of London, or by the name of the mayor and aldermen of the city of London, or by the name of the mayor, citizens, and commonalty of the city of London, or by the name of the mayor and commonalty of the city of London, or by the name of the citizens of the city of London, or by the name of the barons of London, or by the name of the barons of the city of London, or by any other name whatsoever, by reason or force of any letters patent, charters, or confirmations of any of our progenitors kings of England, which in any time or times they had reasonably used or exercised, and them all and singular, to the said mayor and commonalty and citizens of the said city of London, and their successors, do ratify and confirm: To have and hold, enjoy and exercise, all and singular the premises to the said mayor and commonalty and citizens of the said city of London, and their successors for ever, so fully, clearly, and entirely, and in as ample manner and form, as if they were, or had been severally, particularly, and by name in these presents expressed and declared.

And further, we will, and of our special grace, for us, our heirs and successors, do grant, that the said mayor and commonalty, and citizens, and their successors, be restored to all and singular their authorities, jurisdictions, liberties, franchises, privileges, acquittances, immunities, and free customs; and we do restore the same to them and their successors by these presents, as fully, and freely, and entirely, as they or their predecessors, in any time of our progenitors or predecessors, kings of England, used or enjoyed, or ought to have, use, and enjoy the same.

And we will also, and by these presents, for us, our heirs and successors, of our special grace, do grant, that although the same mayor and commonalty of the citizens of the city aforesaid, in some case happening, have not hitherto used, or peradventure have abused the same, or any authorities, jurisdictions, liberties, privileges, franchises, immunities, quittances, and free customs, in the letters patent and charters aforesaid, or any of them contained, and other their customs; they notwithstanding, the mayor, commonalty, and citizens of the said city, and their successors, from henceforth, fully may enjoy and use the same authorities, liberties, privileges, franchises, and immunities, quittances, and free customs whatsoever, totally not used or abused, and every of them, without let or hindrance of us, our heirs or successors, the justices, sheriffs, coroners, escheators, or any other bailiffs or ministers of us, our heirs or successors whatsoever, any cause, matter or thing whatsoever in times past to the contrary thereof notwithstanding; to hold all and singular the premises of us, our heirs and successors, by the same and such-like services, fee-farm rents, sums of money, and demands whatsoever, by which, and as the same of us, and our progenitors or predecessors, before this time [they] were holden.

By the like services, etc., as formerly.

And whereas, within the said city of London, the liberties and suburbs, and port of the same, we are informed the search and surveying of oil, hops, soap, salt, butter, cheese, and such other like things coming or brought to the port of the same city, to the intent to be sold or exposed to sale by way of merchandise, and also the measuring of all corn whatsoever, of any kind, onions, salt, sea-coals, and fruit of all kinds, fish called shell-fish, measurable and used to be measured, which are coming or brought to the said city of London, to the intent to be sold by way of merchandise, hitherto have pertained to the mayor and commonalty and citizens of the city of London, and their predecessors, to be exercised and executed by the mayor of the same city for the time being, according to the laws, ordinances, and statutes made concerning the same, and the custom of the same city; we of our certain knowledge and mere motion, for us and our successors, do ratify the same search, surveying, and measuring abovesaid, in and by all things as the said mayor and commonalty and citizens of the said city, or their successors, lawfully had or enjoyed before this time, and to the said now mayor and commonalty and citizens of the said city of London, and their successors, confirm by these presents.

The search and survey of oil, hops, soap, salt, butter, cheese, etc.

The measuring of corn, sea-coal, fish, and fruits.

And further, we will, and by these presents for us, our heirs and successors, do ordain and grant to the said mayor and commonalty and citizens of the said city of London, and their successors, that the said city of London, and the circuit, bounds, liberties, franchises, and jurisdictions of the same, do extend and stretch forth, and may and can extend and stretch forth, as well in and through all and singular the several circuits, bounds, limits, franchises, and jurisdictions of the late dissolved priory of the church of Trinity near Aldgate, London, commonly called Creedchurch Street, or the Duke's Place; and the late dissolved priory of St. Bartholomew, London, near Smithfield; and the late dissolved hospital of St. Bartholomew, in Smithfield, without Newgate, London, commonly called Great St. Bartholomew and Little St. Bartholomew; and also the late dissolved house or priory of Preaching Friars within and at Ludgate, London, commonly called Blackfriars; and also the late dissolved house or priory of Friars of the Order of the Blessed Virgin Mary of Mount Carmel, called Whitefriars; and also the inn or liberty of Cold Herberge, otherwise Cold Harburgh, and Cold Herburg Lane, within the liberty of London aforesaid; so as from henceforth for ever all and singular the circuits and franchises aforesaid of the late dissolved priory church of St. Trinity, and the said dissolved priory or house of St. Bartholomew; and the said late dissolved hospital of St. Bartholomew; and also the late dissolved house or priory of Preaching Friars; and also the said late dissolved house or priory of Friars of the Blessed Virgin Mary; and also the said inn and liberty of Cold Harbour, be, and every one of them is, and for all times to come shall be and remain within the circuits, precincts, liberties, franchises and jurisdictions of the same our city of London.

And that all and singular the inhabitants and dwellers within the same, or any of them, shall be,

Extends the city liberties through the parish of Trinity, near Aldgate, or Duke's Place, Great St. Bartholomew's, Little St. Bartholomew's, near Smithfield, Blackfriars, Whitefriars, and Cold Harbour.

and every of them is, and for all time to come shall be and remain under the rule, government, jurisdiction, oversight, search, correction, punishment, precepts and arrests of the said mayor and commonalty and citizens of our city of London aforesaid, and their successors, and the sheriffs of our city of London for the time being, and their officers and ministers for ever, any liberties, franchises, privileges, exemption or authority whatsoever to the contrary thereof notwithstanding: Provided nevertheless, and we will and ordain, that all persons now inhabitants, or who shall inhabit in time to come within the liberties and franchises aforesaid of the said late dissolved priory called the Blackfriars, and the late dissolved priory called the Whitefriars, and the whole precinct, circuit, and compass of them, and all buildings therein built, and to be built from henceforth for ever, shall be quit and exonerated of and from all taxes, fifteenths, and other burdens of scot, and of watch and ward, through or within the city of London, to be paid, made, sustained or contributed; except the charges and expenses due and reasonable for setting out of soldiers, and for the defence of our realm, and such-like special services concerning us, our heirs and successors; and except the charges for pavements, and cleansing the lanes, ditches, ways, watercourses, and sewers within the circuits, precincts, liberties and jurisdictions of the same late houses or priories, called Blackfriars and Whitefriars aforesaid, respectively to be paid.

Provided the inhabitants of Blackfriars and Whitefriars be exempt from certain taxes,

and offices.

And that the inhabitants shall be quit and exonerated of and from the office of constable, scavenger, and such offices of charge within the city aforesaid, without the circuits and limits of the said late house or priory called the Blackfriars and the Whitefriars, respectively executed and exercised. Nevertheless, we will, that all freemen of the city aforesaid, for the time being, inhabiting, or who shall inhabit within the said liberties and franchises of the said late house or priory of Blackfriars and Whitefriars, shall be chargeable and eligible unto all offices and charges, as well mayor, sheriffs and aldermen of the said city, as of the company within the said city of London, of which they are or shall be free, as other freemen of the said city are. *But shall be eligible into city and ward offices.*

And furthermore, for the better and common profit of our city of London, and for the accommodation and support of the charges and expenses of the said city, for us, our heirs and successors, we will and grant to the same mayor and commonalty and citizens of the said city, and to their successors, that from henceforth all and singular persons, though they be not free of the same city, who now are, or hereafter shall be dwelling within the said city, the liberties or precincts of the same (except the inhabitants within the liberties and franchises of the aforesaid several late houses or priories of the late Friars, called the Blackfriars and the Whitefriars), in whatsoever aids, tallages, grants, and other contributions whatsoever, to the use and service of us, our heirs and successors, or to the use of the said city, for maintaining the state, good, or benefit of the said city, howsoever to be assessed, shall reasonably be taxed and contribute. *Non-freemen within the city to be taxed equally with the citizens in all aids, etc., except the inhabitants of Blackfriars and Whitefriars.*

And the same mayor and commonalty and citizens of the city aforesaid, may and can levy the said aids, tallages, grants, and other contributions (except before excepted) by their own officers and ministers, by distress of the goods and chattels of such persons, who, from time to time, shall be charged with the payment of such aids, tallages, grants, and other contributions, or any of them; and so levied, they can and may have, hold, and enjoy, to the use and

L

behoof aforesaid: Provided always, nevertheless, that such residents and dwellers in any houses within the aforesaid city, who are not, nor shall be freemen of the aforesaid city, shall be taxed to such aids, tallages, grants, and other contributions, from time to time, only for the houses in which they shall inhabit or reside, or are dwelling within the same city of London, liberties, or precincts of the same, according to the customs of the said city, [they] shall be assessed and taxed, and not otherwise: Provided also, that if anyone, or any of the said inhabitants, residents, or dwellers, who are not, or shall not be a freeman, or freemen of the said city, shall think himself, by reason of the said aids, tallages, grants, or contributions,

May appeal in case of grievance to the lord chancellor. unjustly grieved, that then, and in such case, the chancellor of England, of us, our heirs and successors, for the time being, upon the complaint of any person or persons so grieved, shall moderate and qualify such aids, tallages, grants, and contributions, as to him in that behalf shall be thought fit; which moderation shall stand, and be of force.

Mayor, recorder, and aldermen past the chair to be justices of oyer and terminer. And furthermore we will, and by these presents, for us, our heirs and successors, do grant to the aforesaid mayor and commonalty and citizens, and their successors, that the mayor and recorder of the said city, which now are, and every mayor and recorder of the same city, who hereafter for the time being shall be, as well those aldermen of the said city, as those aldermen who shall for the time to come bear the charge of mayoralty of the same city, after that they have ceased, or be moved from the office of mayoralty of the same city, and so long as they shall continue aldermen of our city of London aforesaid, for ever be, and shall be our justices, and of our heirs and successors, and every one of them be, and shall be justices and keepers of us, our heirs and successors, to keep and make to be kept the peace of us, our heirs and successors, in and through all and singular circuits, precincts, liberties, franchises, and places aforesaid, commonly called the Blackfriars, the Whitefriars, the Duke's Place, otherwise Creedchurch Street, Great St. Bartholomew's, Little St. Bartholomew's, and Cold Harborough aforesaid, and every of them, and to keep, or cause to be kept and executed, all ordinances and statutes of this our realm, made for the good of our peace, and the quiet rule and government of our people, in all their articles, according to the force, form, and effect of the same; and to chastise and punish those who, contrary to the form and effect of those ordinances or statutes, or any of them, within the limits, franchises, and places aforesaid, are found to offend, as ought to be done, according to the form of the said ordinances and statutes; and to make to come before them all those who threaten any of the people of us, our heirs or successors, concerning their bodies, or burning their houses, to find sufficient security of the peace or good behaviour towards us, our heirs or successors; and, if they refuse to find security, them to cause to be safely kept in prison, until they shall find such security. *With power to take security for the peace, and to commit to prison.*

And further, we will and grant for us, our heirs and successors, to the same mayor and commonalty and citizens, and their successors, that the mayor of the said city for the time being, and the recorder of the same now being, and who for the time to come shall be, and every alderman as aforesaid, who has been or hereafter shall be mayor of the said city, after they shall cease or be amoved from the office of mayoralty of the said city, and so long as the aldermen of the said city shall continue, or any four or more of the same, mayor, recorder, and aldermen (whereof the mayor and recorder of the same city *The mayor and recorder to be of the quorum.*

for the time being we will to be two) from henceforth for ever, may be justices of us, our heirs and successors; to enquire of all and all manner of felonies, witchcrafts, enchantments, sorceries, magic art, trespasses, forestallers, regraters, ingrossers, and extortioners whatsoever, and of all and singular other misdeeds and offences, of which our justices of the peace may and ought lawfully to enquire, howsoever and wheresoever done or committed, or which hereafter shall be done or attempted in the liberties, franchises, and places aforesaid; and also, of all other who within the same franchises, liberties, and places, go or ride in assemblies, or with armed force against our peace, and to the disturbance of our people; and also of those who lie in wait to kill our people, or hereafter shall presume to lie in wait; and also of hostlers, and all and singular other persons who have offended or attempted, or hereafter shall presume to offend or attempt, in abuse of weights and measures, and in selling victuals against the form of the ordinances and statutes, or any of them, made for the common profit of our kingdom and people; and also to hear and determine all and singular the same felonies and misdeeds, according to the laws and statutes of our realm of England: And also, to hear and determine, do and execute, all and singular other thing or things, which pertain, have pertained, or in time to come may pertain to justices of the peace within the said city of London; so always that the said mayor, commonalty and citizens, and their successors, may have and hold all and singular their ancient privileges, free, whole, and unhurt; and that no other keeper of the peace, or justice, or other officers or ministers of us, our heirs or successors whatsoever, shall intermeddle in the same, or any of them.

No other justices of the peace to intermeddle.

We will also, and by these presents for us, our heirs and successors, charge and command the sheriffs of the said city of London for the time being, that from time to time they be assisting, aiding, attending, and devising, as it behoveth, to the said mayor, recorder, and aldermen, and every or any of them, in execution of the premises, and according to our true meaning herein expressed. *Sheriffs to aid, etc., the said mayor, etc.*

And furthermore, we do hereby give and grant for us, our heirs and successors, to the said mayor and commonalty and citizens of the said city of London, and their successors, that the said mayor and commonalty and citizens, and their successors, for the time being, may have and enjoy to their own proper use, without any account thereof to be rendered to us, our heirs or successors, all treasure found, or to be found in the said franchises and places called Blackfriars, Whitefriars, Duke's Place, Great St. Bartholomew's, Little St. Bartholomew's, and Cold Harbour abovesaid, and waived goods and chattels, and estrays, goods and chattels of felons and fugitives, for whatsoever felony done or to be done by them, within any the said franchises or places, adjudged, or to be adjudged before us, our heirs or successors, or any of the justices aforesaid; and that it shall be lawful for the said mayor and commonalty and citizens, and their successors, by their deputy or minister, deputies or ministers of the said city, liberties or suburbs of the same, to put themselves in seizin and possession of, and in, all manner of treasure found, goods and chattels waived and estrayed, goods and chattels of felons and fugitives, from time to time, when they shall happen, by virtue of these our letters patent, without any further warrant whatsoever. *City to enjoy all treasure found within the aforesaid liberties. And all waifs, etc.*

We will also, and by these presents grant to the

To have these patents under seal without fine or fees.

said mayor and commonalty and citizens of the said city of London, that they shall have these our letters patent under our great seal of England, in due manner made and sealed, without fine or fee, great or little, to be rendered, paid, or made, to us in our proper hamper, or otherwise to us in any wise for the same; [although] express mention [be not] made of the [true] yearly value, or certainty of the premises, or any of them, or of any other gifts or grants made by us or by our progenitors, or predecessors, to the said mayor and commonalty and citizens of London, before this time; or any statute, ordinance, provision, proclamation, or restriction to the contrary thereof heretofore made or ordained, set forth or provided, or any other thing, cause, or matter whatsoever [notwithstanding]. Whereof these our letters we have caused to be made patent.

 Witness ourself at our Honour of Hampton Court, the twentieth day of September, in the year of our reign of England, France, and Ireland, the sixth, and of Scotland the forty-second.

No. XLIV.

The Third Charter of King James I.

15 September, A.D. 1614.

JAMES, by the grace of God, king of England, Scotland, France and Ireland, defender of the faith, etc., to all to whom these present letters shall come, greeting.

So great is the force of our love towards our city of London, our royal chamber, as whatsoever is in us that we shall see necessary or profitable to the mayor and commonalty and citizens of the same our city, that we have been ready freely to give from our soul to the said mayor, commonalty, and citizens of our said city; and it pleases us well, that all grants made by our predecessors in times past to our city of London be not only confirmed, but also enlarged. Therefore, whereas amongst other things, it appears that the said mayor and commonalty and citizens of London, from all time whereof the memory of man is not to the contrary, have had and lawfully exercised the office of measuring all coals, of what kind or sort soever, in any port of the same city, coming, brought, or carried upon the water of Thames, in any ship, boat, barge, or other vessel whatsoever, floating or being upon what part soever of the said water of Thames, or on what bank, shore, or wharf soever, of the same water of Thames, from the bridge in the town of Staines, in the county of Middlesex, and to

Preamble.

the bridge of London : and from thence to a certain place called Yendale, or Yenland, or Yenleet, toward the sea, and east, and also in Medway, and in the port of London: Nevertheless a question is risen, whether the weighing of coals brought within the limits aforesaid, together with the measuring of coals, doth belong to the mayor and commonalty and citizens of the said city.

<small>Grants the measuring and weighing of coals in the port of London from Yenleet to Staines Bridge.</small>

We therefore, to take away all controversies in this part, as well for the present as for the time to come, and to remove all doubt, and to the intent the said mayor and commonalty and citizens of the said city, may use, have, and enjoy, as well the weighing as measuring, and each, as the wages, rewards, fees, and profits used for the same, of our special grace, have given, granted, and confirmed, and by these presents, for us, and our heirs and successors, do give, grant, and confirm to our beloved the mayor and commonalty and citizens of our said city of London, and to their successors, the weighing of all coals called stone coals, pit coals, earth coals, and all other coals weighable, of what kind or sort soever, in or at the said port of London, coming or brought up the said water of Thames, in any ship, boat, or barge, or other vessel whatsoever, floating, or being in any port of the same water of Thames, and upon whatsoever bank, shore, or wharf of the same water of Thames, from the said bridge of Staines to the said bridge of London, and from thence to the said place called Yendal, towards the sea; and also in Medway, and in the port of London aforesaid, to be sold or put to sale; and also all fees, wages, rewards, profits, and advantages used, or to that time belonging, or any wise appertaining, to be exercised by the mayor of the said city, for the time being, and by the deputies, officers and ministers of the said mayor.

THE THIRD CHARTER OF JAMES I. 153

And further, we do hereby, for us, our heirs and successors, give, grant, and confirm to the said mayor and commonalty and citizens of the said city, and their successors, that they for ever have and enjoy the office of weighing all coals, called stone coals, pit coals, earth coals, and all other coals weighable, of what kind or sort soever, at the port of the said city of London, coming or brought upon the said water of Thames, in any ship, boat, barge or other vessel whatsoever, floating or being in any part of the said water of Thames, or upon any bank, shore or wharf of the same, from the said bridge of Staines to the said bridge of London, from thence to the said place called Yendal, towards the sea, and also in Medway, and in the port of London aforesaid, to be sold or set to sale; and also all fees, wages, profits, rewards and advantages whatsoever used, or to the same office belonging, or any other way appertaining, to be exercised by the mayor of the same city, for the time being, and by the deputies, officers, and ministers of the same mayor.

And we have also constituted, and by these presents, for us, our heirs and successors, do constitute, ordain, create, and make the said mayor and commonalty and citizens of the said city of London, and their successors, by the mayor of the same city for the time being, during the time of his mayoralty, or by his deputies, officers or ministers, to be weigher of all and singular coals, called stone coals, pit coals, earth coals, and all other coals weighable, of what kind soever, in or at the port of the said city of London, coming, carried or brought upon the same water of Thames, in any ship, boat or barge, or any other vessel whatsoever, floating or being in any part of the same water of Thames, and upon any bank, shore or wharf of the same water of Thames, which shall happen to stay, be delivered, or laid down from the said bridge of Staines to the aforesaid place called Yendale, towards the sea; and also in Medway, and in the port of London aforesaid, to be sold or put to sale.

And whereas there is a question risen of the quantity of the fee demanded and received by the mayor of the said city for the time being, and by their deputies, ministers and officers, for the weighing of every ton weight of coals, containing five score and twelve pounds to every ton[1] weight brought within the limits aforesaid:

We, wholly to take away every the said question, and the like question, do declare, establish, and for us, our heirs and successors, do grant to the said mayor and commonalty and citizens of the said city, and their successors, that it shall be lawful for the mayor and commonalty and citizens of the said city, for the time being, by the mayor of the same city, and by the deputy, minister and officers of such mayor for the time being, to ask, demand, take and receive a fee of eightpence of lawful money of England, to the use of the said mayor and commonalty and citizens of the said city, and their successors, for the weighing of every such-like ton of coals aforesaid, and all other coals weighable, of what kind soever; and so, according to the same rate, for a smaller or greater quantity, of the person bringing such-like coals, for and in respect of the charge and costs of them, the said mayor, commonalty and citizens of the said city of London, and their successors, in the beam and weights, and for and in respect of their attendance, labour, and necessary costs and expenses, to be had and expended in and about the premises; which fee of eightpence aforesaid the said mayor and

And to receive a fee of 8d. per ton for the use of the city.

---

[1] Properly this should be "hundredweight".

commonalty and citizens of the said city had and received formerly.

And also we command, and by these presents, for us, our heirs and successors, firmly enjoin and charge all merchants, and other persons whatsoever, who shall bring coals called sea coals, pit coals, and earth coals, of what kind soever the same shall be, within the limits aforesaid, upon the water of Thames aforesaid, in any ship, boat or vessel whatsoever, that none of them henceforth shall unlade, deliver, or lay down, nor cause or permit such-like coals to be unladen, delivered, or laid down, out of such ships, boats or other vessels, being within the limits and bounds aforesaid, upon any wharf, bank or shore, upon either part of the same water of Thames, or to be discharged or laid down, before the mayor of our said city for the time being shall take certain notice of the quantity of such coals, and shall give direction for the unlading of the same, and for the weighing and measuring of such coals; to the intent that the same mayor of the said city for the time being may be able to render a better and more ready reason and accompt to us, our heirs and successors, what quantity of coals, of what sort soever, from time to time, have been brought within the port of our said city, and limits aforesaid, and how the said city, and the parts and places next adjoining, are from time to time provided, and when we, our heirs or successors, shall require the same from the mayor of our said city for the time being; and also, to the intent that the sums and other profits due to us, our heirs and successors, for such coals, so to be brought within the limits aforesaid (if there shall be any due) may be better answered and paid unto the officers and ministers of us, our heirs and successors, to the use of us, our heirs and successors, under pain of

Forbids the unloading of coals till the mayor have notice thereof.

The reason.

contempt of our royal mandate, and incurring all such pains and punishments, which by the laws and statutes of this realm of England may be inflicted upon such neglecters and contemners.

And whereas it is notoriously known, that the river of Thames is so necessary, commodious, and profitable to the said city of London, and without the said river our said city would not long subsist, flourish, and continue; and for that by forestalling, ingrossing, and regrating of coals in and at the port of the said city brought from the water of Thames aforesaid, such coals are made more dear, to the great loss and prejudice as well of us as of our subjects:

And whereas divers ill-disposed persons, more affecting their own private gain and profit than the general and public good and benefit of our said city, little weighing the conservation of the said river, of late and at the present do daily and usually sell coals and other things by retail, in less quantity, in boats commonly called lighters, and other vessels, floating and being on the water of Thames aforesaid, after such coals have been unladen from the ships and other vessels which first brought them within the limits aforesaid, which persons make the same boats or lighters as their common shops and warehouses, and in them do daily hold upon the said water of Thames a common market for selling such coals, and other things, having one, two, three, and sometimes more boats or lighters lying together, and fastened one to the other in the river of Thames aforesaid, by which forestalling, ingrossing, and regrating aforesaid, to the great cozenage, damage, and oppression, as well of the poor as the rich, daily increases and augments, and the price of coals and other things is made dearer:

And for that by the frequent importation, unlading, and measuring of such coals, and such like things, in and from the said boats or lighters, very many of the same coals and other dirt often fall and are cast into the river of Thames, to the great harm and choking up the stream of the same river, and the said boats so placed do greatly hinder the stream of the said river, and the passage of passengers upon the water of the said river:

We, therefore, thinking it fit that such an evil ought not to be permitted to continue, do command, and for us, our heirs and successors, prohibit all persons whatsoever, that they, nor any of them, from henceforth, sell or presume to sell any coals, of what kind soever, upon the water of Thames, in any boat, lighter, or other vessel whatsoever, except only in such ships or other vessels which at first brought the same coals within the port of the said city, and the limits abovesaid, unless upon some port, key, or wharf, near the said river; upon pain of contempt of our royal mandate, and incurring such pains and punishments, which may be inflicted by the laws and statutes of this our kingdom upon such contemners and neglecters. *Prohibits the sale of coals by retail in lighters. Exceptions.*

And because it is our intent that the same mayor and commonalty and citizens of the city aforesaid, and their successors, shall fully enjoy the premises; we, therefore, by these presents, declare and signify, and for us, our heirs and successors, do grant and covenant to and with the said mayor and commonalty and citizens of the said city, and their successors, that they may safely, freely, and quietly have, use, and enjoy, all and singular the premises for ever, without the hindrance of us, our heirs or successors, or any officers or ministers of us, our heirs or successors. *Covenants that the city may enjoy the premises.*

And if any doubt in time to come shall be found in these presents, or any default, scruple, or question concerning the premises shall happen to arise, we, our heirs and successors, shall vouchsafe to make and grant other letters patent under the great seal of England, of our heirs or successors, to the same mayor and commonalty and citizens of the said city, and their successors, for the better giving, granting, and confirming, and for the safer enjoying of the premises, when it shall be desired by the same mayor and commonalty and citizens of the said city, and their successors, although the express mention of the true yearly value, or of the certainty of the premises or of other gifts and grants by us, or by any of our ancestors made in times past to the said mayor and commonalty and citizens of the said city, is not made, or being in these presents, or any other statute, act, ordinance, proclamation, or restriction to the contrary heretofore made, ordained, or published, or any other matter or thing whatsoever in anywise notwithstanding. In witness whereof, we have caused these our letters to be made patent.

And to grant other letters patent if any doubt should arise concerning these.

Witness myself at Westminster, the fifteenth of September, in the twelfth year of our reign of England, France, and Ireland, and of Scotland the forty-eighth.

No. XLV.

First Charter of King Charles I.

18 October, a.d. 1638.

CHARLES, by the grace of God, king of England, Scotland, France, and Ireland, defender of the faith, etc., to all to whom the present letters shall come, greeting.

(1.) We have seen the charter of Lord William, our progenitor, formerly king of England, in this form:—William, king, etc. [See No. i.]

(2.) We have seen also a certain charter of the same William, our progenitor, made after this form: —William, king, etc. [See No. ii.]

(3.) We have also seen the charter of the Lord Henry [I], our progenitor, formely king of England, drawn up in this form:—Henry, etc. [See No. iii.]

(4.) Furthermore, we have seen the charter of Lord Henry the second, our progenitor, formerly king of England, drawn up in the following form:— Henry, etc. [See No. iv.]

(5.) We have also seen the charter of Lord Richard the first, formerly king of England, duke, etc. [See No. v.]

(6.) We have also seen a certain other charter of the said Lord Richard, by the grace of God, king, etc. [See No. vi.]

(7.) We have also seen the charter of Lord John, sometime king of England, our progenitor, in these words:—John, etc. [See No. vii.]

(8.) We have seen other charters of the aforesaid Lord John, our progenitor, made in these words:—John, etc. [See No. IX.]

(9.) We have seen one other charter of the aforesaid Lord John our progenitor, made in this form:—John, etc. [See No. VIII.]

(10.) We have also seen a certain other charter of the aforesaid Lord John, made in this form:—John, etc. [See No. XI.]

(11.) Furthermore, we have seen a certain other charter of the above said Lord John, made in this form:—John, etc. [See No. X.]

(12.) We have also seen a charter of the Lord Henry the third, formerly king of England, our progenitor, made in these terms:—Henry, etc. [See No. XII.]

(13.) We have also seen a certain other charter of the same Lord Henry, made in this form:—Henry, etc. [See No. XIII.]

(14.) We have seen a certain other charter of the said Lord Henry, our progenitor, made in this form:—Henry, etc. [See No. XIV.]

(15.) We have also seen a certain other charter of the above said Lord Henry, made in these words:—Henry, etc. [See No. XV.]

(16.) We have also seen a certain other charter of the aforesaid Lord Henry, made in these words:—Henry, etc. [See No. XVI.]

(17.) We have seen a certain other charter of the said Lord Henry, made in this form:—Henry, etc. [See No. XVII.]

(18.) We have also seen another charter of the aforesaid Lord Henry, made in this form:—Henry, etc. [See No. XVIII.]

(19.) Moreover, we have seen a certain other charter of the aforesaid Lord Henry, bearing date the eleventh day of January, in the fiftieth year of his reign, by which certain charter, among other things, the said Lord Henry granted to the citizens of London, that the said citizens may traffic, etc. [See No. XIX.]

(20.) We have seen a certain other charter of the aforesaid Lord Henry, made in these words:—Henry, etc. [See No. XX.]

(21.) We have seen a certain charter, which the Lord Edward the first, sometime king of England, made to the aforesaid citizens, bearing date the eighteenth day of April, in the twenty-sixth year of his reign, in which charter, among other things, it is continued:—That whereas, etc. [See No. XXI.]

(22.) We have also seen certain letters patent of Lord Edward, son of Edward, sometime king of England, our progenitor made in these words:—Edward, etc. [See No. XXIII.]

(23.) We have also seen the charter of Lord Edward the third, sometime king of England, our progenitor, made in these words:—Edward, etc. [See No. XXIV.]

(24.) We have also seen certain other letters patent of the Lord Edward the third, king of England, made in these words:—Edward, etc. [See No. XXV.]

(25.) We have also seen a certain other charter of the same Lord Edward the third, in these words:—Edward, etc. [See No. XXVI.]

(26.) We have also seen a certain other statute of the said Lord Edward the third, late king of England, made in these words:—Edward, etc. [See No. XXVII.]

(27.) We have also seen certain letters patent of our Lord Edward, late king of England, the third, in these words:—Edward, etc. [See No. XXIX.]

(28.) And we have seen the charter of Lord

A.D. 1400.   Henry the fourth, late king, bearing date the twenty-fifth day of May, in the first year of his reign, made to the citizens aforesaid, in which charter is contained, among other things, as followeth: "And, moreover, of our ample grace, we have granted, for us and our heirs, as much as in us is, to the same citizens, their heirs and successors as aforesaid, that they shall have the custody as well of the gates of Newgate and Ludgate, as all other the gates and posterns of the said city; and also the office of the gathering of the tolls and customs in Cheap and Billingsgate and Smithfield, there rightfully to be taken and accustomed; and also the tronage, that is to say, the weighing of lead, wax, pepper, alum, madder, and other like wares, within the city for ever; as by the said charters among other things more plainly may appear."

(29.) We have seen the charter of Lord Edward the fourth, late king of England, in these words:— Edward, etc. [See No. XXXII.]

(30.) We have also seen certain other letters patent of the same Lord Edward, late king of England, the fourth, made in these words:—Edward, etc. [See No. XXXIII.]

(31.) Moreover, we have seen certain other letters patent of the aforesaid Lord Edward, late king of England, the fourth, made in these words:—Edward, etc. [See No. XXXIV.]

(32.) We have also seen certain other letters patent of the abovesaid Lord Edward, late king of England, the fourth, made in these words:—Edward, etc. [See No. XXXV.]

(33.) And whereas, in and by certain letters patent of Henry, late King of England the seventh, our progenitor, made under the great seal of England, bearing date the twenty-third day of July, in the

twentieth year of his reign, amongst other things A.D. 1505.
it is recited:—That of all time, etc. [See No.
XXXVI.]

(34.) We have also seen the letters patent of Lord
Henry the eighth, late king of England, our progenitor, made in these words:—Henry, etc. [See
No. XXXVII.]

(35.) Moreover, we have seen other letters patent
of the same Lord Henry, our progenitor, late king
of England, made in these words:—Henry, etc. [See
No. XXXVIII.]

(36.) We have seen also the letters patent of Lord
Edward, late king of England, the sixth, our progenitor, made in these words:—Edward, etc. [See
No. XL.]

(37.) We have also seen the letters patent of our
most dear father, Lord James, late king of England,
etc., made in these words:—James, etc. [See No. XLII.]

(38.) We have also seen certain other letters
patent of our said most dear father of blessed
memory, Lord James, late king of England, made in
these words:—James, etc. [See No. XLIII.]

(39.) We have, moreover, seen certain other
letters patent of our said most dear father of blessed
memory, Lord James, late king of England, etc.,
made in these words:—James, etc. [No. XLIV.]

Know ye now, that we, deeply considering and The preamble
calling to memory the good and laudable services
performed by our beloved and faithful subjects, the
said mayor and commonalty and citizens of the city
of London, which we graciously accept; and from
our soul affecting the good and happy estate of our
said city, to increase and enlarge, with the greatest
favour and grace we can, and to establish, with all
care and diligence we can, the rule and government
of our said city, of our especial grace, and from our

certain knowledge and mere motion, and for divers other good causes and considerations especially moving us at present; do accept and approve of, for us, our heirs and successors, as much as in us lies, all and singular the letters patent, charters, and confirmations aforesaid, and all and singular gifts, grants, confirmations, restitutions, customs, ordinances, explanations, articles, and all other things whatsoever in the same letters patent or charters (except as are hereinafter excepted) and all and singular lands, tenements, offices, jurisdictions, authorities, privileges, liberties, franchises, quittals, immunities, free customs, and hereditaments whatsoever, which the said mayor and commonalty and citizens of the city of London, or their predecessors, by the name of mayor and commonalty and citizens of the city of London, or by the name of the mayor and aldermen, citizens, or commonalty, of London, or by the name of mayor and citizens of the city of London, or by the name of the mayor and commonalty of the city of London, or by the name of the citizens of the city of London, or by the names of barons of London, or by any other name whatsoever, by reason and force of the said letters patent, charters, or confirmations, or by use or prescription, or any other lawful means at any time or times heretofore have had ratified and bestowed; and all those we ratify and confirm by these presents to the said mayor and commonalty and citizens of the said city of London, and their successors.

Ratifies and confirms former charters, etc.

We will also, and, for the considerations aforesaid, for us, our heirs and successors, do grant, that the said mayor and commonalty and citizens, and their successors, be fully and wholly restored to all and singular their authorities, jurisdictions, liberties, franchises, privileges, quittals, and free customs

Restores to all liberties, jurisdictions, etc.

whatsoever abovesaid (except such as are hereinafter excepted); and all and singular to the said mayor and commonalty and citizens, and their successors, we for us, our heirs and successors, do restore by these presents, as fully, freely, and wholly, and in as ample a manner and form, as they or their predecessors had used or enjoyed the same in any times of our progenitors or predecessors, once kings and queens of England.

We will, also, and by these presents, for us, our heirs and successors, grant, that it shall be lawful for the said mayor and commonalty and citizens of the city of London aforesaid, any authority, office, jurisdiction, liberty, privilege, franchise, immunity, quittals, and free customs mentioned in the letters patent or charters aforesaid, or any of them, or other their customs which hitherto they have [not] used, or perhaps have abused, or not claimed when they ought to have claimed, that they nevertheless, the mayor and commonalty and citizens of the city of London, and their successors, may henceforth for ever fully have, enjoy, and use, any matter, cause, or thing whatsoever, in times past had, made, or provided to the contrary thereof notwithstanding, without hindrance or impediment of us, our heirs or successors, our justices, sheriffs, coroners, escheators, or any other bailiff or ministers of us, our heirs or successors whatsoever, the same authorities, offices, jurisdictions, liberties, privileges, franchises, immunities, quittals, and free customs whatsoever in [the] like not used or abused, or not claimed, or any of them.

And to the intent the said mayor and commonalty and citizens of the said city, and their successors in time to come, may the more safely, freely, and quietly hold and enjoy to them and their successors for ever, all and singular the premises in the said letters patent, or charters before mentioned, or intended to be given or granted by the same; and for the intent that no ambiguity, controversy, doubtful construction or question of, or about the premises, may henceforth arise, but be altogether taken away:

To hold the same for the like fees, services, etc., as formerly. We, for the consideration aforesaid, and of our special grace, for us, our heirs and successors, do give and grant to the said mayor and commonalty, and citizens of the city of London, and their successors for ever, all and singular, the manors, lands, tenements, offices, fees, rewards, liberties, privileges, jurisdictions, immunities, ordinances, quittals, hereditaments, and all and singular other things whatsoever, in the said letters patent, or charters afore-recited, or any of them contained, or mentioned to have been given or granted, with all and singular the appurtenances (except such as in the same charter, or letters patent, or in these presents are excepted), as fully, plainly, freely, and wholly, to all intents and purposes, as if they had been expressed, named, mentioned, declared, and manifested severally, and namely, and word for word in these presents: to hold all and singular the premises by these presents mentioned to be granted, or confirmed, with all appurtenances, of us, our heirs and successors, by such, the same, or the like services, fees, fee-farm, rent, sums of money, and demands whatsoever, by which or by what, and as all and singular the same premises were formerly held of us, or our predecessors, or were intended to be held by the same letters patent, charters, or otherwise.

And whereas Lord Henry the sixth, late king of England, our predecessor, by his letters patent under the great seal of England, bearing date at Westminster the twenty-sixth day of October, in the twenty-*A.D. 1444.* third year of his reign, granted unto the citizens of the city aforesaid, amongst other things, that the said citizens, and their successors for ever, should have all soils, commons, purprestures, and improvements in all wastes, commons, streets, ways, and other places in the city and suburbs aforesaid, and in the water of Thames within the limits of the same city, together with the profits of the same purprestures and improvements, and that they may improve, and rent and enjoy the rents of them, and their successors for ever, and likewise several other things, as in the said letters patent more fully appears:

To have all soils, commons, purprestures,etc.

And whereas in the parliament of the said Henry the sixth, late king of England, held at Westminster in the twenty-eighth year of his reign, it was enacted by the authority of the same parliament, that the same king should take, resume, seize, and retain into his hands and possession, all honours, castles, lordships, towns, villages, manors, lands, tenements, wastes, rents, reversions, fees, fee-farms, and services, with all appurtenances in England, Wales, and the Marches of the same, Ireland, Guienne, Calais, and the Marches of the same, which the said lord Henry by his letters patent or otherwise had granted from the first day of his reign, and all honours, castles, lordships, towns, villages, manors, lands, tenements, wastes, rents, reversions, fees, fee-farms, and services, with all their appurtenances, which were of the duchy of Lancaster, and by the king himself conveyed by grant or grants of the same king; and the said king [should] have, hold, and retain all the same premises in the like state [that] he had them at the time of such like concession made by the same king of the same; and that all letters patent by the said king, or any other person or persons, at the request and desire of the said king, to any person

A.D. 1449.

or persons made of the premises, or any of them, should be void and of no force in law; as by the same act of parliament (amongst other things) doth more fully appear:

And whereas our most famous progenitor, Henry the seventh, late king of England, etc. by his letters patent, under the great seal of England, bearing date at Westminster the twenty-third day of July, in the twentieth year of his reign, reciting, amongst other things, all and singular donations, confirmations, grants, restitutions, innovations, ordinances, and all other articles and things in the said letters patent contained, did accept, and approved, and ratified, and confirmed all and singular the said things to the said mayor and commonalty and citizens of the said city, and their heirs and successors, by the same letters patent, and did grant and confirm by his said letters patent all and singular those things, as fully, plainly, and wholly as if they had been severally and word for word expressed, declared, and manifested in the said letters patent of the same Lord Henry the seventh, to the same mayor and commonalty and citizens, and their successors; as by the said letters patent amongst other things more plainly appears.

And whereas there are divers questions lately arisen concerning the validity, as well of the said letters patent of the said Lord Henry the sixth, as of the said Lord Henry the seventh, thereupon made by reason or pretence of the same act of parliament concerning resumption aforesaid:

We, willing that all questions thereof be from henceforth taken away, and to the intent the mayor and commonalty and citizens of the city of London, and their successors, may the better, more safely, and quietly have, hold and enjoy some things in the said letters patent of the said late king Henry the sixth, hereinafter expressed; nevertheless, with some provisoes, exceptions, restrictions, and explanations in these presents mentioned, it is our good pleasure, by these our present letters, to grant and confirm to the said mayor and commonalty and citizens, and their successors, the same particular things, and others hereafter specified, in such manner and form as is afterwards mentioned.

Know ye therefore, that we, for divers good causes and considerations especially moving us thereunto, of our special grace, and from our certain knowledge and mere motion, have given and granted, and by these presents, for us, our heirs and successors, do give and grant to the said mayor and commonalty and citizens of the city of London, and their successors, that the mayor and recorder of the said city, who now are, and for the time shall be, as well as those aldermen who formerly have been mayors of the city, as those aldermen who for the time to come shall sustain and bear the burden and office of the mayoralty of the said city, although they shall cease from their mayoralty, or are dismissed from it, so long as nevertheless they stand aldermen, and the three senior aldermen of the said city for the time being, who have stood longest in the office of aldermen, and before that time have not yet borne the burden and the office of mayoralty of that city, [shall be] for ever keepers, and each of them a keeper, of the peace of us, our heirs and successors, within the city of London aforesaid, and the liberties of the same, to be conserved and kept. *The mayor, recorder, all the aldermen who have served the office of mayor, and the three senior aldermen next the chair, shall be justices of the peace.*

And we do constitute, make, and ordain, by these presents, for us, our heirs and successors, the same mayor, recorder, and aldermen aforesaid, our keepers and justices, and each of them the keeper and justice *The mayor, recorder, etc., to hold sessions of the peace.*

of us, our heirs and successors, within the city of London aforesaid, and the liberties of the same; to keep and cause to be kept all and singular the statutes and ordinances made or to be made for the good of the peace of us, our heirs and successors, for the conservation of the same, and for the quiet rule and government of the people of us, our heirs and successors, in all their articles, as well within the said city as the liberty thereof, according to the force, form, and effect of them; and to correct and punish all those whom they shall find offending against the form and effect of the said ordinances and statutes, and any of them, in the city aforesaid, and the liberties thereof, as should be done according to the form of those ordinances and statutes; and to cause all such who shall threaten all or any of the people of us our heirs or successors, concerning their bodies, or burning their houses, to find a sufficient security for his peace and good behaviour towards us, our heirs and successors; and if they shall refuse to find such security, then to cause them to be safely kept in our gaol of Newgate, or in any other prison of us, or our heirs and successors, in the said city of London, until they shall find security; and to do and execute all such things, which the justices and keepers of the peace of us, our heirs and successors, within any county of our kingdom of England, are enabled, may, or ought by virtue of any statutes or ordinances of this our kingdom of England, or by virtue of any commission of us, our heirs or successors, to execute or do for the keeping of the peace in any the like counties.

We will, also, and by these presents, for us, our heirs and successors, do grant to the said mayor, commonalty, and citizens of the city of London, and their successors, that the mayor and recorder of the

FIRST CHARTER OF KING CHARLES I. 171

said city for the time being, and such-like aldermen as is aforesaid for the time being, who have formerly borne and exercised the office or place of mayoralty of that city, and thereof such-like (as aforesaid) senior aldermen for the time being, who have not yet borne the place of mayoralty aforesaid, or four of the same, mayor, recorder, and aldermen (whereof we will the said mayor or recorder for the time being to be one), be the justices of us, our heirs and successors, for us, our heirs and successors for ever; to inquire as often, and when it shall seem best expedient to them, by the oath of honest and lawful men, as well of the city aforesaid, as the liberty of the same, by whom the truth of the thing may better be known, concerning all manner of murders, felonies, punishments, witchcrafts, enchantments, sorceries, magic art, transgressions, forestallings, regratings, engrossings, and extortions whatsoever, and of all and singular other misdemeanours and offences heretofore had or committed, or which shall henceforth happen to be done or attempted, concerning which the justices of the peace of us, our heirs and successors, may, or ought lawfully to inquire within the city aforesaid, or the liberties thereof, and as well of all others who have in companies within the said city, and liberties thereof, gone or rode, or shall from henceforth presume to go or ride armed against us, our heirs and successors, and also of those who there have lain in wait, or shall presume to lie in wait for the time to come, to maim or kill the people of us, our heirs and successors; and also of all hostlers, or other persons who shall offend, or attempt in the said city and the liberty of the same, in the abuse of measures and weights, or in the selling of victuals against the form of the ordinances and statutes, or any of them, made or to be made for the common

And to inquire concerning felonies, etc.

And after all unjust weights and measures.

profit of our kingdom of England, and the same people of us, our heirs and successors; and also of all sheriffs, constables, gaolers, and other officers who have behaved themselves unduly about the premises, or any of them, or shall presume hereafter to behave themselves unduly, or shall have been remiss, or negligent, or shall so be within the city aforesaid, and the liberties of the same; and of all and singular articles, and things whatsoever made and committed, or which henceforth shall be made or attempted anyway concerning the premises, or any of them, in the city aforesaid, and the liberties of the same.

And to see into whatsoever indictments which shall be taken before the mayor or recorder of the city aforesaid for the time being, or such-like (as is aforesaid) aldermen, or four or more of them (whereof we will the said mayor or recorder for the time being to be one) and to make and continue process against all and singular so indicted, or who after shall chance to be indicted, until they be taken, render themselves, or are outlawed: And to hear and determine all and singular murders, felonies, poisonings, witchcrafts, enchantments, sorceries, magic arts, transgressions, false conspiracies, and other misdemeanours, forestallings, regratings, engrossings, extortions, conventicles, and judgments aforesaid, and all and singular the premises, according to the laws and statutes of our kingdom of England, as used and ought to be done in such-like case: And to chastise and punish the same offenders for their faults, by fines, redemptions, amerciaments, forfeitures, and otherwise, as hath been used, and ought to be according to the law and custom of our kingdom of England, and the form of the ordinances and statutes of the same: And to do, exercise, hear, determine, and execute all and singular things within the said city and liberties thereof, which justices of the peace, by the laws and statutes of our kingdom, may and are enabled to do, enquire, or execute, and in as ample manner and form, as any one or other justice of the peace in any counties of this our kingdom of England, may, and are enabled lawfully to do, enquire, punish, or execute; giving it strictly in command by these presents, for us, our heirs and successors, to our sheriffs of our said city for the time being, and their successors, sheriffs of the said city, and to whatsoever citizens of the said city, who now are, and in time to come shall be, that they be attending, counselling, answering, and aiding to the said keepers of the peace, and aforesaid mayor and recorder for the time being, and such aldermen as are aforesaid, in all and singular things, which do or may belong to the office of the keeper of the peace, and such-like justices within the said city, and liberties of the same, according to the said form, as often, and when they shall be duly required by them, or some or one of them, in the behalf of us, our heirs or successors. *That the sheriffs shall be aiding to the said keepers of the peace.*

Know ye also, that we, for the consideration aforesaid, have given and granted, and by these presents for us, our heirs and successors, do give and grant to the said mayor and commonalty and citizens of the said city, and their successors, all recognizances taken or to be taken, acknowledged or to be acknowledged, forfeited or to be forfeited, for appearance at any session or sessions of the peace, holden or to be holden before the mayor, recorder, and aldermen of the city as aforesaid, or any other justices of us, our heirs or successors, assigned or to be assigned for or concerning the peace in the said city of London, and the liberties thereof; and also all and all manner of recognizances taken or to be taken, acknowledged *Also granting all recognizances to be taken and forfeited, and all fines, etc.*

or to be acknowledged, forfeited or to be forfeited, before the justices of us, our heirs and successors, for and concerning the peace in the same city and liberties of the same, assigned or to be assigned, or by one or any of them, for and concerning the keeping and maintaining of bastard children, and the keeping harmless the parishes of the said city, touching such-like children, or of inmates dividing of houses in or for several habitations, or of suppressing of ale houses within the said city and liberties thereof; and for the observation of such-like orders, which from time to time by the said justices of peace or any of them have been made, touching any of the late-mentioned premises; and also all manner of recognizances taken or to be taken, acknowledged or to be acknowledged, forfeited or to be forfeited for non-appearance at any session or sessions of gaol-delivery, of and for prisoners in the same for the time being held or to be held in and for the said city and the liberties thereof: And also fines and issues of jurors, and all other issues, fines and amerciaments, forfeited and to be forfeited, of and for all and singular the matters, causes and occasions aforesaid, and of and for whatsoever transgressions, riots, offences, misprisions, extortions, usurpations, contempts of laws, violations, and other misdemeanours done or to be committed in the said city or liberties of the same, before the mayor, recorder, and aldermen of the said city for the time being, or any of them, or any of the justices of us, our heirs and successors, concerning the peace in the said city, or before the justices of us, our heirs and successors, assigned or to be assigned to hear and determine felonies, transgressions, and misdemeanours in the said city and liberties thereof; or before any justices of us, our heirs and successors, or any of them, in the city aforesaid, judged or to be judged, forfeited or to be forfeited, together with the assessments and levies of the same, as often, and when there shall be need: Saving and always reserving to us, our heirs and successors, all and all manner of issues and amerciaments, commonly called fines or issues royal, hereafter from time to time to be imposed upon these the mayor and aldermen, and sheriffs of London and Middlesex, and for the time or any of them respectively, or by them to be forfeited and paid.

And further, we by these presents, for us, our heirs and successors, do give and grant to the said mayor and commonalty and citizens, and their successors, all and all manner of recognizances taken or to be taken, acknowledged or to be acknowledged, broken or to be broken, not observed or not to be observed, before the said justices of the peace in the said city, and the liberties of the same, or any of them, for the peace and security of the peace and good behaviour; and also all manner of recognizances taken or to be taken, acknowledged or to be acknowledged, before the mayor of the said city for the time being, in his court, or in the conservancy of the river of Thames, within the limits of the same river, or in our said letters patent of our said father, as aforesaid is recited and mentioned, for due fishing and observing of good order in taking of fish, or otherwise for the preservation of small fish in the said river of Thames, as for the conservation of the same water, or shores, or banks of the same river, made or to be made, broken or to be broken; and also all fines and amerciaments, pains and penalties whatsoever, assessed, imposed or adjudged, or to be assessed, imposed or adjudged, by or before the mayor of the said city for the time being, in his courts, as conservator of the said river of the Thames, without *And all forfeitures, fines, etc., in the court of conservancy.*

any account or other thing to be rendered or made to us, or our heirs or successors.

<small>And all fines, etc., imposed by the commissioners of sewers.</small>
And further, for the consideration aforesaid, we have given and granted, and by these presents, for us, our heirs and successors, do give and grant to the said mayor and commonalty and citizens, and their successors, all and all manner of fines, and amerciaments and forfeitures, which by reason of force of any commission or commissions of sewers of us, our heirs or successors, issued or to be issued forth within the city of London, and the liberties of the same, under the great seal of England, of us, our heirs or successors, taxed, imposed, assessed, or adjudged, or from time to time to be taxed, imposed, assessed, or adjudged upon any person or persons, without any account or any other thing to be rendered, paid or made to us, our heirs or successors.

<small>All messuages, houses, etc., erected on void grounds, etc., within the city and its liberties.</small>
And further, for the consideration aforesaid, we, by these presents, for us, our heirs and successors, do give, grant and confirm to the said mayor and commonalty, and citizens of the said city, and their successors, all messuages, houses, edifices, cottages, buildings, courts, yards, gardens, conduits and cisterns, shops, sheds, porches, benches, cellars, doors of cellars, staples, stalls, stages, pales, posts, jutties, and penthouses, signposts, props of signs, and the ground and foundation of them, shores, watercourses, gutters and easements, with their appurtenances, which now are, or at any time hereafter shall have been erected, built, taken, enclosed, obtained, increased, possessed or enjoyed by the said mayor and commonalty and citizens, and their successors, or any person or persons whatsoever of, in, upon or under all or any void grounds, wastes, commons, streets, ways, and other common places within the said city, and the liberties of the same, and in the river or water of Thames, or

ports, banks, creeks, or shores of the same, within the liberties of the said city.

We will, also, and by these presents, for us, our heirs and successors, declare and grant, that the said mayor and commonalty and citizens and their successors for ever, may have, hold and enjoy all those fields, called or known by the name Inward Moor and Outward Moor, in the parish of St. Giles without Cripplegate, London ; St. Stephen, in Coleman Street, London ; and St. Botolph without Bishopsgate, London ; or in some or any of them ; and also all that field called West Smithfield, in the parish of St. Sepulchre's, St. Bartholomew the Great, St. Bartholomew the Less, in the suburbs of London, or in some of them, to the uses, intents and purposes after expressed ; and that the same mayor and commonalty and citizens, and their successors, may be able to hold in the said field called Smithfield, fairs and markets there to be and used to be held, and to take, receive, and have pickage, stallage, tolls, and profits appertaining, happening, belonging, or arising out of the fairs and markets there, to such uses as the same mayor and commonalty and citizens, or their predecessors had, held, or enjoyed, and now have, hold, and enjoy, or ought to have, hold, or enjoy the said premises last-mentioned, and to no other uses, intents, or purposes whatsoever. *To have and hold Moorfields and West Smithfield. And to hold a fair and markets in Smithfield, and to have the tolls, pickage, stallage, etc.*

And that we, our heirs and successors, will not erect, or cause to be erected, nor will permit or give leave to any person or persons, to erect or build a new one, or any messuages, houses, structures, edifices, in or upon the said field called Inner Moor, or the field called Outer Moor, or the said field called West Smithfield ; but that the said separate fields and places be reserved, disposed and continued to such-like common and public uses, as the same here-

N

tofore and now are used, disposed or converted to (saving nevertheless, and always reserving to us, our heirs and successors, all streets, lanes, and alleys, and now waste and void ground and places, as they now are within the city and liberties of the same), to hold and enjoy the said messuages, houses, edifices, courtyards, and all and singular the premises granted or confirmed, or mentioned to be granted and confirmed, with all their appurtenances (except before excepted) to the said mayor and commonalty and citizens of the said city, and their successors for ever, to hold in free and common burgage, and not *in capite*, or by knight's service.

<small>In free and common burgage.</small>

And further, by these presents, for us, our heirs and successors, we pardon, remit and release to the said mayor and commonalty and citizens of the city of London, and their successors, all and singular issues, profits, and rents, of all and singular the same messuages, edifices, houses, structures, penthouses, and other the premises last-mentioned (except before excepted) any way due or incurred before the date of these presents, to us or our predecessors, and the arrearages of the same, without any account, molestation, suit or impediment of us, our heirs or successors, or any justices, officers or ministers of us, our heirs or successors; and this without any writ of *Ad quod damnum*, or any other writ or inquisition to be procured, issued or prosecuted in that behalf.

<small>Without any writ of *Ad quod damnum*.</small>

And that it shall be lawful to the said mayor and commonalty and citizens of the said city, and their successors, to put themselves, by them or their deputies, in full and peaceable possession and seisin of all and singular the premises, as often, and when it shall seem good and expedient; and thereof to have good allowance in any court whatsoever, of us, our heirs and successors, from time to time, without hindrance, impediment or perturbation of us, our heirs and successors, our justices, treasurers of England, barons of the exchequer, or other officers, or ministers whatsoever, of us, our heirs and successors.

And further, for the consideration aforesaid, for us, our heirs and successors, we do pardon, remit, release, and exonerate to the mayor and commonalty and citizens of the said city, and their successors, all and all manner of entries, intrusions, and ingresses whatsoever, at any time heretofore had or made, of, in and upon the premises aforesaid or any part of them, without any right or legal title of the said mayor and commonalty and citizens of the said city, and their predecessors, or their tenants, farmers or assigns, or any other person or persons. We will, nevertheless, and for us, our heirs and successors, do ordain and declare by these presents, that these our letters patent, or anything contained in them, shall not be interpreted or construed to the taking or diminishing the force or effect of any proclamations published hereafter, of or concerning buildings and edifices in the said city, and the liberties of the same, and in the places adjoining, for any contempts or offences whatsoever committed, or to be committed; nor to remit or release any offences or contempts heretofore committed, or hereafter to be committed against the tenor of the same, or any of them; but that the same proclamations may be and remain in their full force, any thing in these presents to the contrary notwithstanding. *Pardons all entries, intrusions, and ingresses. An exception.*

And we will and declare by these presents, for us, our heirs and successors, that such-like edifices, structures, incroachments and purprestures, which before this time have been made, or had upon any churches, or walls of churches, within the said city and liberties *Incroachments upon churches, or their walls, subjected to the privy council.*

thereof, be, and shall be subject to such reformation as shall be appointed by us, our heirs and successors, or our privy council for the time being, in that behalf, any thing in these presents to the contrary notwithstanding.

<small>Grants the office of garbling and garblers.</small>
And moreover we, for us, our heirs and successors, do give, grant and confirm by these presents to the said mayor and commonalty and citizens of the city of London, and their successors, the office or exercise of garbling of whatsoever merchandises and other things which ought to be garbled, at any time arriving or coming to the city of London, by what names or appellations soever that they are at present called or known, or shall happen hereafter to be called or known [by]; and although the same spices and merchandises now or heretofore have not wont to be imported into the kingdom of England or city aforesaid, but shall happen in time to come to be imported.

And we have made, constituted and ordained, by these presents, for us, our heirs and successors, these the mayor and commonalty and citizens, and these successors, garblers of all and singular the said spices, merchandises and things, which, as aforesaid, ought to be garbled, to have, hold and enjoy, and exercise the office and occupation aforesaid, and the disposing, ordering, surveying and correcting of the

<small>With the fees, etc.</small>
same, together with all and singular fees, profits and emoluments lawfully belonging and due to the same office of garbling, to the aforesaid mayor and commonalty and citizens of the said city, and their successors, to be occupied and exercised by them, their deputy and deputies, officer and officers, minister and ministers, without rendering or making any account or other thing to us, our heirs or successors.

And further, we will, and for us, our heirs and successors, do grant to the same mayor and commonalty and citizens of the said city, and their successors, and their deputies, officers and ministers, to ask, demand, take, and receive, to the use of the said mayor and commonalty and citizens of the city aforesaid, and their successors, for garbling of the said spices, things, and merchandises, for which no fee or reward heretofore has been had or taken, which, how great, or of what shall be appointed and allowed for garbling by the lord chancellor, or treasurer of England, or president of the council, of us, our heirs and successors, the lord keeper of the privy seal, lord steward of the house of us, our heirs and successors, and the two chief justices of the king's-bench and common-bench for the time being, or by any four of them at least, and by them subscribed, without any account or any thing to be rendered to us, our heirs or successors; excepting, nevertheless, and out of these presents reserving all such like grants of or for garbling of tobacco, which have hitherto been made by us, or some of our progenitors or predecessors. *Fees, etc., not settled referred to the lord chancellor, etc. Except tobacco.*

And further, for us, our heirs and successors, do give, grant, and confirm by these presents to the said mayor, commonalty, and citizens of the said city, and their successors, the office, occupation, and exercise of gauging of whatsoever wines, oils, and other merchandises and things gaugable within the said city at any time arising, or coming to the said city, by what names or appellations soever they are at present called or known, or hereafter shall be called or known; and although the same wines, oils, things, or merchandises, now or heretofore have not wonted to be imported. *The gauging of wines, oils, etc.*

And we do make, constitute and ordain by these

presents, for us, our heirs and successors, the said mayor and commonalty and citizens, and their successors, gaugers of all and singular the said wines, oils, things, and merchandises which ought to be gauged; to have and to hold, and to enjoy and exercise the office, exercise and occupation aforesaid, and disposing, ordering, surveying, and correcting of the same, together with all and singular fees, profits, and emoluments lawfully belonging or appertaining to the same office, to the said mayor and commonalty and citizens of the said city, and their successors for ever, to be exercised and occupied by them, their deputy or deputies, officer and officers, minister and ministers, without account or any other thing thereof to be made or rendered unto us, our heirs or successors.

And further, we will, and for us, our heirs and successors, do grant to the said mayor and commonalty and citizens of the said city, that it shall and may be lawful to the same mayor and commonalty and citizens of the said city, and their successors, and their deputies, officers, and ministers, to ask, demand, take, and receive, to the use of them, the said mayor and commonalty and citizens, and their successors, for the gauging of the said wines, oils, and other things and merchandises, which ought to be gauged, *With fees, etc.* the fees, wages, and rewards belonging to the said office, and such, so great, and such-like wages, fees, and rewards for gauging such wines, oils, things, and merchandises, for which no fee or reward was heretofore lawfully had or received, which, how great, and what like, shall from henceforth be appointed and allowed for gauging, by the lords chancellor and treasurer of England, and the president of the council of us, our heirs and successors, and the two chief justices of the king's bench and common bench, for

FIRST CHARTER OF KING CHARLES I. 183

the time being, or by any four of them at least, and by them subscribed, without any account or other thing to be rendered or made thereof to us, our heirs and successors.

And further, for the consideration abovesaid, we do by these presents, for us, our heirs and successors, give, grant, and confirm to the said mayor and commonalty and citizens of the city of London, and their successors, the office of keeping the great standard and common balance ordained to weigh between merchant and merchant: and also the office of keeper of the great balance or weight within the said city of London, for weighing all merchandises of avoirdupois; and also all weights whatsoever within the same city, of all sorts of wares, merchandises, and things to be weighed, by what names or appellations soever at present they be called or known, or hereafter shall happen to be called or known; and although the same sort of wares, merchandises, and things heretofore were not accustomed to be weighed; but in time to come shall happen to be weighed, or bought and sold by weight.

The office of keeping the great standard, etc.

To weigh all sorts of wares, etc.

And we do for us, our heirs and successors, by these presents, ordain, make, and constitute the same mayor and commonalty and citizens of the city of London, and their successors, keepers of the great standard, balance and weight, and all weights whatsoever; and also weigher of all sorts of wares, commodities, merchandises, and things to be weighed, and which have been accustomed and used to be bought and sold by weight within our said city, to have and exercise the said office and occupation aforesaid by them, their deputies, officers or ministers, together with the fees, profits, wages, rewards, and emoluments of right belonging or appertaining to the same office, without any account or any other thing

With fees, etc.

to be made, rendered or paid for any of the last-mentioned premises in this behalf, to us, our heirs or successors.

And also of our more ample grace, and mere motion, we will, and by these presents, for us, our heirs and successors, do grant to the said mayor and commonalty and citizens, that it may and shall be lawful to the same mayor and commonalty and citizens of the said city, and their successors, and their deputies, officers and ministers, to ask, demand, take and receive, to the use of the same mayor, commonalty and citizens, for the weighing of all merchandises of avoirdupois aforesaid, and all sort of commodities, wares and things to be weighed, the fees and rewards of weighing the same sort of commodities, merchandises and things to be weighed, of which no fee or reward was heretofore lawfully had or received, which, how great, and what like they shall be for weighing, from henceforth shall be appointed and allowed by the lords chancellors and treasurers of England, president of the council of us, our heirs and successors, lord keeper of the privy seal, lord steward of the house of us, our heirs and successors, the two chief justices of the king's-bench and common-bench for the time being, or by four of them at least, and by them subscribed, without account or any thing to be rendered or made to us, our heirs or successors

The office of common crier in London and Southwark. And also we will, and for us, our heirs and successors, do erect and create, in and through the said city, and liberties thereof, and in and through our borough or town of Southwark, in our county of Surrey, a certain office called outroper, or common crier, to and for the selling of household stuff, apparel, leases of houses, jewels, goods, chattels, and other things of all persons who shall be willing that the said officers shall make sale of the same things by public and open claim, commonly called outcry, and sale in some common and open place or places in the said city and the liberties of the same, and for the borough and town of Southwark aforesaid; and the same office, for the consideration aforesaid, we, for us, our heirs and successors, do give and grant to the said mayor, commonalty, and citizens of London, and their successors for ever; to have and exercise the same by them or their deputy, officer or minister, officers, deputies, or ministers, being first allowed or admitted thereto by the mayor and commonalty and citizens of the said city for the time being, in common council of the same city assembled, or by the major part of them.

And that it shall and may be lawful to the said mayor and commonalty and citizens of the city of London, and their successors, and their deputy or deputies, officers or ministers, to demand, take, and keep for the use of the said mayor and commonalty and citizens aforesaid, the wages and fees expressed in a certain schedule hereunto annexed.

And we will, and for us, our heirs and successors, do strictly appoint, command, and charge all other persons, that neither they, nor any of them, presume to sell any goods, chattels, household stuff, apparel, jewels, and other things, in public claim, called outcry, in the city aforesaid, or the liberties of the same, or in the borough and town of Southwark, under pain of our royal displeasure.

And also, for the consideration aforesaid, we, for us, our heirs and successors, do grant to the said mayor and commonalty and citizens of the said city, and their successors, and by these presents do declare that the relicts and widows of freemen of the said city, using manual arts and occupations, so long as

Widows of freemen empowered to use manual arts and occupations.

they shall continue widows, and remain in the same city, from time to time, and at all times hereafter, may and be licensed to use and execute, and exercise the same arts and manual occupations in the said city, although they were not educated by the space of seven years as apprentices, notwithstanding the statute made and published in parliament of lady Elizabeth, late queen of England, in the fifth year of her reign, or any other statute or ordinance to the contrary notwithstanding.

A.D. 1562-3.

Prohibits markets within seven miles compass.

And further, for the considerations aforesaid, we by these presents, for us, our heirs and successors, do grant and confirm to the said mayor and commonalty and citizens of the city of London, and their successors, that no market shall from henceforth be granted, erected, or permitted by us, our heirs and successors, within seven miles compass of the said city. And because we understand that it has been of an ancient custom of the same city, had and allowed in the circuits of the justices of our progenitors, once kings of England, to the citizens aforesaid, that the mayor and aldermen of the said city

Recorder to plead the city customs without jury or inquiry.

for the time being ought to record by word of mouth all their ancient customs, as often and whensoever anything in act or question touching the said custom happens, and is moved before any justices; we (the same being considered), willing that the customs of the said city be rather enlarged than diminished, of our special grace have granted for us, our heirs and successors, to the said mayor and commonalty and citizens, and their successors, that whensoever and as often as there shall happen any issues to be taken of or upon any custom of the same city between any parties in pleading (although they themselves be parties), or if anything shall be moved or happen in pleading, act, or question, touching the customs aforesaid, before us, our heirs or successors, or justices for holding pleas before us, our justices of the common bench, treasurer and barons of the exchequer, or any other justices of us, our heirs or successors, which shall exact or require inquisition, search or trial, the mayor and aldermen of the same city for the time may record, testify, and declare by word of mouth, by the recorder of the same city for the time being, those customs; and that by such record, testimony, and declaration, without taking any jury thereupon, or making any further process, they may speedily proceed to the caption or determination of the plea, deed, cause or business.

We have also given and granted, and by these presents, for us, our heirs and successors, do give and grant to the said mayor and commonalty and citizens, and their successors, all treasure found in the same city, or the liberty of the same, and also waifed and strayed goods and chattels of all felons and fugitives, for felonies committed, or that shall be committed by them in the said city, or the liberties of the same, judged or to be adjudged before us, our heirs or successors, or any of our justices. *Grants all treasure found, strays, etc.*

We have granted also, and for us, our heirs and successors, by these presents, do grant that the mayor of the said city, and his successors for the time being, may name to the chancellor of England for the time being two of the aldermen of the same city, of which one, at the nomination of the said mayor, shall be one of the keepers of the peace in the county of Middlesex, and the other in the county of Surrey, who shall be inserted with others into all commissions henceforth to be made for the conservation of the peace in the counties aforesaid, and may henceforth do, concern, and execute those things *Mayor to name a justice of the peace for Middlesex, and another for Surrey.*

which are to be done by the keepers of the peace in the counties aforesaid, according to the force and effect of the commissions directed or to be directed to them and others.

And whereas the freedom of the city of London in times past was had in such price and estimation that many merchants thought themselves happy to enjoy the same, and to be reputed members of the same city: and whereas divers persons, being sons of certain freemen of the said city, resident in our said city, and others who were apprentices of freemen of the said city, resident in our said city, in these late times have used and daily do use and exercise merchandise, negotiation, and commerce, from the port of the same city, to parts beyond the seas, and by reason thereof have and do gain and acquire great profits and advantages to themselves, refusing, or at least delaying, to become freemen of the said city, and to be admitted into the liberty of the same city, although they be capable of the same; and so they have privileges, and yet are loose and free from public offices, places, charges and burdens of the said city for our service and honour, and for the upholding of the state and profit of that city, to the weakening of the government of the said city, and impoverishing the freemen, and disparaging of the liberty thereof:

We, considering these things, and intimately desiring, as much as in us is, to strengthen and enlarge the liberties of the said city (our royal chamber) and to conserve, support and protect the rule and government, and good and happy state of that city; we will, appoint, ordain, and declare for us, our heirs and successors, that all they who are, or hereafter shall be sons of freemen of the city, or who are, or hereafter shall be apprentices, or servants of freemen

Obliges merchants in the city and within ten miles to take up their freedom.

of our said city, and now do, or hereafter shall reside, or inhabit in the same city, or the liberties of the same, or within ten miles distant from any part of the same, and do, or shall use merchandise, and who do, or shall refuse, or delay to become freemen of the said city, shall not be permitted at any time henceforth, by themselves or by others, directly or indirectly, to transport any goods, wares, or merchandises, by way of merchandising in any way, from the port of our city of London, to parts foreign, or beyond the seas: willing, and for us, our heirs and successors, we do firmly command the governors, assistants, and merchant adventurers of England; the governors and assistants of the English merchants trafficking in the Baltic Sea; the society of English merchants for discovery of new commerce; the governors and society of merchants of England trading into the Levant Seas; the governor and society of merchants of London trading to France and the dominions of the same; and all other societies of merchants trading or merchandising into foreign parts beyond the seas, by what name or names soever the said distinct societies are known or reputed; that they nor any of them admit, license, or permit any such-like person or persons to merchandise, or traffic, or have commerce as merchants to foreign parts, unless such persons first become freemen of the said city, and bring a testimonial from the chamberlain or under-chamberlain of the said city for the time being, that they are admitted into the liberty of the said city.

And further, for us, our heirs and successors, we will and command, that no merchant, being, or who hereafter shall be, a freeman of the said city, shall take henceforth any apprentice to serve him in such-like merchandise within the city aforesaid, liberties

No merchant to take an apprentice for less than seven years.

or suburbs of the same, or within ten miles of the same city, for less than seven years, to be bound and enrolled according to the custom of the said city, and not otherwise.

<small>Recites the Act 3 Ja. I for confirming and establishing the Court of Requests. A.D. 1605-6.</small>

And whereas by a certain Act of parliament made in the third year of the reign of our most dear father, lord James, late king of England, it is enacted, that every citizen and freeman of the city of London, and every other person or persons inhabiting or which shall inhabit in the said city, or the liberties of the same, being a tradesman, victualler or labourer, who then had, or from thenceforth should have any debt or debts owing to him or them, not amounting to forty shillings, by any citizen, or any other person or persons, being a victualler, tradesman, or labourer, who doth or shall inhabit within the said city, or the liberties of the same, may cause such-like debtor or debtors to be warned or summoned by the beadle or officer of the Court of Requests in the Guildhall of London for the time being, by writing to be left at the dwelling-house of such debtor or debtors, or by any reasonable notice or warning to be given to the said debtor or debtors to appear before the commissioners of the said Court of Requests, holden in the Guildhall of the said city, as by the said act fully appears:

<small>Constitutes a clerk to the said court.</small>

We will, and for us, our heirs and successors, ordain and constitute, that from time to time, and in all future times, there be, and shall be a certain office of the clerk of the Court of Requests aforesaid; and that there be, and shall be from time to time, and in all future times, one fit person to be

<small>How to be chosen.</small>

named and appointed by the mayor and commonalty and citizens of the said city, assembled in common council of the same city, or the greater part of them, to be a clerk of the same court, to make, write, enter and register warrants, precepts, process, acts, orders, and executions of that court; and for labour and attendance to have and receive his fees and wages expressed in a schedule annexed to these presents. _{His duty and fees.}

And that there be from time to time, and in all future times shall be, a certain office of beadle of the Court of Requests aforesaid, to be named and appointed by the said mayor and commonalty and citizens of the said city, assembled in common council of the same city, or the greater part of them; to summon all such persons to appear in the same court, to answer to such-like persons as are appointed in the said Act of parliament, and to serve and execute warrants, precepts and process of the same court, and to receive for his labour in the same office the wages and fees expressed in a certain schedule hereunto annexed. _{And a beadle. How to be chosen. His duty and fees.}

And whereas divers burglaries, felonies, robberies, clandestine stealings and thefts of goods, jewels, apparel and household stuff, and other things, are daily committed within our city of London and liberties of the same, to the grievous damage of some of our subjects inhabiting there, or in the parts adjoining; we, for the better discovery of such-like offenders, and of things so lost, will, and for us, our heirs and successors, by these presents do ordain, grant and constitute, that from henceforth for ever, within the said city of London, and the liberties of the same, there be and shall be a certain office of register of all and for all sales and pawns, made or to be made to retailing brokers within the said city and liberties of the same; and for any goods, jewels, apparel, household stuff and other things so to be sold or pawned by any persons. _{Establishes a register of office of all pawns and sales.}

And for us, our heirs and successors, we now do

give and grant by these presents the same office to the said mayor and commonalty and citizens of the said city, and their successors, to have and exercise the said office by them, or their officer, deputy, or minister, or officers, deputies or ministers, first to be allowed and admitted thereto by the mayor and commonalty and citizens of the said city, assembled in common council of the same city, for the time being, or the greater part of them. And that it may and shall be lawful for the said mayor [and commonalty] and citizens of the said city and their successors, and their deputy or deputies, officer or officers, to demand, take, or have and retain in their power, to the use of them, the mayor and commonalty and citizens of the said city, the wages and fees expressed in a certain schedule annexed to these presents, without any account or any thing else to be rendered or made to us, our heirs or successors.

The mayor, etc., to execute the said office of register of retailing brokers.

Their fees.

And further, we do give and grant to the said mayor and commonalty and citizens of the said city, and their successors, that it may and shall be lawful to the citizens of the same city, and any of them, for the time being, to expose and hang in and over the streets and ways and alleys of the said city, and suburbs of the same, signs and posts of signs affixed to their houses and shops, for the better finding out such citizens' dwellings, shops, arts and occupations, without impediment, molestation or interruption of us, our heirs or successors, or any officers or ministers whatsoever of us, our heirs or successors.

License to hang out signs, etc.

And whereas lord Henry the eighth, late king of England, etc., by his letters patent bearing date at Westminster the thirteenth day of January, in the eight-and-twentieth year of his reign, amongst other things, for him and his successors, did give and grant

Recites King Henry VIII's grant of Bethlem, etc.

A.D. 1537.

FIRST CHARTER OF KING CHARLES I. 193

to the said mayor and commonalty and citizens of the said city, and their successors, the keeping, ordering and governing of the house and hospital of him the late king, called Bethlem, situate without and near Bishopsgate, of the said city of London, and all manors, lands, tenements, possessions, revenues and hereditaments whatsoever, and wheresoever lying and being, belonging and appertaining unto the same hospital or house called Bethlem; and made and constituted by the same his letters patent, these the mayor and commonalty and citizens of the city of London, and their successors, masters, keepers and governors of the said house and hospital called Bethlem, and of the said manors, lands, tenements and other premises belonging to the same house or hospital, to have, hold, and enjoy the said custody, order and government of the said house or hospital called Bethlem, and the said manors, lands, tenements, possessions, revenues and hereditaments belonging to the same house and hospital called Bethlem, to the said mayor and commonalty and citizens of the said city, and their successors for ever, to the uses and intents which are in and upon the foundation ordered and provided by the said late king, his heirs or successors.

And that the said mayor and commonalty and citizens of the said city of London, and their successors, might be better able to support the burthen and expenses of the poor in sustaining the house called the house of the poor in West Smithfield, and other burdens assigned and appointed to the same mayor and commonalty and citizens of the said city, and their successors, by indenture mentioned to be made between the said late king, and those the mayor and commonalty and citizens of the said city, in the said letters patent, as by the same his

And of the house of the poor in West Smithfield.

O

letters patent, amongst other things, more fully appears.

Know ye, that we, from our soul affecting and intimately desiring to support and establish the said works for us, our heirs and successors, do grant and confirm to the said mayor and commonalty and citizens of the said city, and their successors, the said custody, ordering and government of the said house and hospital called Bethlem, and all manors, lands, tenements, possessions and revenues whatsoever, and wheresoever lying and being, belonging and appertaining to the same house and hospital called Bethlem; and do make, ordain and constitute, by these presents, those the mayor and commonalty and citizens of the said city, and their successors, masters, keepers and governors of the said house and hospital called Bethlem, and of the said manors, lands, tenements and other the premises belonging to the same house and hospital called Bethlem, to have, hold, and enjoy the said custody, ordering and government of the same house and hospital called Bethlem, and of the said manors, lands, tenements, possessions, revenues and hereditaments belonging to the same house and hospital called Bethlem, to the said mayor and commonalty and citizens of the said city, and their successors for ever, to the same uses, intents and purposes, as in the said letters patent of lord Henry the eighth are before mentioned, ordained and appointed.

Grants the custody of Bethlem to the mayor, etc.

How to apply its estates.

Willing, moreover, and for us, our heirs and successors, we do declare and ordain, that the said house or hospital of Bethlem, or the manors, lands, tenements, possessions, revenues and hereditaments belonging and appertaining to the same house, or any part thereof, be not delivered, converted or disposed to any other use than to the charitable works now belonging, and applied in the same hospital.

And further, for us, our heirs and successors, we will, and by these presents do declare our good pleasure, and do charge and command the same mayor and commonalty and citizens of the said city, and their successors, that they do not deliver or grant the said manors, lands, tenements, possessions or revenues belonging to the same house or hospital, or any part of them, for any term or terms of years exceeding the number of one-and-twenty years, to commence from the time of the making of such-like grant or lease in possession, and not in reversion, reserving half of the yearly value at the least of such manors, lands, tenements and hereditaments so leased, and granted yearly, to be paid during the said term, to the said mayor and commonalty, and their successors, to the uses, intents and purposes above-mentioned. _{No lease to be granted thereof for more than twenty-one years. With a reserve of half of the yearly value.}

And moreover, for us, our heirs and successors, we grant and give special license to the said mayor and commonalty and citizens of the city of London, and their successors, that it shall and may be lawful to the said mayor and commonalty and citizens of London, and their successors, to purchase and receive, and hold to them, and their successors, of any person or persons whatsoever, five acres of land, situate, lying and being in the parish of St. Giles in the Fields, in our county of Middlesex, and now or late in the tenure or occupation of Margaret Pennell, or her assigns; although the same five acres, or any part of them, be held of us *in capite* by knights' service; to have and hold to the same mayor and commonalty and citizens of the said city, and their successors for ever. _{License to purchase five acres in the parish of St. Giles in the Fields, and occupation of Margaret Pennell.}

And also we give license and power by these presents, to all and singular persons whatsoever, that they, or any of them, may be able to give and grant the said five acres of land, and every parcel thereof, with its appurtenances, to the said mayor and commonalty and citizens, and their successors, although the same five acres of land, or any parcel thereof, be held of us *in capite* by knights' service; the statute of putting of lands and tenements in mortmain notwithstanding, or any other statute, act, ordinance, orders, restitution made, published, ordained or provided to the contrary, or any other thing, cause or matter whatsoever in any thing notwithstanding; and this without any inquisition by pretence of any writ or mandate to be made, presented or taken, and to be returned into the chancery of us, our heirs and successors, or elsewhere: Willing, that the said mayor and commonalty and citizens of the said city, and their successors, by reason or occasion of the premises, shall not be oppressed, molested, disquieted or grieved in any thing by us, our heirs and successors, or by the justices, sheriffs, escheators, or other bailiffs, officers or ministers of us, our heirs or successors, the statute of not putting land into mortmain, or any other statute, act or provision to the contrary in any wise notwithstanding.

We, nevertheless, declare it to be our royal pleasure, by these presents, for us, our heirs and successors, that the said mayor and commonalty and citizens, or their successors, or any other person or persons, by the assent and consent of the same mayor and commonalty and citizens, shall build and erect, without the royal license of us, our heirs or successors, in that behalf first had and obtained, any houses, edifices or structures upon the premises, or any parcel thereof: and as we or our predecessors, by distinct letters patent, made to the said mayor and commonalty and citizens of the said city of London, and their predecessors, have given and granted

To build thereon.

(as in the said letters patent mentioned be given and granted) to them license and power of purchasing, having and receiving to them, and their successors, divers messuages, lands, tenements and hereditaments, to divers distinct yearly values, or sums expressed, as in the same letters patent more fully appears, the statute of not putting lands in mortmain notwithstanding:

We will now and declare, and do to the said mayor and commonalty and citizens of the said city grant, for us, our heirs and successors, by these presents, that these our letters patent, or any grant, thing or matter contained in the same, shall not be reputed or judged to be part or parcel of such yearly value or sum, to which, as aforesaid, they have been made capable and able to purchase.

And further, we will, and by these presents for us, our heirs, and successors, do grant unto the said mayor and commonalty and citizens of the city of London, and their successors, that these our letters patent, and the enrolment of the same, shall be in and through all things firm, valid, good, sufficient, and effectual in law, towards and against us, our heirs and successors, as well in all our courts as elsewhere within our kingdom of England, without any confirmations, licenses or tolerations to be procured or obtained of us, our heirs or successors, by the said mayor and commonalty and citizens of the city of London, and their successors; notwithstanding that any writ or writs *Ad quod damnum* hath not issued, or is not returned before the making of these our letters patent; and notwithstanding the misnaming, or not rightly or certainly naming, or ill-reciting, or not reciting the said messuages, lands, tenements, offices, liberties, authorities, privileges, immunities, quittances, jurisdictions, and all and

This charter declared valid, etc.

Notwithstanding any writ Ad quod damnum being not issued out.

singular other the premises above hereby granted or confirmed, or mentioned to be granted or confirmed, or any part or parcel of them; and notwithstanding the not finding, or ill, or not right or certain finding of office or offices, inquisition or inquisitions of the premises above hereby granted or confirmed, or mentioned to be granted or confirmed, or any part or parcel of it, by which our title in and to the said premises ought to be found, before the making of these our letters patents; and notwithstanding any defect in not reciting or ill-reciting of any lease or leases, grants or grants, heretofore made for term of life or lives, or years, or otherwise, of the premises, or of any part or parcel of them being upon record, or not upon record, or otherwise however; and notwithstanding the ill-naming, or not right or certain naming, any village or hamlet, parish, ward, place, precinct or country, in which the premises, or any part of them, is or are; and notwithstanding any defect in not mentioning, or not fully, rightly or certainly mentioning the name or names of all or any tenements, farms, possessions or occupations aforesaid, and all and singular other the premises, or any parcel thereof, or of the annual rent reserved in and upon the premises, or any part thereof; and notwithstanding any defect, uncertainty or computation, or declaration, or omission of the true value of the premises, or any part of them, in these present letters patent expressed; and notwithstanding any defect in not mentioning our true right, state or title of or to the same premises, or any part or parcel of them; and notwithstanding the statute of lord Henry the sixth, late king of England, our ancestor, made and published in the————year of his reign; and notwithstanding the statute of lord Henry the fourth, late king of England, our ancestor, made and pub-

lished in the first year of his reign; and notwith- A.D. 1399.
standing the statute aforesaid of not putting lands
and tenements in mortmain; and notwithstanding
the statute made in the parliament of Edward the
first, in the third year of his reign; and the statute A.D. 1275.
made in the parliament of Edward the third, in the
twenty-eighth year of his reign, concerning choosing A.D. 1354.
of the coroners; and notwithstanding any other
statute or statutes of this our kingdom of England, or
any other defects whatsoever; and notwithstanding
the not mentioning the natures, kinds, species,
quantities of the premises, or any of them, or any
part or parcel of them.

We will, also, and by these presents grant to the
said mayor and commonalty and citizens of the
said city of London, that they shall and may have
these our letters patent made and sealed under the
great seal of England, without rendering, paying or To be sealed without fine
making fine or fee, great or little to us in our Hamper, or fee.
or otherwise to our use any way, for that express
mention is not made of the true yearly value, or the
certainty of the premises, or any of them, or of other
gifts or grants heretofore made by us, or by any of our
progenitors or ancestors, to the said mayor and
commonalty and citizens of the city of London, or
any other statute, act, ordinance, proclamation,
provision or restriction made, published, ordained or
provided to the contrary, or any other cause or
matter whatsoever in anything notwithstanding. In
witness whereof, we have made these our letters
patent.

Witness myself at Westminster, the eighteenth day
of October, in the fourteenth year of our reign.

The Schedule referred to in the Charter.

Fees to be taken by the outroper or common crier.

For selling of all [sorts of] goods, one farthing in the shilling. For writing and keeping the books, one penny in the pound. To the crier for crying the goods, one shilling.

Fees to be taken by the register for brokers.

For the bond to be entered into by every broker, brogger and huckster, to the chamber, eightpence. For every bargain, contract and pawn, for or upon which there shall be lent or given one shilling, or above, and under five shillings, one farthing.

For every the like, for which shall be lent five shillings or more, and under twenty shillings, one halfpenny.

For every the like, on which shall be lent twenty shillings or more, and under forty shillings, one penny.

For every the like, on which shall be lent forty shillings or more, twopence.

Fees to be taken by the clerks of the Court of Conscience.

For every plaint, twopence. For every appearance, twopence. For every order, fourpence. For every remittance to the common law, fourpence. For every precept or warrant to commit to prison, sixpence. For every search, twopence. For every satisfaction acknowledged to an order, sixpence. For warning every person within the liberties, fourpence. For warning every person without the liberties, sixpence. For serving every precept or warrant, fourpence.

No. XLVI.

Second Charter of King Charles I.

5 September, a.d. 1640.

CHARLES, by the grace of God, of England, Scotland, France and Ireland, king, defender of the faith, etc., to all to whom these present letters shall come, greeting.

Whereas our well-beloved the mayor and commonalty and citizens of the city of London, and their predecessors, within the port of London, within the liberties and franchises of our city of London, and suburbs thereof, have had, exercised, and enjoyed, or claimed to have, exercise and enjoy, the office of package of all cloths, wools, woolfells, calves-skins, goat-skins, bales of tin, and of all other merchandises whatsoever, to be packed, casked, piped, barrelled, or otherwise vesselled out of the said port, to be transported to any the parts beyond the seas, of the goods and merchandises as well of aliens, and persons born under any foreign allegiance, in any parts beyond the seas, wheresoever they should be customed; and also the office as well for surveying, or scavage of all goods, or wares of any merchant, either alien or denizen, whose father was or should be an alien born without our allegiance, and from the parts beyond the seas, to be brought to the said port by way of merchandise; as also for the surveying, delivering, or balliage of all goods and wares of any such *Recites the privileges of package, formerly granted to the citizens.*

And the office of surveying or scavage of all goods.

And of balliage.

merchants aforesaid, to be exported from the said port into the parts beyond the seas, or otherwise, on the account of merchandises upon and through the river Thames, within the said port, in any ship, boat, barge, or vessel whatsoever, floating, laden, remaining, or being off of any shore of the said river of Thames, and upon any wharf, or shore of the same river, which should happen there to remain, and be delivered or unladen, as well by water as by land, within the port aforesaid, within the franchises and liberties of the said city and suburbs thereof; all which they have enjoyed time out of mind, and by virtue of several charters or letters patent of Edward the fourth, late king of England, in the first and eighteenth years of his reign, to them granted.

A.D. 1461-2.
A.D. 1478-9.

And also by virtue of a certain other charter, or letters patent of Henry the eighth, late king of England, to the said mayor and commonalty and citizens aforesaid granted, in the third year of his reign, by whatsoever name or names the same are called in the said letters patent, by authority of parliament confirmed, or by colour of the same letters patent, or any of them, or by the prescription aforesaid, with divers fees and rewards to the said offices belonging and appertaining:

A.D. 1511-2.

And whereas divers questions and differences have of late arisen about and concerning the offices aforesaid, and the execution thereof within the port aforesaid, within the liberties and franchises of the city aforesaid, and suburbs thereof, whereby the said mayor and commonalty and citizens of the city of London aforesaid, have been hindered or disturbed in the offices aforesaid, and in the exercises of them:

Know ye, that we, for the removing and utter taking away all doubts and questions about the said offices, and likewise for the corroborating, amplifying,

SECOND CHARTER OF KING CHARLES I.   203

increasing, declaring and establishing the liberties and privileges of the said city, of our special grace, certain knowledge, and mere motion, and also for and in consideration of four thousand and two hundred pounds of lawful money of England, to the hands of our ancient and faithful servant George Kinge, gentleman of our robes, and one of the grooms of our bedchamber, by a warrant under our privy seal, heretofore paid, or assigned to be paid; whereof we do acknowledge ourself to be fully satisfied and paid, and them the said mayor and commonalty and citizens of the city of London aforesaid, and their successors, to be thereof acquitted and discharged for ever by these presents; and for divers other good causes and considerations us hereunto especially moving, have for us, our heirs and successors, created, ordained, and constituted, and by these presents do create, ordain, and constitute, that from henceforth, for ever after, there shall be within the said port of London, and the limits and bounds thereof, within the liberties and franchises of the said city and suburbs thereof, an office and offices, employment and employments, of package of all woollen cloths, woolfells, calves-skins, goat-skins, bales of tin, and of all other merchandises whatsoever, to be packed, casked, piped, barrelled or any ways vesselled, with a survey of the measure, number, and weight of said merchandizes, and also the survey of all customable merchandises, to the said port within the liberties and franchises of the said city and suburbs thereof coming, and out of the same port going, as well by land as by water, within the liberties and franchises of the city aforesaid, and suburbs thereof, as well of the goods of any denizen, whose father is or shall be an alien, as of the goods of aliens, wheresoever the same shall be customed.

Confirms the said offices for £4,200.

And the package of all cloths, etc.

204   SECOND CHARTER OF KING CHARLES I.

The portage of all wools, woolfells, bales of tin, etc.

As also an office, or employment of carriage and portage of wools, woolfells, bales of tin, and of all other merchandises whatsoever, as well of any denizen, whose father is or shall be an alien, born without the allegiance of us, our heirs or successors, as of aliens born without the allegiance of us, our heirs or successors, and under any foreign allegiance, in any the parts beyond the seas, which shall be carried into London, from the river of Thames to the house or warehouse of such alien, and from thence to the said river: together with the fees, sums of money, profits and emoluments of the said office or employments, and other the premises, in two tables hereunto annexed, mentioned, and respectively limited and appointed; all and singular which fees, sums of money, profits and emoluments, in the said tables or schedules expressed, as due and lawful fees to the said several offices of package and portage annexed and belonging, and in the execution of the same offices, and either of them, respectively, to be had and taken; we do for us, our heirs and successors, ratify, establish, and confirm, by these presents: and

The fees for the said offices.

the same fees, sums of money, profits and emoluments, in the said tables or schedules before-mentioned, we do for us, our heirs and successors, grant unto the said mayor, commonalty and citizens of the city aforesaid, and their successors for ever, by these presents.

And furthermore, of our special grace, certain knowledge, and mere motion, for the consideration aforesaid, we do for us, our heirs and successors, give and grant to the said mayor, commonalty and citizens of the city aforesaid, and their successors, the said office or employment of package of all and all manner of woollen cloths, woolfells, calves-skins, goat-skins, bales of tin, and all other merchandises whatsoever, to be packed, casked, piped, barrelled, or any ways vesselled; with the survey of the measure, number, and weight of the said merchandises, together with the fees, sums of money, profits and emoluments aforesaid.

And also the office or employment of carriage and portage of all wools, woolfells, bales of tin, and all other merchandises whatsoever, as well of any denizen, whose father is or shall be an alien born, without the allegiance of us, our predecessors, heirs or successors, as of any alien born without the allegiance of us, our predecessors, heirs or successors, and under any foreign allegiance, in parts beyond the seas, which shall be carried into London from the river of Thames to the house of such alien, and from thence to the said river; together with the fees, sums of money, profits and emoluments aforesaid; to hold and exercise the offices and employments aforesaid, and either of them, with their appurtenances, and the dispositions, orderings, surveyings and corrections thereof, and of either of them; together with all fees, sums of money, profits and emoluments whatsoever, to the said offices or employments, or either of them, in the said two tables or schedules to these presents annexed, mentioned, and respectively appointed, to the said mayor and commonalty and citizens of the said city, and their successors for ever.

And also, to exercise and occupy the said offices or employments, and every and either of them, by themselves, or by their sufficient minister or ministers, deputy or deputies, without any account or other thing to be therefore rendered or made to us, our heirs or successors (besides the rent hereafter in these presents mentioned to be reserved and paid to us, our heirs and successors), and without incurring any penalty or forfeiture of the offices aforesaid, or either of them, or any parcel thereof; although they or their deputies, officers or servants, do not pack the said goods or merchandises, when they are ready, and upon reasonable request and notice thereof given for the performing the said services. And that no other porter or carrier, or any other person or persons whatsoever, shall presume to intermit or intrude him or themselves to carry or lade any of the said goods or merchandises from any wharf or shore within the limits aforesaid, into any ship or vessel, or to unlade any goods or merchandises from any ship or vessel upon any wharf, shore, or lane within the limits aforesaid, without the special appointment or license of the said mayor, commonalty and citizens of the city aforesaid, or of their officers or deputies, for that purpose first had and obtained.

And that the porter or carrier appointed, and from time to time to be appointed, by the said mayor and commonalty and citizens, and their successors, or by their sufficient officers, or deputies for the time being, shall have, take, or receive, of or from the said merchants, as well aliens born without the allegiance of us, our predecessors, heirs or successors, and under any foreign allegiance in parts beyond the seas, as of the said denizens born, or to be born within the power or allegiance of us, our predecessors, heirs or successors, whose father is, or shall be an alien, born without the allegiance of us, our predecessors, heirs or successors, for the carriage or portage of the said goods and merchandises, such sums of money for their labour aforesaid, as, in a certain schedule to these presents annexed, are mentioned and appointed; without any account or other thing to be therefore rendered or made to us, our heirs or successors, besides the rents hereafter in

SECOND CHARTER OF KING CHARLES I. 207

these presents mentioned to be paid to us, our heirs or successors.

And further, of our more abundant grace, certain knowledge and mere motion, and for the consideration aforesaid, we do, for us, our heirs and successors, give and grant to the said mayor and commonalty and citizens of the city aforesaid, and their successors, the office or employment of the scavage and surveying, and also the scavage of all the goods and wares customable whatsoever, of any merchants, as well aliens as denizens, whose father is or shall be an alien born, or to be born without the allegiance of us, our predecessors, heirs or successors, and to be brought from any parts beyond the seas, within the liberties and franchises of the said city and suburbs thereof, on account of merchandising;

And also the surveying, delivering, or balliage of all goods and wares of any of the said merchants, within the liberties and franchises of the said city, which shall be carried out into parts beyond the seas, by way of merchandise, through and upon the river Thames, within the limits aforesaid, in any ship, boat, barge, or vessel whatsoever, floating, laden, remaining, or being off of any shore of the said river of Thames, and which upon any bank, wharf, or shore of the said river, shall happen to remain, and be delivered or unladen within the liberties and franchises of the said city, and suburbs thereof; together with the fees, sums of money, profits, and emoluments, in a certain table or schedule to these presents annexed, mentioned, and respectively limited and appointed, according to the form of the statute made and published in the twenty-second year A.D. 1530-1. of Henry the eighth, late king of England.

All and singular which said fees, sums of money, profits, and emoluments, in the said table or schedule last-mentioned and expressed, as due and lawful fees to the said several offices of scavage and balliage aforesaid annexed and belonging, and in the execution of the said offices, and either of them respectively, hereafter to be had and taken, we do for us, our heirs, and successors, ratify, establish and confirm, by these presents; and the same fees, sums of money, profits and emoluments in the said last-mentioned table or schedule, we do, for us, our heirs and successors, grant to the said mayor and commonalty and citizens of the city aforesaid, and their successors, for ever, by these presents, to have and exercise the said offices and employments last-mentioned, and either of them, with the appurtenances, and the disputings, orderings, supervisings and corrections of the same, and either of them, together with all the fees, sums of money, profits and emoluments to the said offices or employments, and either of them, in the said table or schedule to the presents annexed, mentioned, and respectively appointed, unto the said mayor and commonalty and citizens of the said city, and their successors for ever.

And also to exercise and occupy the said offices or employments by themselves, or by their sufficient minister or ministers, deputy or deputies, without any account or other matter to be rendered or made to us, our heirs or successors for the same, (besides the rents hereafter in these presents mentioned, to be reserved and paid to us, our heirs and successors), and without incurring any penalty of the said offices or employments, or either of them, or any parcel thereof, although they, or their deputies, officers or servants, shall not survey or deliver the goods and merchandises aforesaid, when they shall be ready, upon reasonable request, or notice thereof given, for the performing the said work or services.

SECOND CHARTER OF KING CHARLES I. 209

Willing, and by these presents, for us, our heirs and successors, enjoining and commanding all and singular such aliens and denizens aforesaid, that they from time to time do make and deliver, or cause to be made and delivered, unto the said mayor and commonalty and citizens, and their successors, or their servants, deputies or collectors of the scavage aforesaid, for the time being, true and perfect bills of entry, of all and every their goods, merchandises and wares, which shall be from time to time brought within the liberties and franchises of the said city and suburbs thereof, under pain of our royal indignation, and of being farther punished for their contempt of our command in this behalf; yielding therefore yearly to us, our heirs and successors, into the receipt of our exchequer at Westminster, three pounds six shillings and eightpence, of lawful money of England, at the feasts of St. Michael the Archangel, and the Annunciation of the Blessed Virgin Mary, by equal portions every year to be paid. *All aliens and denizens shall make and deliver to the mayor, etc., bills of entry.*

And whereas we are informed, that, with intent to defraud and deceive the said mayor and commonalty and citizens of the city aforesaid, of the fees and profits to the said several offices belonging and appertaining, several goods and merchandises have been fraudulently laden and unladen by divers persons at certain wharfs or places, commonly called St. Katharine's, Tower Wharf, Southwark, Bickshoar, Wapping, Redrith, Deptford, Greenwich, and Blackwall, and other places between Blackwall and London Bridge, on both sides of the river of Thames aforesaid, supposing the same places to be without the port of London aforesaid, and the liberties, franchises, and suburbs thereof: *Fraudulent ladings, etc., how punished.*

We will, and by these presents, for us, our heirs and successors, do ordain and declare, that for ever

P

hereafter all and singular merchant-strangers born without our allegiance in parts beyond the seas, and under foreign obedience, and also the sons of such merchant-strangers, who henceforth shall lade or unlade any goods or merchandises customable in the port of the city of London aforesaid, or in any of the said places or wharfs above mentioned, shall from time to time render and pay, or make and cause to be rendered and paid, unto the said mayor, commonalty and citizens of the city aforesaid, and their successors, or their officers, deputies and servants, such wages and fees as are in the said tables or schedules mentioned and expressed.

And further, because we are given to understand that divers goods and merchandises of merchants as well aliens born without our allegiance, under foreign obedience, in parts beyond the seas, as also of such denizens, whose father is or shall be an alien, and born under foreign allegiance in parts beyond the seas, which are carried out of the port of the said city, and brought into the said port from foreign parts, and beyond the seas, are very often subtly concealed and coloured, under the names of other persons, to defraud us of our customs, and other things to us belonging, for such goods and merchandises, to the prejudice and loss of us, our heirs and successors, and also of the said mayor and commonalty and citizens of the said city, of the fees and sums of money, so as aforesaid respectively limited, appointed and ordained by reason of the exercise of the offices aforesaid, or any of them.

We, therefore, being willing to look after our indemnity in this behalf, and also to the intent that the said mayor and commonalty and citizens may the better detect the frauds, covins and deceits of all persons so concealing and withdrawing the said goods and merchandises, and the fees aforesaid, we do, for us, our heirs and successors, give, and by these presents grant, to the said mayor and commonalty and citizens and their successors, that the mayor of the city aforesaid, for the time being, and the sufficient deputies, servants or officers of the said mayor, commonalty and citizens of the city aforesaid in that behalf, from time to time duly assigned, shall and may have full power and authority to give and administer the oath upon the Holy Evangelists, from time to time, to all such persons suspected, or to be suspected, of the said withdrawings, concealments, colourings, frauds and covins; and that it shall and may be lawful to the said mayor, his minister and deputy, or officer for the time being, by all lawful ways and means to compel all such persons, suspected, or to be suspected (as shall refuse or deny to take the said oath) to take the same oath; *In such cases the mayor, etc., may administer an oath.*

Although express mention of the true yearly value, or of the certainty of the premises, or any of them, or of any other gifts or grants by us, or by any of our progenitors or predecessors, to the said mayor and commonalty and citizens of the city aforesaid, or any of them heretofore made, is not made in these presents, or any statute, act, ordinance, provision, proclamation or restraint to the contrary thereof, heretofore had, made, published, ordained or provided, or any other thing, cause or matter whatsoever, in any wise, notwithstanding. In witness whereof, we have caused these our letters to be made patent.

Witness ourself at Westminster, the fifth day of September, in the sixteenth year of our reign.

The TABLES *or* SCHEDULES *referred to in the above-recited Charter.*

The Scavage Table of Rates Inwards.

	s.	d.
Allum, the cwt. qt. 112 lb... ...	0	2
Amotto, the c. qt. five score ...	0	4
Apples and pears, the little barrel ...	0	0¼
Aqua vitæ, the hogshead	0	6
Argil, white or red, the cwt. qt. 112 lb...	0	1½
Babies heads, the dozen	0	0½
Bacon, the cwt. qt. 112 lb.... ...	0	3
Bandstrings, the dozen knots ...	0	0¼
Balks, great, the c. qt. six score ...	1	6
Balks, middle, c. qt. six score ...	0	9
Balks, small, c. qt. six score ...	0	4
Barlings, the c. qt. six score ...	0	4
Barley, the quarter, qt. eight bushels ...	0	0½
Barilla or saffora, the barrel, qt. cwt. ...	0	4
Basket rods, the dozen bundles ...	0	4
Bast ropes, the cwt. qt. 112 lb. ...	0	0½
Battery, basherows or kettles, the cwt. qt. 112 lb.	0	6
Beef, the barrel	0	1
Bell-metal, the cwt. qt. 112 lb. ...	0	2
Beans, the quarter	0	0½
Blacking, or lamb-black, the cwt. qt. 112 lb.	0	3
Bottles of all sorts, the dozen ...	0	0½
Barrel boards, the thousand ...	0	4
Boards-clap, the c. qt. six score ...	0	1
Boards-pipe, the c. qt. six score ...	0	1
Borattos, narrow, the single piece, qt. 15 yards	0	2
Bombassins, broad, the single piece, qt. 15 yards	0	3
Books, unbound, the basket or maund...	0	8
Bow staves, the c. qt. six score ...	0	2
Brass and irons, livercocks, chafing-dishes, and all other brass or lattin wrt. the c. qt. five score ...	0	3
Brimstone, the cwt. qt. 112 lb. ...	0	0½
Bristles, the dozen pounds	0	0½
Buckromes of Germany, the dozen pieces	0	3
Buckromes of France, the dozen pieces...	0	2
Buffins, liles and mocadoes, narrow, the single piece of 15 yards... ...	0	1
Buffins, liles, mocadoes, broad, the single piece of 15 yards	0	2
Bulrushes, the load	0	1
Burs for millstones, the cwt. five score...	0	3
Butter, the cwt. qt. 112 lb.... ...	0	1
Cable ropes for cordage, cwt. qt. 112 lb	0	1
Cabinets, great, the piece	0	2
Cabinets, small, the piece	0	1
Caddas, or cruel ribbons, the dozen pieces, qt. 36 yards each ...	0	1
Candleweeks, the cwt. qt. 112 lbs. ...	0	1
Candles of tallow, the dozen pound ...	0	0¼
Capers, the cwt. five score	0	2
Capravans, the cwt. six score ...	0	3
Cards, playing, the small gross, 12 dozen pair	0	2
Cards, wool, the dozen pair... ...	0	0½
Carpets, Turkey. Persia, India, and Venice, long, the piece	0	6
Carpets, of the same, or like sorts, short, the piece	0	4
Carpets, of all other sorts, the piece ...	0	0½
Cases for looking-glasses, gilt, from No. 3 to No. 10, the dozen ...	0	1½
Cases for looking-glasses, ungilt, the dozen	0	0½
Chamlets, moyhair and Turkey gro-grams, each 15 yards	0	1½
Cheese, the cwt. qt. 112 lb.	0	1
Cherries, the cwt. qt. 112 lb. ...	0	1½
Cloth, French woollen, each twenty yards	0	8
Cloth, scarlet, the yard	0	1
Cochenele, Silvester or Campecha, the pound	0	0½
Cochenele, of all other sorts, the pound	0	1
Combs, of box or light wood, the gross, qt. 12 dozen	0	0¼
Copper bricks, or plates, round or square, the cwt.	0	4
Copperas, the cwt. qt. 112 lb. ...	0	1
Coral, rough or polished, the mast, qt. 27 lb.	0	2
Cork, the cwt. qt. 112 lb.	0	1
Cork, the dozen pieces for shoemakers ...	0	0¼
Deal boards of all sorts, the c. qt. six score	1	0
Dogs of earth, the small gross, qt. 12 dozen	0	1½
Durance of duretty, with thread, each 15 yards	0	1½
Durance of duretty, with silk, each 15 yards	0	2
Drugs, ambergreese, the ounce ...	0	1½
Ditto, allonficatrina, the pound ...	0	0½
Ditto, barley hulled, the cwt. qt. 112 lb.	0	1½
Ditto, carway and comin seed, the cwt. 112 lb.	0	1½
Ditto, China roots, the cwt. qt. five score	1	6
Ditto, civet, the ounce	0	1
Ditto, gum armoniack, the c. qt. score	0	6
Ditto, musk, ounce	0	1
Ditto, musk cods, the dozen ...	0	1
Ditto, saunders, white or red, the c. qt. five score	0	6
Ditto, treacle, common, the cwt. qt. five score	0	2
Ditto, turpentine, common, the cwt. qt. 112 lb.	0	1
Feathers for beds, the cwt. qt. 112 lb. ...	0	2
Fish, cod, the cwt. qt. six score ...	0	4
Fish, cole, the cwt. qt. six score ...	0	1
Fish, eeles, the barrel	0	1
Fish, eeles, quick, ship lading ...	10	0
Fish, herrings, white or red, the last ...	0	6
Fish, lings, the cwt. qt. six score ...	0	6
Fish, lub, the c. qt. six score ...	0	2
Fish, croplings, the c. qt. six score ...	0	1
Fish, titlings, the c. qt. six score ...	0	0½
Fish, sturgeon, the firkin	0	1

	s.	d.
Fish, sturgeon, the keg	0	0½
Fish, salmon, the barrel	0	1½
Flax, the cwt. qt. 112 lb.	0	2
Flax undrest, the cwt. qt. 112 lb. ...	0	1½
Flax, drest or wrought, the cwt. qt. 112 lb.	0	4
Frankincense, the cwt. qt. 112 lb. ...	0	1½
Fustian, Barmillion, each piece, qt. 30 yards	0	2
Fustian, Neapolitan, Tripe or Velver, the piece, 15 yards	0	2
Furs, bever skins, the piece ...	0	0½
Furs, bever bellies or wombs, the dozen	0	4
Furs, budge, tawed or untawed, the cwt. qt. five score	0	2
Furs, fox-skins, the cwt. five score ...	0	4
Furs, foines, without tales, the dozen ...	0	1½
Galley dishes, each twelve dozen ...	0	1
Gauls, the cwt. qt. 112 lb.	0	2
Glass for windows, the chest or case ...	0	3
Glass called Venice drinking glasses, the dozen	0	0½
Glass, looking, halfpenny ware, the gross qt. 12 dozen	0	0¼
Glass, ditto, penny ware, the gross, qt. 12 dozen	0	0½
Glass, ditto, of steel, the small dozen ...	0	0½
Glass, ditto, of steel, the large dozen ...	0	1
Glass, ditto, of chrystal, small, the dozen under No. 6...	0	1
Glass, ditto, of chrystal, middle, the dozen, No. 6...	0	2
Glass, ditto, of chrystal, the dozen, No. 7, 8, 9, and 10	0	4
Glass, ditto, of chrystal, the dozen No. 11 and 12	1	6
Glass stone plates for spectacles, rough, the dozen	0	0½
Glass plates of chrystal, small, under No. 6, the dozen	0	0½
Glass looking-plates of chrystal, No. 6, the dozen	0	1
Glass, ditto, of chrystal, No. 7, 8, 9, and 10, the dozen	0	2
Glass, ditto, of chrystal No. 11 and 12, the dozen	1	0
Gloves of Spanish leather, the dozen pair	0	0½
Grain for dyers, scarlet powder, the lb....	0	0½
Grain of Sevil, in berries, and that of Portugal or Rotta, the pound ...	0	0½
Grocery wares, almonds, the cwt. qt. 112 lb.	0	3
Ditto, anniseeds, the cwt. qt. 112 lb. ...	0	2
Ditto, cloves, the cwt. qt. five score ...	1	6
Ditto, currants, the cwt. qt. 112 lb. ...	0	2
Ditto, dates, the cwt. qt. 112 lb. ...	0	3
Ditto, figgs, the cwt. qt. 112 lb. ...	0	1
Ditto, fusses of cloves, the cwt. qt. five score	0	8
Ditto, ginger, the cwt. qt. five score ...	1	0
Ditto, liquorish, the cwt. qt. 112 lb. ...	0	1½
Ditto, mace, the cwt. qt. five score ...	2	0
Ditto, nutmegs, the cwt. qt. five score...	1	6
Ditto, pepper, the cwt. qt. five score ...	0	6
Ditto, prunes, the cwt. qt. 112 lb. ...	0	1
Ditto, raisons of the sun, the cwt. qt. 112 lb.	0	2
Ditto, Malaga raisons, the cwt. qt. 112 lb.	0	1

	s.	d.
Ditto, cinnamon, the cwt. qt. five score	1	0
Ditto, sugar refined, the cwt. qt. 112 lb.	0	10
Ditto, sugar candied, brown or white, the cwt.	0	8
Ditto, sugar, muskavadoes, and white, the cwt.	0	4
Ditto, St. Thomæ & Pennellis, the cwt....	0	2
Goats'-hair, the cwt. qt. five score ...	0	6
Gunpowder, the barrel, qt. 112 lb. ...	0	3
Gum arabick, the cwt. qt. 112 lb. ...	0	2
Hawks, of all sorts, each	0	2
Hats, beast or straw, the dozen ...	0	0¼
Hats, ditto, plain, the gross, qt. 12 dozen	0	1½
Hats, woolfells, the dozen	0	1½
Hats, demycasters, the piece ...	0	0½
Hats, beaver, the piece	0	2
Headlings for pipes, hogsheads, or barrels, the thousand	0	2
Heath for brushes, the cwt. qt. 112 lb....	0	1
Hemp undrest, the cwt. qt. 112 lb. ...	0	1
Hemp drest, the cwt. qt. 112 lb. ...	0	2
Hides, buff, the piece	0	0½
Hides, cow or horse, the dozen ...	0	3
Honey, the barrel	0	1½
Horses and mares, each	0	6
Hops, the cwt. qt. 112 lb.	0	2
Indico, the cwt. qt. five score ...	2	0
Indico dust, the cwt. qt. five score ...	0	8
Incle, wrought, the dozen lb. ...	0	1½
Incle roles, the doz. pieces, qt. 36 yds. each	0	1
Incle, unwrought, the cwt. qt. five score	0	4
Iron, wrought, the cwt. qt. 112 lb. ...	0	1
Iron, unwrought, the ton	0	6
Iron pots, the dozen	0	1½
Lattin, shaven, the cwt. qt. 112 lb. ...	0	6
Lattin, black, the cwt. 112 lb. ...	0	3
Lace, bone, of thread, the dozen yards	0	0½
Lace, bone, of silk, the pound, qt. 16 oz.	0	2
Lace, silk, of all other sorts, qt. 16 oz....	0	1
Leamonds or limons, the thousand ...	0	1
Leamon juice, the pipe	0	6
Leamonds, pickled, the pipe ...	0	3
Linseed, the quarter	0	1
Leaves of gold, the c. five score ...	0	0¼
Lewres for hawks, the dozen ...	0	0½
Leather, bazel, the dozen skins ...	0	0½
Leather hangings, gilt, the piece ...	0	3
Leather for masks, the dozen pounds ...	0	2
Lutes, the dozen...	0	4
Lutestrings, catling, the great gross ...	0	1
Lutestrings, minikins, the gross, qt. 12 dozen of knots	0	0½
Linen, British, the c. ells, qt. five score	0	2
Ditto, of Brabant, Embden, Flemish, Freeze, Gentish, Holland, Issingham, Overisily, Rowse, Crowfield, or Platts, each piece of thirty ells ...	0	2
Ditto, callicoes or dutties, the piece ...	0	0½
Ditto, cambricks, the piece, qt. 13 ells ...	0	2
Ditto, Holland table damask, the doz. yards	0	4
Ditto, Silesia ditto, the dozen yards ...	0	2
Ditto, Holland ditto, for napkins and towels, the dozen yards ...	0	1
Ditto, of Silesia, for ditto, the doz. yards	0	2
Ditto, Holland diaper, for tabling, the dozen yards	0	1
Ditto, of Silesia, for ditto, the dozen yards	0	0½

214 SECOND CHARTER OF KING CHARLES I.

Item	s.	d.
Linen, of Holland, for napkins and towels, the dozen yards...	0	1
Ditto, of Silesia, for ditto, the doz. yds.	0	0½
Ditto, French canvas and line, ell and half-quarter broad, or upwards, the c. ells, qt. six score	0	3
Ditto, Norman canvas and line, narrow vandales, or vittry canvas, Dutch barras, and Hessen canvas, the c. ells, qt. six score	0	2
Ditto, gutting and spruce canvas, drillinges pack, duck hinderlands, middle good headlock, narrow Muscovia linen, narrow ditto Hamburg, and Irish ditto, the c. ells, qt. six score	0	1
Ditto Hamburg and Silesia, broad, the c. ells, qt. six score	0	3
Ditto, poldavis, the bolt	0	1
Ditto, lawns, the whole piece, qt. 15 ells	0	2
Ditto, callicoe lawns, the piece	0	0½
Ditto, French lawns, the piece	0	0½
Ditto, lockrams of all sorts, the piece, qt. 106 ells	0	1½
Ditto, Southwick, the c. ells, qt. six score	0	1½
Ditto, Strasbrow, each piece, qt. 30 ells	0	1
Ditto, striped or tufted canvas, with thread, the piece, 15 yards	0	1
Ditto, striped, tufted, or quilted canvas, with silk, the piece, 15 yards	0	1
Littimus, the cwt. qt. 112 lb.	0	1
Malt, the quarter	0	0½
Magnus, the cwt.	0	1
Masks of velvet, or sattin, the dozen	0	1
Masts, the great sort, each...	0	2
Masts, the middle sort, each	0	1
Masts, the smaller sort, each	0	0½
Maps, printed, the ream	0	1
Madder, crop and all other bale madder, the cwt. qt. 112 lb.	0	2
Madder, fat, the cwt. 112 lb.	0	1½
Madder, mull, the cwt. 112 lb.	0	0½
Meal, the last, qt. 12 barrels	0	4
Mocado ends, the dozen pounds	0	1½
Oars, the c. qt. six score	0	2
Oats, the quarter	0	0½
Oyls, of Seville, Majorca, Minorca, Provence, Portugal and sallad oyl, the ton	2	8
Oyl, rape and linseed, the ton	2	6
Oyl, train, the ton	1	4
Olives, the hogshead	0	4
Onions, the hundred bunches	0	1
Onion seed, the cwt. qt. 112 lb.	0	3
Oranges, the thousand	0	1
Orchal, the cwt. qt. 112 lb. ...	0	1½
Packthread, the cwt. qt. five score	0	1½
Pans, dripping or frying, the cwt. qt. 112 lb.	0	1½
Pans, warming, the dozen ...	0	1½
Paper, brown, the hundred bundles	0	6
Paper, of all other sorts, each five score reams	1	8
Pens, the quarter	0	0½
Pitch and tar, the last	0	3
Plates, single, white or black, the c. plates	0	1
Plates, double, white or black, the c. plates	0	2
Pomegranates, the thousand	0	2
Pork, the barrel	0	1½
Pots of earth or stone, covered, the c. qt. five score	0	1
Pots of ditto, uncovered, the c. cast. qt. a gallon	0	2
Quales, the dozen	0	0¼
Quicksilver, the cwt. qt. five score	0	10
Quinces, the c. qt. five score	0	0½
Rapeseed, the quarter	0	1
Rosin, the ton	0	8
Rice, the cwt. qt. 112 lb.	0	1
Rye, the quarter ...	0	0¼
Rims for sieves, the gross, qt. twelve dozen	0	0½
Saffron, the pound	0	0½
Safflore, the cwt. qt. five score	0	4
Salt, the cwt.	0	2
Salt petre, the cwt. qt. 112 lb.	0	1½
Sayes, double, or Flanders serges, the piece	0	3
Sayes, hounscot, and middle sayes, the piece	0	2
Shumack, the cwt. qt. 112 lb.	0	1¼
Silk, of Bruges, Granadoes, Naples, Organsine, Pole and Spanish, sattin, silk, slear silk, fine and thrown silk, the pound, qt. sixteen ounces	0	1
Ditto, raw, of China, the pound, qt. 24 oz.	0	1
Ditto, ferret or florret silk, fillozel, sleave silk, coarse, the pound, qt. 16 oz. ...	0	0¼
Ditto, raw, long, the pound, qt. 14 oz.	0	0¼
Ditto, raw, short, and raw Morea, the pound, qt. 24 ounces	0	0¼
Silk stockings, the pair	0	0¼
Silk of Boradoes, Catalapha, China, damask, chamlet, China grogram, tabby grogram, phillosellas, narrow tabbies, of silk towers, taffaty the dozen yards...	0	2
Ditto, grograms, narrow, say calunsaucoes and phillosellas broad, the dozen yards ..	0	3
Ditto, grograms, broad, caff or damask, the dozen yards	0	4
Ditto, wrought sattins, of Bolonia, lukes, jean, and other of like making, the dozen yards...	0	6
Ditto, sattin, of Bruges, China and Turkey, the dozen yards	0	1½
Ditto, sarcenets of Bolonia or Florence, the dozen ells	0	1½
Ditto, of China, the dozen ells	0	1
Ditto, of Cypress, broad, the dozen yards	0	0½
Ditto, of Cypress, narrow, each 24 yards	0	0¼
Ditto, taffaties, ell broad, each dozen yards	0	2
Ditto, taffaties, of China and the Levant, the dozen yards	0	0½
Ditto, velvets of China, each doz. yards	0	1
Ditto, all other sorts of velvets and plushes, the dozen yards	0	6
Skins, cordovant, the dozen	0	2
Skins, goat, in the hair, the dozen	0	1
Skins, kid, of all sorts, the c. qt. five score	0	3
Smalts, the cwt. qt. five score	0	4

	s.	d.		s.	d.
Spars, bonny, the c. qt. five score	0	3	Whale fins, the dozen fins	0	1
Spars, cant, the c. qt. six score	0	2	Wheat, the quarter, eight bushels	0	1
Spars, small, the c. qt. six score	0	1	Woad, island, the ton	1	0
Stones, dog. the last	0	6	Woad, Tholouse, the cwt. qt. 112lb.	0	1
Stones, marble, the ton	0	8	Wood, box, the thousand pieces	0	2
Stones, mill, the piece	0	6	Wood, Brazil or Fernando, buck, the cwt. qt. 112 lb.	0	3
Stones, quern, the last	0	2			
Sword blades, the dozen	0	1	Wood, Brazaletto or Jamaica, the cwt. qt. 112 lb.	0	1
Staves, pipe or hogshead, the thousand	0	6			
Staves, barrel, the thousand	0	3	Wood, fustick, the cwt. five score	0	0¼
Staves, firkin, the thousand	0	1½	Wood, red or Guinea, the cwt. qt. 112 lb.	0	2
Steel, long, wisp, and such-like, the cwt. qt. 112lb.	0	2	Wood, sipeet, of East India, the cwt. qt. 112 lb.	0	1
Steel, gad, the half barrel	0	4	Wool, beaver, the pound	0	1
Succads, wet or dry, the cwt. qt. five score	0	10	Wool, cotton, the cwt. qt. five score	0	3
			Wool, Irish, combed, the cwt. five score	0	4
Syder, the ton	0	4	Wool, Irish, uncombed, the cwt. five score	0	2
Tallow, the cwt. qt. 112lb.	0	1	Wool, estridge, the cwt. qt. 112 lb.	0	2
Tapistry, with hair, the c. Flemish ells, qt. five score	0	4	Wool, Polonia, the cwt. qt. 112 lb.	0	3
			Wool, French, the cwt. qt. 112 lb.	0	2
Tapistry, with wool, the c. Flemish ells, qt. five score	0	6	Wool, lambs, the cwt. qt. 112 lbs.	0	3
			Wool, Spanish, the cwt. qt. 112 lbs.	0	4
Tapistry, with caddas, the c. Flemish ells, qt. five score	1	0	Wool, red, the pound	0	0¼
			Wyer, lattin, and all other sorts, the cwt.	0	4
Tapistry, with silk, the doz. Flemish ells	0	2	Wine, eager, the tun	0	6
Tarras, the barrel	0	0¼	Wine, Gascoyne, and all other sorts of French, the ton	2	0
Tazells, the thousand	0	0¼			
Tykes of all sorts, the tyke	0	1½	Wine, rhenish, the awm	0	6
Thred, Bruges, the dozen pounds	0	1	Wine, muskadell, and all other sorts of Levant, the butt	1	0
Thred, Outnal, the dozen pounds	0	1			
Thred, whited-brown or piecing, the dozen pounds	0	1½	Wines, sack, Canaries, Malagaes, Madeiraes, Romneys, bastards, tents and Alicants, the pipe	1	0
Thred, sisters, the pound	0	0¼			
Thred, Lyons or Paris, the bale, qt. c. bolts	0	8	Yarn, cable, the cwt. qt. 112 lb.	0	1
			Yarn, grogram or moyhair, the cwt. qt. five score	1	6
Tobacco, Spanish, Verins and Brazil, the cwt. qt. five score	2	0	Yarn, cotton, the cwt. qt. five score	0	4
Tobacco, St. Christopher's, or the like, the c. qt. five score	0	2	Yarn, Irish, the pack, qt. four cwt. at six score per c.	0	6
Tow, the cwt. qt. 112 lb.	0	0½	Yarn, raw linen, Dutch or French, the c. qt. five score	0	4
Tyles, pan or Flanders, the thousand	0	2			
Wax, the cwt. qt. 112lb.	0	4	Yarn, spruce or Muscovia, the cwt. qt. 112 lb.	0	2
Wainscot, the c. qt. five score	0	6			

All other goods not mentioned in this table shall pay for scavage-duties inward after the rate of one penny in the pound, according as they are expressed or valued in His Majesty's book of rates; and all other not expressed therein shall pay the same rate, according to their value.

The Balliage Table of Rates Outwards.

	s.	d.		s.	d.
Beer, the ton	0	4	Fustians, English, each fifteen yards	0	0½
Canvas, the hundred ells, at six score	0	2	Indico, the c. qt. five score	0	4
Coals, the chaldron	0	1	Iron, the ton, unwrought	0	6
Cloth, broad, the piece	0	1½	Iron, the ton, wrought, the cwt. qt. 112lb.	0	1
Cloves, mace, nutmegs and cinnamon, the cwt. qt. five score	0	6	Kersies, of all sorts, the piece	0	0¼
			Lamprones, the thousand	0	0¼
Cochinele, the c. qt. five score	0	7	Lead, the fodder	0	6

	s.	d.		s.	d.
Pepper or ginger, the cwt. qt. five score	0	2	Skins, fitches, the timber ...	0	1
Perpetuannoes, the piece ...	0	0¼	Skins, morkins, the c. qt. six score	0	2
Raisons, the piece or frail ...	0	0½	Skins, otter, the c. qt. five score	0	6
Raisons of the sun, the cwt. ...	0	1	Skins, sheep or lamb, the c. qt. six score	0	2
Saffron, the pound ...	0	0½	Skins, squirrel, the thousand ...	0	1
Salt, the cwt. ...	0	2	Stuffs, woollen or worsted, the single piece	0	0¼
Salt petre, the cwt. qt. 112 lb. ...	0	1	Stuffs, woollen or worsted, the double piece ...	0	1
Silk, raw or thrown, the pound, qt.16 oz.	0	0¼	Tin or pewter, the cwt. qt. 112 lb. ...	0	2
Skins, bever, the c. qt. five score	1	6	Wax, the cwt. qt. 112 lb. ...	0	2
Skins, badger, the c. qt. five score ...	0	6	Wood, of all sorts for dyers, the cwt. qt. 112 lb. ...	0	1
Skins, coney, black, the c. qt. five score	0	2	Wool of all sorts, the cwt. qt. 112 lb. ...	0	2
Skins, cat, the c. qt. five score	0	2			
Skins, calf, the c. qt. five score ...	0	2			
Skins, fox, the c. qt. five score ...	0	6			

A Table of other Merchandize, Liquid and Dry, not particularly rated in the foregoing Table, shall pay Balliage-Duties Outwards, according to their undermentioned Bulks.

	s.	d.		s.	d.
A great pack, truss or fardel, containing betwixt fifteen or twenty cloths, or other goods to that proportion	1	6	For a butt or pipe ...	0	8
			For a hogshead or puncheon ...	0	4
			For a barrel ...	0	2
An ordinary pack, truss or fardel, containing in bigness about ten, or twelve, or fourteen bays, or the like proportion in freezes, cottons, or other goods ...	1	0	For a firkin ...	0	0¼
			For a dry fatt ...	0	8
			For a drum fatt ...	0	4
			For a bale ...	0	6
			For a great chest or case ...	0	8
A bale containing three or four cloths, or four or five bays, or the like proportion in other goods ...	0	6	For a small chest or case, poize three hundred weight or under	0	4
For a great maund, or great basket ...	0	8	For a small box ...	0	2
			For a small trunk ...	0	6
For a small maund or basket, poize three hundred weight or under ...	0	8	For a small trunk, poize not above two hundred weight ...	0	3
For a hamper or coffer, poize two hundred weight or under ...	0	3	For a bag or sack ...	0	4
			For a seron ...	0	3

The Package Table of Rates.

	s.	d.		s.	d.
Arnetto, the hundred, qt. five score ...	0	3	Caps for sailors, Monmouth and others, the dozen ...	0	1
Aqua Vitæ, the hogshead ...	0	4			
Argal, white or red, the cwt. qt. 112 lb.	0	1½	Canary seed, the bushel ...	0	0½
Ashes, pot, the barrel, qt. 200 weight ...	0	2	Cloaks, old, the piece ...	0	0½
Ashes, sope, the last ...	1	0	Copperas, the cwt. qt. 112 lb. ...	0	1¼
Awl blades for shoemakers, the thousand	0	0½	Cochenele, Silvester or Campecha, the pound ...	0	0½
Barilla or saffora, the barrel, qt. 200wt.	0	4			
Beer, the ton ...	0	6	Cochenele, of all other sorts, the pound	0	1
Birding shot-lead, the cwt. qt. 112 lb. ...	0	2	Cobweb lawns, each fifteen yards	0	1
Books, the maund ...	1	0	Drugs, assa fœtida, gum armoniack, gum lac, olibanum, and sassafras, the cwt. qt. five score ...	0	6
Bottles of glass covered with leather, the dozen ...	0	1			
Brimstone, the cwt. qt. 112 lb. ...	0	1	Ditto, cassia fistula, the cwt. qt. five score	0	8
Brushes, the dozen ...	0	0½	Ditto, cassia lignea, the cwt. qt. five score	0	8
Broken glass, the barrel ...	0	0¼	Ditto, cubebs, the cwt. qt. five score ...	0	6
Buttons, brass, steel, copper or lattin, the great gross, qt. twelve small gross	0	1	Ditto, rhubarb, the pound ...	0	1
			Ditto, scammony, the pound ...	0	1
Buttons, hair, the great gross ...	0	1	Elephants teeth, the c. qt. five score ...	0	4
Buttons, silk, the great gross ...	0	0½	Estridge feathers, the pound, undrest ...	0	0½
Buttons, thred, the great gross ...	0	0¼	Fileings of iron, called swarfe, the barrel	0	2
Buckrams of all sorts, the dozen pieces	0	2	Flasks of horn, the dozen ...	0	1
Buckweed, the quarter ...	0	1	Flaxs, drest, the cwt. qt. 112 lb. ...	0	4

	s.	d.
Flax, undrest, the cwt. qt. 112 lb. ...	0	2
Frankincense, the cwt. qt. 112 lb. ...	0	1½
Fish, herrings, full or shotten, the last	0	6
Fish, stock, of all sorts, the last ...	0	6
Fustians, English million, qt. thirty yds. the piece	0	1
Fustians, Venetian, English, fifteen yds. each piece	0	1
Gauls, the cwt. qt. 112 lb.	0	2
Glew, the cwt. qt. 112 lb.	0	1
Glovers clippings, the maund or basket	0	1½
Grain, scarlet powder, Seville berries, and grain of Portugal or Rotta, the cwt.	2	6
Grain, French or Guinea, the cwt. ...	0	4
Garble, of cloves, the cwt. qt. five score	0	4
Ditto, of almonds, the cwt. qt. 112 lb....	0	1
Ditto, of ginger, the cwt. qt. five score	0	1
Ditto, of mace, the cwt. qt. five score...	0	9
Ditto, of pepper, the cwt. qt. five score	0	3
Gloves, buck leather, the dozen pair ...	0	1
Gloves, with silk fringe, and faced with taffaty, the dozen pair... ...	0	1
Gloves, lined with coney or lamb skins or plain, the dozen pair ...	0	0½
Grocery, almonds, the cwt. qt. 112 lb....	0	2
Ditto, anniseeds, the cwt. qt. 112 lb. ...	0	2
Ditto, cloves, the cwt. qt. five score ...	1	0
Ditto, currants, the cwt. qt. 112 lb. ...	0	3
Ditto, dates, the cwt. 112 lb. ...	0	4
Ditto, figgs, the cwt. qt. 112 lb. ...	0	0½
Ditto, ginger, the cwt. qt. five score ...	0	9
Ditto, licorish, the cwt. qt. 112 lb. ...	0	1½
Ditto, mace, the cwt. qt. five score ...	1	6
Ditto, nutmegs, the cwt. qt. five score...	1	1
Ditto, prunes, the cwt. qt. 112 lb. ...	0	0½
Ditto, raisons, great and Malaga, the cwt. qt. 112 lb.	0	1
Ditto, raisons of the sun, the cwt. qt. 112 lb.	0	2
Ditto, sugar candy, the cwt. qt. 112 lb.	0	8
Ditto, sugar of St. Thomæ and Pennellis, the c. qt. 112 lb.	0	3
Ditto, sugar of all sorts, the cwt. qt. 112 lb.	0	6
Ditto, cinnamon, the cwt. five score ...	1	0
Hemp, the cwt. qt. 112 lb.	0	1½
Hatts, bever, the piece	0	2
Hatts, demi-casters, the piece ...	0	1
Hatts, plain felts, the dozen ...	0	1½
Hatts, felts, lined or faced, the dozen ...	0	2
Hair, coney, the cwt. five score ...	0	4
Hair, of goats or kids, the cwt. qt. five score	0	4
Hair, of ox or cow tails, the cwt. qt. 112 lbs	0	0½
Horns, ink, the small gross, qt. 12 dozen	0	0½
Horns, lanthorn leaves, the thousand ...	0	2
Horns, tipps, the thousand ...	0	1
Hops, the cwt. qt. 112 lb.	0	2
Indico, of all sorts, the cwt. qt. five score	1	0
Indico dust, the cwt. qt. five score ...	0	6
India hides, the c. qt. five score ...	1	6
Irish rugs, the piece	0	1
Iron, the ton, unwrought	0	6
Iron, wrought, the cwt.	0	1
Iron spurs, the dozen pair	0	1
Ivory combs, the dozen pounds ...	0	2
Knives, London, ordinary, the small gross	0	3
Knives, Sheffield, the small gross ...	0	1½

	s.	d.
Knives, shoemakers paring, the small gross	0	0½
Lace, bone, of thred, the dozen yards	0	0½
Lace, silk, the pound, qt. 16 ounces ...	0	1½
Lamparnes, the thousand	0	1½
Lead, the fodder	0	8
Leamonds, pickled, the pipe ...	0	3
Leamond juice, the pipe	0	6
Linseed, the quarter	0	0½
Linnen, callico, the piece	0	0½
Ditto. cambricks, two half pieces, 13 ells	0	1½
Ditto, damask for tabling, of all sorts, the dozen	0	2
Ditto, for napkins and towels, and all other sorts, the dozen	0	1
Ditto, diaper, of all sorts, for tabling, the dozen yards	0	1
Ditto, diaper, for napkins and towels, of all sorts, the dozen yards ...	0	0½
Ditto, lawns, the piece, qt. thirteen ells	0	1½
Ditto, of Brabant, Emden, Flemish Freeze, Gentish, Holland, Isingham, Overisilis and Rows, each 30 ells ...	0	2
Ditto, French or Norman canvas, the c. ells. qt. six score	0	3
Ditto, Dutch barras, hessens and vittry canvas, the c. ells, six score ...	0	3
Ditto, canvas tufted, striped or quilted, with copper, silk, or thread, or such like, the piece, qt. 15 yards ...	0	1
Ditto, shreds, the maund	0	2
Madder, all but mull madder, the cwt. qt. 112 lb.	0	2
Mellasses, the hogshead	0	4
Mustard seed, the cwt. qt. 112 lb. ...	0	0½
Nails, chair, brass or copper, the thousand	0	0½
Nails, copper, rose and saddle, in number ten thousand	0	0½
Oaker, red or yellow, the cwt. qt. 112 lb.	0	1
Onion seed, the cwt. qt. 112 lb. ...	0	4
Orchal, the cwt. qt. 112 lb.... ...	0	1
Ox bones, the thousand	0	1
Ox gutts, the barrel	0	2
Oyl, Seville, Majorca, Minorca, Province, Portugal, linseed and rape, the ton	1	4
Oyl, train or whale, the ton ...	0	8
Paper, printed or copy paper, the c. reams, qt. five score	1	6
Pewter, the cwt. qt. 112 lb. ...	0	4
Rapeseed, the quarter	0	1
Rape cakes, the thousand	0	0½
Red lead, the cwt. qt. 112 lb. ...	0	1
Red earth, the cwt. qt. 112 lb. ...	0	0½
Rice, the cwt. qt. 112 lb.	0	1
Rozen, the ton	0	6
Saffron, the pound	0	1
Salt, the weigh	0	2
Salt petre, the cwt. qt. 112 lb. ...	0	2
Sea-horse teeth, the cwt. qt. five score	0	10
Sea-coals, the chaldron	0	4
Stockings, children, the dozen pair ...	0	0½
Ditto, kersey or leather, the dozen pair	0	1
Ditto, silk, the pair	0	0½
Ditto, worsted, the dozen pair ...	0	2
Ditto, woollen, knit, the dozen pair ...	0	1½
Shumack, the cwt. qt. 112 lb. ...	0	2
Skins, badger, the c. qt. five score ...	0	6
Ditto, beaver, the c. qt. five score ...	2	6

	s.	d.
Skins, cat, the c. qt. five score ...	0	4
Ditto, calf, the c. qt. five score ...	0	8
Ditto, coney, grey, tawed, seasoned, or stag, the c. six score	0	2
Ditto, coney, black, the c. qt. six score	0	2½
Ditto, elk, the piece	0	0½
Ditto, fitches, the timber	0	1
Ditto, fox, the c. qt. five score ...	0	8
Ditto, jennet, black, seasoned or raw...	0	0½
Ditto, kid, the cwt. qt. five score ...	0	2
Ditto, lamb, tawed or in oil, the c. qt. six score	0	6
Ditto, morkins, tawed or raw, the c. qt. six score	0	4
Ditto, otter, the c. qt. five score ...	0	8
Ditto, rabbit, the c. qt. five score ...	0	1
Ditto, sheep, the c. qt. six score ...	0	6
Ditto, sheep pelts, the c. qt. five score ..	0	3
Ditto, squirrel, the thousand ...	0	3
Silks of all sorts, raw, the pound, 16 ounces	0	1
Silk nubs or husks, the cwt. qt. 21 ounces to the pound	0	4
Silk, English, thrown, the pound, 16 ounces	0	1
Silver, quick, the cwt. qt. five score ...	0	8
Slip, the barrel	0	1
Stuffs, buffins, broad, qt. 14 yards the piece	0	2
Ditto, buffins, narrow, qt. 14 yards the piece	0	1
Ditto, Bridgewaters, the piece ...	0	2
Ditto, carral, the piece	0	1
Ditto, cametians, the piece. qt. 25 yards	0	2
Ditto, camblets, or grograms, the piece, about 14 or 15 yards	0	2
Ditto, damasellours or damasins, the piece	0	2
Ditto, durance, the piece	0	1
Ditto, dimaty, each thirty yards ...	0	1
Ditto, floramedas, the piece ...	0	1
Ditto, fugaratoes, the piece ...	0	2
Ditto, hangings of Bristol, or striped, the piece	0	4
Ditto, lindsey woollsey, the piece ...	0	1½
Ditto, liles, broad or narrow, the piece not above 15 yards	0	2
Ditto, mocadoes, double, the piece, qt. 28 yards	0	2
Ditto, mocadoes, single or tufted, the piece, qt. 14 yards	0	1
Ditto, mohair, the piece, qt. about 15 yards	0	1½
Ditto, messellawny, the piece, qt. 30 yards	0	1
Ditto, perpetuanoes, the piece, ell broad	0	2½
Ditto, paragon or parapos, the piece ...	0	2
Ditto, piramides or maramuffe, the piece, narrow	0	1
Ditto, piramides or maramuffe, the piece, broad	0	2
Ditto, rashes of all sorts, the piece about 24 yards	0	4
Ditto, says, called hounscot or milled, the piece	0	3
Ditto, says of all sorts, the piece ...	0	2½
Ditto, serges, yard broad, the double piece, 24 yards	0	3
Soap, hard castle, the cwt. qt. 112 lb....	0	2
Soap, the barrel...	0	3
Spectacles, without cases, the gross 12 dozen	0	0½

	s.	d.
Succads, wet or dry, the cwt. qt. five score	0	8
Tallow, the cwt. qt. 112 lb.... ...	0	1
Tapistry, with hair, the c. Flemish ells, qt. five score	0	4
Tapistry, with wool, the c. Flemish ells, qt. five score	0	6
Ditto, with caddas, the c. Flemish ells, qt. five score	1	0
Ditto, with silk, the dozen Flemish ells	0	2
Taffaty, ell broad, the dozen yards ...	0	2
Ditto, silk, broad, the dozen yards ...	0	4
Ditto, silk, narrow, the dozen yards ...	0	2
Thred, white, brown or coloured, the dozen yards...	0	1
Thred, points, the great gross ...	0	0½
Tiffany, each dozen yards	0	1
Tobacco, Spanish, the cwt. qt. five score	2	0
Tobacco, of all other sorts, the c. qt. five score	0	6
Tyn, unwrought, the cwt. qt. 112 lb. ...	0	3½
Tyn, wrought, the cwt. qt. 112 lb. ...	0	4
Velures, English, the single piece ...	0	2
Velures, English, the double piece ...	0	3
Vinegar or wine, the ton	0	2½
Wax, English, the cwt. qt. 112 lb. ...	0	4
Wax, English, hard, the cwt. qt. five score	0	8
Woollen bays, single, the piece ...	0	2
Ditto, bays, double, the piece ...	0	4
Ditto, minikin bays, the piece ...	0	6
Ditto, broad cloth, the short piece, qt. 24 yards	0	
Ditto, broad cloth, the long piece, qt. 32 yards	0	8
Ditto, cotton of all sorts, the c. goads...	0	6
Ditto, Devonshire dozens, the piece ...	0	1
Ditto, fitzadoes, the piece	0	3
Ditto, kersies of all sorts	0	2
Ditto, lists of cloth, the thousand yards	0	6
Ditto, northern dozens, the single piece	0	3
Ditto, northern dozens, the double piece	0	6
Ditto, penny stones, the piece ...	0	2
Ditto, Spanish cloth of English making, each 20 yards	0	6
Waistcoats, of kersey or flannel, the doz.	0	2
Ditto, of woollen knit, the dozen ...	0	4
Ditto, of worsted knit, the dozen ...	0	0½
Ditto, wrought with cruel, the piece ...	0	0¼
Ditto, wrought with silk, the piece ...	0	1
Wool, cotton, the cwt. qt. five score ...	0	3
Ditto, estridge, the cwt. qt. 112 lb. ...	0	2
Ditto, French, the cwt. qt. 112 lb. ...	0	2
Ditto, Spanish, the cwt. qt. 112 lb. ...	0	4
Wormseed, the cwt. qt. five score ...	0	6
Wood, box, the cwt. qt. 112 lb. ...	0	0½
Ditto, brazil, the cwt. qt. 112 lb. ...	0	3
Ditto, ebony, the cwt. qt. 112 lb. ...	0	1½
Ditto, fustick, the cwt. qt. 112 lb. ...	0	0½
Wood, red, the cwt. qt. 112 lb. ...	0	1½
Wine, French, of all sorts, the ton ...	0	8
Ditto, muskadels and Levant, the butt	0	6
Ditto, sack Canary, Maderoes, romneys and hullucks, the butt or pipe ...	0	6
Yarn, cotton, the cwt. qt. five score ...	0	4
Ditto, grogram or mohair, the cwt. qt. five score	1	6
Ditto, raw linen of all sorts, the cwt. qt. five score	0	4

SECOND CHARTER OF KING CHARLES I.

All other goods not mentioned in this table shall pay for package duties after the rate of one penny in the pound, according as they are expressed or valued in His Majesty's late book of rates; and all other not expressed therein shall pay the same rate according to their value.

For every entry in the packer's book, for writing bills to each entry outward, as usually they have done, twelve pence.

The strangers shall pay the labouring porters for making up their goods, at their own charge, as always they have done.

The strangers shall pay the water-side porters, belonging to the package office, such fees and duties, for landing and shipping their goods, as they have usually paid within these ten years last past (*i.e.* from the date hereof, 16 Car. I).

A Table of Fees taken by the PACKERS *and Water-side Porters, for shipping and landing the Goods or Merchandize of Strangers.*

	s.	d.		s.	d.
Imprimis, for a butt of currants	1	4	For a great mast	5	0
For a carratel of currants	0	8	For a middle mast	2	6
For a quarter roll of currants	0	4	For a small mast	1	3
For a bag of currants	0	4	For great balks, the c. qt. six score	5	0
For pieces of raisons, the ton	1	8	For middle balks, the c. qt. six score	2	6
For a barrel of raisons	0	4	For small balks, the c. qt. six score	1	3
For all sorts of puncheons	0	6	For a millstone	5	0
For a barrel of figgs	0	2	For a dogstone	2	6
For tapnets and frails of figs, per ton	1	8	For a wolfstone	2	0
For brazil or other wood for dying, per ton	1	8	For a yardstone	0	3
			For a grindlestone	1	0
For iron, the ton	1	2	For a stepstone or gravestone	0	8
For copperas, the ton	1	2	For quern-stones, the last	1	0
For oyl, wine or vinegar, per ton	1	2	For emery-stones, the ton	1	2
For hemp and flax, the last	1	8	For ten hundred weight of Holland cheese	1	0
For loose flax and tow, the hundred weight	0	2	For rosin, the ton	1	2
For a great bag of tow	0	8	For woad, the ton	1	2
For a small bag of tow	0	4	For a chest of sugar	0	6
For a great bag of hops	0	8	For half wainscots, the c. qt. six score	2	6
For a pocket or little bag of hops	0	4	For raw hides, the c. qt. five score	5	0
For packs, trusses, flats or maunds, per piece	0	8	For bonnispars, the c. qt. six score	0	4
For a great chest	0	8	For small spars, the c. qt. six score	0	4
For a small chest	0	4	For ends of bonnispars, the c. qt. six score	0	9
For all cases, barrels, or bales, per piece	0	4	For a horse, gelding, or mare	2	6
For a bale of madder	0	8	For allum, the ton	1	8
For a bale of ginger, shumack, qt. 400 weight	0	8	For heath for brushes, the c. qt. 112 lb.	0	1
For a faggot of steel	0	1	For iron pots, the dozen	0	3
For any serrions, the piece	0	4	For rings of wire loose, the ring	0	0½
For a fat of pot-ashes	0	8	For pipe staves, the thousand	2	6
For a last of sope-ashes	1	0	For rhenish wine, the aum	0	6
For a last of pitch or tar	1	0	For bur-stones, the c. qt. five score	2	6
For a last of fish	1	0	For half packs of tazels, the piece	0	4
For wainscots, the c. qt. six score	5	0	For wicker bottles, the dozen	0	0½
For clapboards, the c. qt. six score	0	6	For stone, the c. qt. five score	0	1
For deal boards, the ct. qt. six score	1	4	For loose fish, the hundred landing	0	3
			For a barrel of salmon	0	2
			For a barrel of stubb eeles	0	2

		s.	d.
For a bundle of basket rods	...	0	0½
For a ton of cork	...	1	8
For a thousand of oxen bones	...	1	0
For a thousand tips of horns	...	0	6
For a thousand of shank-bones	...	1	0
For brimstone, the ton, loose	...	1	3
For a fodder of lead	...	1	2
For rims of sieves, the load	...	1	0
For a load of fans	...	1	0
For a load of bullrushes	...	0	8
For an hundred reams of paper, loose	...	1	0
For a barrel of terras	...	0	2
For a barrel of ling	...	0	2
For a keg of sturgeon	...	0	0½
For iron backs of chimneys	...	0	1
For an hundredweight of elephants teeth	...	0	1
For copper and iron plates, per piece	...	0	0½
For an hundred small barrels of blacking		1	0
For a dozen of scales	...	0	1
For an hundred of oars	...	2	6
For every twenty sugar flags	...	0	4
For a barrel of shot	...	0	4
For a bundle of canes	...	0	1
For a cage of quails	...	0	4
For a cage of pheasants	...	0	4
For a winch of cable yarn	...	0	4
For a firkin of shot	...	0	2

All other goods not mentioned in this table shall pay portage duties as other goods do, of like bulk or condition, herein expressed.

No. XLVII.

Confirmation of the City Charters by King Charles II.

24 June, a.d. 1663.

CHARLES the second, by the grace of God, of England, Scotland, France and Ireland, king, defender of the Faith, etc., to all to whom these present letters shall come, greeting.

(1.) We have seen the charter of Lord William, our progenitor, formerly king of England, made in this form:—William, king, etc. [See No. I.]

(2.) We have also seen a certain other charter of the said Lord William, our progenitor, made in this form:—William, king, etc. [See No. II.]

(3.) We have also seen another charter of our most dear father, Lord Charles the first, late king of England, of blessed memory, made in this form:—Charles, etc. [See No. XLV.]

(4.) We have also seen a certain other charter of our said most dear father, Charles the first, late king of England, of blessed memory, made in these words:—Charles, etc. [See No. XLVI.]

Now know ye, that we, at the humble petition of the mayor and commonalty and citizens of our city of London aforesaid, of our special grace, certain knowledge, and mere motion, and for divers good causes and considerations us hereunto especially moving, all and singular the letters patent, charters and confirmations aforesaid, and all and singular the gifts, grants, confirmations, restitutions, customs, ordinances, explanations, and articles, and all other things whatsoever in the said letters patent, charters, grants, and confirmations, or any of them, contained, recited, specified, confirmed, explained or mentioned, and all and singular the lands, tenements, offices, jurisdictions, authorities, privileges, liberties, franchises, freedoms, immunities, liberties, customs, and hereditaments whatsoever; which the said mayor and commonalty and citizens of our city of London, or their predecessors, by the name of mayor and commonalty and citizens of the city of London; or by the name of the mayor, aldermen, citizens, and commonalty of London; or by the name of the mayor and citizens of London; or by the name of the mayor and commonalty of the city of London; or by the name of the citizens of the city of London; or by the name of the barons of London; or by the name of the barons of the city of London; or by any other name whatsoever, by reason or force of the said letters patent, charters, or confirmations before-mentioned; or of any use or uses, prescription or prescriptions, or any other lawful means whatsoever, at any time or times heretofore have had, or reasonably used or exercised (except as above is excepted) ratifying, and gratefully for us, our heirs and successors (as much as in us lies) accepting and approving, do them, and every of them, to the said mayor and commonalty and citizens of our city of London aforesaid, and their successors, ratify and confirm, by these presents, to have, hold, enjoy, and exercise all and singular the premises aforesaid (except before excepted) to the said mayor and commonalty and citizens of our city of London aforesaid, and their successors for ever, as fully, freely, and entirely, and in as ample manner and form, as the same are above-mentioned to be given or granted, or as the same otherwise by use, prescription, or any legal way or right whatsoever, have been heretofore respectively had, obtained, or enjoyed, as if the same were separately, singly, and nominally, in and by these presents expressed, named, declared, granted, and manifested. And further, we will, and by these presents we do, for us, our heirs and successors, grant to the said mayor and commonalty and citizens of the city of London aforesaid, and their successors, that these our letters patent shall be in and by all things, according to the true intent thereof, good, firm, valid, and effectual in the law, notwithstanding any misnaming, or any ill or false naming or recital in the same contained; or any statute, ordinance, provision, proclamation, or restriction heretofore in any wise had or made. We will also, etc., without any fine in our hanaper, etc., although express mention, etc.

Witness ourself at Westminster, the twenty-fourth day of June, in the fifteenth year of our reign.

No. XLVIII.

Proclamation issued by King Charles II,

To prohibit the Rebuilding of Houses after the Great Fire of London, without conforming to the General Regulations therein premised.

13 SEPTEMBER, A D. 1666.

CHARLES, R.—As no particular man hath sustained any loss or damage by the late terrible and deplorable fire in his fortune or estate, in any degree to be compared with the loss and damage we ourself have sustained, so it is not possible for any man to take the same more to heart, and to be more concerned and solicitous for the rebuilding this famous city with as much expedition as is possible; and since it hath pleased God to lay this heavy judgment upon us all in this time, as an evidence of his displeasure for our sins, we do comfort ourself with some hope, that he will, upon our due humiliation before him, as a new instance of his signal blessing upon us, give us life, not only to see the foundations laid, but the buildings finished, of a much more beautiful city than is at this time consumed; and that as the seat and situation of it is the most convenient and noble for the advancement of trade of any city in Europe, so that such care will be taken for the re-edification of it, both for use and beauty, and such provision made for the future against the ordinary and casual accidents by fire, as may, as far as human wisdom can provide, upon the sad experience we have had, reasonably secure the same, and make it rather appear to the world, as purged with the fire (in how lamentable a manner soever) to a wonderful beauty and comeliness, than consumed by it: and we receive no small encouragement in this our hope, by the alacrity and cheerfulness we observe in those who have undergone the greatest loss, and seem the most undone; who, with undaunted courage, appear to desire the same as we do, and resolve to contribute their utmost assistance thereunto. We have therefore thought fit, most necessary, and agreeable to the great and constant affection we have always had, and always shall retain for this our native city, to use this expedition in publishing our thoughts, resolutions, and intentions upon this great affair; that though such present rules and directions cannot be formed, as must, upon more mature deliberation, be established for the re-edification; yet such inconveniences may and shall be prevented, which may arise by the hasty and unskilful buildings many may purpose to erect for their present conveniences, before they can know how the same will suit and consist with the design that shall be made; and if this candour of ours, which resolves, with the blessing of God, so to provide for the just right and interest of all, that no man shall have cause to complain of wrong and oppression; and if this our seasonable animadversion shall not meet with that prudent submission we expect, but that some obstinate and refractory persons will presume to erect such buildings as they shall think fit, upon pretence that the ground is their own, and that they may do with it what they please, such their obstinacy shall not prevail to the public prejudice: but we do hereby require the lord mayor, and the other magistrates of the city of London, in their several limits, to be very watchful in such cases, and speedy to pull down whatsoever such men shall presume to set up, so much to the disturbance of public order and decency; and that they forthwith give notice to us or our privy council of such their proceedings, and return the names of such refractory persons who presume to contemn this our injunction, and we shall give order for their exemplary punishment, without the violation of the public justice.

And because no man shall complain or apprehend, that by this caution or restraint of ours they shall or may for a long time be kept from providing habitations for themselves, and for carrying on their trades, though we make no question, but in a short time, with the assistance and advice of the lord mayor and court of aldermen (who have besought us for some time to put this restraint) to finish the whole design, even before any man can make provision of materials for any valuable edifice; we do declare, that if any considerable number of men (for it is impossible to comply with the humour of every particular man) shall address themselves to the court of aldermen, and manifest to them in what places their ground lies, upon which they design to build, they shall in a short time receive such order and direction for their proceeding therein, that they shall have no cause to complain; and so we proceed to the setting down such general, to which all particular designs must conform themselves.

In the first place, the woeful experience in this late heavy visitation hath sufficiently convinced all men of the pernicious consequences which have attended the building with timber, and even with stone itself, and the notable benefit of brick, which in so many places hath resisted and even extinguished the fire: and we do therefore hereby declare our express will and pleasure, that no man whatsoever shall presume to erect any house or building, great or small, but of brick or stone; and if any man shall do the contrary, the next magistrate shall forthwith cause it to be pulled down, and such further course shall be taken for his punishment as he deserves. And we suppose that the notable benefit many men have received from those cellars which have been well and strongly arched, will persuade most men, who build good houses, to practise that good husbandry, by arching all convenient places.

We do declare, that Fleet Street, Cheapside, Cornhill, and all other eminent and notorious streets, shall be of such a breadth, as may, with God's blessing, prevent the mischief that one side may suffer if the other be on fire; which was the case lately in Cheapside; the precise breadth of which several streets shall be, upon advice with the lord mayor and aldermen, shortly published, with many other particular orders and rules, which cannot yet be adjusted: in the mean time we resolve, though all streets cannot be of equal breadth, yet none shall be so narrow as to make the passage uneasy or inconvenient, especially towards the water-side; nor will we suffer any lanes or alleys to be erected, but where, upon mature deliberation, the same shall be found absolutely necessary; except such places shall be set aside, which shall be designed only for buildings of that kind, and from whence no public mischief may probably arise.

The irreparable damage and loss by the late fire being, next to the hand of God in the terrible wind, to be imputed to the place in which it first broke out, amongst small timber houses standing so close together, that as no remedy could be applied from the river for the quenching thereof, to the contiguousness of the buildings hindering and keeping all possible relief from the land-side, we do resolve and declare, that there shall be a fair key or wharf on all the river-side; that no house shall be erected within so many feet of the river, as shall be within few days declared in the rules formerly mentioned; nor shall there be in those buildings which shall be erected next the river, which we desire may be fair structures, for the ornament of the city, any houses to be inhabited by brewers, or dyers, or sugar-bakers; which trades, by their continual smokes, contribute very much to the unhealthiness of the adjacent places; but we require the lord mayor and aldermen of London, upon a full consideration, and weighing all conveniences and inconveniences that can be foreseen, to propose such a place as may be fit for all those trades which are carried on by smoke to inhabit together, or at least several places for the several quarters of the town for those occupations, and in which they shall find their account in convenience and profit, as well as other places shall receive the benefit in the distance of the neighbourhood; it being our purpose, that they who exercise those necessary professions, shall be in all respects as well provided for and encouraged as ever they have been, and undergo as little prejudice as may be by being less inconvenient to their neighbours.

These grounds and foundations being laid, from the substance whereof we shall not depart, and which, being published, are sufficient advertisements to prevent any man's running into, or bringing an inconvenience upon himself, by a precipitate engagement in any act which may cross these foundations: we have, in order to the reducing this great and glorious design into practice, directed, and we do hereby direct, that the lord mayor and court of aldermen do, with all possible expedition, cause an exact survey to be made and taken of the whole ruins occasioned by the late lamentable fire, to the end that it may appear to whom all the houses and ground did in truth belong, what term the several occupiers were possessed of, and at what rents, and to whom, either corporations, companies, or single persons, the reversion and inheritance appertained; that so provision may be made, that though every man must not be suffered to erect what buildings and where he pleases, he shall not in any degree be debarred from receiving the reasonable benefit of what ought to accrue to him from such houses or lands; there being nothing less in our thoughts, than that any particular person's right and interest should be sacrificed to the public benefit or convenience, without such recompense as in justice he ought to receive for the same: and when all things of this kind shall be prepared and adjusted, by such commissioners, and otherwise, which shall be found expedient, we make no doubt but such an Act of Parliament will pass, as shall secure all men in what they shall and ought to possess.

By the time that this survey shall be taken, we shall cause a plot or model to be made for the whole building through those ruined places; which being well examined by all those persons who have most concernment as well as experience, we make no question but all men will be pleased with it, and very willingly conform to those orders and rules which shall be agreed for the pursuing thereof.

In the mean time, we do heartily recommend it to the charity and magnanimity of all well-disposed persons, and we do heartily pray unto Almighty God, that he will infuse it into the hearts of men, speedily to endeavour by degrees to re-edify some of those many churches, which, in this lamentable fire, have been burned down and defaced; that so men may have those public places of God's worship to resort to, to humble themselves together before him upon this his heavy displeasure, and join in their devotion for his future mercy and blessing upon us; and, as soon as we shall be informed of any readiness to begin such a good work, we shall not only give our assistance and direction for the model of it, and freeing it from buildings at too near a distance, but shall encourage it by our own bounty, and all other ways we shall be desired.

Lastly, that we may encourage men by our own example, we will use all the expedition we can to re-build our custom-house in the place where it formerly stood, and enlarge it with the most conveniencies for the merchants that can be devised; and, upon all the other lands which belong unto us, we shall depart with any thing of our own right and benefit, for the advancement of the public service and beauty of the the city; and shall further remit, to all those who shall erect any buildings according to this declaration, all duties arising to us upon the hearth-money for the space of seven years.

> Given at our court at Whitehall the thirteenth day of September, one thousand six hundred and sixty-six, in the eighteenth year of our reign.

No. XLIX.

Confirmation of the Order of Common Council,

For the laying new foundations, and for widening the streets of London, after the Great Fire.

AT THE COURT AT WHITEHALL, THE EIGHTH OF MAY, A.D. 1667, PRESENT,—

The KING's Most Excellent Majesty.

His Royal Highness the Duke of York,
Lord Archbishop of Canterbury,
Lord Chancellor,
Lord Privy-Seal,
Duke of Albemarle,
Marquess of Dorchester,
Lord Chamberlain,
Earl of Bridgwater,
Earl of Berkshire,
Earl of Bath,
Earl of Carlisle,
Earl of Craven,
Earl of Lauderdale,
Earl of Middleton,
Lord Arlington,
Lord Ashley,
Mr. Comptroller,
Mr. Secretary Morice,
Mr. Chancellor of the Duchy,
Sir William Coventry.

An order made by the lord mayor, aldermen and common council of the city of London, of the twenty-ninth of April past, in the ensuing words, viz.—

"It is ordered, that the surveyors take special care, that the breast-summer of all houses do range of an equal height house with house, so far as shall be convenient, and there to make breaks by directions.

"And that they do encourage and give directions to all builders for ornament-sake, that the ornaments and projections of the front buildings be of rubbed bricks; and that all the naked part of the walls may be done of rough bricks neatly wrought, or all rubbed, at the discretion of the builder; or that the builders may otherwise enrich their fronts as they please.

"That, if any person or persons shall desire in any street or lane of note to build on each side of the street or lane (opposite one to the other) six or more houses of the third rate, or that the upper rooms or garrets may be flat roofs, encompassed with battlements of bricks covered with stone, or table ends, or rails and bannisters of iron or stone, or to vary their roofs for the greater ornament of building; the surveyors, or one of them, shall certify their opinions therein to the committee for rebuilding, who shall have liberty to give leave for the same, if they see cause.

"That in all the streets no sign-posts shall hang cross, but the signs shall be fixed against the balconies, or some other convenient part of the side of the house.

"It is ordered, that a postern shall be made on the north side of Newgate, for conveniency of foot passengers; and that Holborn Bridge shall be enlarged to run straight on a bevel line from the timber-house on the north side thereof, known by the sign of the Cock, to the front of the building at the Swan Inn on the said north side of Holborn Hill.

"Forasmuch as it is provided in the late Act for rebuilding, that the surveyors shall take care for the equal setting out of all party walls and piers, and no person be permitted to build till that be done; therefore, for prevention of any exaction in the taking of such surveys, and of all quarrels and contentions that may arise between the builders, it is ordered, that no builder shall lay his foundation, until the surveyors, or one of them (according to the Act) shall view it, and see the party walls and piers equally set out; and that all persons observe the surveyors' directions concerning the superstructure to be erected over the said foundation.

"And that, for the defraying that and all other incident charges of measuring, staking out, taking the level, and surveying the streets and ground, each builder, before he lays his foundation, or such survey shall be taken, do repair to the chamber of London, and there enter his name, with the place where his building is to be set out, and to pay to the chamberlain the sum of six shillings and eight pence for every foundation to be rebuilt; for which Mr. Chamberlain shall give acquittances; upon receipt of which acquittances the surveyors shall proceed to set out such persons' foundations.

"And it is ordered, that all persons, who have already laid any foundations, shall forthwith pay into the chamber of London six shillings and eightpence for every foundation.

"And this court is consenting and desirous, that all straight and narrow passages, which shall be found convenient for common benefit and accommodation, and shall receive his majesty's order and approbation, shall and may be enlarged and made wider, and otherwise altered, before the twentieth day of May now next ensuing, as shall be fitting for the beauty, ornament, and conveniency thereof, and staked and set out accordingly.

"Several late inhabitants of Fleet Street intending to rebuild their houses, which did formerly stand backward, of other foundations near adjoining, and desiring liberty to advance their houses, that the whole front may run on a straight line; the committee did agree to the same, if the right honourable the lord high chancellor of England and the other lords shall approve thereof, and procure His Majesty's approbation to the same; and the committee do desire liberty may be given for other persons in other places, where it shall be found convenient.

"And it is ordered, that the committee for rebuilding do present the particulars aforesaid to the right honourable the lord high chancellor of England and the other lords, and that the same (if they receive His Majesty's approbation) shall be forthwith printed and published."

Which being this day represented to the board by the right honourable the lord high chancellor of England, the same was allowed and approved of; and it was ordered, that the same be punctually observed in every part thereof. And all persons concerned are required and commanded to yield due obedience and conform themselves thereunto.

No. L.

Act of Common Council,

For Paving, Cleansing, and for preventing Nuisances in, the Streets of London and the Liberties thereof.

OCTOBER 27, A.D. 1671.

THAT the several pieces or parcels of ground hereafter named; that is to say, a piece or parcel of waste ground on the south side of the hither end of Mile End Green, to the highway there, extending from the place called the Fort, to the hither end of the wall of the house and ground called the Red Lion; a piece of ground on the west side of, and contiguous to, Dowgate Dock, now or late in the possession of Job Clark; a piece or parcel of ground on the east side of, and contiguous to Puddle Dock, now or late in the possession of John Cock; and a piece or parcel of ground on the west side of and contiguous to White Friars Dock, now or late in the tenure and possession of Robert Gosling; shall be from henceforth places for common laystalls, to be employed for the public use and benefit of this city, and liberties thereof, in such manner as the commissioners authorised or to be authorised by this court, according to the said Act of parliament, or any seven of them, shall order and direct; to be purchased out of the moneys arising by the imposition of two shillings per chaldron upon coals, according to the aforesaid Act of parliament.

And that the said commissioners, or any seven or more of them, are hereby farther authorised, as need shall require, to appoint and set out such and so many other parcels of ground for common laystalls, and for public stores, for all sorts of fuel, and for all sorts of materials for pitching, paving, and cleansing the streets, and for other commodities for public use, as from time to time shall be by them found requisite and necessary; and to make agreement with the proprietors of the said grounds, and to order payment for the same, in manner as aforesaid; and the ordering and managing of the said places, when set out and appointed, shall be in the said commissioners, or any seven or more of them. And that all the profits thereof shall be paid unto the chamberlain of this city for the time being, for the use of the mayor, commonalty, and citizens of the same; and distinct books of accompts shall be kept concerning the same. And the said profits shall be disposed of from time to time, as the said commissioners, or any seven or more of them, shall appoint, to be approved of by this court.

And that the said commissioners, or any seven or more of them, shall from henceforth have authority and are hereby empowered, from time to time, to summon, enquire after, examine, and in default of appearance upon such summons, or submission to the censure or judgment of the said commissioners, or any seven or more of them, to cause to be indicted or informed against at the sessions of the peace to be held for this city, all such persons as have made, and shall continue within this city and liberties thereof, any bulks or stalls, contrary to the ancient usage and custom of this city, and several late Acts of parliament; or have made and shall continue any stall boards above the breadth allowable by the said ancient usage and custom, and Acts of parliament; or shall set goods and commodities, or materials for building, into the common streets and common passages within this city or liberties thereof; or shall hang out goods, to the hindrance or damage of passengers, or their neighbours' trade, or streightening the common passage; or shall throw out or cast into the streets any dust, soil, or rubbish; or shall dig any pits or drains, or otherwise intermeddle with the pavements (without license from the said commissioners, or any seven or more of them) which shall tend to the obstructing or annoyance of the ways, passages, or water-courses of this city.

And farther, that from henceforth no beggars or vagrants, tankard-bearers, porters, or other persons whatsoever, bearing any kind of burdens on their heads, backs, or arms, horses, or any kind of cattle, shall be permitted at any time of the day, from six of the clock in the morning until nine of the clock at night, to go or pass, or be led upon the said flat pavements in any street between the houses and the posts adjoining to the said flat pavements, except only for going into the said houses directly cross the said pavements, under the penalty of five shillings for every horse, or other kind of cattle whatsoever, and three shillings and fourpence for every tankard-bearer, porter, and other person carrying burden as aforesaid, for every offence, and the said beggars and vagrants to be punished according to the laws already in force: and that all constables within this city and liberties thereof, and other officers, employed or to be employed by the said commissioners, or any seven or more of them (who shall have power, and are hereby authorised and directed to employ such persons accordingly) and all marshals and their men, and warders, are to take special care to prevent the said offences, and to apprehend all such offenders. And, in case the said marshals or their men, or warders, shall be negligent in doing their duty herein, it shall be lawful for the lord mayor for the time being, and his successors, upon due proof of such neglect, to amove such marshals and their men, and other inferior warders, and others to put in their places.

And farther, that no street car, or brewer's dray, shall, from and after the tenth day of December next ensuing, be drawn with more than one horse within this city or liberties thereof, unless in such case only where the load cannot be divided, and that the weight thereof shall require more than one horse for the draught thereof, and in case also of drawing up any the hills from Thames Street, and up Holborn Hill, upon the penalty of ten shillings, by the owner of such car or dray which shall break this law, for the first offence, twenty shillings for the second offence, and thirty shillings for the third and every other offences; and that the supernumerary horse and horses shall and may be seized and impounded by the officers appointed to take care of the before-mentioned offences, or any of them, or by such officer or officers as are or shall be appointed by the president, treasurer, and governors of Christ's Hospital for the time being, for taking care of cars and carmen, until the said penalty be paid.

And that all cars, waggons, drays, and other carriages, during all the time of their loading and unloading within the streets of this city and liberties thereof, unless before six of the clock in the morning and after eight of the clock in the evening from Lady day to Michaelmas, and before eight in the morning and after six in the evening from Michaelmas to Lady day, shall stand sideways the long way of the street, and not cross the same, that so passengers may safely go between the houses and carriages (except for such goods and commodities as are not portable); and that no dray, upon any occasion whatsoever, shall from henceforth stand in any street or passage within this city or liberties thereof, but where a coach or other dray may pass by such cart or dray so standing, nor shall stand any longer time than for loading or unloading, or other case of absolute necessity; and that, if any person or persons shall cause his or their car or carriages to be set otherwise in loading or unloading, he or they shall forfeit three shillings and fourpence for every such offence; and the horse and dray shall be impounded by any of the officers aforesaid, till payment thereof.

And that all pains, penalties, and forfeitures, in and by this act before limited and appointed, in case the same shall not be paid to the said commissioners or seven or more of them, upon summons to the respective offenders beforehand made for their appearance before the said commissioners concerning payment thereof, shall and may be recovered by action of debt, bill, or information, in the name of the chamberlain of this city for the time being, in His Majesty's court holden before the mayor and aldermen of the said city in the chamber of Guildhall of the city of London, wherein no essoign or wager of law shall be admitted or allowed for the defendant: one third part shall be to the prosecutor, and the other two parts and residue thereof (after all charges out of the said two parts deducted) to the poor of Christ's Hospital in London. In all which suits to be brought by this Act, the chamberlain shall recover his ordinary costs and charges, to be expended in and for recovery of all such forfeitures against the offender or offenders: and in case the same pains, penalties, and forfeitures shall be paid to the said commissioners, or any seven or more of them, upon summons as aforesaid, without any farther process, one third part shall be disposed by the said commissioners, for encouragement of their officers, who shall take pains in the matter aforesaid, in such manner as they shall think fit, and the other two parts shall be disposed to the poor of the Hospital, as is aforesaid.

Rules, Orders, and Directions.

I. *Item*, That hereafter all streets within this city, called, known, or set down to be High Streets, shall be paved round, or causeway fashion: and upon notice given to the commissioners of any defective pavements in any of the streets, lanes, and passages within this city and liberties, the same shall be forthwith made good and amended, unless by general consent some better expedient be found and published.

Paviours. II. That, inasmuch as it hath been found by common experience that the paviours, to hide and cover their bad workmanship, have oftentimes spread and laid great quantities of gravel over their pavements, to greater charge of the persons setting them on work than was needful, and which, upon a sudden rain, did either choke the common sewers, or turn to dirt and mire in the streets; therefore the said paviours are required, that hereafter they do forbear to lay or spread any more gravel on the pavements than will only fill up the joints of their work, and cause the same to be swept and well rammed, and leave the pavements bare of gravel, and keep a regular method of paving, not paving one door higher than another, upon pain of paying five shillings for every complaint.

III. That the breadth of six foot at the least from

the foundation of the houses, in such of the said High streets which shall be allowed to be posted, shall be paved by the inhabitants or owners with flat or broad stone for a foot passage; unless such parts thereof as shall lie before any gateway, which may be done with square rag by the said breadth of six feet, upon pain of paying five shillings for every week the same shall be omitted to be done after notice given.

IV. That every person having occasion to rebuild or repair any house or houses fronting any street, lane, or common passage, do first procure licence of Mr. Chamberlain for the time being to board in a piece of ground before his building, within which to lay his materials for building; or in default shall pay forty shillings, and twenty shillings for every week's omission so to do.

V. That a fall or cestpool of convenient bigness shall be made and continued to every grate of the common sewer within this city and liberties, to receive the sand or gravel coming to the same, so to prevent the choking thereof. And upon complaint at any time made of the want, decay, or defect thereof, the commissioners will forthwith cause the same to be made or amended.

VI. That the fellowship of carmen of this city, Carmen. having undertaken for one year, to commence from the first of January 1671, to sweep and cleanse the streets, lanes, and common passages within the said city and liberties from dung, soil, filth, and dirt, and to carry the same, together with what shall be brought out of the houses of the inhabitants, unto certain laystalls appointed, or that shall be appointed by the said commissioners for the time being, the several persons by them employed in and about this affair (whose names, places of abode, number of tunbrels or cars, and the wards to which they are respectively designed, are hereafter set down), or such others as (by death, or removal of any of them) shall be employed therein, shall keep, observe, and follow the rules and orders hereafter following, viz.:

VII. That they, their agents, or servants, shall come out with their tunbrels or cars and horses on Mondays, Wednesdays, Thursdays, and Fridays, in every week of the year, from the eleventh of October to the eleventh of February, by five of the clock every morning of the same days; and not to continue and remain in the streets, lanes, or passages after the hour of nine of the clock the same morning; and from the eleventh of February to the eleventh of October, to come out, as aforesaid, by four of the clock every morning of the same days, and not to continue or remain in the streets, lanes, or passages, after the hour of seven of the clock the same morning; and upon every Saturday in the year to come out as aforesaid, by two of the clock in the afternoon of the same day, to remain and continue till night, if need be: and within the hours and times aforesaid shall cleanse all the streets, lanes, and passages, every man within his or their respective divisions, from its soil, filth, and dirt, by sweeping of the same, and carrying it away, together with what shall be brought out of the houses of the inhabitants, to the laystalls appointed, or that shall be appointed, upon pain to forfeit for every offence ten shillings.

VIII. That the several inhabitants within this city and liberties, or their servants, do take care that the dirt, ashes, and soil of their houses be in a readiness for the carmen, their agents, or servants, either by setting out the same over night in tubs, boxes, baskets, or other vessel, near and contiguous to their houses, or by bringing out the same within convenient time, before the hours for their departure as aforesaid.

IX. That the said carmen, their agents or servants, in their several wards or divisions (with the assistance of the servants of the inhabitants, who are hereby directed to give such assistance) shall in times of frost and snow daily employ themselves in the opening of the channels, and heaping up the ice and snow, that so the passages may be cleared, and upon a thaw of the same, that all the soil and filth found in the streets, lanes, and passages be carried away, upon pain of ten shillings for every day's omission.

X. That no person whatsoever do presume to cast out any soil, horse dung, or filth, or carry the same into any street, lane, or common passage, after the hours aforesaid, either by night or by day, upon the penalty that the person offending, if known (and if a servant, his or her master or mistress), to forfeit and pay five shillings; and if not known, the party against whose house the same shall be found (having been laid there in the day time after the hours before-mentioned) shall forfeit one shilling; which said several forfeitures shall be paid, the one moiety to the discoverer, and the other to the carman or carmen appointed to cleanse that ward wherein the offence shall be committed.

XI. That the several tunbrels or cars employed in this work shall be marked or numbered according to the number of cars appointed for each ward, upon the penalty of two shillings for every load carried without such mark.

XII. That the several carmen, undertakers in this affair, shall set upon the fore part of his tunbrel or car, open and plain to view, a board, whereon to be painted the city arms, the ward to which he or they are appointed, the mark or number of his tunbrel or car, upon penalty of paying three shillings and fourpence a day for want thereof; which said marking is to betoken the allowance of the commissioners, and to caution the inhabitants from employing of foreign cars.

XIII. That the said carmen undertakers, their agents or servants, shall give notice of their being in the street with their tunbrels or cars by loudly knocking a wooden clapper, especially in courts, alleys, and other back passages, upon pain to forfeit three shillings and fourpence upon every complaint duly proved.

XIV. That the said carmen, their agents or servants, do take care that the falls or cestpools belonging to any grate within their respective wards be once in every week, or oftener, if need require, cleansed of its dirt and filth, and the same carried away, upon pain to forfeit five shillings for every complaint duly proved.

XV. That the aforesaid carmen, their agents or servants, and no other, shall also carry away to the laystalls aforesaid all such oils, dirt, and dung (rubbish or earth excepted) that shall be made or found in any of the houses or stables of any inn-keeper, livery-stable-keeper, brewer, dyer, sugar-baker, soap-maker, or other trader or inhabitant with any the wards to which they are respectively appointed and designed. For which such quarterly allowance (over and above the customary rates by the scavenger's book) shall be made by the assessors of each ward according to their best discretion, respect being had to the trade or other occasions in the making of more or less dung or soil by such traders or inhabitants.

XVI. That the aforesaid carmen, their agents or servants, and no other, shall take up and carry away to such persons or places, as will receive the same, all such rubbish or earth that shall be made or found within their respective wards or divisions. For which there shall be paid them by the owners or proprietors thereof twelvepence per load, and no more. Provided they carry it away within one day after notice given for the conveniency of the owners, and to avoid complaint of them, upon pain that the person offending in either of these cases shall pay two shillings per load.

XVII. That no other tunbrel or car, than what is or shall be appointed and allowed by the said commissioners for doing the works aforesaid, shall be employed, or shall intermeddle with the carrying of any soil, rubbish, earth, dung, paving-stones, Thames gravel, or the like, within this city or liberties; bricks or tiles from the waterside within the city or liberties; upon pain to pay to the carman or carmen employed in cleansing the streets as aforesaid, of the ward where this offence shall be committed, two shillings for every load so taken up or carried in a tunbrel or car: and for non-payment, that such tunbrel or car shall be carried to the city's pound, called the Green Yard, and there to remain till payment thereof. Provided, that if any the said carmen shall not, immediately after notice, employ himself in carrying the said materials, to forfeit and pay two shillings for every load thereof, and the owners at liberty to employ foreign cars.

XVIII. That no coachman, carman, carter, drayman, or other person, shall feed his or their horse or horses with hay or grains in the streets, lanes, or common passages within this city and liberties, upon pain to forfeit and pay for every offence two shillings and sixpence (over and above the like sum formerly imposed to be paid to the Governors of Christ's Hospital), the one moiety to the discoverer and prosecutor, and the other to the carman or carmen of the ward in which the said offence shall be committed; and in case of non-payment, to carry the horse or horses to the city's pound, called the Green Yard; there to remain till payment thereof.

XIX. That none of the aforesaid carmen, their agents or servants, or other person or persons, do sweep the filth or soil of the streets, lanes, or passages, into any the channels of this city, in time of rain, or otherwise, upon pain to pay six shillings and eightpence for every complaint duly proved.

XX. That no man shall cast or lay in the streets, lanes, or common passages, or channels within this city or liberties, any dogs, cats, inwards of beasts, cleaves of beasts feet, bones, horns, dregs or dross of ale or beer, or any noisome thing, upon pain of ten shillings for every offence.

XXI. That no person set a tunbrel, car, or cart, in the street by night time, upon pain to pay two shillings, besides satisfaction to any person hurt thereby.

XXII. That no person do ride or drive a tunbrel, car, cart, or dray, a-trot in the street (or sit on any part of the car, cart, tunbrel, or dray, unless another skilful person lead the horse) upon pain to forfeit and pay two shillings; and in case of non-payment, to carry the horse to the pound, as aforesaid, to remain till payment thereof.

XXIII. That no waggon, car, or cart, shod with iron, or spignails, or having more horses than is allowed by the aforesaid act of Common Council, shall take up any goods within this city or liberties, to carry for hire about the streets, upon pain to pay five shillings for every offence: and in case of nonpayment, to carry the horse or horses to the aforesaid pound till payment thereof.

XXIV. That no goung-fermer shall carry any ordure till after ten o'clock in the winter, and eleven o'clock in the summer, at night, nor shall spill any ordure in the streets, upon pain to forfeit and pay thirteen shillings and fourpence.

XXV. That no pudding-cart of shambles shall go out till after the hours last before-mentioned, upon pain to forfeit six shillings and eightpence.

XXVI. That no artificer, labourer, or other person, shall make any stop or dam in any channel, nor shall slake any lime in the streets, lanes, or passages, upon pain to pay two shillings for every offence.

XXVII. That no man shall feed any kine, goats, hogs, or any kind of poultry, in the open streets, upon pain to forfeit three shillings and fourpence for every offence.

XXVIII. That no man shall cast into the ditches or sewers, grates or gullets of the city, any manner of carrion, stinking flesh, rotten oranges or onions, rubbish, dung, sand, gravel, or any other thing that may stop the course of the same, upon pain of forfeiting forty shillings for every offence.

XXIX. That no man shall make or continue any widraughts, seat or seats, for houses of easement over, or drains, into, any the common sewers, without license of the commissioners for the time being, upon pain to forfeit forty shillings, and forty shillings a month for so long time as the same shall be continued after warning.

XXX. That no person or persons do presume to keep any laystall for dung, rubbish, earth, or other soil, either at the water-side, or other place within this city or liberties, other than the common or public laystalls appointed, or to be set out and appointed by the said commissioners for the time being; upon pain to forfeit and pay fifty-three shillings and four pence, and forty shillings a week for every week he or they shall so continue to do after warning, or be indicted from time to time, as a common nuisance.

XXXI. That no tyler, bricklayer, or other person, do throw out of gutters, or off roofs or other parts of houses, any tyles, loam, or rubbish, into any street, lane, or common passage; but do bring down the same in baskets or trays; upon pain to forfeit three shillings and four pence for every offence.

XXXII. That no person or persons do set out in the streets, lanes, or passages, any hogsheads, barrels, or other casks or vessels, to hoop, wash, or dry, or otherwise encumber the passage; upon pain to forfeit and pay twenty shillings for every offence.

XXXIII. That the dung, mud, filth, and soil of the wards of Billingsgate, Bridge, Langbourn, Cornhill, Candlewick, Walbrook, Vintry, and Dowgate, shall be carried down to the laystall at Dowgate Dock; of the wards of Portsoken, Tower, Aldgate, Duke's Place, and Lyme Street, to the laystall set out at Mile End: of the ward of Bishopsgate Within and Without to the laystall at Holloway Lane end, being part of a meadow there belonging to the city: of the ward of Cripplegate Within and Without, Aldersgate without, Bassishaw, Coleman Street and Broad Street, to the laystall at Bunhill: of the wards of Cheap, Cordwainer, Queenhithe, and Bread Street, to the laystall at or near the Three Cranes, and in Dunghill Lane near Broken Wharf, until such time as the public wharf or key at the riverside shall be laid open, and afterwards to the laystall at Puddle Dock: of the wards of Farringdon Within, Castle Baynard, Aldersgate Within, and St. Martin's-le-Grand, to the laystall at Puddle Dock: of the ward of Farringdon Without, to the laystall at White Friars: and this course to be used until the commissioners shall see cause to alter the same; and whoso shall offend herein shall forfeit and pay five shillings for every offence.

XXXIV. That the carmen undertakers, their agents or servants, shall have liberty to carry rubbish from all parts of the city or liberties, into the Vineyard near [without] Aldgate, for levelling the same, till the first of May next, and to shoot the same there gratis, and after that time to pay such sum for what they there shoot as the commissioners shall require.

XXXV. That inasmuch as the said carmen have undertaken to do this work in a better manner and to greater satisfaction than heretofore hath been done; and the commissioners believing from what they have already observed, that they will accordingly perform the same, do therefore exhort all persons, that shall be rated towards this work, willingly and readily to pay the same; so to prevent trouble to themselves, and discouragement to the said carmen, in a work of this nature, so requisite and necessary to the health and trade of the inhabitants of this city.

XXXVI. That the several pains and penalties before-mentioned, not particularly expressed to whom to be paid, shall be paid into the chamber of London, upon summons or warning by the officers attending the commissioners, or either of them; or, in default, the offender or offenders to be indicted at the sessions for his or their respective offences.

XXXVII. That if any the aforesaid carmen, their agents or servants, do offend in any the particulars aforesaid, or otherwise relating to this affair; that complaint be made thereof to the commissioners at the Guildhall, who will deal with them according to their offences.

XXXVIII. That the scavengers for the time being, in the several wards and precincts within this city and liberties, do take care, either by their own observations, or complaints to them by any of the inhabitants, that the said carmen, their agents or servants, do accordingly perform the several branches aforementioned to them relating; or to make complaint thereof to the commissioners; upon pain that the said scavengers shall, from time to time, for their negligence or remissness, be indicted at the sessions: unless they shall submit to the censure and judgment of the said commissioners for the time being.

No. LI.

Act of Common Council,

For regulating the Markets for Woollen Goods at Blackwell Hall, Leaden Hall and Welch Hall.

THAT all Essex and Suffolk cloths, and all cloths commonly called Coventry cloths, Hampshire and Surry kerseys, and all sorts of Suffolk and Essex flannels, baize, perpetuanes, rashes, serges and sayes, and all other commodities that go under the name of the new drapery, made or mixed with wool, worsted, jersey, or cruel, or with cotton-wool, or either or any of them, brought, or which shall be brought to the city of London, or liberties thereof, either by land or water, except Norwich and Canterbury stuffs, be brought unto, pitched and harboured in Leaden-hall, there to remain till they be entered, and the duties of hallage herein after-mentioned paid, or agreed and secured to be paid for the same; which entry of the said cloths, or other woollen manufactures, brought, or to be brought as aforesaid to the said hall, shall be immediately made after such bringing the said commodities to the said hall, upon pain that every person that shall offend herein shall forfeit, for his first offence the sum of fifty shillings, for his second offence four pounds nineteen shillings, and for every other offence the like sum of four pounds nineteen shillings: which cloth, cloths, and other woollen manufactures, or any of them, shall not from thence be removed to any other place out of this city, or liberties thereof, till after the three first market-days of their being brought to the said market, unless sold in the mean time, or removed and carried to be sold in any other market without the liberties of this city.

That all other sorts of broad and narrow cloths, by what name soever called, distinguished, or known, in what place soever made, and all other kerseys, baize, tammies, sayes, rashes, perpetuanes, serges, rugs, blankets, motleys, of what sort or nature soever, pennistones, half-thicks, plains, friezes, cottons, linsey-woolseys, stockings of all sorts, carpetings and hangings of all sorts, fustians of all sorts, and all other commodities and manufactures made or mixed with wool, worsted, jersey, or cruel, or with cotton-wool, or either or any of them, brought, or which shall be brought to the city of London, and liberties thereof, either by land or water, be brought unto, pitched, and harboured in Blackwell-hall, and the Welch-hall, or one of them, there to remain till they be entered, and the duties of hallage herein after-mentioned also paid, or agreed and secured to be paid for the same; which entry of the said cloths, stuffs, and other woollen commodities, brought, or to be brought as aforesaid, to the said halls, or either of them, shall be immediately made after such bringing those commodities to the said halls, or any of them; upon pain that every person which shall offend herein shall forfeit, for his first offence the sum of fifty shillings, for his second offence four pounds nineteen shillings, and for every other offence the like sum of four pounds nineteen shillings. Which cloth, cloths, and other woollen manufactures, or any of them, shall not from thence be removed to any other place out of this city, or liberties thereof, till after the three first market-days of their being brought to the said market, unless sold in the mean time, or removed and carried to be sold in any other market without the liberties of this city, except the cloth, cloths, and other commodities made or mixed with wool, worsted, jersey, or cruel, bought by any merchant, draper, or any other that are freemen of the said city, and inhabiting therein (and not being a factor in that commodity) by pre-contract with the said clothier, which cloth, cloths, and other woollen manufactures, shall be brought to the hall appointed by this act to receive the same; which being done, the said cloths may be taken thence by the owners as soon as they please; and except such small parcels as being contracted for in the country by persons that have bought, or shall buy, the same for their own private use or wearing, and not to sell again; and except such cloths and other woollen manufactures, as, having received damage, by wet or otherwise upon the road, shall require drying or new dressing before they can be fit for sale.

And that no person or persons whatsoever, free or not free of this city, shall, at any time or times hereafter, buy, sell, or barter any of the aforesaid cloths, or any other the commodities aforesaid, or shall permit or suffer them, or any of them, to be sold, bartered, or put to sale, or opened to be put to sale, within any part of his or their houses, yards, inns, stables, chambers, shops, warehouses, or workhouses, or other place or places within the said city, or liberties thereof before the same be brought, pitched and harboured within some of the said public markets of Blackwell-hall, Welch-hall or Leaden-hall, respectively, appointed as aforesaid, and therein sold, or from thence removed and carried to be sold in some other market without the liberties of this city, or shall buy, sell, or barter, or permit any of the said commodities, which shall at any time hereafter be taken out of any of the said markets of Blackwell-hall, Welch-hall, or Leaden-hall (before the same shall be there bought and sold as aforesaid) to be bought, sold, bartered, or put to sale, or opened to be put to sale, in any of his or their inns, yards, houses, stables, or any part thereof, as aforesaid, within the said city and liberties thereof, other than in any of the said markets of Blackwell-hall, Leaden-hall, or Welch-hall, appointed as aforesaid (except as is before excepted).

And that neither factor nor broker belonging to Blackwell-hall or Leaden-hall, although a freeman of this city, so long as he is in the capacity of a factor or broker for foreigners, during his being so, shall buy any of the said cloth, cloths, kerseys, baize, fustians, or other commodities aforesaid, within the said markets or market-places aforesaid, on pain that every such person, who shall offend herein, shall forfeit and lose, for the first offence three pounds, for the second offence, four pounds nineteen shillings, and for every other offence, the like sum of four pounds nineteen shillings.

Provided, that neither such factor nor broker, being a freeman of this city, shall by this act be restrained from buying any sort of cloth, cloths, or other woollen manufactures aforesaid, within the said markets or market-places, within the hours hereafter limited, which he himself doth not sell, so that the same be transported beyond the seas upon his own account.

And further, that all persons, as well carriers as cloth-men, or clothiers, and others, shall, at the bringing of their cloth, cloths, and other woollen manufactures, either by land or water, to this city or liberties thereof as aforesaid, bring, or cause to be brought to Blackwell-hall, Leaden-hall, or Welch-hall respectively, such of them as by this act are appointed to be brought thither respectively, to the end they may be entered, and the duties paid for the same; upon pain of twenty shillings for every pack of cloth, cloths, or other commodities, to be forfeited and paid by every such carrier, cloth-man, clothier, or others, for every offence to the contrary, and for every single cloth, or other woollen commodities, the piece ten shillings.

And further, that the markets at the aforesaid Blackwell-hall, Leaden-hall and Welch-hall, shall be and begin on every Thursday, between the twenty-fifth day of March and the twenty-ninth day of September, at eight of the clock in the forenoon, and continue till eleven of the clock in the same forenoon, and between the twenty-ninth day of September and the twenty-fifth day of March, at nine of the clock in the forenoon, and continue till eleven of the clock in the same forenoon; and on every Thursday at one of the clock in the afternoon, and continue till four of the clock in the same afternoon; and on every Friday at eight of the clock in the forenoon, and continue till eleven of the clock in the same forenoon; and shall begin in the afternoon of the same Friday at one of the clock, and shall continue till four of the clock in the same afternoon; and shall begin on every Saturday at eight of the clock in the forenoon, and shall continue till eleven of the clock in the same forenoon; and that the said hours for the beginning and ending of the said market times shall be known by the ringing of the market bells in the halls aforesaid, appointed for that use and purpose; and the same to be held and continued weekly throughout the whole year, except days of humiliation or thanksgiving, appointed to be otherwise set apart by Act of parliament, or public authority; and that the respective hall-keepers shall not permit or suffer any buying or selling of any the aforesaid woollen cloths or commodities in or at any of the said halls in or upon any other days or hours than on the market-days and hours appointed.

And further, that the respective hall-keepers, clerks, and master-porters of every the halls aforesaid, shall take care that all the rules and orders, appointed to be observed by this act, in every branch of it be carefully put into execution; and shall also diligently and faithfully keep their books and weekly registers of all the cloths and woollen commodities aforesaid bought and sold in any of the said halls, or bought and pitched there; in which books and registers they and every of them, as they are concerned in their respective halls, shall truly enter the names of baptism, surnames, place of habitation, and addition, both of the owner, buyer, and seller of every of the said commodities; to the end all clothiers, their factors, and others concerned, may be satisfied how their cloths and other woollen commodities are disposed of from time to time; and if any hall-keeper, clerk, or master-porter, shall refuse or neglect to perform his duty herein, for the first offence he shall forfeit twenty shillings, for his second offence forty shillings, and for his third offence be discharged from his office.

And further, that the hall-keepers of every the halls aforesaid for the time being, shall attend in their respective markets in their gown, and hinder all foreigners and aliens from coming into the said market; upon pain that every hall-keeper that shall fail in his duty herein, shall forfeit for his first offence twenty shillings, for his second offence forty shillings, and for his third offence be discharged from his office.

And further, that the hall-keepers of every the halls aforesaid for the time being, shall attend in their respective markets in their gown, and hinder all foreigners and aliens from coming into the said markets; upon pain that every hall-keeper that shall fail in his duty herein, shall forfeit for his first offence twenty shillings, for his second offence forty shillings, and for his third offence be discharged from his office.

And further, that every freeman of this city that shall introduce any foreigner or stranger into any of the aforesaid markets, to buy or make inspection into any of the aforesaid commodities, shall for his first offence forfeit and pay the sum of five pounds, and for his second offence the sum of ten pounds, and for his third offence the sum of twenty pounds; and, if any such freeman shall again offend in the like manner, then upon his conviction thereof in the king's majesty's court, holden within the Guildhall of this city, before the lord mayor and aldermen of the same city for the time being, he and they shall stand and be utterly disfranchised, as unworthy members of this city, and shall not be re-admitted but by order and consent of common council.

And that every factor who shall, either himself, or by his servant, knowingly sell any of the commodities aforesaid, in any of the common markets before-mentioned, to any foreigner or foreigners, or for his or their use (except to such persons as by Act of parliament are allowed),—that every such factor so selling the same, whether a freeman or foreigner, shall for his first offence forfeit and pay one-third-part of the real value of every piece of woollen commodity so sold to foreigner or foreigners.

And further, that every hall-keeper of the several halls aforesaid respectively do and shall, within fourteen days next after the publishing of this act, present a note in writing to the president, treasurer, and governors of Christ's Hospital, of the names and surnames of all persons who then take upon them to be and to act and deal as factors and brokers in any of the said halls respectively, and shall likewise hereafter, from time to time, at every three months' end, make like certificate in writing to the said governors, of the names and surnames of all factors or brokers, or such as take upon them to act as factors or brokers in either of the said halls respectively, together with the offence or offences by them or any of them committed, contrary to this act, or any other orders made for the good government of the said halls, upon pain that every hall-keeper, wilfully neglecting to do his duty herein, shall for his first offence forfeit the sum of three pounds, and for his second offence be dismissed from his place or employment of hall-keeper.

And that, for the observation of this act and all the parts thereof, there be every year six able, experienced freemen, dealers in those commodities, surveyors, chosen by the president and governors of Christ's Hospital at the next court to be holden after the second day of February next ensuing, and so yearly from year to year; whose office shall be, by themselves, or such others as they shall think fit to use for their assistance, to enquire of all abuses and offences against this act; and any two of them to present the same to the said court from time to time, as often as they shall find cause, that so due punishment may be inflicted upon the offenders.

And further, that the ensuing rates, and no other, shall be paid, demanded, and received of and from every the respective owner or owners, or his and their servant and agent, for the commodities hereafter mentioned, brought and to be brought to the several halls, or any of them, for the said hallage duty thereof, and for the entering, harbouring, and safe keeping thereof, from the time of their first pitching the three first market days, and no longer:—

All broad cloths, of what kind or name soever, shall pay a piece for hallage, one penny.

All broad rashes, twenty yards or above, two pence.

All kersey cottons, one penny.

All Devonshire, Wiltshire, and Dorsetshire baize shall pay for each piece, one penny.

Dutch baize, the piece, three halfpence.

All other Essex, Norfolk, and Suffolk, and Minakin baize, by what name soever called, shall pay for each piece, two pence.

All Yorkshire broad cloths, kerseys, cottons, and all other commodities made of wool, shall pay for the horse-pack coming from those parts, eight pence.

All Lancaster woollen wares, as broad cloths, kerseys, cottons, baize, penistones, friezes, and all other commodities made with wool, coming from those parts, the horse-pack, eight pence.

All commodities coming from Wales, Salop, and any of those parts, commonly known by the names of Welch cottons, rolls, plains, baize, flannels, or friezes, shall pay for every horse-pack, eight pence.

All flannels, venetians, wagmols, dimities, fustians, and bustins, made in England and Wales, shall pay for each horse-pack, eight pence.

All stuffs, of what name or kind soever, made of wool, worsted, jersey, or cruel, or mixed with them, or any of them, the piece to pay one penny.

Bed rugs, or caddows for beds, being five breadths, or any of the same largeness, shall pay for every rug, one penny.

For every rug of four breadths, or of the same largeness, an halfpenny.

For every rug of three breadths, or of the same largeness, a farthing.

Cradle rugs, for every two rugs a farthing.

Blankets, the dozen pair, three halfpence.

Birdsey carpeting, Bristol carpeting, and all other sorts of carpeting and darnix, the piece, being twenty yards or more, two pence.

But if the piece be less than twenty yards, one penny.

Carpets of needle-work or trent-work, for every carpet, to pay one penny.

Coverlets, the horse-pack to pay eight pence.

If less than a horse-pack, every one an halfpenny.

Worsted stockings, the twenty pair shall pay two pence.

Yarn, being woollen, cruel, linnen, worsted, or jersey, every dozen pound shall pay one penny.

Bolters and bewpers, the dozen pieces, one penny.

The single piece, a farthing.

Darnix, narrow, for garments, the piece, one penny.

Hair-cloth, the piece, an halfpenny.

Lindsey-woolsey broad, the piece, one penny.

Narrow, the piece, an halfpenny.

Loom-work for waistcoats and children's coats an halfpenny.

Says, plained or milled, the piece, one penny.

Every half piece of above thirty shillings price, or more, one penny.

But the half piece under thirty shillings price, an halfpenny.

Serges of all sorts, the piece one penny.

Muckaddo ends, the dozen pounds one penny.

Cushions of all sorts, unstuffed and unbottomed, the dozen, one penny.

Irish rugs, the hundred yards, four pence.

Irish mantlets of all sorts, being made within this kingdom, twenty yards and upwards, to pay one penny.

Motleys for mariners, the piece, an halfpenny.

Pedegny, the horse-pack, eight pence.

Swadling-bands, the gross, one penny.

Woollen stockings, for every three dozen, one penny.

All of which duties of hallage are to be, from time to time, employed for and towards the maintenance of the poor children harboured in Christ's Hospital.

And further, that if any owner or owners of the commodities aforesaid, or his or their servant, shall refuse to pay, agree, or secure to pay the hallage before-mentioned, at the first pitching of the same at any of the halls aforesaid, he shall forfeit and pay for such his refusal six shillings and eight pence for every cloth, or any other single piece of woollen manufacture unpacked, and twenty shillings for every pack of cloth, cloths, or other woollen manufacture.

And further, that if the owner or owners of any the aforesaid commodities, or his or their servant, cannot, within the time and space of the three first market-days next after the bringing of them to the said respective markets, sell all the cloth, cloths, or other woollen manufactures brought to Blackwell-hall, Leaden-hall, or the aforesaid Welch-hall, then it shall be lawful for the said owner or owners, or his or their servant by his appointment, to remove any of the said commodities, which shall remain unsold after the said market-days are over, to any other market or markets forth of this city and liberties thereof, or otherwise to dispose of them as they shall think fit.

And that what cloth, cloths, or other woollen manufacture, shall remain in any of the halls or market-places, or storehouses in Blackwell-hall aforesaid, after the three first market-days, if the owner or owners do not remove the same to some other place or market forth of this city, but will continue them to be lodged and safe kept therein, that then the owner or owners of any such cloth, cloths, or other woollen manufactures aforesaid, their factor or servant, shall pay for the lodging and safe keeping of the said commodities half so much every week as was the rate of their hallage at first pitching (under penalty of five shillings for every neglect or refusal upon demand), which money is likewise to go for and towards the relief of the poor children harboured in Christ's Hospital, and to defray the charges of officers that must of necessity be employed therein, and repairs of the said halls. Provided, that this extend not to Devonshire packs, for which consideration is paid at the first pitching; nor to Yorkshire packs, Kidderminster stuffs, serges, Welch cottons, plains, or flannels, in Blackwell-hall, and the Welch-hall, nor to any bays or says at Leaden-hall, nor to cloths lodged in any private store-houses or warehouses, for which an annual rent is paid to the said hospital.

And that no common porter, or any other person or persons whatsoever (except the clothier, or his factor, in his or their own person) shall be admitted to carry any of the commodities aforesaid out of or from the said Blackwell-hall, Leaden-hall, or the Welch-hall, or any of the rooms adjoining thereunto (except such commodities as the clothier or his factor shall send out to be refreshed and prepared for sale by his cloth-worker or packer, for whom he will answer); but the same shall be carried out by the chief porters of Blackwell-hall, Leaden-hall, or the

Welch-hall aforesaid (for the time being) or such as shall be appointed by the chief porters of Blackwell-hall, Leaden-hall, or the Welch-hall, as anciently it hath been accustomed, and for whom they shall be respectively responsible. And to the end there may be no exaction of rates and prices for the carriage of the aforesaid commodities out of the said Blackwell-hall, Leaden-hall, or the Welch-hall, of any merchant, or other buyer or seller of the said commodities, otherwise than the rates hereafter mentioned, as are appointed for their several carriages, be it enacted and ordained by the authority afoaesaid, That the several rates hereafter mentioned shall be fairly written in a table, and hung up in some public place in each of the said halls, and that these rates, and no greater, shall or may be taken by the said porters, or by any other employed by them: and, if any chief porter, or any employed by them, shall exact and receive more than shall be expressed in such tables, he or they so offending shall forfeit ten times as much as shall be so received:

Imprimis, every Kentish whole cloth, or two half cloths, shall pay two pence.

Every long Worcester whole cloth, or two half cloths, shall pay one penny halfpenny.

Every long Gloucester whole cloth, or two half cloths, shall pay one penny halfpenny.

Every long Western whole cloth, or two half cloths, shall pay two pence.

Every Norfolk, Suffolk, or Essex cloth, one penny halfpenny.

Every Spanish cloth, one penny.

Northern dozen kerseys or cotton, the pack, six pence.

Devonshire baize, for each piece, one penny farthing.

Minakin baize, for each piece, three pence.

All Essex, Norfolk, and Suffolk baize, one penny halfpenny.

All Welch wares, the horse-pack, six pence.

All Manchester wares, the horse-pack, six pence.

Blankets, twelve pair in a bundle, three pence.

Rugs, for every score, ten pence.

Stockings and yarn, for every horse-pack of two hundred weight, six pence.

All fustians and bustians, or dimities, the horse-pack of two hundred weight, six pence.

And all other manufactures mentioned in this act, and not provided for in the table, shall pay for every horse-pack of two hundred weight, six pence.

And that it shall and may be lawful to and for the governors of Christ's Hospital aforesaid, or any three of them, or hall-keeper by their direction, from time to time, to regulate the aforesaid markets of the said Blackwell-hall, Leaden-hall, and the Welch-hall, as to the standing of the clothier and factor in the said markets, having always regard to the clothier who sells in his own person, or his household servant, that he or they have always convenient room reserved in the said markets for the sale of the aforesaid commodities.

And that all and singular the pains, penalties, forfeitures, and sum and sums of money, duties, and other things whatsoever, which shall be forfeited, incurred, or due by virtue of this Act, or by reason of any clause, branch, or article of the same, shall be obtained, levied by distress, or recovered, as the case shall require, either by action of debt, plaint, bill, or information, in the name of the chamberlain of the said city for the time being, in the king's majesty's court, holden in the chamber of the Guildhall, before the lord mayor of the city of London, and aldermen of the same city for the time being: and the chamberlain of the said city for the time being, in all matters or things to be prosecuted by virtue of this present act against the offender or offenders, shall recover the ordinary costs of suit to be expended in or about the prosecution of them, or any of them. And, in case upon a trial a verdict shall pass for the defendant, or the plaintiff shall become nonsuit, or discontinue his suit; in every such case the defendant shall also recover his reasonable costs.

And that all pains, penalties and forfeitures, to be had and recovered by virtue of this act for the regulating of Blackwell-hall, Leaden-hall and the Welch-hall, and other the premises as aforesaid (the charges of suit for recovery thereof being first deducted) shall be divided into two equal parts; the one moiety thereof, together with the whole duties of hallage, to be paid unto the treasurer of Christ's Hospital for the time being, to be employed towards the maintenance of the poor children harboured and kept in the said hospital; and the other moiety to him or them that will sue for the same: any other act or ordinance of this court to the contrary thereof notwithstanding.

No. LII.

𝕮𝖍𝖊 𝕾𝖙𝖆𝖙𝖚𝖙𝖊

2 *W. & M.* c. 8., *vacating the Judgments on the* Quo Warranto, *against the City of London, and confirming all the Privileges of the Corporation.* A.D. 1690.

A.D. 1683.

WHEREAS a judgment was given in the court of King's Bench, in or about Trinity-term, in the thirty-fifth year of the reign of the late king Charles the second, upon an information, in the nature of a *Quo Warranto*, exhibited in the said court against the mayor and commonalty and citizens of the city of London, That the liberty, privilege and franchise of the said mayor and commonalty and citizens, being a body politick and corporate, should be seized into the king's hands as forfeited : and forasmuch as the said judgment, and the proceedings thereupon, is and were illegal and arbitrary; and for that the restoring of the said mayor and commonalty and citizens to their ancient liberties, of which they had been deprived, tends very much to the peace and good settlement of this kingdom :

2. Be it declared and enacted, by the king and queen's most excellent majesties, by and with the advice and consent of the lords spiritual and temporal, and commons, in this present parliament assembled, and by authority of the same, That the said judgment given in the said court of King's bench in the said Trinity-term, in the thirty-fifth year of

the reign of the said king Charles the second, or in any other term; and all and every other judgment given or recorded in the said court, for the seizing into the late king's hands the liberty, privilege, or franchise of the mayor and commonalty and citizens of the city of London, of being of themselves a body corporate and politick, by the name of the mayor and commonalty and citizens of the city of London, and by that name to plead and be impleaded, and to answer and to be answered, and in what manner or words soever such judgment was entered; is, shall be, and are hereby reversed, annulled, and made void, to all intents and purposes whatsover; and that *vacates* be entered upon the rolls of the said judgment, for the vacating and reversal of the same accordingly.

3. And be it further declared and enacted, by the authority aforesaid, That the mayor and commonalty and citizens of the city of London, shall and may forever hereafter remain, continue, and be, and prescribe to be a body corporate and politick, *in re, facto et nomine*, by the name of mayor and commonalty and citizens of the city of London, and by that name, and all and every other name and names of incorporation, by which they at any time before the said judgment were incorporated, to sue, plead and be impleaded, and to answer and be answered, without any seizure or forejudger of the said franchise, liberty and privilege, or being thereof excluded or ousted, for or upon any pretence of any forfeiture or misdemeanor at any time heretofore or hereafter to be done, committed, or suffered; and the said mayor and commonalty and citizens of the said city, shall and may, as by law they ought, peaceably have and enjoy all and every their rights, gifts, charters, grants, liberties, privileges, franchises, customs, usages, constitutions, prescriptions, immunities, markets, duties, tolls, lands,

tenements, estates, and hereditaments whatsoever, which they lawfully had, or had lawful right, title, or interest of, in, or to, at the time of recording or giving the said judgment, or at the time or times of the said pretended forfeitures.

4. And be it enacted, by the authority aforesaid, that all charters, letters patents, and grants for incorporating the citizens and commonalty of the said city, or any of them, and all charters, grants, letters patents, and commissions touching or concerning any of their liberties or franchises, or the liberties, privileges, franchises, immunities, lands, tenements, and hereditaments, rights, titles, or estates of the mayor and commonalty and citizens of the city of London, made or granted to any person or persons whatsoever, by the late king Charles the second, since the said judgment given, or by the late king James the second, be and are hereby declared and adjudged null and void to all intents and purposes whatsoever.

5. Provided nevertheless, that no recoveries, verdicts, judgments, statutes, recognisances, inquisitions, indictments, presentments, informations, decrees, sentences, executions, nor any plaints, process, or proceedings in law or equity, had, made, given, taken, or done, or depending in the mayor or either of the sheriff's courts, or any other court within the said city or liberties thereof, since the said judgment given, shall be avoided for want or defect of any legal power in those that acted as judges, justices, officers or ministers of, in, or as belonging to any of the said courts; but that all and every such recoveries, verdicts, judgments, and other things abovementioned, and the actings, doings, and proceedings thereupon, shall be of such and no other force, effect, and virtue, than as if such judges, justices, officers

and ministers had acted by virtue of legal authority; and that no person or persons shall be in any wise prosecuted, sued, impeached, or molested for any cause or thing by him or them lawfully acted or done, in pursuance of any such charters, letters patents, grants, or commissions.

6. Provided, that this Act shall not extend to discharge any person or persons from any penalty or penalties, or forfeitures by him or them incurred, for not duly qualifying him or themselves to act upon the said charters, letters patents, grants, or commissions.

7. And be it enacted, by the authority aforesaid, that all officers and ministers of the said city, that rightfully held any office or place in the said city or liberties thereof, or in the borough of Southwark, at the time when the said judgment was given, are hereby confirmed, and shall have and enjoy the same as fully as they held them at the time of the said judgment given, except such as have voluntarily surrendered any such office or place, or have been removed for any just cause; and that every person who, since the said judgment given, hath been chosen, admitted, and placed into any office or employment within the said city, upon the death, surrender, or removal, as aforesaid, of the former officers, shall be, and is hereby confirmed in his said office or employment, and shall have and enjoy the same in as full and ample manner as if he had been admitted or placed therein according to the ancient customs of the said city.

8. Provided also, and be it enacted, by the authority aforesaid, that all leases and grants of any of the lands, tenements, hereditaments, and other things, before the time of the said judgments given, belonging to the said mayor and commonalty and citizens,

and usually leased or granted by them, made since the time of the said judgment given by the said late king Charles the second, or king James the second, or by any person or persons taking upon them to be trustees for the said city, for the preservation or maintenance of the government, or publick offices of the said city, by or upon pretence of any grant or commission by their said late majesties king Charles the second and king James the second, or either of them, such grants and leases being made for just, good, and valuable considerations, and whereupon the old-accustomed yearly rent, or more, hath been reserved, payable into the chamber or Bridge-house, or any of the hospitals of the said city, shall be as good and valid for the terms, and under the rents, payments, provisos, conditions, covenants, and agreements therein respectively contained, against the mayor and commonalty and citizens of the said city, and their successors, as if the same had been made by the mayor and commonalty and citizens of the said city, under their common seal, and the said judgment had never been given, and not otherwise; and the said mayor and commonalty and citizens, and their successors, shall have the benefit and advantage of all rents, reservations, payments, conditions, covenants, clauses, and agreements in every such grant or lease contained; and the like remedy for non-payment, breach, or non-observance thereof, as if the said grants or leases had been made by the said mayor and commonalty and citizens, and the said rents, payments, conditions, covenants, clauses and agreements had been made payable, reserved, covenanted, or agreed to and with the said mayor and commonalty and citizens.

9. And be it further enacted, by the authority aforesaid, that all judgments, decrees, and sentences,

had or obtained by any person or persons taking upon them to be trustees, as aforesaid, for or concerning any lands, tenements, duties, tolls, and interests whatsoever, of or belonging to the said mayor and commonalty and citizens of the said city, shall stand and remain in force, and shall be prosecuted and executed by and to, and for the use of, the said mayor and commonalty and citizens, as if the same had been obtained in the name of the said mayor and commonalty and citizens; and that all persons being natural-born subjects, or denizens, that have been admitted into the freedom of the said city since the said judgment given, shall be free thereof, and have and enjoy the said freedom to all intents and purposes, as if they had been thereunto admitted before the said judgment given.

10. Provided always, that the present mayor, sheriffs, chamberlain, and common council of the said city, shall continue until a new election shall be made of such officers, and the persons elected sworn into their respective offices, and that such new election be made at the times hereafter mentioned; that is to say, the election of the mayor, sheriffs, and chamberlain shall be on the twenty-sixth day of May, in the year one thousand six hundred and ninety; and the election of the common council shall be made on the tenth day of June, in the year one thousand six hundred and ninety; and such person so elected shall continue till the usual times of election of such officers, according to the ancient usage and custom of the said city, and from thence shall continue for the year ensuing.

11. Provided nevertheless, and be it enacted, that, if the mayor, sheriffs, chamberlain, and common council, shall not be elected at the times hereby limited, the mayor, sheriffs, chamberlain, and com-

mon council, which were in being at the time of the said judgment given, shall be and continue in those respective offices and places till new elections be made of the like officers and common council, according to the ancient usage and custom of the said city.

12. And be it farther enacted, that all persons so to be restored and continued, shall be, and are hereby required, to take the oaths appointed by a certain Act, made in the first year of their majesties' reign, entitled, *An Act for the abrogating of the oaths of supremacy and allegiance, and appointing other oaths*, the next term after Restitution, under the penalties, forfeitures, disabilities and incapacities in the said Act provided and appointed.

13. And be it enacted, that the mayor, sheriffs, and chamberlain, so to be elected, shall be sworn, in the usual manner, on or before the twentieth day of June next ensuing.

14. And be it enacted, by the authority aforesaid, that all and every of the several companies and corporations of the said city, shall from henceforth stand and be incorporated by such name and names, and in such sort and manner, as they respectively were at the time of the said judgment given, and every of them are hereby restored to all and every the lands, tenements, hereditaments, rights, titles, estates, liberties, powers, privileges, precedencies, and immunities which they lawfully had and enjoyed at the time of giving the said judgment; and that as well all surrenders, as charters, letters patents, and grants for new incorporating any of the said companies, or touching or concerning any of their liberties, privileges or franchises, made or granted by the said late king James, or by the said king Charles the second, since the giving of the said judgment, shall be void,

and are hereby declared null and void, to all intents and purposes whatsoever. Provided nevertheless, That no person or persons shall be in any wise prosecuted, sued, impeached or molested for any cause or thing by him or them lawfully acted or done in pursuance of any such charters, letters patents or grants.

15. Provided also nevertheless, and it is hereby farther enacted, by the authority aforesaid, That all leases, terms, and estates made or granted by any of the said companies since the giving of the said judgment for just and valuable considerations, and whereupon the old accustomed yearly rents or more are reserved, shall stand and be of the same force and effect, as if the same had been made or granted by the said several companies as hereby restored; and the said respective companies, and their successors, shall have the benefit and advantage of all rents, reservations, payments, conditions, covenants, clauses and agreements in all and every such lease or grant contained, and the like remedy therefore, as if the same grants and leases had been made by the said respective companies as now restored, and the said rents, payments, conditions, covenants, clauses, and agreements had been made payable, reserved, covenanted and agreed to, or with them respectively.

16. Provided also, and be it enacted, That all and every person or persons, who, at any time since the said judgment, have been admitted into the freedoms of, or into the liveries of the said companies, according to the usages and customs of the said city, and their respective companies, shall be and enjoy all the rights and privileges of a freeman, and of a liveryman, to all intents and purposes, as if they had been admitted before the said judgment.

17. Provided always, and be it enacted, by the

authority aforesaid, That this present Act of parliament shall be accepted, taken and reputed to be a general and publick Act of parliament; of which all and every the judge and judges of this kingdom in all courts shall take notice, on all occasions whatsoever, as if it were a public Act of parliament relating to the whole kingdom; any thing herein contained to the contrary thereof in any wise notwithstanding.

No. LIII.

The Act

11 George I, c. 18, *for regulating Elections within the City of London, and for preserving the Peace, good Order, and Government of the said City.*

A.D. 1725.

---

1. **WHEREAS** of late years great controversies Preamble. and dissentions have arisen in the city of London at the elections of citizens to serve in parliament, and of mayors, aldermen, sheriffs, and other officers of the said city; and many evil-minded persons, having no right of voting, have unlawfully intruded themselves into the assemblies of the citizens, and presumed to give their votes at such elections, in manifest violation of the rights and privileges of the citizens, and of the freedom of their elections, and to the disturbance of their public peace: and whereas great numbers of wealthy persons, not free of the said city, do inhabit, and carry on the trade of merchandize, and other imployments, within the said city, and refuse or decline to become freemen of the same, by reason of an ancient custom within the said city, restraining the freemen of the same from disposing of their personal-estates by their last wills and testaments; and whereas great dissentions have arisen between the aldermen and commons of the common-council of London, in or concerning the making or passing of acts, orders or ordinances in common-

276 ACT FOR REGULATING ELECTIONS.

council, which, if not timely settled and determined, may occasion great obstructions of the public business and concerns of the said city, and create many expensive controversies and suits at law, and be attended with other dangerous consequences: now to the intent that suitable remedies may be provided for preserving the privileges of the city of London, and the freedom of elections therein, and for settling the right of such elections, and putting a stop to the aforesaid controversies and dissentions, and the ill consequences of the same, and that a constant supply may be had of able officers, capable of supporting the dignity of, and maintaining good order and government within that ancient, populous and loyal city, which is of the greatest consequence to the whole kingdom: be it enacted by the king's most excellent majesty, by and with the advice and consent of the lords spiritual and temporal, and commons, in this present parliament assembled, and by the authority of the same, That at all times from and after the first day of June, in the year of our Lord 1725, upon every election of a citizen or citizens to serve for the said city of London, in parliament, and upon all elections of mayors, sheriffs, chamberlains, bridge-masters, auditors of chamberlain and bridge-masters' accounts, and all and every other officer and officers to be chosen in and for the said city, by the liverymen thereof, and upon all elections of aldermen and common-council men chosen at the respective wardmotes of the said city, the presiding officer or officers at such elections shall, in case a poll be demanded by any of the candidates, or any two or more of the electors, appoint a convenient number of clerks to take the same; which clerks shall take the said poll in the presence of the presiding officer or officers, and be sworn by such officer or officers, truly and indifferently to take

On all elections by the livery-men, and at the ward-motes, presiding officer to appoint a convenient number of clerks to take the poll, etc. None to be polled who is not sworn.

the same, and to set down the name of each voter, and his place of residence or abode, and for whom he shall poll; and to poll no person who shall not be sworn, or, being a quaker, shall not affirm, according to the direction of this act: and every person, before he is admitted to poll at any election of any citizen or citizens to serve in parliament, or of any officer or officers usually chosen by the liverymen of the said city, as aforesaid, shall take the oath herein after mentioned, or, being one of the people called quakers, shall solemnly affirm the effect thereof, that is to say,

YOU do swear, That you are a freeman of London, and a liveryman of the company of   and have so been for the space of twelve kalendar months; and that the place of your abode is at   in and that you have not polled at this election. So help you God. Liveryman's oath at elections.

And in case of any election of any alderman or common-council-man, every person, before he is admitted to poll, shall take the oath herein after mentioned, or, being one of the people called quakers, shall solemnly affirm the effect thereof, that is to say,

YOU do swear, That you are a freeman of London, and an householder in the ward of   and have not polled at this election. So help you God. Oath at wardmotes.

And if any person or persons shall refuse or neglect to take the oaths respectively appointed to be taken, or, being a quaker, shall refuse or neglect to make such solemn affirmation, as aforesaid, then, and in every such case, the poll or vote of such person or persons, so neglecting or refusing, shall be, and the same is hereby declared to be null and void, and as such shall be rejected and disallowed. On refusal to swear, poll to be rejected.

ACT FOR REGULATING ELECTIONS.

The oath 1 Geo. I to be taken, if required.

2. And be it further enacted, by the authority aforesaid, That at all times, from and after the said first day of June, in the year of our Lord 1725, upon every election of such citizen or citizens, officer or officers by the liverymen of the said city, and upon every election of such officer or officers at any wardmote of the said city, as aforesaid, all and every person and persons, having a right to vote or poll at such election or elections, shall, before he be admitted to vote or poll thereat (if required by any of the candidates, or any two or more of the electors) first take the oaths in and by an Act made in the first year of his majesty's reign, intituled, *An Act for the further security of his majesty's person and government, and the succession of the crown in the heirs of the late princess Sophia, being Protestants, and for extinguishing the hopes of the pretended prince of Wales, and his open and secret abettors*, appointed to be taken; or being one of the people called quakers, shall, if required, as aforesaid, solemnly affirm the effect thereof; and if any person or persons shall, being required thereunto, as aforesaid, refuse or neglect to take the said oaths, by the said act appointed to be taken, or to affirm the effect thereof, as aforesaid; that then the poll or vote of such person or persons so neglecting or refusing, shall be, and the same is hereby declared to be null and void, and as such shall be rejected and disallowed; and the presiding officers at all and every the respective elections aforesaid, and such sworn clerks as shall be by them appointed, are hereby respectively authorized and impowered to administer the above mentioned oaths and affirmations; and if any such presiding officer or officers, sworn clerk or clerks, shall neglect or refuse so to do, or shall otherwise offend in the premises, contrary to the true intent and meaning of this act, every such

Presiding officer and sworn clerk to administer the oaths, on penalty of £60.

ACT FOR REGULATING ELECTIONS. 279

officer and sworn clerk shall, for every such offence, forfeit the sum of sixty pounds of lawful money of Great Britain, besides costs of suit.

3. And it is hereby further enacted, That if any person or persons shall wilfully, falsely, and corruptly take the said oaths or affirmations, set forth and appointed in and by this act, or either of them, and be thereof lawfully convicted by indictment or information; or if any person or persons shall corruptly procure or suborn any other person to take the said oaths or affirmations, or either of them, whereby he shall wilfully and falsely take the said oaths or affirmations, or either of them, and the person so procuring or suborning, shall be thereof convicted by indictment or information; every person so offending shall, for every such offence, incur and suffer such penalties, forfeitures, and disabilities, as persons convicted of wilful and corrupt perjury at the common law are liable unto. *Penalty on falsely taking the oaths, or suborning.*

4. And to the intent that the poll at every such election may be expeditiously and duly taken, be it further enacted by the authority aforesaid, That if a poll shall be demanded at any of the elections before mentioned, after the said first day of June, in the year of our Lord 1725, the presiding officer or officers at such election shall begin such poll the day the same shall be demanded, or the next day following at furthest, unless the same shall happen on a Sunday, and then on the next day after, and shall duly and orderly proceed thereon, from day to day (Sundays excepted) until such poll be finished, and shall finish the poll at elections by the liverymen within seven days, exclusive of Sundays; and the poll at the wardmote within three days exclusive of Sundays, after the commencing the same respectively, and shall, upon adjourning the poll on each day, at all and *Presiding officer, how to act if a poll be demanded. When the poll to be finished, etc.*

every the elections aforesaid, seal up the poll books with the seals, and in the presence of such of the respective candidates, or persons deputed by them, as shall desire the same; and the said poll-book shall not be opened again, but at the time and place of meeting, in pursuance of such adjournment; and after the said poll is finished, the said poll-books being sealed, as aforesaid, shall within two days after be publickly opened at the place of election, and be duly and truly cast up; and within two days after such casting up, the numbers of the votes or polls for each candidate shall be truly, fairly, and publickly declared to the electors, at the place of election, by the officer or officers presiding at such election; and *If a scrutiny be demanded* if a scrutiny shall, upon such declaration made, be lawfully demanded, the same shall be granted and proceeded upon, and the respective candidates shall immediately nominate to the presiding officer or officers at such elections, any number of persons qualified to vote at such election, not exceeding six, *Scrutineers not to exceed six on each side.* to be scrutineers for and on behalf of the candidate or candidates on each side, to whom the presiding officer or officers at such elections shall, within six days next after such scrutiny shall be demanded, upon request, and at the charge of the candidate or candidates, or any the scrutineers on his or their behalfs, deliver, or cause to be delivered to him or them, a true copy, signed by such officer or officers *Scrutinies when to begin, and when finished on elections by liverymen.* of the poll taken at such election; and all and every the scrutinies to be had or taken upon any election to be made by the liverymen of the said city, shall begin within ten days after the delivery of the copies of the said polls, and be proceeded on day by day (Sundays excepted) and shall be finished within fifteen days after the commencement of such scrutiny; and thereupon the presiding officer or officers shall, within four days after the finishing such scrutiny, publickly declare at the place of such election which of the candidates is or are duly elected, and the number of legal votes for each candidate appearing to him or them upon such scrutiny; and on the election of any officer or officers at the respective wardmotes of the said city, if a scrutiny be demanded, the candidates or scrutineers, nominated on their behalfs respectively, shall, within ten days next after the receipt of the copy or copies of the polls taken at such election, deliver or cause to be delivered to the presiding officer or officers, the names in writing of the several persons, who have polled in the said election, against whose votes they shall object, with the particular objections against each respective name; and the presiding officer or officers shall thereupon, within three days then next following, at the request and charges of any candidate or candidates, or the scrutineers named on his or their behalfs, deliver or cause to be delivered to him or them, one or more true copy or copies (signed as aforesaid) of the paper containing such names and objections, as aforesaid; and the said presiding officer or officers, within ten days then next following (exclusive of Sundays) after having fully heard such of the said candidates, as shall desire the same, or some person appointed by him or them, touching such objections, shall, at or in the place of election, openly and publickly declare which of the said candidates is or are duly elected, and the number of legal votes for each candidate appearing to him or them upon such scrutiny; and if the said presiding officer or officers, or any other person or persons, shall offend in the premisses, every such offender shall forfeit for every such offence the sum of two hundred pounds of lawful money of Great Britain, with full costs of suit, over and above all

Scrutinies on elections at wardmotes.

True copies of the objections against the pollers.

Penalty £200 with costs.

other penalties and forfeitures inflicted by any other Act or Acts of parliament.

<small>A true list to be given of the voters disallowed.</small>

5. And be it further enacted by the authority aforesaid, That after any election made, and scrutiny taken, as is hereinbefore provided and directed, the presiding officer or officers at such election and scrutiny shall deliver, under his or their hand or hands, a true list of the voters by him or them disallowed upon such scrutiny, to any of the candidates, who shall, upon the final declaration of the election, as aforesaid, demand the same, within six days after such demand made, such candidate paying for the same; provided always, that no such list, as is hereby directed to be given, nor anything therein contained, shall be admitted to be given in evidence on any action or occasion whatsoever.

<small>Mayor to issue precepts to the companies to bring in lists.</small>

6. And be it further enacted by the authority aforesaid, That the mayor of the city of London for the time being, upon request to him made by any candidate or candidates, his or their agent or agents, at any election of a citizen or citizens to serve in parliament for the said city, or of a mayor, or any other officer or officers to be chosen by the liverymen thereof, where a scrutiny is demanded and granted, shall issue his precepts as has been usual, requiring the masters and wardens of the livery-companies of the said city respectively, to cause their clerks forthwith to return to him two true lists of all the liverymen of their respective companies; and the said clerks shall return such their respective lists upon oath, within three days after the receipt of any such precepts; one of which lists so returned, the said mayor shall, and he is hereby required forthwith to deliver or cause to be delivered to the candidate or candidates on each side at such election, or to his or their agent or agents respectively.

7. And whereas divers controversies and disputes have arisen in the said city of London, touching the right of election of aldermen and common-council-men for the respective wards of the said city, for quieting all such disputes and controversies for the future, it is hereby further enacted by the authority aforesaid, That from and after the said first day of June, in the year of our Lord 1725, the right of election of aldermen and common-council men, for the several and respective wards of the said city, shall belong and appertain to freemen of the said city of London, being householders, paying scot, as herein after is mentioned and provided, and bearing lot, when required, in their several and respective wards, and to none other whatsoever. *Election of aldermen and common-council-men to be by freemen paying scot and lot,*

8. Provided nevertheless, That the houses of such householders be respectively of the true and real value of ten pounds a year at the least; and that such householders be respectively the sole occupiers of such houses, and have been actually in the possession respectively of a house of such value, in the ward wherein the election is made, by the space of twelve kalendar months next before such election. *and paying £10 per ann. rent.*

9. Provided also, and for the better ascertaining what are the rates and taxes, to which such householders ought to contribute and pay their scot, the same are hereby declared and enacted to be a rate to the church, to the poor, to the scavenger, to the orphans, and to the rates in lieu of or for the watch and ward, and to such other annual rates, as the citizens of London, inhabiting therein, shall hereafter be liable unto, other than and except annual aids granted or to be granted by parliament; and in case any such householder, within the space aforesaid, shall have been rated and charged, and contributed and paid his scot to all the said rates or taxes, or thirty *The scot ascertained.*

284   ACT FOR REGULATING ELECTIONS.

Householder paying 30s. a year in all may vote. shillings a year to all, or some of them, except as aforesaid; every such person shall be deemed and taken to be a person paying of scot.

10. Provided always that such householder, within the space aforesaid, shall have been rated or charged, and contributed or paid his scot, to all and singular the rates and taxes (other than and except annual aids granted by parliament) whereunto the citizens of London, inhabiting therein, are or shall be liable, or shall have paid in the whole to the said rates and taxes, or some of them, except as aforesaid, thirty shillings a year at least: and in case any two or more *Partners in trade may vote, each paying £10 per annum rent.* partners carry on a joint trade in any such house together, and shall have been householders of such house by such space of time as aforesaid; such partners shall, paying their scot in manner aforesaid, and bearing their respective proper lots, if required, have votes at the elections aforesaid; so as such house, wherein such partners carry on their trade, be of the true and real yearly value of as many respective sums of ten pounds a year, computed together, as there are partners.

Two inhabiting the same house, each paying scot and £10 per annum rent may vote. 11. Provided also, That where two persons and no more, not being partners, shall have by the space aforesaid, severally inhabited in the same house, such two persons, severally paying their scots, and bearing their respective lots as aforesaid, shall have votes at the elections aforesaid; so as such house, wherein such two persons inhabit, be of the true and real yearly value of twenty pounds or upwards, and that each of the said persons doth pay the yearly rent of ten pounds at the least for his respective part of such house.

Persons exempted from scot and lot may vote. 12. Provided always, That nothing in this Act contained shall extend, or be construed to extend, to oblige any person or persons to pay any scot, or bear any lot, from the doing of which they are or shall be exempted and discharged by Act of parliament, charter, or writ of privilege; but that such person and persons, so exempted and discharged, shall and may vote at any election of any alderman, common-council man, or other officer, usually chosen at the wardmotes of the said city, notwithstanding he or they shall not have borne such lot, or paid such scot, in such manner as he or they should or might have done, in case this Act had not been made, and no otherwise.

13. And to the intent that the citizens and inhabitants of London may have a proper remedy and relief in case they, or any of them, shall be aggrieved by any tax, rate, or assessment, made in or for the said city, or by any misbehaviour of any officer in relation thereto, or to the collecting the same, be it further enacted by the authority aforesaid, That it shall and may be lawful to and for all and every person and persons, who, from and after the said first day of June in the year of our Lord 1725, shall be aggrieved by any of the assessments that shall or may be made in or for the said city, towards payment of the rate or tax for the orphans, and also to the rate or tax in lieu of, or for keeping watch and ward in the said city, or by any breach or neglect of duty committed by any officer concerning the same, to appeal, in respect thereof, to the mayor and court of aldermen of London; and it shall and may be lawful to and for any such person or persons, in case he or they shall be in any wise aggrieved by any other rate or assessment, that shall be made in or for the said city, or any of the wards, precincts, parishes, or inhabitants of the same, or by any breach or neglect of duty committed by any officer relating thereto, to appeal to the proper persons, unto whom by law such

Complainants about assessments may appeal to the mayor and aldermen, or to the proper officer,

ACT FOR REGULATING ELECTIONS.

whose determination shall be final. appeal lies; and the said mayor and court of aldermen, and the said other persons, to whom such appeal shall be lawfully made respectively, shall and may hear, and finally determine the matter so complained of, and correct and settle the said rates.

Persons excluded from voting. 14. And it is hereby further enacted, That no person or persons whatsoever, shall, from and after the said first day of June 1725, have any right or title to vote at any election of a citizen or citizens to serve in parliament for the said city, or of any mayor, or other officer or officers to be chosen by the liverymen thereof, who have not been upon the livery by the space of twelve kalendar months before such election, and who shall not have paid their respective livery-fines, or, who having paid the same, shall have received such fines back again in part or in all, or shall have had any allowance in respect thereof; and no person or persons whatsoever shall have any right to vote at any election of a citizen or citizens to serve in parliament, or of any mayor, alderman, or other officer or officers of or for the said city, or any the wards or precincts thereof, who have at any time, within the space of two years next before such election or elections, requested to be, and accordingly have been discharged from paying to the rates and taxes, to which the citizens of London, inhabiting therein, are or shall be liable as aforesaid, or any of them, or have, within the time aforesaid, had or received any alms whatsoever; and the vote of every such person shall be void.

15. And to the intent that a final end may be put to all disputes between the mayor and aldermen and the commons of the common-council of the said city, touching the making or passing of acts, orders, or ordinances in common-council, and that no act, order or ordinance, may for the future be made or

passed in common-council, without the full consent of the representative body of the said city, according to the ancient constitution of the same; be it enacted by the authority aforesaid, That no act, order, or ordinance whatsoever, at any time, from and after the said first day of June 1725, shall be made or passed in the common-council of the said city, without the assent of the mayor and aldermen present at such common-council, or the major part of them, nor without the assent of the commons present at such common council, or the major part of them.* Mayor and aldermen to have a negative in passing acts, etc., as also the commons.

16. Provided always, That nothing in this act contained shall extend, or be construed to extend, to any election, nomination, or appointment in common-council, of any common-serjeant, town-clerk, judges of the sheriffs' court, coroner, common cryer, commissioners of sewers, garbler, and the governor and assistants of London of the new plantation of Ulster in Ireland; but that the election, nomination, or appointment of all or any of the said officers shall and may, from and after the said first day of June 1725, be made by the mayor, aldermen, and commons in common-council assembled, or the major part of them; any thing in this act contained to the contrary thereof notwithstanding. Exception.

17. And to the intent that persons of wealth and ability, who exercise the business of merchandize, and other laudable employments, within the said city, may not be discouraged from becoming free of the same, by reason of the custom restraining the citizens and freemen thereof from disposing of their personal estates by their last wills and testaments; be it further enacted by the authority aforesaid, That it shall and may be lawful to and for all and

* This clause was repealed by 19 Geo. II, c. 8.

288   ACT FOR REGULATING ELECTIONS.

<small>Freemen made after 1 June 1725, may dispose of their personal estate as they think fit.</small>

every person and persons, who shall, at any time from and after the said first day of June 1725, be made, or become free of the said city, and also to and for all and every person and persons, who are already free of the said city, and on the said first day of June, shall be unmarried, and not have issue by any former marriage, to give, devise, will, and dispose of his and their personal estate and estates, to such person and persons, and to such use and uses, as he or they shall think fit; any custom or usage of or in the said city, or any by-law or ordinance, made or observed within the same, to the contrary thereof in any wise notwithstanding.

<small>Exception.</small>

18. Provided nevertheless, That in case any person, who shall at any time or times, from and after the said first day of June 1725, become free of the said city, and any person or persons, who are already free of the said city, and on the said first day of June 1725, shall be unmarried, and not have issue by any former marriage, hath agreed or shall agree, by any writing under his hand, upon or in consideration of his marriage, or otherwise, that his personal estate shall be subject to, or be distributed or distributable, according to the custom of the city of London; or in case any person so free, or becoming free as aforesaid, shall die intestate; in every such case, the personal estate of such person so making such agreement, or so dying intestate, shall be subject to, and be distributed or distributable according to the custom of the said city; any thing herein contained to the contrary in any wise notwithstanding.

<small>Words to be omitted in the oath of a freeman.</small>

19. And it is hereby further enacted, That there shall from and after the said first day of June 1725, be omitted and left out of the oath of a freeman of the said city, the words following, that is to say

[*Ye shall know no foreigner to buy or sell any merchandize with any other foreigner within the city, or the franchise thereof; but ye shall warn the chamberlain thereof, or some minister of the chamber*] and also these words following, that is to say [*Ye shall implead or sue no freeman out of the city, whilst ye may have right and law within the same city*] and after these words [*Ye shall take no apprentice*] the words immediately following shall also be omitted, that is to say [*but if he be free-born, that is to say, no bondsman's son, nor the child of any alien*] and for [*no*] and instead thereof these words [*for any*] shall be inserted in the said oath.

20. And be it further enacted by the authority aforesaid, That all and every the forfeitures hereby enacted or inflicted, shall be distributed in manner following; that is to say, one third part thereof to the king's most excellent majesty; one other third part thereof, to the chamberlain of the said city, to the use of the mayor, commonalty, and citizens of the said city; and the remaining third part thereof, to him or them that will sue for the same, within six kalender months next after the same shall be incurred; to be recovered by action of debt, bill, plaint, or information, in any of his majesty's courts of record at Westminster; wherein no essoign, privilege, protection, or wager of law, shall be allowed, nor any more than one imparlance. *Forfeitures how to be distributed.*

21. And be it further enacted by the authority aforesaid, that this act shall in all courts and places be deemed and taken to be a publick act, and shall be judicially taken notice of as such by all judges, justices, and courts whatsoever, without specially pleading the same. *Publick act.*

No. LIV.

Charter of George II,

Constituting all the Aldermen of the City of London Justices of the Peace.

25 AUGUST, A.D. 1741.

A.D. 1638.

GEORGE the second, by the grace of God, of Great Britain, France and Ireland, king, defender of the faith, and so forth. To all to whom these presents shall come greeting: Whereas our royal predecessor king Charles the first, late king of England, by his letters patent under the great seal of England, bearing date at Westminster, the eighteenth day of October, in the fourteenth year of his reign, did give and grant unto the mayor and commonalty and citizens of the city of London, and their successors, amongst other things, that the then mayor and recorder of the said city, and the mayor and recorder of the said city for the time being; and as well those aldermen who before that time had sustained and had borne, as those aldermen who thereafter should have sustained and borne, the charge and office of mayoralty of the said city, although they should cease from the mayoralty or should be dismissed therefrom, so long as they should remain aldermen there; and the three senior aldermen of the said city, for the time being, who should have been longest in the office of aldermanship, and had not before sustained and borne the charge and office of mayoralty of that city for ever should be all and every of them a justice and justices, to preserve and keep the peace of the said king, his heirs and successors, within the said city of London and liberties of the same, and appointed the said lord mayor and recorder, for the time being, to be of the Quorum. And whereas our royal predecessors, king William and queen Mary, by certain other letters patent, under their great seal of England, bearing date, at Westminster, the eight-and-twentieth day of July, in ^{A.D. 1692.} the fourth year of their reign, reciting the said former letters patent of king Charles the first, and reciting also, that the said mayor and aldermen, by their humble petition, had represented to their majesties, that the number of justices of the peace constituted within the said city, by the said letters patent of king Charles the first, were so few, that by reason thereof, it frequently happened that justice could not be administered within the said city with so much expedition, so commodiously, and in such a manner as might be most expedient for their said late majesties service, and the utility of their subjects; their said late majesties, therefore, by their said recited letters patent, did grant to the said mayor and commonalty and citizens of the city of London, and their successors, that six other aldermen of the said city for the time being, who then were, or for the future should be next in the office of aldermanship to the three senior aldermen mentioned and constituted justices of the peace in the said first-mentioned charter, and who then had borne, and thereafter should have borne the office of sheriff of the said city, besides and beyond the three senior aldermen, as aforesaid, should for ever thereafter be justices of the peace, within the said city of London, and liberties thereof; and these six aldermen, with the mayor and recorder, for the time being, as well as those aldermen who had borne the office of mayoralty, and the aforesaid three senior aldermen, or any four of them, whereof the said mayor or recorder for the time being to be one, are, by the said last-recited letters patent constituted justices of the peace for the said city and liberties, with the same powers as are granted to the justices of the peace of any county of this kingdom, as by the said several recited letters patent (amongst divers other matters and things therein contained, relation being thereto respectively had) may more fully and at large appear: And whereas the lord mayor and aldermen of the said city of London have, by their petition, humbly represented unto us, that, since the granting the said last-mentioned letters patent, the duties of the justices of the peace, within the said city and liberties, are, by many acts of parliament, very much increased, so that the petitioners, who are constituted justices by the said charter, have, for the more speedy and effectual execution of justice, agreed amongst themselves, to sit daily by turns, in the Guildhall of the said city, for the publick administration of justice; and that the petitioners most humbly conceive it will be for the publick utility of all our subjects, within the said city and liberties, and that justice may still be more commodiously and expeditiously administered, if the present number of justices of the peace, within the said city of London and liberties thereof, was increased: And the petitioners further represent, that the lord mayor and recorder being the only justices of the Quorum, if by sickness, or other unavoidable accident, it should happen that neither may be able to attend the session, great inconveniences may arise; the petitioners, therefore, have humbly besought us to grant to our good subjects, the mayor and commonalty and citizens of the said city, that, for the future, the mayor, recorder, and all the aldermen of the said city, for the time being, may be justices of the peace for the said city of London and liberties thereof; and that all those aldermen for the time being, who shall have borne and sustained the office of mayoralty of the said city, may be of the Quorum, as well as the mayor and recorder:

We, being willing to gratify the petitioners in their request; know ye, therefore, that we, of our special grace, certain knowledge and meer motion, have given, granted, and by these presents, for us, our heirs and successors, do give, and grant, to the mayor and commonalty of the city of London, and their successors, that the mayor, recorder, and all the aldermen of the said city of London, for the time being, and every of them, be for ever hereafter a justice and justices of the peace, of us, our heirs and successors, within the said city of London and liberties thereof: And we do, by these presents, for us, our heirs and successors, constitute, make, and ordain the mayor, recorder, and all the aldermen of the said city of London, for the time being, and every of them, or any four of them, (of whom the mayor and recorder, or any one of the aldermen who have sustained the office of mayoralty, for the time·being, we will shall be always one) justices of us, our heirs and successors, within the said city of London and liberties thereof, to keep, and cause to be kept all and singular statutes and ordinances, in all their articles made, and to be made, for the preservation of the peace of us, our heirs and successors, and for the peaceable ruling and governing the people of us, our heirs and successors, as well within the said city as the liberties thereof, according to the form and effect of the same; and to correct

Mayor, recorder and all the aldermen made justices of the peace.

and punish, in the manner prescribed by those statutes and ordinances all such persons who shall be found offending, within the said city and liberties thereof, against the form and effect of the same statutes and ordinances, or any, or either of them, and to demand such sufficient security for the peace, or good behaviour towards us, our heirs and successors, and all the subjects of us, our heirs and successors, of all such persons who shall send threatenings to any subject, or subjects, of us, our heirs or successors, concerning their bodies, or the burning their houses; and if they shall refuse to find such security, then to cause them to be safely kept in our gaol of Newgate, or in any other prison of us, our heirs and successors, in our said city of London, until they shall have found such security; and to do and perform all and singular other matters and things, which any justices or keepers of the peace, of us, our heirs and successors, within any county of that part of our kingdom of Great Britain, called England, may, can, or ought to do, and perform, by virtue of any statutes and ordinances of this part of our kingdom of Great Britain, called England, or by virtue of any commission of us, our heirs and successors, to preserve the peace in any such county. In witness whereof we have caused these our letters to be made patent.

John Potter.   Witnesses. John, archbishop of Canterbury, and other guardians and justices of the kingdom, at Westminster, the twenty-fifth day of August, in the fifteenth year of our reign.

No. LV.

An Act

For repealing all former Acts, Orders and Ordinances, touching the Nomination and Election of Sheriffs of the City of London and County of Middlesex, and for regulating and enforcing such Nominations and Elections for the future.

7 APRIL, A.D. 1748.

WHEREAS from time immemorial there have Preamble. been, and of right ought to be, two sheriffs of this city, which said two sheriffs, during all the time aforesaid, have constituted, and of right ought to constitute, one Sheriff of the county of Middlesex:

And whereas the sheriffwick of this city, and the sheriffwick of the said county of Middlesex have, from time immemorial, belonged, and do of right belong, to the mayor and commonalty and citizens of the city of London:

And whereas the several acts, orders and ordinances heretofore made and passed in this city, touching the choice of election of persons to the offices of sheriffalty of this city and county of Middlesex, and for compelling the persons so chosen, or elected, to accept and serve the said offices, have hitherto proved ineffectual to answer the several purposes in and by such acts, orders and ordinances expressed or intended:

For remedy thereof, be it enacted, and it is hereby Former acts enacted and ordained by the right honourable the repealed. lord mayor, the right worshipful the aldermen, and the commons of this city, in this present common council assembled, and by the authority of the same, that all and every the said acts, orders and ordinances, so far as the same relate to the said offices of sheriffalty, shall from henceforth be, and the same are hereby repealed, annulled, and made utterly void and of none effect.

Who to elect sheriffs, and what to be the general election day.
And it is hereby further enacted, that the right of electing persons to the said offices of sheriffalty shall be, and the same is hereby vested in the liverymen of the several companies of this city, to be for that purpose from time to time assembled in the common hall of the Guildhall of this city, and that the general day of election of persons to the said offices shall be, yearly, the twenty-fourth day of June, unless the same shall happen to be Sunday; in which case, the said election shall be on the day then next following.

In what instances elections to be on other days.
Provided always, that whensoever it shall happen, that any person or persons elected to the said offices of sheriffalty, shall in any instance refuse or neglect to conform to this act, or shall depart this life, or be lawfully removed or discharged from the said offices, or from his or their respective election thereunto; or that upon any other occasion whatsoever, there shall be just cause to proceed to a new election; then, and in every such case, it shall and may be lawful, to and for the liverymen of the said several companies of this city, duly assembled as aforesaid, to proceed to, and make such new election at such day and time as by the court of lord-mayor and aldermen of this city for the time being shall be ordered or appointed.

When persons elected are to take, and how long to hold the office.
And it is hereby further ordained, that every person who shall hereafter be elected to the said offices of sheriffalty upon the said general election day, or at any other time between the said general election day and the twenty-second day of September in the same year, when there shall be no actual

vacancy in the said offices, shall take the same upon him on the vigil of St. Michael the Archangel next following his said election, and shall hold the same for and during the space of one whole year from thence next ensuing; and that every person who shall be elected to the said offices on the said twenty-second day of September, or at any time between the said twenty-second and twenty-eighth days of September, or upon a vacancy happening in the said offices, or when the sheriffs of this city and county of Middlesex for the time being, or either of them, shall hold over, as is herein after mentioned and provided, shall take the said offices upon him on the seventh day next after notice of his said election, and shall hold the same until the swearing in of the new sheriffs upon the vigil of St. Michael the Archangel next following the day of his taking the said offices upon him as aforesaid.

Provided always, and it is hereby further ordained, that if, upon any future vigil of St. Michael the Archangel, it shall happen, that neither of the persons elected to the said offices of sheriffalty shall appear in the Guildhall aforesaid, and take the said offices upon him, then, and in every such case, both the then sheriffs shall hold over and continue in the said offices until some other persons shall be duly elected and sworn into the same in their stead; and if upon any such vigil it happen, that only one of the persons elected to the said offices shall so appear and take the said offices upon him, then, and in every such last mentioned case, the junior in office of the then sheriffs shall hold over and continue in the said offices, until some other person shall be duly elected and sworn into the same in his stead. *In what instances to hold over.*

Provided also, and it is further ordained, that from henceforth, at every assembly for the election of a person or persons to the said offices of sheriffalty, *In what order the aldermen to be put up and take lace.*

every alderman of this city who shall not have actually served the same, shall according to his seniority in the said court of lord mayor and aldermen, and before any commoner of this city, be publickly put in nomination for the said offices; and every alderman of this city, who shall be elected to the said offices, shall therein take place according to his seniority in the said court, and have precedence of every commoner of this court.

<small>Power to lord mayor to nominate persons, and how they shall be put up.</small>

And that from henceforth for ever, it shall and may be lawful, to and for the lord mayor of this city for the time being, at such time or times as he shall think proper, between the fourteenth day of April and the fourteenth day of June in every year, to nominate, in the said court of lord mayor and aldermen of this city, one or more fit and able person or persons (not exceeding the number of nine persons in the whole), being free of this city, to be publickly put in nomination for the said offices of sheriffalty, to the liverymen of the several companies of this city, to be thereafter in the common-hall aforesaid assembled for the election of a person or persons to the said offices; and the person or persons so nominated by any lord mayor of this city, shall at every such assembly of the said liverymen, after his and their respective nominations by the lord mayor as aforesaid, be publickly put in nomination for the said offices, before any other commoner of this city, and in the same order as he or they shall stand nominated by the lord mayor, until he or they shall respectively have been duly elected to the said offices, or shall have been duly discharged of and from such nomination, in such manner as is herein after mentioned.

Provided always, that if any person so nominated shall, within six days after notice thereof, pay to the chamberlain of this city for the time being, the sum of four hundred pounds of lawful money of Great Britain, for the uses herein after mentioned, and twenty marks towards the maintenance of the several ministers of the several prisons within this city, together with the usual fees, every such person shall be for ever exempted and discharged from such nomination, and from serving the said offices of sheriffalty, unless he shall afterwards take upon him the office of an alderman of this city, in which case he shall be liable to be elected to the said offices of sheriffalty. *What fine to be paid to discharge persons nominated by the lord mayor.*

And it is further ordained, that at every assembly for the election of one or more person or persons to the said offices of sheriffalty, all, and every such person and persons being free of this city, and then not exempted or discharged from the said offices, as shall then and there be for that purpose nominated by any two or more of the said liverymen then and there present, and having a right of voting at such election, shall be publickly put in nomination for the said offices, next after such person or persons as shall have been so nominated for the said offices by any lord-mayor of this city, and shall not then have been discharged from such nomination (if any such shall then be); or in default of such person or persons last mentioned, then next after such of the aldermen of this city as shall not have served the said offices. *In what order persons nominated by two liverymen to be put up.*

And it is further ordained, that no freeman of this city shall be discharged from such election or nomination for insufficiency of wealth, unless he shall and do voluntarily take his corporal oath, before the said court of lord mayor and aldermen, that he then is not of the value of fifteen thousand pounds, in lands, goods and separate debts: and also unless six other citizens, freemen of this city, to be brought by him, and being men of good credit and reputation, such *In what cases, by whom, and how far persons to be excused for insufficiency of wealth.*

as the said court shall approve of, shall and do likewise, before the same court, voluntarily testify, upon their corporal oaths, that in their consciences they believe the said person so elected by the said liverymen, or so nominated by the lord mayor (as the case shall happen to be) hath deposed and sworn truly concerning his value as aforesaid.

<small>In what instances the persons elected to give bond, and the forfeiture in case of default.</small>

Provided always, that every person who shall be elected to the said offices of sheriffalty upon the said general election day, as any other time between the said general election day and the fourteenth of September in the same year, when there shall be no actual vacancy in the said offices, shall personally appear before the said court of lord mayor and aldermen in the inner chamber of the Guildhall aforesaid, at the first court there to be holden next after notice of his election, unless such reasonable excuse shall then and there be offered on his behalf, as the said court shall allow, and in case of such excuse allowed, then at such other subsequent court or courts as the said court shall appoint, and shall then and there become bound to the chamberlain of this city for the time being, his executors and administrators, by his bond or obligation, in the penal sum of one thousand pounds; with condition there underwritten, or thereupon endorsed, that if he shall personally appear on the vigil of St. Michael the Archangel then next following, between the hours of twelve of the clock at noon, and three of the clock in the afternoon, in the publick assembly in the said Guildhall, in the place where the court of hustings is usually holden, and then and there, in the presence of the lord-mayor of this city for the time being, and two of the aldermen of this city for the time being, or in case of the absence of the lord mayor, then in the presence of four of the aldermen of this city for the time being, take the oath of office there usually taken by the sheriffs of this city and county of Middlesex, then the said bond or obligation shall be void; upon pain that every person so elected, who shall not appear and become bound as aforesaid, shall (if any alderman of this city, or a commoner previously nominated by the lord mayor of this city, as aforesaid) forfeit and pay to the uses herein after mentioned, the sum of six hundred pounds of lawful money of Great Britain; or, if he shall not then be an alderman of this city, or a commoner so previously nominated by the lord mayor of this city, the sum of four hundred pounds of like lawful money.

Provided also, that if any freeman of this city who shall be duly elected to the said offices of sheriffalty, upon the said fourteenth day of September, or at any other time between the said fourteenth and twenty-second days of September in the same year, when there shall be no actual vacancy in the said offices, and shall have six days' notice thereof as aforesaid, shall not appear on the vigil of St. Michael the Archangel next after such notice, between the hours of twelve of the clock at noon, and three of the clock in the afternoon, in the publick assembly in the Guildhall aforesaid, in the place where the said court of hustings is usually holden, and then and there, in the presence of the lord mayor of this city for the time being, and two of the aldermen of this city for the time being, or in case of the absence of the lord mayor, then in the presence of four of the aldermen of this city for the time being, take the oath of office there usually taken by the sheriffs of this city and county of Middlesex, then, and in every such case, such person shall (if an alderman of this city, or a commoner previously nominated by the lord mayor as aforesaid) forfeit and pay to the uses herein after

Penalties on persons elected on the 14th, or between the 14th and 22nd of September, when no vacancy, who shall not take the said offices in time.

mentioned, the sum of six hundred pounds of lawful money of Great Britain; or, if he shall not then be an alderman of this city, or a commoner so nominated by the lord mayor, the sum of four hundred pounds of like lawful money.

Provided also, that if any freeman of this city, who shall be duly elected to the said offices of sheriffalty, shall not personally appear on the seventh day next after notice of his election, between the hours of twelve of the clock at noon, and three of the clock in the afternoon, in the publick assembly in the Guildhall aforesaid, in the place where the said court of hustings is usually holden, and then and there, in the presence of the lord-mayor and two aldermen, or in case of the absence of the lord-mayor, then in the presence of four aldermen, take the oath of office there usually taken by the sheriffs of this city and county of Middlesex, then, and in every such case, such person shall (if an alderman of this city, or a commoner previously nominated by the lord mayor as aforesaid) forfeit and pay to the uses herein after mentioned, the sum of six hundred pounds of lawful money of Great Britain; or, if he shall not then be an alderman of this city, or a commoner so previously nominated by the lord-mayor, the sum of four hundred pounds of like lawful money.

How the said penalties to be recovered. And it is further ordained, that all penalties and sums of money to be forfeited by virtue of this act or ordinance, shall be recovered by action of debt, to be commenced and prosecuted in the name of the chamberlain of this city for the time being, in one of the courts of record of the king's majesty, his heirs and successors, within this city, wherein no essoign or wager of law shall be admitted or allowed for the defendant; and that the chamberlain of this city for the time being, in all such actions to be prosecuted by virtue of this act, wherein he shall obtain judgment, by verdict, *Nil dicit*, or confession, or upon demurrer, shall and may recover his costs of suit; and, if a verdict shall be given for the defendant, or if the plaintiff shall be nonsuited, or discontinue his action after the defendant shall have appeared, or if upon demurrer, judgment shall be given against the plaintiff, the defendant or defendants shall and may recover costs, and have the like remedy for the same as any defendant or defendants hath or have in other cases by law.

And it is further ordained, that if it shall happen, that two or more persons nominated by any lord mayor or lord mayors of this city, for the said offices of sheriffalty, shall, between the fourteenth day of April, and the twenty-fourth day of June, in any one year, pay unto the chamberlain of this city for the time being, the sum of four hundred pounds each, to be exempted and discharged from their said nomination, and from serving the said offices according to the proviso for that purpose herein before contained, then, and in every such case, the said chamberlain for the time being shall, out of the monies so paid to him, issue and pay the sum of one hundred pounds to each of the two persons, who, upon the vigil of St. Michael the Archangel in that year, or at any other time thereafter, shall first and next take the said offices upon them; and if it shall happen that only one person so nominated by any lord mayor, shall pay the said sum of four hundred pounds within the time, and for the purpose aforesaid, then, and in every such last mentioned case, the said chamberlain for the time being shall thereout issue and pay the sum of fifty pounds to each of the two persons, who, upon the said vigil in that year, or at any other time thereafter, shall first and next take the said offices upon

In what cases the sheriffs to have part of the fines, and how the rest of the fines and forfeitures are to be applied.

them; and that the residue of all and every the sums of four hundred pounds, which shall hereafter be paid to the chamberlain of this city for the time being, within the time, and for the purpose aforesaid, and also all penalties and sums of money to be forfeited and paid by virtue of, and in pursuance of this act, shall go and be applied to the use of the said mayor and commonalty and citizens of London, subject to such orders and resolutions of this court as have heretofore been made, touching the monies paid into the chamber of London as a fine for not holding the said offices, and to such further orders and resolutions of this court hereafter as shall be made touching the same.

No person who has been fined upon any former act, to be eligible. Provided always, and it is further ordained, that every person who hath at any time heretofore paid to the chamberlain of this city for the time being, for the use of the mayor and commonalty and citizens of the same city, any sum of money to be exempted or discharged from the said offices of sheriffalty, shall be, and is hereby for ever exempted and absolutely discharged from the said offices of sheriffalty, unless such person shall at any time hereereafter take upon him the office of an alderman of this city, in which case he shall be, and is hereby declared to be subject and liable to be elected to the said offices, such payment or anything herein before contained to the contrary thereof in any wise notwithstanding.

No person to serve a second time. Provided also, and it is further ordained, that no person who now hath, or hereafter shall have, duly served the said offices of sheriffalty of this city and county of Middlesex, according to the true intent and meaning of this present act, or of any former act of common council, shall hereafter be eligible to the said offices a second time, any thing herein before contained to the contrary thereof in any wise notwithstanding.

No. LVI.

Substance of the Act of Common Council

For licensing Foreigners to work in the City of London.

22 NOVEMBER, A.D. 1750.

THAT, after the first day of December next, the court of lord-mayor and aldermen may grant a licence to a free master, who has used his best endeavours, and cannot procure a sufficient number of fit and able free journeymen to carry on his business, to employ such a number of foreigners, for or during such time or times, and under such restrictions, as to the said court shall seem fit and necessary.

That on any Tuesday, on which no court of lord-mayor and aldermen shall be holden, the power above-mentioned, so as the same do not exceed the space of six weeks, shall be vested in the lord-mayor for the time being.

That no licence shall be granted, by virtue of this act, to any freeman to employ any foreigner, unless he has one apprentice at least, or has had one apprentice within twelve calendar months next before his application for such licence.

That no freeman shall be enabled to employ any foreigner by virtue of this licence, until he has registered the christian and surnames, and place of abode of the said foreigner, and in what business he is to be employed, with the town-clerk of this city for the time being, who is to enter the same in a book to be kept for that purpose, he being paid two shillings and six pence for every licence so to be registered; which book any freeman of this city shall have liberty to inspect gratis, every day between twelve o'clock at noon and two in the afternoon (Sundays excepted); and if any person registered by virtue of this licence shall leave his master's service, or be discharged the same, the town clerk is, upon application, to insert and enter in the licence and register another person's name, in the room of the person discharged, for the remaining term of the licence, without any fee.

That the court of lord-mayor and aldermen have a power to revoke, or call in any licence, though the time limited therein be not expired.

APPENDIX,

OR

REFERENCE TABLE TO THE TEXTS OF THE FOREGOING COLLECTION OF CHARTERS AND DOCUMENTS; WITH NOTICES OF SOME ADDITIONAL TEXTS.

I. FIRST CHARTER OF WILLIAM THE CONQUEROR.

British Museum, MS. Cotton, Vespasian D. xvi, ff. 57; 57, b. A.D. 1067 :—MS. Sloane 754, f. 1 :—MS. Harley, 1464, f. 1 :—cf. MS. Harley, 2058, f. 4.

Liber Albus. ed. Riley in Rolls series, *Liber Custumarum*, pp. 25, 246, 247 (two texts), 504 (*Lat.* and *Sax.*), 594 (*Engl.*) :—J. E., *Charters*, p. 2 :—Stow, *Hist. of Lond.*, p. 449, col. 1 (*Sax.*) and col. 2 (*Engl.*) :— Maitland, *Hist. of Lond.*, p. 37 (*Sax.* and *Engl.*) :— Noorthouck, *Hist of Lond.*, p. 773 : — Luffman, *Charters*, p. 1 :—Stubbs, *Select Charters*, p. 79.

II. SECOND CHARTER OF WILLIAM THE CONQUEROR.

cf. MS. Harl., 2058, f. 4.

J. E., p. 2 :—Maitland, p. 38 :—Noorthouck, p. 773 :—Luffman, p. 4 :—Alex. Ellis, *Proclam. of Hen. III.*

III. CHARTER OF HENRY I.

MS. Cott., Vespasian D. xvi, ff. 7, b; 64 (*Lat.*):— MS. Harl., 2058, f. 4 (*Lat.*) :—MS. Sloane, 754, f. 1 :— MS. Soc. of Antiquaries of London, 105, f. 1.

Rymer's *Fœdera*, Record Edition by Clarke and Holbrooke, vol. I, p. 11 :—Stow, p. 449 (*Lat.*) :—J. E., p. 2 :—Maitl., p. 39 :—Noort., p. 773 :—Luffm., p. 5 :—Stubbs, p. 103.

Charter of King Stephen to the Barons, etc., of England claimed by the City of London to be entitled to place among their charters, Stow, p. 450 (*Lat.*) :—Stubbs.

IV. CHARTER OF HENRY II.

MS. Cott., Claudius D. ii, f. 70*b* (*Lat*) :—MS. Cott., Vespasian D. xvi, ff. 58, 64*b* (*Lat.* :—MS. Hargrave 313,[1] f. 79*b* (*Lat*) :—MS. Sloane, 754, f. 2 :—MS. Soc. Antiq., 105, f. 1*b* :—MS. Harl., 2058, f. 4 :—*Liber Albus* :—MS. Harl., 311, f. 94 (*Lat.*).

Riley, p. 31 (*Lat*) :—J. E., p. 5 :—Maitl., p. 53 :—Noort., p. 774 :—Luffm., p. 10.

V. FIRST CHARTER OF RICHARD I.

MS. Cott., Claudius D. ii, f. 111 (*Lat.*) :—MS. Cott., Vespasian D. xvi, f. 58*b* (*Lat.*) :—MS. Sloane 754, f. 2*b* :—MS. Harl., 2058, f. 4*b* (*Lat.*).

J. E., p. 7 :—Maitl., p. 55 :—Noort. p. 775 :—Luffm., p. 13 :—Riley, p. 248 (*Lat.*).

VI. SECOND CHARTER OF RICHARD I.

MS. Sloane, 754, f. 2*b* :—MS. Harl., 2058, f. 4*b* (*Lat.*).

Fœdera, I. 67 :—cf. Hardy, *Syllabus*, p. 10 :—J. E., p. 8 :—Maitl., p. 56 :—Noort., p. 776 :—Luffm., p. 16.

VII. FIRST CHARTER OF JOHN.

MS. Harl., 1125, f. 1 :—Harl. 84, f. 37*b* :—MS. Sloane, 754, f. 3 :—MS. Soc. Antiq., 105, f. 3 :—MS. Harl., 2058, f. 5 (*Lat.*)

Fœdera, I. 76 :—*Fœdera* (Hague ed.) I. 36 :—Hardy, *Syll.*, p. 11 :—J. E., p. 9 :—Maitl., p. 73 :—Noort., p. 776 :—Luffm., p. 19.

---

[1] With these variations of witnesses :—"Th' Archiep'o Cant', R. ep'o London', Ph. ep'o Bai', Er' ep'o Oxon', Th' Cancella'io, R. de Novoburgo, T. de S'c'o Waleriano, R. de Waran', Walt' Mam'n', R. de Luci, Warino fil' Ger', Com' Man' Bigot Dapif', Jocio de Baliolo."

APPENDIX. 309

VIII. SECOND CHARTER OF JOHN.

MS. Sloane, 754, f. 4b :—MS. Harl., 1125, f. 5 :—MS. Harl., 2058, f. 5b.

J. E., p. 12 :—Maitl., p. 59 (Extract); p. 74 :— Noort., p. 777 :—Luffm. p. 23.

IX. THIRD CHARTER OF JOHN.

MS. Cott., Vespasian D. xvi, f. 59 (*Lat.*) :—MS. Sloane, 754, f. 4 :—MS. Harl., 1125, f. 3 :—MS. Harl., 2058, f. 5 (*Lat.*).

Riley, II. p. 251 :—J. E. p. 11 :—Maitl., p. 74 :— Noort., p. 777 —Luffm., p. 25.

X. FOURTH CHARTER OF JOHN.

MS. Sloane, 754, f. 5b :—MS. Harl., 1125, f. 7 :— MS. Harl., 2058, f. 5b (*Lat.*).

J. E., p. 14 :—Maitl. p. 75 :—Noort, p. 778 :— Luffm., p. 29.

XI. FIFTH CHARTER OF JOHN.[1]

MS. Hargrave, 142, ff. 3, 4 (9 May, *Lat.*) :—MS. Sloane 754, f. 5 :—MS. Harl., 1125, f. 6 :—MS. Harl., 2058, f. 5b (9 May).

J. E., p. 13 (19 May) :—Stubbs, p. 305, from Charter Rolls, p. 307 :—Maitl., p. 76 :—Noort., p. 778 (19 May) :—Luffm., p. 31 (19 May).

Charter of John to the City of London, recommending Isembert, Master of the School of Xainctes in France, to be employed in finishing the building of London Bridge, dated Molineux, Normandy, 18 April A.D. 1202[2], and other deeds relating to the bridge : in Maitland's *History*. Among them

[1] 9 May, A.D. 1214, and 9 May, A.D. 1215, both fall in the sixteenth regnal year of King John, who always commences his regnal year on the moveable feast of Ascension Day, as shown by Sir Harris Nicolas in his *Chronology of History*, pp. 289, 335 ; W. de G. Birch, *Regnal Years*, in *English Cyclopædia*, Art and Sciences *Supplement*, and other writers. The sixteenth year of John is included in the period 8 May 1214—27 May 1215. The *Itinerary of King John*, by Sir T. D. Hardy, shows that 9 May 1215 is the correct date, 19th May incorrect.

[2] Hardy, *Itin. K. John*.

brief for repairing bridge. *Walsingham*, 8 Jan. 9 Edw. I [A.D. 1281] :—and appointment of the tolls for three years. *Chester*, 6 July, 10 Edw. I [A.D. 1282].

XII. FIRST CHARTER OF HENRY III.

MS. Cott., Vespasian D. xvi, f. 63 (*Lat.*) :—MS. Cott., App. xi, ff. 1, 14*b* (*Lat.*) :—Inspex. in Add. MS. 4563, f. 189*b* :—MS. Lansd. 558, f. 207 (*Lat.*) :— MS. Harl. 2058, f. 6 (*Lat.*).

J. E., p. 15 :—Maitl. p. 79 :—Noort., p. 778 :— Luffm., p. 33.

XIII. SECOND CHARTER OF HENRY III.

MS. Cott., Vespasian D. xvi, f. 62 (*Lat.*) :—MS. Sloane 754, f. 6 :—Inspex. in Add. MS. 4563, f. 189*b* :—MS. Lansd. 558, f. 207*b* :—MS. Harl. 2058, f. 6.

Riley, p 46 :—J. E., p. 17 :—Stow. p, 450 (*Lat.*) : —Maitl. p. 80 :—Noort., p. 779 :—Luffm., p. 37.

XIV. THIRD CHARTER OF HENRY III.

MS. Cott., Vespasian D. xvi, ff. 60, 74 (*Lat.*) :—MS. Cott., App. xi, ff. 1*b*, 15 (*Lat.*).

J. E., p. 18 :—Maitl., p. 80 :—Noort., p. 780 :— Luffm., p. 39.

XV. FOURTH CHARTER OF HENRY III.

MS. Cott., Vespasian D. xvi, f. 74 (*Lat.*) :—MS. Cott., App. xi, ff. 2, 15*b* (*Lat.*) :—MS. Sloane 754, f. 6 :— Inspex. in MS. Lansd. 558,[1] f. 207*b* :—MS. Harl. 2058, f. 6*b* (*Lat.*).

Riley, p. 259 (*Lat.*) :—J. E., p. 19 :—Maitl., p. 80 : —Noort., p. 780 :—Luffm., p. 41.

XVI. FIFTH CHARTER OF HENRY III.

MS. Cott., Vespasian D. xvi, f. 59*b* ; 75 (*Lat.*) :—MS. Cott., App. xi, ff. 2*b* ; 16 (*Lat.*) :—MS. Sloane 754, f.

---

[1] With these variations of witnesses :—" D. Eustachio London', Jocelino Bathon', Ric'o Sar', et Petro Wynton' ep'is; Huberto de Burgo, Com' Cane', Justic' n'ro, Gilb'to de Clare, Com' Glouc' et Hertford', Rad'o fil' Nich'i et Ric'o de Argentein, sen' n'ris, Heu' de Capell' et aliis."

APPENDIX. 311

6 :—MS. Soc. Antiq., 105, f. 5 :—Inspex. in MS. Lansd. 558, f. 208*b* (*Lat.*) :—Add. MS. 4563, f. 189*b*. Riley, pp. 44, 261 (two texts) :—J. E., p. 20 :—Maitl., p. 81 :—Noort. p. 781 :—Luffm., p. 45.

XVII. QUEENHITHE CONFIRMATION CHARTER OF HENRY III.

MS. Harl., 2058, f. 7 (*Lat.*) :—MS. Sloane 754, f. 6*b*. Riley, pp. 46, 47 (*Lat.*) :—J. E., p. 21 :—Maitl., p. 86 :—Noort., p. 781 :—Luffm., p. 48.

XVIII. SIXTH CHARTER OF HENRY III.

MS. Cott., Vespasian D. xvi, f. 75 (*Lat.*) :—MS. Cott., App. xi, ff. 3*b*, 16*b* (*Lat.*) :—MS. Sloane 754, f. 7 :—MS. Harl., 2058, f. 7 (*Lat.*) :—Inspex. in MS. Lansd., f. 208*b* (*Lat.*) :—Add. MS. 4563, f. 189*b*. Riley, pp. 37, 262 (*Lat.*) :—J. E., p. 23 :—Maitl., p. 88 :—Noort., p. 782 :—Luffm., p. 50.

XIX. SEVENTH CHARTER OF HENRY III.

MS. Sloane, 754, f. 7*b* : —MS. Harl., 2058, f. 7 (*Lat.*) : —Maitl., p. 98, with extract from another charter, also in Luffm., p. 56 (see Introd.) :—Noort., p. 782 :— The text of the paragraph which I have marked in p. 161 as taking the place of No. XIX. in the Great Confirmation Charter of King Charles I, inspected by King Charles II, printed by J. E., is as follows :—

"Moreover we have seen a certain other Charter of the aforesaid Lord Henry, bearing date the eleventh day of January, in the fiftieth year of his reign, by which certain Charters, amongst other things, the said Lord Henry granted to the citizens of London, that the said citizens may traffick with their commodities and merchandizes wheresoever they please, throughout his kingdoms and dominions, as well by sea as by land, without interruption of him or his, as they see expedient; quit from all custom, tolls, and paying; and may abide for their trading wheresoever they please in the same his kingdom, as in times past they were accustomed, till such time it be more fully ordered by his counsel, touching the state of the city; as by the said letters patents among other things more fully appeareth." P. 24.

XX. EIGHTH CHARTER OF HENRY III.

MS. Cott.., Vespasian D. xvi, f. 60 (*Lat.*) :—MS. Cott., App. xi, ff. 3*b*; 17 (*Lat.*) :—MS. Sloane 754, f. 8*b* :—MS. Harl., 2058, f. 7*b* (*Lat.*) :—Inspex. in MS. Lansd. 558, f. 209 (*Lat.*) :—Add. MS. 4563, f. 189*b*. See a Charter dated 26 *May*, 52 Hen. III, quoted in an inspex. of 17 April, 27 Edw. I, MS. Cott., Vespasian D. xvi, f. 75*b* (*Lat.*).

Riley, pp. 251, 264 (*Lat.*) :—J. E., p. 24 :—Maitl., p. 99 :—Noort., p. 783 :—Luffm., p. 56.

Charter in J. E., p. 27, date 18 April, 16th year of Edw. I. A.D. 1288.

Magna Carta of Edward I, 12 October, 21st year, A.D. 1293, in MS. Harl., 2058, f. 9 (*Lat. Inspex.*).

XXI. CONFIRMATION CHARTER OF EDWARD I.

Stow, p. 452 (*Engl.*, second part only) :—cf. Riley, p. 266 (reads "pavage" for "pannage" in p. 44, l. 1 of this collection) (*Lat.*) :—Maitl., p. 108 :—Noort., p. 784 :—Luffm., p. 64-67.

See also Charters 17 April, 27th year, MS. Lansd., 558, ff. 209, 209*b*. confirmed, with others, at York, 8 June, 12 Edw. II, A.D. 1319 :—MS. Cott., App. xi, ff. 4*b*, 18 (*Lat.*) :— MS. Cott., Vespasian D. xvi, f. 76*b* (*Lat.*) :—Add. MS. 4563, f. 189 (Inspex.) 17 April and 26 May, 27 Edw I. :—See also MS. Sloane 754, f. 10, a Charter dated 12 October, 25 Edw. I, A.D. 1297, inspecting a Charter dated 11 February, 9 Hen. III, A.D. 1225 ; and another of Edw. I, not dated.

Brief to the assessors of the County of Oxford forbidding them to tax the citizens of London among the inhabitants of Henley to the tallage, 13 February, 6 Edw II, A.D. 1313 : —Maitl., p. 111.

XXII. CONSTITUTION OF EDWARD II.

MS. Lansd., 558, f. 210 (*Lat.*) :—MS. Harl., 2058, f. 9*b* (*Lat.*) both preceded by inspeximus of preceding Charters :—MS. Cott., Nero A. vi, f. 87*b* (*French*, with variation at the close of the text).

Riley, p. 268 (*Lat.*) :—Maitl., p. 115 (preceded by other documents of Edw. II) :—Noort., p. 785 :—Luffm., p. 67.

XXIII. CHARTER OF EDWARD II.

MS. Soc. Antiq., 105, f. 7.
J. E., p. 29 (" 5th year," in error) :—Maitl., p. 118 : —Noort., p. 787 :—Luffm., p. 78 :—Hartshorne, Itin. of Edw. II, in *Collectanea Archæologica, Brit. Arch. Assoc.*

Charter " de perdonatione," by Edward III, 28 February, 1st year, A.D. 1327, MS. Cott., Faustina B.I., f. 211 (*Lat.*) :— MS., Lansd., 558, f. 211 (*Lat.*) dat. 29 February, 1st year.

Charter " de adnullatione obligationum" by Edward III, 4 March, 1st year, A.D. 1327, MS. Cott., Faustina B.I., f. 211*b* (*Lat.*) ; and MS. Lansd., 558, f. 218*b* (*Lat.*).

XXIV. FIRST CHARTER OF EDWARD III.

MS. Cott., App. xi, f. 7*b* (*Lat.*) :—MS. Cott., Faustina B.I., f. 212 (*Lat.*) :—MS. Cott., Nero A. vi,[1] f. 104 (*Lat.*) :—MS. Soc. Antiq., 105 :—MS. Harl., 2058, f. 10*b* (*Lat.*) :—MS. Lansd., 558, f. 219 (*Lat.*, imperfect).

J. E., p. 29 :—Maitl., p. 120 :—Noort., p. 787 :— Luffm., p. 80.

XXV. SECOND CHARTER OF EDWARD III.

MS. Cott., App. xi, f. 10 (*Lat.*) :—MS. Cott., Faustina B.I., f. 214 (*Lat.*) :—MS. Lansd., 558, f. 218*b* (*Lat.*) :—MS. Harl., 2058, f. 14 (*Lat.*).

Riley, p. 435 (*Lat.*) :—J. E., p. 35 :—Maitl., p. 122 :—Noort., p. 789 :—Luffm., p. 94.

[1] With the following full list of witnesses :—" W[alter Reynolds], Archbishop of Canterbury, Primate of all England ; J[ohn Hotham], Bishop of Ely, our chancellor ; A[dam de Orleton], Bishop of Hereford, our Treasurer ; W[illiam Ayremyn], Bishop of Norwich ; Thomas [Plantagenet], Earl of Norfolk and Marshal of England ; Ed[mund Plantagenet], Earl of Kent ; Henry [Plantagenet], Earl of Lancaster ; Roger de Mortnomari (Mortimer), of Wygemore ; Thomas de Wake ; John de Roos, Steward of our household, and others. Given by our hand at Westminster, 6 March, first year of our reign [A.D. 1327].

Charter "de pesagio," by Edward III, 20 March, 1st year, A.D. 1327, MS. Cott., App. xi, f. 12 (*French*) :—and MS. Cott., Faustina B.I., f. 215 (*French*), followed by several other documents not included in the present collection.

XXVI. THIRD CHARTER OF EDWARD III.

MS. Cott., App. xi, f. 10*b* (*Lat.*) :—MS. Harl., 2058, f. 11*b* (*Lat.*).

J. E., p. 36 :—Maitl., p. 124 :—Noort., p. 790 :— Luffm., p. 96, with another called a Confirmation or Fourth Charter, p. 99.

XXVII. FOURTH CHARTER OF EDWARD III.

MS. Cott., App. xi, f. 11 (*Lat.*) :—MS. Harl., 2058, f. 13*b* (*Lat.*) :—MS. Soc. Antiq., 105, f. 7*b*.

J. E., p. 37 :—Maitl., p. 128 :—Noort., p. 790 :— Luffm., p. 100 (called *Fifth*).

XXVIII. FIFTH CHARTER OF EDWARD III.

MS. Cott., App. xi, f. 11*b* (22 Nov. 50=37 F. Edward III) (*Lat.*).

Maitl., p. 132 :—Noort., p. 791 :—Luffm., p. 102 (called *Sixth*).

XXIX. SIXTH CHARTER OF EDWARD III.

J. E., p. 38 :—Maitl., p. 133 :—Noort., p. 791 :— Luffm., p. 105 (called *Seventh*).

Richard II's Charter of Inspeximus of several foregoing Charters. MS. Cott., App. xi, f. 14 (*Lat.* and *Fr.*). The date is 4 December, 1 Ric. II, A.D. 1377. Cf. MS. Harl. 2058, f. 15 :—Luffm., p. 111.

XXX. CHARTER OF RICHARD II.

Cf. Noort., p. 792 :—Luffm., p. 109 :—MS. Bodl. Barlow 15, entitled "Charta Libertatum Civitatis Londoniæ", 26 November, 7 Ric. II, A.D. 1383 :— Maitl., pp. 143, 144 :—Luffm., p. 109.

APPENDIX.

XXXI. PROCLAMATION BY THE MAYOR.

Maitl., p. 144 :—Noort., p. 793.

Charter of Henry VI, apparently unfinished and without date, MS. Harl. 1125, f. 8.

XXXII. FIRST CHARTER OF EDWARD IV.

MS. Harl., 2058, f. 19 (*Lat.*) :—MS. Harl., 1125, f. 17. J. E., p. 41 :—Maitl., p. 200 :—Noort., p. 793 :— Luffm., p. 115.

XXXIII. SECOND CHARTER OF EDWARD IV.

MS. Harl. 2058. f. 20*b* (*Lat.*) :—MS. Harl., 1125, f. 27. J. E., p. 50 :—Maitl., p. 204 :—Noort., p. 797 :— Luffm., p. 134.

XXXIV. THIRD CHARTER OF EDWARD IV.

MS. Harl., 2058, f. 21 (*Lat.*) :—MS. Harl., 1125, f. 28. J. E., p. 51 :—Maitl. p. 208 :—Noort., p. 797 :— Luffm., p. 137.

XXXV. FOURTH CHARTER OF EDWARD IV.

J. E., p. 53 :—Maitl., p. 209 :—Noort., p. 798 :— Luffm., p. 141.

XXXVI. REGULATIONS IN HENRY VII's CHARTER.

J. E., p. 56 :—Maitl., p. 221 :—Noort., p. 799.

Charter of Inspeximus by Henry VIII, inspecting Henry VII's inspeximus of several foregoing Charters. MS. Harl., 2058, f. 4, etc.

XXXVII. FIRST CHARTER OF HENRY VIII.

J. E., p. 58 :—Maitl., p. 226 :—Noort., p. 800 ; Luffm., p. 151.

XXXVIII. SECOND CHARTER OF HENRY VIII.

J. E., p. 59 :—Maitl., p. 230 :—Noort., p. 801 :— Luffm., p. 153.

APPENDIX.

XXXIX. ACT OF COMMON COUNCIL.
Maitl., p. 64 :—Noort., p. 803.

XL. CHARTER OF EDWARD VI.
MS. Harl., 1125, f. 30 (with additional paragraph of ratification at the end).
J. E., p. 64 :—Maitl., p. 242 :—Noort., p. 804 :—Luffm., p. 164.

XLI. PROCLAMATION BY ELIZABETH.
Maitl., p. 264 :—Noort., p. 810, etc.

XLII. FIRST CHARTER OF JAMES I.
J. E., p. 80 :—Maitl., p. 284 :—Noort., p. 811 :—Luffm., p. 196.

XLIII. SECOND CHARTER OF JAMES I.
J. E., p. 85 :—Maitl., p. 290 :—Noort., p. 813 :—Luffm., 206.

XLIV. THIRD CHARTER OF JAMES I.
J. E., p. 95 :—Maitl., 295 :—Noort., p. 817 :—Luffm., p. 226.

XLV. FIRST CHARTER OF JAMES I.
J. E., p. 102 :—Maitl., p. 308 :—Noort., p. 820 :—Luffm., p. 239.

XLVI. SECOND CHARTER OF JAMES I.
J. E., p. 134 :—Maitl., p. 322 :—Noort., p. 832 :—Luffm., p. 303.

XLVII. CONFIRMATION CHARTER BY CHARLES II.
J. E., prints the whole Charter *in extenso;* see p. 174, for the ratificatory clauses :—Maitl., p. 429 :—Noort., p. 845 :—Luffm., p. 340.

XLVIII. PROCLAMATION BY CHARLES II.
Maitl., p. 438 :—Noort., p. 846, etc

APPENDIX. 317

XLIX. CONFIRMATION OF ORDER OF COMMON COUNCIL.
Maitl., p. 443 :—Noort., p. 848, etc.

L. ACT OF COMMON COUNCIL FOR PAVING.
Maitl., p. 452 :—Noort., p. 850, etc.

LI. ACT OF COMMON COUNCIL REGULATING WOOL MARKETS.
Maitl., p. 462 :—Noort., p. 855, etc.

Arguments in the suit concerning the Charter, A.D. 1683. MS. Harl., 2206 :—MS. Hargrave, 153, and other numbers in the Hargrave Collections.

LII. STATUTE OF WILLIAM AND MARY.
Maitl., p. 492 :—Noort., p. 860 :—Luffm., p. 346.

LIII. ACT OF GEORGE I.
Maitl., p. 534:—Noort., p. 863, etc., etc.

LIV. CHARTER OF GEORGE II.
J. E., Appendix :—Noort., p. 868 :—Luffm., 360, etc.

LV. ACT CONCERNING ELECTION OF SHERIFFS.
Noort., p. 869, etc., etc.

LVI. ACT OF COMMON COUNCIL.
Maitl., p. 664:—Noort., p. 373, etc., etc.

Many other copies of the foregoing Charters and Documents may be collected without difficulty—and more particularly of the later ones—but those tabulated above are sufficient to point out to the student the most useful texts. Subjoined are a few notes from the Record Edition of the *Statutes of the Realm*, relating to London.

Liberties confirmed. *Magna Charta*, cap. 9, 14 Edw. III, stat. I, cap. 1; stat. II, cap. 2.
Regulations for peace—securing of offenders ; Foreigners not to be Innkeepers nor Brokers. Stat. Civ. Lond., 13 Edw. I.
Regulation of Sale of Victuals. 31 Edw. III, stat. I, cap. 10 ; 42 Edw. III, cap. 7.

Statute of Labourers extended to London. 31 Edw. III, stat. I, cap. 7.

Preservation of Salmon in the River Thames. 17 Ric. II, cap. 9.

Aldermen not to be removed without cause. 17 Ric. II, cap. 11.

Citizens may carry wares to any Fair or Market. 3 Henry VII, cap. 10.

Jurisdiction of Mayor over Thames. 4 Henry VII, cap. 15.

Among manuscripts and special works concerning the Charters of London, in various libraries and not already pointed out, may be mentioned the following titles:—

MS. Trin. Coll., Oxon., No. 82 (2019). *An extract of the several Charters and Privileges from the Conquest down to Henry VI. Granted to the City of London.*

MS. Yelverton, xx (5259). Now in possession of Lord Calthorp. *The Charter of London granted and confirmed by divers Kings,* f. 197.

Ditto. Vol. XXXII (5271). *A monument of all the Charters, etc., granted to the Mayor, Commonalty, and Citizens of London by all the Kings successively from William I to Queen Elizabeth,* f. 1-140. *Beneficial Charters granted to the City of London by King Henry VI, King Edward IV, and King Henry VII, not confirmed by Parliament,* f. 152.

Bishop More's MS. (Public Library, Cambridge), 243. *Extract de Chart. Civitatis London.*

Charters of London, MS., Trinity College, Dublin. Fourth Report Historical Commission, p. 598.

"*Privilegia Londini:* or the Rights, Liberties, Privileges, Laws, and Customs of the City of London, wherein are contained, 1. The several Charters granted to the said City," etc. By W. Bohun, of the Middle Temple, Esquire. 1723. Third Edition. This work contains *précis* of most of the Charters included in this series, and some valuable notes on the meaning of the words occurring in them, as well as much general information on the subject of the Charters, Laws, and Customs of London.

INDEX,

GLOSSARY, NOTES, AND CORRECTIONS.

The following abbreviations have been used :—

[B.] Boyer : *French Dictionary.*
[C.] Cunningham : *Law Dictionary.*
[D.] Dugdale : *Monasticon Anglicanum.*
[G.] S. F. Gray : *Supplement to the Pharmacopœia*, ed. Redwood.
[H.] J. O. Halliwell : *Archaic Dictionary.*
[Haydn] : *Book of Dates,* and *Book of Dignities.*
[J.] Jacobs : *Law Dictionary.*
[N.] Sir H. Nicolas : *Synopsis of the Peerage.*
[P.] Bohun's *Privilegia Londini.*
[R.] H. T. Riley : *Liber Albus,* and *Liber Custumarum, Rolls Series.*
[V.] Virtue : *Gazetteer.*

The names of persons are under the Christian names.

Acquittal of murder, *i.e.*, that the place where it was committed should not be fined or amerced though the murderer escaped, 5, 11, 39. *Murder* signifies not only crime, but the pecuniary result or punishment due for that crime. [P.]; [J.E.]
Acquittals, 83, 119
Act regulating election of sheriff, 205
—— for licensing foreigners to work in the city, 305
Ad quod damnum, 88, 89, 178, 197. A writ authorising the sheriff to inquire *what damage* a grant may do to others
Aids, 46, 49
Albemarle, George Monk, Duke of, 231
Aldermanston, co. Berks, 51
Aldermen, election of, 46, 65
—— taxation of, 49
—— maces of, 63
—— to be justices, 75, 290
—— exemption from certain duties, 79, 80
—— duties of, as justices, 84, 169, *et seq.*
—— to survey ruins after the great fire, 229
Aldersgate ward, 248
Aldgate ward, 248
Ale-houses, suppression of, 174
Alicante wine, 215
Aliens, 201, *et seq.*
Alloficatrina (? Aloe Socotrina), 212
Almaine, High ; merchants of, 69, 79
Almaines, Guildhall of the, 79
Almonds, 217
Alum, or Allum, 101, 103, 212, 219
Alured of Toteneys, witness to charter of Henry I., 4
Amber, vessels of, 91

Ambergrease, 212
Amerciaments, 4, 5, 7, 11, 12, 15, 16, 22, 28, 82, 83, 117, 118, 119, 121, 172, 174, *et seq.* Pecuniary penalty [J.E.]. An arbitrary and pecuniary penalty which was inflicted " at the mercy" of the Court, whereas a fine was a certain penalty. There was a difference between a " misericordia" and an " amercement" ; the penalty being called by the latter name after it had been reduced to a certain sum by being assessed, and a " misericordia" both before and afterwards. Norton also (*Constit. City of London*, p. 371) is of opinion that the being " amerced" and the being " in mercy" were different; the real derivation of the word " amercement" being from " merces," and its genuine signification a " mulct admeasured," or " affeered". On close examination, however, it will be found that these distinctions can hardly be supported. Madox, *Hist. Excheq.*, who has devoted a chapter to this subject; also Thorpe's *Ancient Laws and Instit. of England*, Glossary, s.v. Misericordia. Mercia was an amercement, inflicted upon a hundred for murders or other offences there committed. [R.]
Amotto, 212 ; probably the same as arnetto, 216
Andely, Isle of, in Normandy (Hardy, *Itin. of King John*), 10
Andirons, 212. Ornamental irons on each side of the hearth with rests for the ends of the logs. [H.]
Anniseeds, 213, 217
" Antelope, The", in Southwark, grant of, 112

INDEX.

Anthony Widvile, second Earl Rivers, chief butler of England, 92
Apparel, sale of, etc., 184
Apples, 133, 135, 137, 212
Apprentices, 47, 186, 188, 189, *et seq.*
—— none to be taken for less than seven years, 189
Aqua vitæ, 212, 216
Archbishop of Canterbury, privileges of the,'122
—— Gilbert Sheldon, 231
Arching, recommending in rebuilding, 227
Argil, 212; argal, 216; argal, hard lees sticking to the sides of wine vessels and, other wine called *tartar* [G.] [H.], but probably here used for the famous dye *archil*, from the Rocella tinctoria. [G.]
Arlington, Henry Bennet, first Baron, 231
Armed companies, 171
Arnetto. *See* Amotto
Arnulph, Bishop of Lisieux, witness to charter of Henry II, 6
Arrest, 83
Ashley, Sir Anthony Cooper, first Baron Ashley, 231
Ashes, pot, and sope, 216
Assa-fœtida, a gum-resin, 216
Assay (trial or proof) and assise of bread, etc., 82
Assize of bread, etc., 118
Assise, assessment, or fixing of price of provisions. The power of making the assize of victuals within the City of London lay in general with the civic authorities, but in other instances it was effected by proclamation immediately enjoined by the sovereign. [R.]
Assaia Panis. Assay of bread; the right of proving its weight and quality. [R.]
Attach, to take or apprehend by commandment of a writ or precept. [C], 59. Attachment, a summary process issuing against a person for contempt of court. [C.], 71, 87, 119. Attachment differs from "arrest" in that the latter is only upon the body of a man; the former sometimes on his body, and sometimes on his goods. [R.]
Averdupois, 103, 183, 184; explanation of the word, 61
Averia ponderis, fine goods, or *avoirs-du-poys*, goods weighed by the pound weight. Thus called because weighed by the small balance in ascertaining the duties upon them; and not by the king's great beam, or tron, which was used for weighing coarse goods by the hundredweight; goods sold by the hundredweight, as wax, alum, and the like, were weighed by the king's beam; but other wares, which are valued by *the pound*, such as pepper, ginger, brasil, grains (of paradise), and the like, were wont to be weighed by the measures and balances in the hostelers' houses, or else (to be valued) by the basket. In the *Nominale* of the 15th century (Wright's *Vol. Vocab.*, p. 227), this word, given in Latin as "ponderale", appears under the form of "haburdepays, whence probably our expression *haberdasher* of "small wares", though it seems much more likely that the word is derived from the cloth called "hapertas". [R.]
Awl blades, 216. [B.]

B.

Babies' heads, (dolls), 212. [H.]
Bacon, 212
Badger skins, 216, 217
Bailiff of London, 6, 8
Bailiffs, 88, 165. A bailiff, superior officer, or judge; in early times, the sheriffs of London and Middlesex were commonly thus called, and not improbably under this name the mayor was included. Baillifs de la Cite, sheriffs of the City of London. [R.]
Baize, 251, 252, 259
—— Devonshire, 263; minakin, 264
Balance of weight, 99, 102, 103, 104
—— the common, and the great, 183
Bale, a, 216
Balo, the, in Southwark, 113
Bales of tin, 201, *et seq.*
Balliage, 201, *et seq.*
Baltic merchants company, 189
Band strings, 212. Strings going across the breast for tying in an ornamental way. [H.]
Barilla, 212, 216. Impure soda made by burning sea weeds, chiefly of the genus Salsola, in Spain and the Levant. [G.]
Barley, 212
Barlings, 212; firepoles. [H.]
Barmillion fustain, 213
Barns, 112
Barons of Exchequer, 34, 43, 44, 179, 186
Barrel boards, 212
Basherows, 212. Bashrone, a kettle. [H.]
Basket rods, 212, 220
Bassishaw ward, 248
Bastard children, maintenance of, 174
Bast ropes, 212; bast straw [H.], or bark of the Tilia intermedia. [G.]
Bastards, wine, 215
Bath, John Granville, seventh Earl of, 231. [N.]
Battery. *See* basherows, 212
Battle, to wage, 357. *See* Wager Battle
Bays (stuff), 218
Beadle of the Court of Requests, 191
Beans, 212
Beasts, offal of, 246
Beaver hats, 213, 217
Beaver skins, 216, 217
Bed rugs, 259
Beef, 212
Beer, 82, 118, 215, 216
Beggars, regulation concerning, 237
Bell-metal, 212
Berkshire, Thomas Howard, second Earl of, 231
Bermondsey, monastery of; grant of lands, etc., late belonging to, 113, 116, 122
Bertram de Kyriolle, witness to charter of Henry III, 35
Bethlehem hospital, 192, *et seq.*
Bever furs, 213. *See* Beaver
Bewpers, 260
Bickshoar wharf, 209
Billingsgate, 162
—— ward, 248
Birding shot, 216
Bishopsgate wards, 248
Blackfriars, exemption of inhabitants, 144, 145, 149. The black or preaching friars of London came, shortly after A.D. 1221, on the west side of Chancery lane, on or near the present site

INDEX.

of Lincoln's inn ; afterwards they acquired ground near Castle Baynard, within the city, where they built a handsome church and convent. The liberties were retained for some time after the dissolution. [D. vi, p. 1487.]
Blacking, 212, 220
Blackman street, Southwark, 117
Blackwall wharf, 209
Blackwell hall, 251, 252, et seq.
Blank sterling money, 15, 21. Blanci, white money or sterling, was silver melted down or *blanched*, to ascertain its fineness or freedom from alloy. Hence a payment in "blank" or "blanched" money meant a payment of so many pounds of blanched and genuine silver. In practice, however, it was the custom to melt down but a small part of the silver coin paid upon any particular occasion into the King's exchequer; if satisfactory, the goodness of the rest, as "blank" money, was taken for granted. See Madox, *Hist. Excheq.*, i, p. 275. [R.]
Blankets, 252, 260, 264
"Blue Mead," The, in Southwark, 11
Boards, clap and pipe, 212, 219 ; boards cut to make casks. [H.]
Bolonia, silk, 214
Bolters, kind of cloth for sifting flour, 260
Bombassins, 212
Bones, 220
Bonneville-sur-Toncque, in Normandy (see Hardy, *Itin. of K. John*), 17
Bonny spars, 215, 219, ? rafters [H.]
Books, 212, 216
Boradoes, silks, 214. Perhaps same as next entry.
Borattos, 212. Bombasin [H.]
Bottles, 212, 216
Boundaries of city, 143
Bow-staves, 212
Brabant linen, 213, 217
Brass work, 212
Brazaletto-wood, wood of the *Picramnia antidesma*, used to dye red [G.], 215
Brazil-wood, wood of the *Cæsalpina Braziliensis*, etc. ; a red dye-wood [G.], 215, 218, 219
Bread-street ward, 248
Bread, assise of, 82, 118. See Assise
Brewers, houses of, 229
Bricklayers, 107
—— regulations of, 247
Bridge masters, 49
—— election of, 276
Bridge ward, 248
Bridge House, masters of the, 114
Bridgewater, John Egerton, third Earl of, 231. [N.]
Bridgewater stuffs, 218
Bridtoll, 6, 8, 12, 29. Bridtol, or Bridtoll, or Bridge toll, money paid for passing a bridge. [J. E.]
Brimstone, 212, 216, 220
Bristles, 212
Bristol carpets, 260
—— stuffs, 218
Broadcloth, 259
Broad-street ward, 248

Brogger, a badger who deals in corn, 200 [H.]
Broken wharf, 248
Brokers (broccatores), 49, 67, 68, 69, 200, 258. Those that contrive bargains for a fee [C.]
Buckromes, 212 ; buckrams, 216
Buckweed, probably buckwheat. *Polygonum fagopyrum* [G.]
Bruges, commodities from, 214, 215
Brushes, 216
Budge, lamb's fur, 213 [C. H.],
Buffins, a kind of coarse cloth, 212, 218 [H.]
Buildings in London, proclamation against, by Qn. Elizabeth, 128
Bulrushes, 212, 220
Bunbill, 248
Burgage, free, 178. Burgage, a tenure proper to cities and towns, whereby they hold their lands and tenements of the king or other person for a certain yearly rent
Burs for millstones, 212, 219
Bustians, a coarse cloth, perhaps the same as fustian, 264 [H.]
Bustins (cloths), 259 [H.]
Butler of England, office of, 92
Butter, search and survey of, 142, 212
Buttons, 216

C.

Cabinets, 212
Cable ropes, 212
Caddas, 212, 215, 218. There seems to have been a kind of woollen stuff, so called, used for stuffing dresses [H.]
Caddows for beds, 259. Perhaps same as preceding word.
Caff, silk, 214. Perhaps taffata [H.]
Calais, 167
Callicoes, 213, 214
Calves' skins, 91, 201, *et seq.*; 216, 218
Camblets, 218
Cambricks, 213, 217
Cametians, 218. (? Camelyne) [H.]
Campecha cochinele, 212, 216
Canary seed, 216
Canary wine, 215, 218
Candles, 212
Candleweeks, 212
Candlewick ward, 248
Candy sugar, 217
Canes, 212
Canterbury, 251 ; possessions of the archbishopric, and bishopric, 115, 116
Canvas, various, 214, 215
Capers, 212
Capite, tenures in, 195, 196; or "*in chief*", were held immediately of the king as of his Crown, by knight's service or socage, and not as of any honour, castle, or manor. Abolished by the Act 12 Chas. II.
Capravans, 212
Caps, 216
Caraway seeds, 212
Cards, 212
Carlisle, Charles Howard, fourth Earl of, 231
Carmen, regulations of the fellowship of, 241
Carpets, 212
Carpetings, 252, 260, 261
Carral, 218, fustian cloth [H.]
Carratel, a measure, 219

Y

322   INDEX.

Carrier, 206
Cassia, various, 216
Castle (Castile) soap, 218
Castles, 167
Castle Baynard ward, 248
Catalapha silk, 214
Catling lutestrings, 213
Cats, dead, 246
—— skins, 216, 218
Cellars, 176
—— benefit of, 227
Chaces, or huntings, 4, 6, 8, 12, 29, 30. The chase was of a middle nature between a forest and a park; like the former it was open, but had no courts of attachment, swainmote, or justice-seat; while it was of larger compass than the latter, provided with more keepers, and stored with a greater variety of beasts of chase and game. [R.]
Chafingdishes, 212
Chamberlain, Lord; Robert Bertie, Earl of Lindsey, 231 [Haydn]
——, the king's chamberlain, 49, 264. In early times the chamberlain of the city was also an officer of the King. He collected the customs from foreign merchants, and accounted for them at the Exchequer; and he also took to the king's use the duties on tonnage, tolls for passing through the city gates, prisage of wines, and sometimes escheats. [R.]
Chamberlain, duties of the, 189
—— election of, 272, 276
Chamberlainship of London reserved, called Skamberlengeria, correctly "Camberlengeria", 19, 24. In early times the chamberlain of London was an officer of the king, and payments were made to him in the king's behalf. Hence, the term "Camberlengeria Londoniarium", technically used to signify the King's prisage on wines. [R.]
Chamlets, Camelot [H.], 212, 214
Chancellor, 181, 182, 184
—— Lord, Sir Edward Hyde, Earl of Clarendon, 231
—— of the Duchy, Mr.; Charles, Lord Seymour of Trowbridge, 231
Charles I, first charter of, 159; second charter of, 201; charters of, confirmed by Charles II, 221
Charles II, confirmation charter of, 221; proclamation prohibiting buildings after the great fire, 224; note of, 231; deeds of, annulled, 268; letters patent of, referred to, 290, 291; reversal of the judgment against the city in his reign, 266
Charles Brandon, Duke of Suffolk, 111; lands of, 114, 116
—— notice of, 122
Charter, the Great, of England, to be observed, 62; charters confirmed by Charles II, 221; charters, restoration of, 267
Chattels, all goods of the nature of freehold, 112, 149 [C.]
—— sale of, 184 et seq.
Cheap, 162
Cheap ward, 248
Cheapside, breadth of, 227
Cheese, search and survey of, 142, 212, 219

Cherries, 212
Childwite, 6, 8, 12, 29, 40. The same as leirwite or lecherwite, i.e., money paid, as a punishment for corrupting a bondmaid. [J. E.] Childwite is a fine taken of a bond-woman for suffering herself to be got with child without consent of her lord and master [Maitland]. The penalty for begetting a bastard on a lord's bondwoman. The wite was, under the A.-S. system, the fine paid to the magistrate of the district; whereas the were was the sum paid in compensation to the party injured. [R.]
Chiltre, chaces in, 4. Part of the county of Hertford, about St. Albans [J. E.] The district now known as the "Chilterns", a range of hills commencing in Oxford, and running across Buckingham into Bedford, near Dunstable. The whole of this district was formerly covered with wood, and in it, from the days of Henry I, by royal charter, the citizens of London had right of hunting. The name is derived by Camden from the British "cylt", or "chilt", chalk. "Chylturne grounde and flyntye grounde be light groundes, and dry and full of small stones, and chalke grounde is moche of the same nature." Fitzherbert's Surveyenge, 1539. [R.]
Chimney backs, 220
China roots, 212. The rhizoma of Smilax China eaten as an invigorating medicine [G.]
China silk, 214
Chirograph, 33. A public conveyance or deed of gift [J. E.] It consisted of a script and rescript, or part and counterpart, written upon one sheet divided in the middle with indentations; the letters of the alphabet, or the word "chirographum", in capital letters, being written between the two copies in the place where the severance was made [R.]
Christ's hospital, duties of the officers, 238 et seq., 258, 261, 262, 264, 265
"Christopher", The, in Southwark, 114
Chrystal glass, 213
Cinnamon, 213, 215, 217
Circot, a messuage so called, 115. A surcoat. [H.]
Circuits, 53, 54, 56, 57, 58, 97, 98
Cisterns, 176
Civet, 212
Clapboards, 212, 219. Boards cut to make casks. [H.] See Boards
Clerk of the Court of Requests, 190
—— of the market, 55, 122
Clerkenwell, 33
Cloaks, 216
Cloth, 212, 216, 218; measures of, 216
—— various; markets of, 251, et seq.
Cloves, 213, 215, 217
Coals, 215, measuring of, 133, et seq.
—— measuring of and tax on, 151, et seq.
—— application of money arising from dues of, 235
Cobweb laws, 216 (? misty) [H.]
Cochinele, 212, 216
"Cock", The, a timber-house so called, 232

INDEX. 323

Cod-fish, 212
Coffer, a measure, 216
Cold Herberge, Harburgh, or Herburg lane, 143, 147, 149
Colman-street ward, 248
Combs, 212, 217
Comin seeds, 212. Cumin [G.]
Commissioners of Sewers, 176
Commodities, fees due on various, 212, et seq.
Commons, 112, 176
Common balance, keeping of the, 183
Common bench, L. C. Justice of, 181, 182, 184, 186
Common clerk, 49
Common council, Act of, concerning navigation of the Thames, 106; order of, for new foundations after the fire, 231; Act of, for paving and cleansing streets of London and of the liberties, 235; Act of, 251
Common-rakers, 108
Common serjeant, 49
Companies, merchant, 189
—— incorporation of, 272; to give lists of the liverymen to the mayor, 282
Comptroller, Mr., 231
Conduits, 176
Coney hair, 217
Coneyskins, 216, 217, 218
Conservation of the water of the Thames, 132, et seq.
Conservancy of Thames, 175
Constable of Tower, 43, 55
Conspiracy, 172
Copper, 212
Copperas, 212, 216, 219
Coral, 212
Cordovant skins, 214; Spanish leather from Cordova. Also spelt cordewayne. [H.]
Cordwainer ward, 248
Corks, 212, 220
Cornhill, breadth of, 227
—— ward, 248
Coroner, 88, 165, et seq.
—— office of, 92
—— of Southwark, 121
Corporations, incorporation of, 272
Corrody, a defalcation from an allowance or salary for some other than the original purpose, 126
Cotton wool, 251, 252
Court leet, 112. A court for the election of officers. [C.]
—— leets, 125
—— of requests, 190, 191; also called a "court of conscience," first instituted in the reign of Henry VII, 1493, and remodelled by Henry VIII, 1517, according to Stow, for the summary recovery of small debts under forty shillings, but in the City of London the jurisdiction extends to debts of five pounds. [Haydn.]
Court of conscience, fees due to the, 200
Coventry cloths, 251
Coverlets, 260
Craven, William Craven, first Earl of, 231
Creedchurch street, 143
Crier, common, of Southwark, 184, et seq.
Cripplegate wards, 248
Crocard, a spurious coin, so called from its crookedness, resulting from extreme thinness. [R.]
Croplings, fish, 212
Crowfield linen, 213
"Crown" The, in Southwark, 114
Cruel, fine worsted [H.], 251, 252, 255, 260; ribbons, 212, 218
Cubebs, 216. Piper cubeba. [G.]
Currants, 213, 217, 219
Cushions, 260
Customs, 40, 44, 52, 53, 83; manner of pleading, 186-7; restoration of, 267
Cypress (Cyprus) silk, 214

D.

Damasellours, or damasins, 218
Damask linen, 217; silk, 214
Danegeld, 3. This tax, first levied by Ethelred II, as a payment to propitiate the Danish invaders, was continued in active force so late as the reign of Henry II, and is mentioned in a charter of the 15th Henry III. For an elaborate account of it, see Madox, Hist. Excheq., i, pp. 685-693. [R.] A tax imposed on our Saxon ancestors by King Æthelred, first of one, then of two shillings on every hide of land, for clearing the seas of Danish pirates that then infested our coasts. This was given to the Danes on terms of peace and departure, who received at first £10,000, then £16,000, then £24,000, then £34,000, and at last £48,000, Henry I and Stephen released them finally from paying this tax. [J.E.]
Darnix, 260. A coarse damask used for carpets, curtains, etc. [H.]
Dates, 217
Deal-boards, 219
Dewarrenning of Staines, 7
Deawarennare, to unwarren, or diswarren; to throw open what has hitherto been preserved as a warren, 7. [R.]
Debts, recovery of small, 190
—— enrolling of, 41
Debtors to citizens, 4
Demy-caster hats, 213, 217
Denizens, 201, et seq.
Deodand, 117. Anything which causes a man's death, forfeited to the king. A deodand, or gift to God, is a personal chattel that has been the immediate cause of the death of a human being, which was forfeited to the king, to be applied by him to pious uses. It is only at a recent period that deodands have been abolished. [R.]
Deorman, king's homo, charter grant to, 2
Deptford wharf, 209
Deputies of sheriffs, 48
Devonshire baize, 259, 263
—— cloths, 218; packs of cloth, 262
Diaper linen, 213, 217
Dimity, 218, 259, 264
Discharge, 39. Disrationare, to deraign, or dereyn, i.e., to discharge or clear one's self of an accusation. The word "rationes" was used for a legal account of one's actions; whence derationare and disrationare. Fr. desrener, "to darraign", to clear the legal account, to answer an accusation. Wedg-

Y 2

wood's *Dict. Engl. Etym.*, i, p. 138. Spelman gives a number of significations representing the Fr. "desrener" or "deraisnier", there can be little doubt that its primary meaning is, to disprove the case of an opponent, and its necessary result, to prove one's own. See Hearne's Glossary to R. de Brunne's Translation of Langtoft's *Chronicle*, p. 564. [R.]

Distress, 108; the thing taken or distrained upon any land for rent or other duty, or for hurt done. [C.]

Dogs of earth, 212. Pitchers [H.]

Dogs, dead, 246

Dog-stones, 215, 219. Gilt buttons. [H.]

Dorsetshire baize, 259

Dorcester, Harry Pierrepoint, Marquis of, 231. [N.]

Dovehouses, 112

Dowgate dock, 235, 248

—— ward, 248

Dregs of ale and beer, 246

Drugs, 212

Duke's-place, 143, 147, 149

—— ward, 248

Dunghill lane, 248

Durance of duretty, 212, 218. Durance: a kind of durable stuff made with thread or silk. [H.]

Duretty, 212. Same as durance. [H.]

Dust and rubbish, rules for the removal of, 241, *et seq.*

Dutch baize, 259; commodities, 214, 217; yarn, 215

Dyers, houses of, 228

—— wood, 216

E.

Easement, 176. A service which one neighbour has of another by charter or agreement without payment. [C.]

East-Greenwich, manor of, 125

East-India wood, 215

Easter, close of; (the Sunday after Easter), 33

Ebony, 218

Edward, the Confessor, 52

Edward, son of Henry III, offences of the city against him, 36, 37, same personage as Edward, Prince, witness to charter of Henry III, 42, and

Edward I, extracts from charter of, 43; confirmation of his charter, 161; reference to a statute of A.D. 1275, 199

Edward II, constitutions of, 45; charter of, 51; reference to, 56, 65; reference to charter of, 101; confirmation of his charter, 161

Edward III, first charter of, 52; second, 59; third, 61; fourth, 63; fifth, 65; sixth, 67; reference to charters of, 80, 97; confirmation of his charters, 161; reference to a statute of, 190

Edward IV, first charter of, 74; second, 85; third, 87; fourth, 90; confirmation of his charters, 162; reference to charters of, 202

Edward VI, grant of the manor of, and lands in, Southwark, 110; confirmation of his charter, 163

Eeles, 212

Eeles, stubb, 219

Elephants' teeth, 216

Elizabeth, proclamation of, against new buildings, 128; reference to a statute of, 186

Elk-skins, 218

Embden linen, 213, 217

Emery-stone, 219

Enchantment, 171, 172

Encroachments, 179

Engrossers, 148

Engrossing, 171, 172

Escheator, 55, 73, 82, 83, 88

—— mayor to be an, 122, 165 *et seq.*, 196. An officer who looked after the lands and profits that fell into the king within his manor, either by forfeiture or death. The escheator was appointed in every county to make inquest of titles by escheat; such inquests to be taken by good and lawful men of the county, empannelled by the sheriff. [R.]

Escheats, 117

Essex, charter addressed to the thanes of, 2

—— cloths, 251, 263; flannels, 259 *ib.*; baize, 259

Essoign, 109, 239. The allegation of an excuse for one that is summoned to answer to an action real. [C.]

Estray, or stray, 81, 112, 117, 125, 149, 187. A valuable animal not wild, found within a lordship, and whose owner is not known. According to an ancient law, it was proclaimed in the church of the parish and in the two nearest market towns, on two market days; if not claimed by the owner within a year and a day, it belonged to the king, or, by grant of the crown, to the lord of the soke or liberty. [R.]

Estridge feathers, 216; wool, 215, 218 (ostrich)

Eustace, Dean of Salisbury, vice-chancellor, charter of Richard I issued by, (afterwards Bishop of Ely), 10, 18

—— Bishop of Ely, witness to charters of John, 12, 14, 17, 18

—— de Fauconberge, Bishop of London, witness to charters of Henry III, 23, 25, 27, 29

Exchequer, 34, 41, 60; receipt of, 87, 90. *See* Barons

Execution, 71; of writs, 82, 118

Exigent, 117. Exigenda, or exigent: the condition of a person who has been proclaimed and summoned by the sheriff on five county court days to appear, upon pain of outlawry, and has failed to do so [R.]. Also a writ in an indictment for felony where the party indicted cannot be found.

Extortion, 171, 172, 174

F.

Factors, 258

Fairs, 55, 61, 118, 177; in Southwark, 82

Fans, 220

Fardel, a, 216

Farringdon wards, 248

Fatt, a measure, 216, 219

Fealty, 125. An oath taken by the tenant on his admission, to be true to the lord of whom he holds.

Fee-farm, 16, 32, 34. An annual rent of at least one-fourth the true value paid for land granted or given to the tenant. [C.]

Farm, 60 *i.e.*, rent paid. From the A.-S. feorme, "food", because rents were originally paid in produce. This ferm was at an early period, in favour of some localities, estimated at a specific sum, and made perpetual; upon which it was denominated a "feodi firma", and such places were said to be held of the king *in capite*, or "in chief", at "fee ferm". See Madox, *Firma Burgi*, and Thorpe's *Ancient Laws and Instit. of England*, Glossary. [R.]
Feathers, 212
Fees, table of various, 200, *et seq.*
Feedings, 112. Grazing lands. [H.]
Felons, 47, 119
Felony, 75, 81, 82, 83, 148, 171, 172, 174, 187
Felt hats, 207
Fernando-wood, 215
Ferret silk, 214
Figs, 213, 217, 219
Fillozel silk, 214; flowered silk. *Ital.* [H.]
Fines, 83, 172
Fire, the great, prohibition of buildings after, 224; confirmation of order for new buildings after, 231
Fish, search and survey of, 142
—— various, 212, 217, 219
Fishmongers, company of, 113
Fishing, regulations, 175
Fitch-skins, 216, 218
Fitzadoes (cloths), 218
Flags, 220
Flanders commodities, 214, 215
Flannel. 218, 251, 259
Flasks of horn, 216
Flat, a measure, 219
Flax, 213, 216, 217, 219
Fleet street, breadth of, 227, 233; rebuilding of, 223
Flemish linen, 213, 217
Floramedas, 218
Florence silks, 214
Florret silk, 214
"Flower-de-luce," The; in Southwark, 113
Foines, fur, 213. Polecat-skins. [H.]
Folkmote, 4. The general assembly of the citizens. [J.E.; *Spelman*.] The general meetings of the people. In the 13th century the folkmotes of London were held at stated times in the year: at Michaelmas, for election of the sheriffs; at Christmas, for setting watch and ward throughout the wards; and in June, on St. John's day, to take precautions against fire. [*Liber Albus*, pp. 118-9.] Extraordinary folkmotes were also held for proceeding to outlawry, discussing political grievances, electing mayor, and receiving messages from the sovereign, or hearing addresses from him in person, more particularly when about to visit his foreign dominions. These meetings were held in a vacant space at the east end of St. Paul's Churchyard, near the cross there, the citizens being summoned by the great bell of St. Paul's. The assertion that the wardmotes of London were the same as the Saxon folkmotes does not appear to be strictly accurate. In the laws of Edward the Conf. (Thorpe's *Anc. Laws and Instit. of England*, p. 197) it is stated that folkmotes were summoned in counties and provinces twice in the year. This is treated by Mr. Thorpe as an interpolation. See Norton's *Constit. City of London*, p. 377. [R.]
Foreigners, *i.e.*, persons not free of the city, 49, 67; not to be admitted into woollen-markets, 257; licensed to work in the city, 305
Forests, 31
Forfeitures, 117
Forestalling, 40, 76, 148, 171, 172. The penalty due to the sovereign for an assault upon a person in the king's highway; from *fore*, "before", and *stellan*, "to spring out upon". The act of thus doing was the original meaning, but at a later period it came solely to mean the act of intercepting a person on his way with merchandise or provisions to market, for the purpose of buying his wares, still known as "forestalling". [R.]
Fort, at Mile-end green, 235
Fox-skins, 213, 216, 218
France, commodities from, 212
Franchises, 83, 84, 164, *et seq.*; restoration of, 267
Frankincense, 213, 217. The gum of the Norway and Alpine spruce fir, *Abies excelsa*. [G.]
Frankpledge, view of, 83, 112, 119. Frankpledge, surety for freemen aged 14 or upwards, except clerks or knights. All the former class were to find security towards the king and his subjects, or to go to prison.
Freedom of sale, 61; restricted, 62
Freemen, 47; widows of, 185; merchants to become, 188; of companies, 272; disposal of property of, 283
Free-soccage (called by J. E. and Luffman, fee soccage), a certain tenure of lands held by inferior husbandry services. It consisted of free soccage, soccage of ancient tenure, and base soccage, 125
Freewarren, 112, 125
Freeze linen, 213, 217
"French and English," 1, 2, 3, 5, 7, 11, 28
French commodities, 214, 215, 217, 218
Friezes, 252, 259
Fruit, search and survey of, 142
Fugaratoes, 218, figured stuffs
Fugitives, 81, 117, 149, 187
Furs, 213
Fusses of cloves, 213; mother-cloves, *antophylli*, larger and less aromatic than the true cloves, flower buds of the *Caryophyllus aromaticus*. [G.]
Fustian, 213, 215, 217; cloth, 252, 259, 264
Fustick, 215, 218. Wood of the *Morus tinctoria* of the West Indies, used as a dye. [G.]

G.

Galley-dishes, 213
Gaol-delivery, 53, 58; Newgate, 97, 98
Garble, various (mixture or selection), 217
Garbling of spices, 91; of merchandise, etc., 180
Gardens, 112
Gascony, merchants of, 49
Gascoyne wines, 215

INDEX

Gates, to be erected along waterside, 107; custody of, 162
Gauger, office of, 91, 96
Gauging of merchandise, 181, 182
Gauls, 213. 217 (Galls)
Gelding, 219
Gentish linen, 213, 217
Gentlemen of the royal robes, 203
Geoffrey, son of Peter, witness to charter of Richard I, 8; and (as Earl of Essex) of John, 12, 14
Geoffrey de Lucy, witness to charter of John, 20
George I, act for regulating election, 275
George II, charter of, 290
George Kinge, Gentleman of the Royal Robes, etc., 203
George Neville, Bishop of Exeter, witness to charter of Edward IV, 84
George Plantagenet, Duke of Clarence, witness to charter of Edward IV, 84
Germany, commodities from, 212
Gifts, restoration of, 267
Gilbert, Bishop of Rochester, witness to charter of Richard I, 8; witness to charter of John, 12
Gilbert de Clare, Earl of Gloucester and Hertford, witness to charter of Henry III, 25, 27, 29
Giles Athorn, land of, 114
Ginger, 213, 216, 217, 219
Glass, various kinds, 213, 216
"Gleyne", The; in Southwark, 113
Gloucester cloth, 263
Gloves, 213; glovers, 217
Glue, 217
Goat's hair, 213, 217
Goats in the streets forbidden, 247
Goat skins, 91, 201, *et seq.*, 214
Goceline de Balliol, witness to charter of Henry II, 6
Godfrey, portreeve of London, charter addressed to, 1
Godfrey, Bishop of Winchester, witness to charters of John, 12, 14
Godfrey, Gyffarde (master), chancellor, witness to charter of Henry III, 42
Gold, leaves of, 213
Goung - fermor, regulations concerning the duties of the, 246 (Gong, = *cloaca*)
Gournay, 18
Grain for dyers, 213, 217
Granadoes silks, 214
Grants, restoration of, 267
Gratings, dimensions of, for watercourses, 107
Gravel, 247
—— in the Thames, 106, 107
Grave-stones, 219
Graves of the dead, 39
Great beam, 99, 102, 103, 104
Greenwich wharf, 209
Gregory (St.) Pope, 46, 65, 66
Grindle stone, 219
Grocery, various, 219
Grograms, 212, 218; grograin, a coarse kind of silk taffety, usually stiffened with gum. [H.]
—— silk, 214
Groom of the Bedchamber, 203

Guarine, son of Gerold, witness to charter of Henry II, 6
Guienne, 167
—— Duke of, title of Henry III, 36
Guild, a company or incorporated society
Guildhall, sessions removed to, 97; notice of, 120, 239
—— of Almaine, 79
—— Court of Requests in, 190
Guinea, grain, 217
—— wood, 215
Gum arabic, 213; from *Acacia Arabica*. [G.]
Gum armoniack, 212, 216. A fœtid gum-resin from the *Dorema ammoniacum* of Persia, used as a stimulating plaster. [G.]
Gum-lac, 216, from the *Ficus indica*, or banyan tree. [G.]
Gunpowder, 213
Gutters, 176
Gyddesdene, royal grant of land at, 2; an unknown site; but in the hundred of Chafford, co. Essex; see Domesday Book, *Essex*, fol. 15 A.

H.

Hair, 217
Haircloth, 260
Half-thicks (cloths), 252
Hamburg linen, 214
Hameline, Earl of Warren, witness to charters of John, 12, 14
Hamper, 150; Hamper or Hanaper, an office in Chancery wherein are paid all moneys due to the king for the seal of charters, patents, etc., and to the officers for enrolling the same.
—— a measure, 216
Hampshire kerseys, 251
Hampton Court, 150
Hangings, 218
Hangulf de Taney, witness to charter of Henry I, 4
Harbourers, 49
Hats, 213, 217
Hawks, 213
Headlings for pipes, 213
Heath for brushes, 213, 219
Heirship of children, in succession to their fathers, 1
"Helmet", The, in Southwark, 113
Hemp, 213, 217, 219
Henry I, charter of, 3; referred to, by Henry II, 5. 6; by Richard I, 7, 8; by John, 11, 12; and by Henry III, 28, 29; charters of, confirmed by Charles I, 159
Henry II, charter of, 5; confirmed by Charles I, 159; charter for soul of, 12
Henry III, first charter of, 21; second, 24; third, 26; fourth, 28; fifth, 30; sixth, 34; remission, 36; eighth, 38; confirmed by Charles I, 160, 161; reference to, 56
Henry IV, reference to a charter of, 101; extract from a charter of, 162; reference to a statute of, A.D. 1399, 198
Henry VI, reference to charters of, and statutes of, 166; reference to a statute of, 198
Henry VII, regulations concerning strangers, from a charter of, 94; confirmation of extract of his charter, 162, 163; reference to charter of, 168

INDEX.

Henry VIII, first charter, 97; second, 99; reference to charters of, 101, 116, 202, 207; act for enforcing a statute, of, 106; reference to lands purchased by, 111; reference to holdings of, in Southwark, 123; confirmation of his charters, 163; recitation of his grant of Bethlem Hospital, etc., 192, 193
Henry de Wyngham, witness to charter of Henry III, 35
Hereditaments, 112; restoration of, 269
Herrings, 212
Hervey de Stantone, Justice, 56
Hessen canvas, 214, 217
Hides (skins), 213, 217, 219
Hida, hide, 2. A carucate, or plough-land. It is ascertained that the hide did not contain any fixed number of acres, it being set down at 80, 120, 140, and in an ancient table at p. 284 of Hearne's *Hist. Johan. Glaston.*, as much as 160 acres; while again, in a MS. of Malmesbury Abbey, cited by Spelman, the hide is made to be four virgates of 24 acres, or 96 acres. See Introduction to Archdeacon Hale's *Domesday of St. Paul's*, pp. lxiii, cxxij. The word *hida* in several passages evidently means a "family". In Beda, *Hist. Eccles.*, iii, 24, there is a passage where the word written elsewhere as "hides" is replaced by "familiæ". On the dimensions of land in England in general, the reader may consult Hearne's *Collection of Curious Discourses* (ed. 1773), i, pp. 40-50 [R.], Kemble, *Saxons in England*, 2nd edit., etc.
Hogs in the streets, forbidden, 247
Holborn bridge, to be enlarged, 232
Holborn hill, 232; traffic of, regulated, 238
Holland linen, 213, 214, 217
Holloway lane, 248
Honey, 213
Honours, 167
Hops, search and survey of, 142; tax on, 213, 219
Horn, 216, 217
Horns, 220
"Horsehead," The, in Southwark, 113
Horsepacks, 259, etc.
Horses, 213, 219
Hounscot sayes, 214, 218
Hubert de Burgh, Earl of Kent; Justice, witness to charters of Henry III, 25, 27, 31
Hubert, the king's chamberlain, witness to charter of Henry I, 4
Hubert, Walter, Archbishop of Canterbury, witness to charters of Richard I, 8, 10; mentioned, 9, 13, 26; witness to charter of John, 12, 14; charter of John issued by, 17, 18
Huckster, 200
Hugh Bardolfe, witness to charter of Richard I, 8; and of John, 12, 14
Hugh, Bygot, witness to charter of Henry I, 4
Hugh, Bishop of Coventry, witness to charter of Richard I, 10
Hugh, Bishop of Durham, witness to charter of Richard I, 8
Hugh de Gournai, witness to charter of John, 18
Hugh, Bishop of Lincoln, witness to charter of Richard I, 8
Hullucks (wine), 218. Hollocks [H.]
Hustings, 4, 5, 7, 11, 28, 40, 46, 120. Or hustins,

from "hus", a house, and "thing", a cause, *i.e.*, a house where causes are tried; or according to Somner, from the Saxon word "hyhst", highest, and "thing". The highest court of the city of London. [J. E.] The king's court of Hustings, anciently held each week in the city of London. Spelman derives it from the A.-S. "hus", a house, and "thing", a cause; and Somner from "hyst thing", supreme court; but the most probable origin, according to Riley, is husthing, "court held in a house"; the other courts in Saxon times being held in the open air. See Thorpe's *Anc. Laws and Inst. of England*, s. v. *Husteng.* [R.]

I.

Immunity, 164 *et seq.*
In capite. See Capite
Incle, 213, tape. *Ruban de fil.* [B.
India, commodities from, 212; hides, 217
Indico, indigo, 213, 215, 217
Infangtheof, 53; a liberty granted to lords of manors to try and judge anything taken in their fee; "fang" or "fong", to catch; and "thefe", a thief. [C.] The privilege or liberty granted to the lord of a manor of judging a thief taken within his demesne. In some instances this privilege extended to all delinquents whatsoever; in others to only the men, or homagers, belonging to that manor. [R.]
Innovations, 168
Inquisitions, 48, 58; removed from St. Martin's-le-Grand to Guildhall, 97. A process of search or examination, used in the king's behalf in temporal causes. [C.]
Ireland, 167
Irish rugs, 215, 217, 261; mantlets, 261; wools, 215
Iron, 219; plates, 220; pots, 219; various, 213, 215, 216, 217
Irreplagiable (=Irrepleviable), 108
Issingham linen, 213; Isingham, 217
Issue, 83. Profit arising from amerciaments or fines, profits of lands, or tenements. [C.]
Ivory, 217

J.

Jamaica wood, 215
James I, first charter of, 132; second, 139; third, 151; confirmation of his charters, 163
James II, deeds of, annulled, 268
Jean silk, 214. Of Genoa. [H.]
Jennet skin, 218
Jeresgive, 6, 8, 12, 29, 40. A toll or fine taken by the king's officers on a person entering into an office; or rather a sum or bribe given to them to connive at extortion, or other offence in him that gives it. [J. E.] The meaning of this word, which is found written in several forms, is unknown. Norton suggests that it has been originally a miswriting for "heregeat" or "beregeld", a tax common among the Danes and Saxons—the same, in fact, as the "heriot" (and perhaps the "relief") originally a contribution of military stores by a vassal, according to his rank; but after-

wards degenerated to a fine, on death of a tenant, paid out of his goods, usually his best beast. The word has also been explained as a toll or fine, taken by the king's officers on a person entering upon an office. It seems, however, not improbable that it is from the A.-S. "gear", a year, and "gifan", to give, as meaning a new year's gift; extorted, perhaps, on certain grounds, in favour of the sovereign; for in Madox, *Hist. Excheq.*, i, p. 504, we read of the citizens of London giving £300 to King John as a *New Year's Gift*. In *Prompt. Parv.*, p. 343, is a somewhat similar form, "*moryve*," a corruption of the *morgen gifu*, or nuptial gift, of the Anglo-Saxons. [R.]

Jersey (wool), 251, 252, 253, 259, 260
Jewels, sale of, 184, etc.
Jews, 41
Job Clark, land of, 235
John, Earl of Moreton (afterwards King of England), witness to charter of Richard I, 10
John, first charter of, 11; second, 13; third, 15; fourth, 17; fifth, 19; mention of charters by, 22, 27, 29, 57; charter given for his soul's health, 26; charters of, confirmed by Charles I, 159, 160. It is said by Calthorp, in his *Tract of the City Liberties*, "that the king's hand, as well as seal, was set to one of his charters the like of which I never did hear or read before". [J. F., p. 13.]
Joceline, Bishop of Bath, witness to charters of Henry III, 25, 29
John Bellet, witness to charter of Henry I, 4
John Billington, grant of land held by, 111
John Burcetor, Knt., lands of, 112
John de Cheshulle, Archdeacon of London, witness to charter of Henry III, 42
John Cock, land of, 235
John Gate, Sir, Knt, gentleman of the Privy Chamber, reservation in favour of, 125
John Gisors, Mayor of London, 32
John, brother of Richard de Grey, witness to charter of Henry III, 33
John de Grey, witness to charter of Henry III, 35
John Gumband, witness to charter of Henry III, 33
John Hotham, Bishop of Ely, chancellor, witness to charter of Henry III, 38
John, son of Hugh, witness to charter of John, 20
John de Lexingtone, witness to charter of Henry III, 35
John de la Lynde, witness to charter of Henry III, 42
John Maunsel, Provost of Beverley, witness to charter of Henry III, 35
John, son of Philip, witness to charter of Henry III, 31
John Parrow, grant of land held by, 111
John Potter, Archbishop of Canterbury, witness to charter of George II, 294
John Solas, field of, 115
John, Bishop of Worcester, witness to charter of Richard I, 10
Jurors, fines, etc., of, 174

Justices, 83, 97, 98, 124, 165, etc., 176; mayors and aldermen to be, 146; of the peace, *ex officio*, 169, *et seq.*, 290, etc.; pleading before, 186; nomination of, 187, 188
Jury, default of, 120

K.

Kentish cloths, 263
Kentish street, Southwark, 117
Keeper of the Great Beam, office of, 99, 102
Keeper of the Privy Seal, 181, 184
Kersies, 215, 218, 251, 252, 259
Kettles, 212
Kidderminster stuffs, etc., 262
Kid's hair, 217; skins, 214, 218
Kine in streets, forbidden, 247
King's Bench, the prison so called, in Southwark, 124
King's Bench, L. C. Justice of, 181, 182, 184; reversal of the judgment of, against the city, 266
Knight's service, 178, 195, 196
Knives, 217

L.

Lace, 213, 217
"Lamb", The, in Southwark, 113
Lambblack, 212. Lampblack
Lambskins, 91, 216, 217, 218
Lambeth, co. Surrey, grant of land in the parish, 111
Lamprones, 215; lamparnes, 217. Lampreys.
Lands, restoration of, 267
Lancaster, Duchy of, 167
—— woollen ware, 259
Langbourn ward, 248
Lantern horn, 217
Last, a measure, 219
Lastage, or Lestage, 3, 5, 7, 11, 28, 39. A toll paid for liberty for persons to carry their goods up and down to marts, markets, and fairs. [J. E.]
Lattin, 212, 213, 215 (a mixed metal)
Lauderdale, John Maitland, second earl of, 231
Lawns, 217
Laws, 214
Lawworthy, citizens made, 1. See notice in preface, p. x.
Law merchant, 38. Law proper to merchants, administered in the mercantile boroughs among those foreign to the borough jurisdiction who were then trading there; the judges being ordinarily the mayor, bailiff, or principal officer of the borough; though, as to London, the citizens exercised the privilege of appointing wardens of their own in other towns, to adjudicate on litigated points. Gerard Malynes published a work (A.D. 1623) on this subject, intituled *Lex Mercatoria*.[R.]
Lay-stalls, 235, etc., 247. Dunghills. [H.]
Lead, 101, 103, 215, 217, 219, 220
Leadenhall, 85, 251, 253, etc.
Leamonds, 213, 217. Lemons
Leather, Spanish, 213
——, various, 213
Leases, sale of, 184, etc.
Leeds Castle, co. Kent, 51
Levant, commodities from, 214, 215; wines, 218
Levant Merchants Company, 189

INDEX. 329

Levies of men-at-arms, 51 ; outside London, 55
Lewres for hawks, 213. Lures
Liberties, 56, 57, 72, 73, 83, 84, 164, *et seq.*; restoration of, 267. A privilege held by grant or prescription, conferring some unusual benefit or favour. [C.]
Liberty of St. Paul's, 35
Lighters, or coal barges, 156
Liles, 212
Lilies (stuffs), 218
Linen, 213, 217
——, various, 213
——, yarn, 260
Ling, fish, 212, 220
Linseed oil, 214, 217 ; linseed, 213, 217
Linsey woollsey, 218, 252, 260
Liquorish, 213, 217 Liquorice, root of the *Glycyrrhiza glabra*. [G.]
Littimus, 214. Litmus, a dye from the *Rocella tinctoria*. [G.]
Livercocks, 212
Liverymen's oath, 277
Lock, at Southwark, 113, 115
Lockrams, linen, 214. A cheap linen worn by the lower classes. [H.]
London Bridge, 132, 133, 135, 136, 209
London knives, 217
London, sheriffwick of, 15, 16, 21, 22, 23, 53
London, Tower of, 77
Looking-glass cases, 212
Loomwork, 260
Lot, 3, 47, 283. Lot and Scot, from A.-S. lot, scot, or sceat, contribution and tribute ; signifying a contribution levied upon all subjects rateably, and according to their ability. See Norton's *Constit. Cit. Lond.*, pp. 356-8. [R.]
Lordships, 167
Lub fish, 212
Ludgate, custody of the gate, 162
Lukes, silk, 214 ; Velvet. [H.]
Lutes, 213
Lutestrings, 213
Lyme street ward, 248
Lyons thread, 215

M.

Mace, 213, 215, 217, Outer membrane of the nutmeg, *Myristica officinalis*. [G.]
Maces, to be used of gold or silver, etc., 63, 64
Madder, 101, 103, 214, 217, 219. Dye from the root of *Rubia tinctorum*, South Europe. [G.]
Madeira wine, 215, 218
Magic, 148 ; arts, 171, 172
Magnus, 214 (? Magnesia)
Majorca oil, 214, 217
Malaga wine, 215
Malefactors, 119
Malt, 214
Manasser Biset, witness to charter of Henry II, 6
Manchester wares, 264
Mantlets, 261. Short mantles. [H.]
Maps, 214
Maramuffe stuff, 218
Marble, 215
Mares, 213, 219
Margaret Pennell, lands of, 195
Markets, limitation of 58

Markets, 61, 82, 177; in Southwark, 124; limit of, 186; restoration of, 267
Marshal, 5, 7, 11, 28, 39, 55; of the household, 125. The marshal of the king's household, otherwise called the "Knight Marshal". As to the nature and duties of this office, see Madox, *Hist. Excheq.*, i, pp. 43-48, and Hearne's *Col. of Cur. Disc.*, ii, 90-154 (ed. 1773). [R.]
Marshals, 238
Marshalsea, the prison so called, in Southwark, 124
Masks, 213, 214
Masons, 107
Masts, 214, 219
Matthew, brother of Peter son of Herbert, witness to charter of Richard I, 10
Maund, 212, 219 ; or basket, 216, 217
Mayor, election of, 272, 276
—— free choice of, 19, 24, 25, 46 ; presentation of the, 19, 24, 34, 43
—— to be escheator, 55, 122; maces of, 63, 94 ; to name justices of peace, 187
—— to be justices, 75, 147, 169, 192, 293. The term was probably borrowed from the French, and the name seems to imply (like the A.-S. ealdorman) advanced age and experience, as being *major natu*, "older by birth". See Norton's *Constit. City of London*, p. 403. [R.]
Meadows, 112
Meal, 214
Measures of various commodities, 133, etc.
Medway, river, 132, 133, 135, 136, 152, 153, 154; weirs in the, 54
Melasses, 217. Molasses, uncrystallisable liquor drained from sugar. [G.]
Merchant Adventurers Company, 189
Merchants-denizens and aliens, 91
Merchant-strangers, 41, 54, 61, 67, 68
Merchants, foreign, not to trade in London, 70
Merchants trading to France, company of, 189
Merchants for discovery of new commerce, company of, 189
"Mermaid", The. in Southwark, 113
Messelawny (stuff), 218
Middleton (John Middleton, first) Earl of, 231
Middlesex, grant of, to farm, 3 ; huntings in, 4 ; sheriffwick of, 15, 16, 21, 22, 23 ; sheriffs of, 295, etc. ; mentioned, 63 ; justice of peace of, 187
Mile end, 248
Mile End Green, land at, 235
Mill stones, 215, 219
Minakin, or Minikin, baize, 218, 259, 264 ; delicate, elegant. [H.]
—— lutestrings, 213 ; properly treble strings. [H.]
Minorca oil, 214, 217
Miskenning, 4, 5, 7, 11, 28. Changing a plea in court, when one leaves his first declaration or plea and gives another. [J. E.] A fine exacted for the offence of mispleading or proffering false pleas, afterwards known as "miscounting." The word seems to be derived from "mis", wrong, and "can", to know (or perhaps "to aver as in one's

*

knowledge)." Although Stephen, in a proclamation, prohibited "Miskennings wrongfully exacted by sheriffs and others", it is erroneous to suppose that he finally abolished them, as they are named at a much later date. It seems probable that "miskenning" was identical with "stultiloquium", for which fines are often accounted for in early times of the Exchequer, and down to the reign of Henry III. [R.]
Mocadoes, 212, 214, 218. Or mock velvet, a woollen stuff made in imitation of velvet. [H.]
Mohair, or Moyhair, 212, 218.
Moneyers, 5, 7, 11, 28. These officers were ministers of the mint, who coined the king's money, such mints being established in several counties. [R.]
Monmouth caps, 216
Moor, the inner and the outward, 177
Morea, silk, 214
Morice, Mr. Secretary, 231 ; Sir William Morrice
Morkins, skins, 216, 218. A morkin is a beast that dies by disease or accident. [H.]
Mortmain, 196, 197, 199
Mortmain, power to purchase land in, 54, 55, 87, 89. An alienation of lands and tenements to any guild, corporation, or fraternity, and their successors, which might not be done without the king's licence.
Motleys, 252. A king of mottled cloth. [H.]
Motleys (cloths) for mariners, 261
Moulter's close, grant of land so called, 111
Muckaddo ends (cloths), 260. See Mocadoes
Murage, 44. A contribution towards repairing the walls and edifices of a city. [J. E.]
Murder, 3, 5, 7, 11, 171, 172. See acquittal
Muscovia linen, 214 ; yarn, 215
Musk ; musk-cods, 212. See G., p. 128
Muskadel wines, 215, 218. See G., p. 254
Muskavado sugar, 213 ; raw sugar. [G.]
Mustard seed, 217
Mysteries, 46, 47, 50. A trade, or mystery ; from the old Fr. "mestier", which came from the med. Lat. "ministerium", a term used to signify a trade. The English word "mystery" is derived from the same source, and in this sense has nothing in common with the same word as signifying a religious or secret ceremony. [R.]

N.

Nails, 217
Naples silks, 214
Navigation of the Thames, 106-109
Neapolitan fustian, 213
Needlework carpets, 260
"New-drapery," 251
Newgate, goal of, 58, 83, 119, 173 ; custody of the gate, 162 ; a postern to be built at, 232
Newington, co. Surrey, grant of land in, 111 ; lands in, 114, 115, 117
New Temple, London, 20
Nicholas Brembre, mayor, 71
Nicholas de St. Maur, witness to charter of Henry III, 35
Non-freeman, 48, 49
Norfolk cloth, 263 ; baize, 259, 264
Norman linen, 217 ; canvas, 214
Northampton, 37

Northern-dozen, kerseys, 263
Norton (Geo.) notice of his work, viii, 325, 329
Norwich stuffs, 251
Nutmegs, 213, 215, 217

O.

Oaker (ochre), 217
Oars, 214, 220
Oaths, Act, for abrogation of, mentioned, 272 ; of liverymen, etc., 277-279, 289 ; to be taken on the Holy Evangelists, 211
Oats, 214
Octave of St. Michael, the eighth day after Michaelmas, 33. [J. E.]
Oil, search and survey of. 142 ; gauging of, 181, 182 ; rates on, 214, 217, 219
Olibanum, 216. A resin from the *Boswellia serrata*, used as a stimulant, etc. [G.]
Olives, 214
Onions, 133, 135, 137, 214, 217, 247
Oranges, 214, 247
Orchal, 214, 217 (orchil ; see Argal)
Orchards, 112
Organsine silks, 214
Osbert Giffard, witness to charter of Henry III, 31
Otter skins, 216, 218
Outcry, public sale or, 185
Outfangtheof, 53 ; a liberty to judge any thief taken out of a fee. The word is also spelled Outfangenetheof. A liberty or privilege whereby the lord of a manor was enabled to summon any man of his manor, taken for felony in a place out of his fee, to judgment in his court. [R.]
Overisily, linen, 213, 217 (Overyssel in Germany)
Outlaws, 81
Outnal thread, 215
Outroper, or common crier of Southwark, etc., 184
—— fees of the, 200. Outrop, a public auction. [H.]
Ox bones, etc., 217
—— hair, 217

P.

Pack, a, 216
Packthread, 214
Package, office of, 91
Package, 201, et seq.
Pales, 176
Pannage, 44. Or pawnage, a duty paid to the king for pasturage of cattle, but by some thought to be an error for pavage. Pannage also signifies the mast of the oak and beech, fed on by swine. [H.] A licence granted to feed swine in the lord's woods, as also the money paid for a licence, derived from the old Fr. "pasnage", and that probably from the Lat. "pastio". See the *Charta de Foresta*, 2 Henry III, c. 9. In A.-S. times this remuneration was called æfesn, and consisted of every third hog belonging to him who enjoyed the privilege, when the fat was three fingers thick. At the time of the Domesday survey payment in money had become customary ; but in the grant by Edward the Confessor, of Calcbythe, to the Abbey of St. Peter, Westminster, he makes

INDEX. 331

grant of "the pannage hog", swine of sevesen. [R.]
Pans, various, 214
Paper, 214, 217, 220
Parliament, 59, 60, 61, 67, 68, 72, 80
—— Acts of, 167, 168, 186
Paragon, or parapos, stuff, 218. Paragon, excellent. [H.]
Paris thread, 215
Passage, 3. Through a town or port, gates, or bridges. [J. E.] Paagium has been said to be identical with the tax called "passagium"; but as both are named together in *Lib. Cust.*, p. 655, it seems not improbable that "pavnsium", pavage, is meant. [R.]
Pastures, 112
Paulinus Peyvre, witness to charter of Henry III, 33
Paving, orders for, 235, *et seq.*
Paviours, 107; regulations concerning, 240
Pawns, office of registration of, 191
—— fees for, 200
Peas, 214
Pears, 133, 135, 137, 212
Pedegny (cloths), 261. Cf. Pedesay, a kind of cloth. [H.]
Penellis sugar, 213, 217
Pennistones, or penistones, 252, 259. A kind of coarse woollen cloth. [H.]
Pennystones, cloths, 218
Penny-ware, 213. ? penne-vair, a kind of fur. [H.]
Penthouses, 176, 178
Pepper, 101, 103, 213, 216, 217
Perpetuanoes, or perpetuanes, 216, 218, 251, 252. A kind of glossy cloth called everlasting. [H.]
Persia, commodities from, 212
Pesage, pesagium. A custom or duty paid for weighing commodities. [R.]
Peter, son of Herbert, witness to charter of Richard I, 10; and of John, 20
Peter de Egeblancke], Bishop of Hereford, witness to charter of Henry III, 35
Peter [de Rupibus], Bishop of Winchester, witness to charters of John, 20; and of Henry III, 25, 27, 29
Peter de Sabandia or Savoy, witness to charter of Henry III, 35
Peter de Stoke, witness to charter of John, 18.
Petition of the city to King Edward III, 68
Pewter, 216, 217
Pheasants, 220
Philip de Albeniaco, witness to charter of Henry III, 31
Philip, Bishop of Bayeux, witness to charter of Henry II, 6
Philosellas, 214. See Filozelle
Pickage, 122, 177. A payment for breaking ground to erect a stall. [J. E.]
Piepowder courts, 55, 82, 83, 118. A summary court of justice held at fairs. [C. J. H.]
Piramides (stuff), 218
Pitch, 214, 219
Plates, 214
Platts, linen, 213
Plea, 3, 7, 11, 46, 55. Is what either the plaintiff or defendant alleges for himself in court. [J.E.]

Pleas of the crown, 3, 5, 39, 55. Suits in the king's name for offences committed against his crown and dignity
—— of foreign tenures, 5, 7, 11, 28
Pleading outside walls, 38, 55
Plums, 133, 135, 137
Plush, 214
Poisoning, 171, 172
Poldavis, 214. A kind of coarse cloth or canvas. [H.]
Pole (? Polish) silk, 214. See [H.] Polgarments, cloth like velvet, smooth on one side and rough on the other.
Pollard. An unlawful coin much imported into England from Flanders upon occasion of the disorganisation of its monetary system during the latter years of Henry III. Pollards and crocards were often prohibited by proclamation, as also by statute 27 Edw. I, *De Falsa Moneta*; and when allowed to be circulated were only estimated at one-half of their asserted value. The former, as Camden says, were probably so called from being polled or clipped, and the latter from being made so thin as easily to become crooked. [R.]
Polonia, wools, 215
Pomegranates, 214
Ponds, 112
Pontage, 44. A duty paid to the king for passing over bridges with horses, carts, and carriages, or under them with ships, etc., towards repairing such bridges, etc. [J. E.]
Pools, 112
Pork, 214
Porter, 206
Portgreve, or portreeve, 1. Signifies a governor or ruler of a port, city, or forest, by which name the Lord Mayor of London was called before the Conquest, until Richard II. mounted the throne, by whom were appointed two bailiffs; but soon afterwards King John granted them a mayor for their chief magistrate. [J. E.]
Portsoken, 5, 7, 11, 28, 39. An extent of jurisdiction or liberty, from without the gates of the city, or, as some take it, the liberty within the port or city of London.
—— ward, 248
Portugal, grain from, 213, 217
—— oil, 214, 217
Posterns, custody of, 162
Potashes, 219
Pots, various, 214
Poultry in the streets forbidden, 247
Pound, or greenyard, 246
Poundering, 91. See H. under *Auncel*, a kind of weight or weighing with scales on hooks at each end of a staff, prohibited on account of its great uncertainty
Preaching friars, at Ludgate or Blackfriars, 143, 147, 149
President of the council, 181, 182, 184
Pretended Prince of Wales, the, 278
Prisons of Southwark, 124, 125
Privileges, 83, 119, 164, *et seq.*
Privy Council, 180
Privy Seal, Lord; John, second Baron Robartes, 231
Processes, 120

332   INDEX.

Provence, oil, 214, 217
Prunes, 213, 217
Pudding-cart of shambles, 247. Cf. puddings, intestines. [H.]
Puddle-dock, 235, 248
Purprestures, 167, 179. Enclosures or encroachments on anything that belongs to the king or public. See "A brief discovery of the great purpresture of new buildings nere to the cittie, with means howe to restraine the same". *Archæologia*, xxiii, 121. [H.]
Purveyors, 57

Q.

Quales (Quails), 214, 220
Quakers, exception of, from taking oaths, 277, 278
Queenhithe, grant of, to the city, 32
——— ward, 218. In the city of London. In early times this hythe, or landing-place, was known as "Edred's Hithe", which name it retained until the time of King Stephen. Stow says "that it afterwards came to the king's hands, and pertained unto the queen, and therefore was called 'Ripa Reginæ,' the queenes bank, or queenes hithe, and great profit thereof was made to her use". In documents of the 12th century this locality is called "Cornhith" (see Newcourt's *Repertor*, i. p. 487); and in the 9th of Henry III. it was ordered that ships of the Cinque Ports should bring *corn* to this hithe only. From Cornheth (or Quernhethe) we may perhaps trace the corruption of the name to "Queenhithe", in the same manner that the Church of St. Michael, at the west end of Cheapside, was called indifferently "St. Michael le Quern" and "atte corn." [R.]
Quern-stones, 215, 219. *Mola* in the Nominale MS. [H.]
Quicksilver, 214, 218
Quinces, 214. *Cydonia vulgaris.* [G.]
Quittals, 164, *et seq.*
Quo warranto, 266. Two statutes (6 Edw. I. and 18 Edw. I, stat. 2) were so called as making writs of quo warranto returnable not before the Justiciars in Eyre; such writs commanding the defendant to show "by what warrant" he claims such a franchise, office, or liberty. [R.] See William and Mary.

R.

R. de Ryuuers, witness to charter of John, 18
R. de St. Walery, witness to charter of Henry II, 6
R. de Warren, witness to charter of Henry II, 6
Rabbit skins, 218
Raisons, 213, 216, 217, 219
Ralph, Earl of Chester, witness to charter of Richard I., 10. See Rannulph
Ralph, Neville, Bishop of Chichester, charters of Henry III issued by, 23, 25, 27, 29, 31
Ralph, son of Nicholas, witness of charters of Henry III, 25, 27, 33
Ralph de Wauncy, witness to charter of Henry III, 33
Rain, provision for carrying off rain water, 107

Rannulph, Earl of Chester, witness to charter of Richard I. See Ralph
Randulph, Earl of Chester, witness to charter of John, 17
Rape oil, 214, 217. Expressed from *Brassica rapa oleifera.* [G.]
Rapeseed, 214, 217
Rashes. 218, 251, 252, 259. A kind of inferior silk. [H.]
Rates on woollen commodities, 258, etc.
Rebellion of the city, 36, 38
Recognizances, 173, 174, *et seq.*
Recorder, 75-77; to be justice, 75, 293
———, privileges of, 147, 186, *et seq.*
———, duties of, 169, 170, 174, *et seq.*
Rectati (accused), 39. Rectare, to accuse; Fr. retter, to diffame. The word *rette* used in early English, to charge, impute, accuse. See Arette [H.]. To rate or chide [R.]
Red-earth, 217
Red-lead, 217
Redemptions, 118, 119
"Red Lion", Mile End, 235
Redrith wharf (? Rotherhithe), 209
Regrating, regraters, 76, 145, 171, 172. Retailing. [R.]
Reversions, 112
Rhenish wines, 215, 219
Rhubarb, 216
Rice, 214
Richard I, first charter of, 7; second charter of, 9; charters of, confirmed by Charles I, 159
Richard II, extract from charter of, 70; proclamation in time of. 71
Richard de Argentein, king's steward, witness to charters of Henry III, 25, 27, 31
Richard de Belmeis, Bishop of London, witness to charters of Henry II, 6; and of Richard I, 8
Richard, Earl of Clare, witness to charter of Richard I, 8; and of John, 12, 14
Richard, Earl of Cornwall, royal confirmation of a charter granted by, 32; witness to charter of Henry III, 35 (see next name); offences against him by the city, 36
Richard, King of Germany, witness to charter
Richard de Grey, witness to charter of Henry of Henry III, 42. (Same as above.)
Richard, son of Hugh, witness to charter of Henry III, 31
Richard de Luci, witness to charter of Henry II, 6
Richard de Mariscis, Chancellor, charter of John issued by, 20
Richard de Newburgh, witness to charter of Henry II, 6
Richard Plantagenet, Duke of Gloucester, witness to charter of Edward IV, 84
Richard Poore, Bishop of Salisbury, witness to charter of Henry III, 29
Rights, 83, 84
Rights, restoration of, 267
Rings of wire, 219
Riots, 174
Robert Aguillum, witness to charter of Henry III, 42
Robert Gosling, land of, 235

INDEX. 333

Robert de Harcourt, witness to charter of John, 18
Robert, Earl of Leicester, witness to charter of Richard I, 10
Robert Linled, land of, 114
Robert (de Bingham), Bishop of Salisbury, witness to charters of Henry III, 25, 27
Robert, son of Richier, witness to charter of Henry I, 4
Robert, son of Roger, witness to charters of John, 12, 14
Robert, son of Siward, witness to charter of Henry I, 4
Robert Waleraunde, witness to charter of Henry III, 42. (Same as following name.)
Robert Walravensis, witness to charter of Henry III, 35. (See previous name.)
Robert, son of Walter, witness to charter of John, 17
Roger Bigot, witness to charter of Richard I, 8; and (as Earl Roger de Bigot), of John, 12, 14
Roger de Clifforde, witness to charter of Henry III, 42
Roger de Leyburne, witness to charter of Henry III, 42
Roger de Mortimer, witness to charter of Henry III, 42
Romney wine, 215, 218. A kind of Spanish wine. [H.]
Rosin, 214, 217, 219
Rotta, grain from, 213, 217
Rowse linen, 213, 217 (? Rough, cf. rousing.) [H.]
Rugs, 252, 259, 260, 261, 264
Rushes, burning of, 108
Rye, 214

S.

Sac, saccha. A privilege dating from Anglo-Saxon times, which enabled the inferior lord to hold a court for the adjudication of causes between his own vassals. This, however, is also one of the meanings of "soc"; and, in fact, the exact shades of meaning of "sac" and "soc" cannot, perhaps, with any satisfactory degree of certainty be ascertained [R.]
Sack (wine resembling sherry), 215, 218
Safflore, 214. *Carthamus tinctorius*. [G.]
Saffora, 212, 216
Saffron, 214, 216, 217. See Safflore
St. Bartholomew Priory, or Great St. Bartholomew, 143, 147, 149; parish, 177
St. Bartholomew Hospital, or Little St. Bartholomew, 143, 147, 149
St. Bartholomew the Less, parish of, 177. The Priory of St. Bartholomew in Smithfield, as well as the hospital, founded by Rahere in the time of Henry I, about A.D. 1123. A convent of Black, or Preaching, Friars was placed here by Queen Mary, but ejected in the first year of Queen Elizabeth. Dugd. *Mon. Angl.*, vi, 291. For the hospital, see Dugd., *Mon. Angl.* vi., 626
St. Botolph-without, Cripplegate, parish of, 177
St. Christopher tobacco, 215
St. George, Southwark, grant of lands in the parish of, 111; parish of, 117

St. Giles-without, Cripplegate, parish of, 177
St. Giles-in-the-Fields, lands in, 195
St. Katharine's wharf, 209
St. Martin's-le-Grand, 58; sessions removed from, 97. Ecclesia Sancti Martini: the collegiate church of St. Martin's-le-Grand. (See the *History of St. Martin's-le-Grand*, by A. J. Kempe.) [R.]
St. Martin's-le-Grand, ward, 248
St. Mary, B.V., Feast of the Annunciation, 209
St. Mary Overy, co. Surrey, priory of, 123
St. Michael Archangel, vigil of, 297; feast of, 209; octave of, 33
St. Olave, Southwark, parish of, 116
St. Paul's, liberty of, 35
St. Saviour's, monastery of, 122
St. Saviour, Southwark, parish of, 116
St. Sepulchre's parish, 177
St. Stephen, Coleman street, parish of, 177
St. Thomas's, or the King's, Hospital, Southwark, 117, 122
St. Thomas, sugar (from the island of), 213, 217
Sales, registration of, 191
Salmon, 213, 219
Salop, woollen goods of, 259
Salt, search and survey of, 142
—— 214, 216, 217
Saltpetre, 214, 216, 217
Sand, 247
Sand in the Thames, 106, 107
Sarcenets, 214. Thin slight kind of silk. [H.]
Sassafras, 216. *Laurus sassafras*, N. America. Used as a sudorific drug. [G.]
Sattin, 214
Savaric, Bishop of Bath, witness to charter of John, 17
Say, a delicate serge or woollen cloth. [H.]
Say calunaucoes, 214. Error in the texts for calamanco, a kind of woollen stuff with shiny satin-like surface. [H.]
Sayes, 214, 218, 251, 252, 260
Saunders, 212. Sandal-wood. [H.]
Scales, 220. Thin outside pieces of timber with the bark on. [H.]
Scammony, 216. *Convolvulus scammonia*. [G.]
Scavage, 201, *et seq*. Shewage, the custom, or duty on imported goods, known as "scavage". Spelman terms this toll levied by the owners of markets for licence given to chapmen of *shewing* their wares, and derives it from the A.-S. scefian, to "shew" or "inspect." Scavage is so called as being a *demonstraunce*, or "shewing". In the second charter of James I it is called "search" and "surveying". The A.-S. sccawian, "to look at", is the basis of the word. [R.]
Scot and lot, 3, 47, 283. Contributions laid upon subjects. *See* Lot
Scotale, 6, 8, 12, 29, 40. A practice of the king's officers who kept alehouses or brewed liquors, and forced men to come to their houses and pay contributions (called Scotales), for fear of their displeasure. [J. E.] The meaning of this term is obscure, but most probably it originally signified a scot, tax, or payment, in reference to the sale of ale; the word re-

ceiving different complexions of meaning at later periods. Is evidently a tax hitherto levied by the crown upon the citizens of London for the privilege either of making or of selling ale. In 1212 it is pretty clear that one meaning of "scotale" was a licence in reference to ale, granted as a distinctive privilege by the city dignitaries, and extending probably not only to the selling, but to the brewing of ale. Foresters and bedels are forbidden to make scotales, in reference apparently to a right which they had assumed of granting such licences within the verge of their respective forests, or of keeping this right in their own hands, and compelling the people of the vicinity to deal with them. The term evidently extends also to certain meeting or assemblies, the nature of which is now unknown, but which probably resembled the "beoracipes" of the Anglo-Saxons and ancient Germans; the name, not improbably, being given to them by reason of the contributions made by the persons, so meeting, for liberty to brew on such occasions. From these meetings, perhaps, were derived "bride-ales" and "bid-ales", or meetings for the purpose of drinking ale, of a comparatively recent period. The word "scotale" seems also to have been applied to the ale made by those who had licence to brew. Under this name also the "church-ale", or potations upon anniversaries of the dedication of churches, were probably included; as we find such "Scotallæ" mentioned and prohibited in the Provincial Constitutions of the Archbishop of Canterbury in 1209 and 1236, and in the several Diocesan Canons. See Hale's *Domesday of St. Paul's*, Introd. p. cix. Spelman considers the word "scotale" a general term for taxes payable under the name of "scot", and grounds that conjecture on the various modes in which the word is spelt; this opinion, however, seems to Riley untenable, as it bears reference to the making, sale, and drinking of ale. Somner, again, takes it as identical with the A.-S. drinc-lean, or "contribution for drink", made by the tenants for the purchase of ale for entertaining the superior lord, or his steward, on the fee. ("Potus" seems to have been a similar payment in France, in the 13th century, for the purchase of wine.) If this is the case, it is still clear that scotale had other meanings. The word does not occur in Anglo-Saxon times. See Du Cange, *Glossar. s. v. Scotallum*, etc. [R.]

Sea-coals, 217
Seahorse, teeth, 217
Seal, common, 48; charter to be sealed without fine, 199
Seher de Quincy, witness to charter of Richard I, 10
Seizin, 117. Actual or legal possession
Serges, 214, 218, 251, 252, 260
Serjeants, 63, 64
—— at mace, 120
Seron, a measure, 216. Serone, a barrel or package of soap. [H.]
Serrion, a measure, 219

Sessions, 97, 173
Sevile grain, 213, 217
—— oil, 214, 217
Sewers, 247
Sheepskins, 91, 216, 218
Sheffield knives, 217
Shelves or banks of the Thames, 106
Sheriff, appointment of, 3, 15, 16, 21; not to take scotale, 6, 8, 12, 29
—— duties and liberties of the, 22
—— 40, 44, 45, 46, 57, 76, 82, 84, 88, 173, etc.
—— amercement of, 44, 54
—— maces of, 63, 64
—— of Surrey, 122
—— to assist the mayor, 149
—— election of, 272, 276
—— act regulating election of, 295. A sheriff, vicecomes; literally a "vice-count" or "vice-earl." In Anglo-Saxon times governor of a county or province; he was an "earl" or "comes"; originally a higher dignitary than the "ealdor-man", but identified with him in the time of Cnut, and known also as the "reve" or "gerefa". After the Conquest the "vice-comes" supplanted the "comes", or earl, as the scirgerefa, and hence, as being invested with the functions of the "comes", his Latin name. [R. See also C. and J.]
Sheriffwicks of London and Middlesex, 15, 16, 21, 22, 23, 53; sheriff's jurisdiction
Shoemakers' knives, 217
Shoreham, 12, 14
Shores, 176
Shot, 220
Shumack, 214, 217, 219. *Sumach*, or *Rhus Cotinus*. [G.]
Sieves, rims for, 214, 220
Signposts, 176
Signs and signposts, use of, 192
Silesian linen, 213, 214
Silk, various, 214, 216, 218
Silvester, cochinele, 212, 216
Simon de Kyma, witness to charter of Richard I, 10
Simon Sebatson, grant of his tenement, 110
Simon de Pateshille, witness to charter of John, 12, 14
Sipeet-wood, 215
Skins, various, 214, 216, 217
Slip, 218
Smithfield, 162
—— West, 177, 193
Smoke nuisance, 228
Soap, search and survey of, 142
Soaps, 218; sope-ashes, 219
Soles, 212
Soccage, free, 125. See Free Soccage
Soilage, sweeping of, 107, 108
Sokes, 3, 4. Liberty of jurisdiction or court held within it. [J. E.] Socca, liberty of exemption from customary payments and imposts. [R.] Sokne, a soke or soken, or rather the liberty of holding a soke, or court of exclusive jurisdiction; a French form of the A.-S. word *soc*. In the city each trade or guild originally inhabited its separate district, and the baron or alderman of the guild held exclusive jurisdiction. Later, these local guilds were changed into wards,

INDEX. 335

the lordship of which was in general no longer inheritable by the baron, or alderman, who was then elected to the office; but so late as Edwd. II. Nich. de Farndone was owner of Farringdon Ward, hence its name. Long after men of wealth and title had sokes of exclusive jurisdiction in the midst of the city, the Bishop of London, on Cornhill, for example. See Charter of Henry I. *New Fœdera*, v, 1 [R.]
Sophia, Princess, 278
Sorcery, 148, 171, 172
Southmead, in Walworth, co. Surrey, 115
Southwark, resorted to by malefactors, 59; the village or town granted to the city, 59, 60; grant of the town, 80, 81; manor of, and various lands in, granted, 110-112; duties of the Outroper of, 184, etc.; wharf, 209; borough officers, 260
Southwick, linen, 214
Spanish commodities, 214, 215; goods, 215, 218; cloth, 263
Spars, various, 215, 219
Spectacle, glass, 213
Spectacles, 218
Spices, 91
Spignails, 246 (spike-nails)
Springs, 112
Spruce, yarn, 215
Spurs, 217
Squirrel skins, 216, 218
Stag (skin), 218
Stages, 176
Staines, 151, 152, 153, 154; warren of, unwarrened, 30; bridge of, the western limit of jurisdiction on the river, 132, 133, 135, 136. Staines, co. Middlesex, 18 miles S.W. of London is a place of great antiquity on the south bank of the Thames at the spot where a *stone*, bearing the date 1285, marks the boundary of the jurisdiction of the corporation of London over the river to the west [V.]
Stallage, 122, 177. A payment for having erected a stall [J. E.]
Stalls, 176
Standard, keeping of the great, 183
Staple, 176. A market or place where storehouses are kept to lay up commodities for better vending them wholesale.
Staves, various, 215; pipe, 219
Steel, 219; glass, 213; various kinds, 215
Step-stone, 219
Stephen Middleton, land of, 115
Stephen de Turneham, witness to charters of John, 12, 14
Sterling, 26, etc.
Sterlingus, a sterling or English silver penny. In a statute of uncertain date, *Stat. Realm.* (1810), i, p. 200, as also in the *Assisa de Pond. et Mensur.* of uncertain date, p. 204, it is mentioned as "Denarius Anglicus, qui dicitur *sterlingus*". The origin of the word "sterlingus" (or, as it is not unfrequently written, "esterlingus") is involved in obscurity. The most probable opinion is that certain coins were first so called from the Easterlings, members of the Hanseatic League, coming from eastern parts of Germany; or from the Anglo-Saxons, who,

it has been alleged, were called "Esterlingi" by the Normans, in consequence of the countries from which they emigrated lying to the east; the Normans giving this name to the Saxon coin in contradistinction to their own. Du Cange seems to think that the word is derived from the Osterlingi, a people who inhabited the southern part of Saxony. [R.]
Steward of the Household, 181, 184
Stillyard, beam of the, 100, 102, 104
Stockings, 214, 217, 252, 260, 264
Stones, various, 215, 219
Strangers, 46; buying and selling within the city, regulations of, 94
Strasbrow (Strasburg) linen, 214
Straw, burning of, 108
Stuffs, various, 216, 218
Sturgeon, 212, 213, 220
Styles of incorporation, 140
Search of various commodities, 142. etc. See Scavage.
Succads, 215, 218
Sugar, 213, 217, 219
—— bakers, houses of, 228
Suffolk baize, 259, 264; cloths, 251; flannels, *ib.*
Summons, 71, 83
Surrey, huntings in, 4; sheriff of, 122; justices of the peace of, 187; kerseys, 251
Survey of commodities, 142, etc.
—— of the ruins after the great fire ordered, 229, 230
Swadling bands, 261
"Swan" inn, Holborn hill, 232
—— The, in Southwark, 113
Swarfe, or Iron fillings, 216. (? Grit worn away from grinding-stones used in wet grinding). [H.]
Swegn, sheriff; charter addressed to, 2
Sword-staves, 215
Syder, 215 (cider)

T.

Tabby grogram, 215; Tabby, a kind of cloth. [H.]
Taffaty, 214, 218. Taffeta, a kind of thin silk. [H.]
Tallage, 46, 49, 50. A certain rate according to which barons and knights were taxed by the king towards the expenses of the state, and inferior tenants by their lords on certain occasions.
Tallow, 212, 215, 218
Tammies (cloth), 252
Tankard-bearers, 23. Those who fetched water from conduits for the use of the citizens; before the New River was brought to London this was the usual custom. [H.]
Tapistry, 215, 218
Tapnet, a measure, 219
Tar, 214, 219
Tarrass, 215
Taxation, liability to, 78
Tazells, 215. (? Tassel, a male goshawk). [H.]
Tent - wine, 215. A kind of alicant wine. [H.]
Terras, 220

Thames, river, 151, 152, 153, 154, 155, 156, 157, 167, 175, 176, et seq.
—— weirs in the, 9, 13, 26, 54; act for enforcing statute concerning navigation of, 106, 109; conservation of the river, 132, etc.
—— merchandise on the, 202
—— street, traffic regulations, 238
Tenements, restoration of, 268
Theobald, Archbishop of Canterbury, witness to charter of Henry II, 6
Thomas Basset, witness to charter of John, 18
Thomas Bourchier, Archbishop of Canterbury, rights of reserved, 84; witness to charter of Edward IV, ib.
Thomas, the Chancellor, witness to charter of Henry II, 6 (Abp. Thomas a' Becket)
Thomas, Lord Poynings, messuage of, 114. For pedigree see Collins, *Peerage*, ix, 475. Sir Edward Poynings, who died 14 Hen. VIII, had among other issue, Sir Thomas Poynings, created Lord Poynings, A.D. 1544, extinct 1560; and a daughter, name not known, married to Sir Thomas Wilford. Sir Thomas distinguished himself at the siege of Bures and Bulloign, under Charles Brandon, Duke of Suffolk, also mentioned in the same charter.
Thoulouse woad, 215
Thread, 215, 218
"Three Cranes," 248
Tiffany, 218. A portable flour sieve. [H.]
Tilers, 107
Timberhouses, 227
Tin, 216, 218
"Tipping-in-the-bole," land at Southwark so called, 114
Titlings, fish, 212
Tobacco, 215, 218; garbling of, reserved, 181
Toll, 3, 4, 5, 6, 7, 11, 12, 28, 39, 122, 177
Tow, 215, 219
Tower of London, keeper of the, 9, 13, 26; notice of, 54, 55, 56, 58, 97, 98; constable of the, 43, 55
Tower wharf, 209
Trading companies, 189
Traffic regulations, 237, et seq.
Treacle, 212
Treasure trove, 149; treasure found, 187
Treasurers of England, 179, 181, 182, 184, 186
Trent, 54; Trent-work carpets, 260; (?) handmade. [H.]
Trinity, Church, near Aldgate, 143. The priory of Christ Church, or the Holy Trinity within Aldgate, London, at the south-east corner of Leadenhall street, founded in A.D. 1108, as a monastery for canons regular of the order of St. Austin, by Queen Maud, who placed the church solely under the Bishop of London, giving the canons the gate of Aldgate, with the soken thereof. Afterwards the Knighten Gild, or Portsoken Ward, was conferred on it, and thereby the priors became aldermen of the City of London of Portsoken Ward, and so continued until the time of the dissolution. [D. vi. 150]
Tripe, fustian, 213
Trone, 41

Tronage, 85, 101, 103; Tronare, to weigh at the tron; a balance or beam; derived, not improbably, from the Latin "trutina." The "trona" seems to have been the "large beam" (in contradistinction to the small beam, for weighing only fine wares) used for weighing coarse and heavy commodities, wool, for example, the "tron" for which, at one time, was at Leadenhall, and at a later period at Wool Wharf, near the Tower, and the king's custom payable on which was called "tronage". A distinction is made between goods sold by the hundredweight, as wax, alum, and the like, which were weighed in the king's balance, and those valued by the pound, as pepper, ginger, brasil, and similar commodities, which were weighed by scales carried to the houses where the vendors were harboured. [R.]
Tun, 39
Tunbrels, 242, et. seq. Tumbrel, a dung-cart. [H.]
Turkey, commodities from, 212
—— silk, 214
Turpentine, 212
Tyke, 215. A bullock, etc. [H.]
Tyler, 247
Tyles, 215
Tyn (tin), 216, 218

U.

Ulster, new plantation of, 287
Underchamberlain, duties of the, 189
Underwoods, 125

V.

Vandales, 214
Velver-fustian, 213
Velvets, 214
Velures, 218 (velvets)
Venetians (cloths), 259
Venice, commodities from, 212
—— glass, 213
Verge, the, 125
Verins, tobacco, 215
Victuals, sale of, 171
Views of frankpledge, 121
Vinegar, 218, 219
Vineyard near Aldgate, 240
Vintry ward, 248
Violation, 174
Vittry canvas, 214, 217
Void grounds, 176, etc.; void ground-rents, 112

W.

Wage battle, 5, 7. A species of trial of great antiquity, but much disused, though still in force (1772) if the parties choose to abide by it. This mode of trial was used in the court martial, or court of chivalry and honour, in appeals of felony, and on issues joined in writs of right. [J.] See also [C.]
Wager of law, 239. Wager of law is where an action of debt is brought against anyone upon a simple contract between the parties without deed or record, and the defendant swears that he owes the defendant nothing

INDEX. 337

in manner and form as declared. [J.] See also [C.]

Wagmols (cloths), 259

Waif, 81, 112, 117, 125, 149, 187. The legal name given to goods stolen by a felon, and waived, or abandoned, on being closely pursued or overloaded, such waifs becoming forfeited to the king, or to the lord of the manor (if he had the franchise of waif), unless certain formalities were complied with by the owner of the goods. The word has probably a Norman origin, and is not derived, as some authorities suppose, from the Saxon word "wafian". See Du Cange. [R.] [J. E.]

Wainscot, 215, 219
Waistcoats, 218, 260
Walbrook ward, 248
Wales, 167; woollen goods of, 259
Walls of churches, 179
Walkeline Maminot, witness to charter of Henry II, 6
Walter de Evermue, witness to charter of Henry III, 31
Walter de Gray, Bishop of Worcester, witness to charter of John, 20
Walter de Meitone, witness to charter of Henry III, 42
Walter Reynolds, Archbishop of Canterbury, witness to charter of Henry III, 58
Walworth's field, co. Surr., 115
Wapping wharf, 209
Warren, of Staines, 30. See Staines. Warren, a place, either enclosed or not, privileged by prescription, or grant from the king, for keeping "beasts and fowls of warren", namely, hares, rabbits, partridges, and pheasants; to which some authorities add quails, woodcocks, and waterfowl. [R.]
Wastes, 167, 176, etc.
Waste-street, 112
Watercourses, 176
Wax, 101, 103, 215, 216, 218
Weavers, guild of, 18. See Introduction
Weighing, method of, 183, 184
Weights and scales, 48
Weights and measures, 171
Welch hall, 251, 252, etc.
Welsh stuffs, 262, 263
Wears, or weirs, in the Thames, 9, 13, 14, 26. Wears, tanks, or great dams for taking fish, also for conveying the stream to a mill. J. E. calls them "stanks". [J. E.; L.] Kidelle, a net for taking fish, more generally signifies a "wear" adapted for such nets for taking fish. "Kettles", or "kettle-nets", are still used on the coast of Kent and Cornwall, and, under certain restrictions, on the Thames. [R.]
Western cloth, 263
Westminster, 4, 6, 25, 27, 29, 32, 34, 42, 43. 52, 58, 59, 60, 62, 64, 66, 69, 80, 84, 85, 86, 89, 93, 98, 105, 127, 158, 166–168, 199, 209, 211, 223, 294
—— liberty of, 41
West Smithfield, 177; poorhouse, 193, *et seq.*
Whale fins, 215
Wharves, 209, 210
Wheat, 215

Whitefriars, or Carmelites, 143, 147, 149, 248. The Carmelites, or Whitefriars, of London, were founded in A.D. 1241, by Sir Richard Gray, Knt. Edward I gave them land in Fleet street, and the mayor and commonalty of London granted a lane called Croker's lane, reaching from Fleet street to the Thames, to build in the west end of the church. [D. vi, 1572]
—— exemption of inhabitants, 144, 145, 149
Whitehall, 230, 231
"**White Hart**", The, in Southwark, 114
Wicker bottles, 219
Widows of freemen, privileges of, 185, *et seq.* See Introduction
Wilford, Lord, land of, 113. See Thomas, Lord Poynings
William, the Conqueror, first charter of, 1; second charter of, 2; charters confirmed by Charles I, 159; confirmed by Charles II, 221
—— reference to, 52
William and Mary, statute vacating the judgment on the *quo warranto* against the city, 266; references to letters patent of, 291
William de Aette, witness to charter of Henry III, 42
William of Alba-Spina, witness to charter of Henry I, 4
William de Albeniaco, witness to charter of John, 17
William, Earl of Arundel, witness to charter of Richard I, 10; and of John, 12, 17
William, Bishop of Avranches, witness to charter of John, 18
William Basley, grant of land held by, 111
William Booth, Archbishop of York, witness to charter of Edward IV, 84
William de Braose, witness to charter of John, 12, 14
William Briwere, Brywerre, Briewer, or Briewerre, witness to charter of Richard I, 8; and of John, 12, 14, 20
William Champion, land of, 115
William de Cornhull, Bishop of Coventry, witness to charter of John, 20
William Coventry, Sir, 231
William Gernoun, witness to charter of Henry III, 35
William Giffard, Bishop of Winchester, witness to charter of Henry I, 4
William Glassock, Esquire, lands of, 112
William, brother of Richard de Grey, witness to charter of Henry III, 33 (see next name.)
William de Grey, witness to charter of Henry III, 35
William de Grey, Bishop of Ely, witness to charter of Edward IV, 84
William Kilkenni (Master); Archdeacon of Coventry, witness to charter of Henry III, 35
William, Bishop of London, witness to charter of John, 12, 14
William Longchamp, Bishop of Ely, Chancellor, charter of Richard I, issued by, 8
William Malton, messuage of, 114
William Marshall, witness to charters of Richard I, 8, 10; and (as Earl of Pembroke), of John, 12, 14, 17; and of Henry III, 31
William, of St. Mary's Church, witness to charter of Richard I, 10

Z

William de Montfitchet, witness to charter of Henry I, 4
William the Norman, Bishop of London, charters addressed to, 1, 2
William Salisbury, messuage of, 114
William Sidney (Sir), Knt., keeper of the great beam, 99, 100, 101
William Stafford, keeper of the great beam, 99
William de Warenne, witness to charter of Richard I, 8; witness to charter of John, 12, 14
Wiltshire baize, 259
Winchester, 8
Windsor, 33, 35
Wine-drawer, 91
Wines, 39, 48, 67, 82, 118, 215, 218, 219
—— gauging of, 181, 182
Witchcraft, 148, 171, 172
Woad, 215, 219. *Isatis tinctoria*, used as a blue dye. [G.]
Wolf-stone, 219
Woods and underwoods, 115
—— various, 215, 216, 218, 219
Woodstock, 31
Wool, 201, *et seq.*, 215, 216, 218, 251, 252, 325, 259
Wool-weighing, 85
—— hats, 213
Wool fells, 201, *et seq.*
Woollen cloth, 91
—— goods, regulation of the markets of, 251
—— yarn, 260
Worcester cloth, 263
Wormseed, herb, vermifuge. *Erysimum cheiranthoides*. [G.]

Worsted, 218, 251, 252, 253, 259, 260
Wyer, 215, 219. (Wire)

Y.

Yard-stone, 219
Yarn, 220, 260, 264
Yarns, various, 215, 218
Yenland, Yendale, or Yenleet, the eastern limit of jurisdiction on the river, 132, 133, 135, 136, 152, 153, 154. Another form is Yanlade. Now called "Yantlet Creek", running from the river Medway into the Thames, and forming the Isle of Grain. This word seems to have been a general name for an inlet or creek. [R.] Yantlet, an islet and creek in the parish of Allhallows, in Kent, nine miles N.E. of Chatham. The creek forms one of the mouths of the Medway delta, and separates the Isle of Grain from the mainland. The island is a coastguard station on the Thames, and has the "London stone", marking the boundary of the city jurisdiction. The "London stone" is on the foreshore of the Isle of Grain, a little to the east of the creek; and the boundary of the jurisdiction of the Lord Mayor of London as conservator of the Thames is taken as running due north to the "cross stone" on the Essex shore, just behind the Leigh Sands. [V.]
York, 44, 50, 61
York, Duke of (James Stuart), 231
Yorkshire baize, 259; cloth, 262

ERRATA.

For accoased *read* accused, p. 39, l. 17.
P. 59, *for* 1227 *read* 1327.
P. 67, title, *for* November *read* December.

TO BE COMPLETED IN ABOUT TWENTY-FIVE PARTS, PRICE 2s. 6d. EACH.
Issued at Intervals of Two Months.
PARTS I, II, AND III, NOW READY; PART IV, MARCH 1, 1884.

CARTULARIUM SAXONICUM:

A COLLECTION OF

Charters Relating to Anglo-Saxon History.

BY

WALTER DE GRAY BIRCH, F.S.A.,

Of the Department of MSS., British Museum, Honorary Secretary of the British Archæological Association; Member of the Committee of the Palæographical Society; Author of the "History, Art, and Palæography of the Utrecht Psalter", the "Fasti Monastici Ævi Saxonici," etc.

COLLATION.		Shelf Catalogue.
338.	18.12.1919	

Checked by	Stamped by	Cut by
..........Issues from.................to.................
.... ,, ...to..............
.... ,, ...to..............

l-known "Codex Diplomaticus shed by the English Historical ters, not alone of English, but publication of that work, the Mr. B. Thorpe, 1865; the J. Cameron, R.E., C.B., F.R.S. n the British Museum", edited he "Councils and Ecclesiastical v. A. W. Haddan, B.D., and brought to light many new n it. To these, not a few may ish Museum from the Earl of the Deputy Keeper of Records, Antiquarian and Archæological documents in a general series, ed being preceded by a short *précis*, and collated with the oldest and best copies, either manuscript or printed. The variations will be placed in foot-notes. At the foot of each deed will be given a summary of the principal sources from which the text and various readings are derived, so as to form a Bibliography of Saxon Diplomatics.

From a careful calculation it has been considered that the "Cartularium" can be contained in about twenty-five parts, embracing between two and three thousand documents—in many cases printed from the original and contemporary manuscripts—in a series which, it is hoped, will form a standard of reference to all matters connected with the early diplomatic history of England, as written in the charters, from the fifth century to the termination of the Saxon dynasties on the advent of the Normans. The work will be closed with copious Tables and Indexes.

As this work cannot be carried on without the support of subscribers, and as the impression is limited, it is requested that those who desire to subscribe to the work will signify their names at an early opportunity to the publishers,

Messrs. WHITING & CO., Limited,
30 & 32, SARDINIA STREET, LINCOLN'S INN FIELDS, W.C.

William de Montfitchet, witness to charter of Henry I, 4
William the Norman, Bishop of London, charters addressed to, 1, 2
William Salisbury, messuage of, 114
William Sidney (Sir), Knt., keeper of the great beam, 99, 100, 101
William Stafford, keeper of the great beam, 99
William de Warenne, witness to charter of Richard I, 8; witness to charter of John, 12, 14
Wiltshire baize, 259
Winchester, 8
Windsor, 33, 35
Wine-drawer, 91
Wines, 39, 48, 67, 82, 118, 215, 218, 219
—— gauging of, 181, 182
Witchcraft, 148, 171, 172
Woad, 215, 219. *Isatis tinctoria*, used as a blue dye. [G.]
Wolf-stone, 219
Woods and underwoods, 115
—— various, 215, 216, 218, 219
Woodstock, 31
Wool, 201, *et seq.*, 215, 216, 218, 259
Wool-weighing, 85
—— hats, 213
Wool fells, 201, *et seq.*
Woollen cloth, 91
—— goods, regulation of the ma
—— yarn, 260
Worcester cloth, 263
Wormseed, herb, vermifuge. *cheiranthoides*. [G.]

Worsted, 218, 251, 252, 253, 259, 260
Wyer, 215, 219. (Wire)

Y.

Yard-stone, 219
Yarn, 220, 260, 264
Yarns, various, 215, 218
Yenland, Yendale, or Yenleet, the eastern limit of jurisdiction on the river, 132, 133, 135, 136, 152, 153, 154. Another form is Yanlade. Now called "Yantlet Creek", running from the river Medway into the Thames, and forming the Isle of Grain. This word seems to have been a general name for an inlet or creek. [R.] Yantlet, an islet and creek in the parish of Allhallows, in Kent, nine miles N.E. of Chatham. The creek forms one of the mouths of the Medway delta, and separates the Isle of Grain from the mainland. The island is a

ERRATA.

For accased *read* accused, p. 39, l. 17.
P. 59, *for* 1227 *read* 1327.
P. 67, title, *for* November *read* December.

TO BE COMPLETED IN ABOUT TWENTY-FIVE PARTS, PRICE 2s. 6d. EACH.
Issued at Intervals of Two Months.
PARTS I, II, AND III, Now READY; PART IV, MARCH 1, 1884.

CARTULARIUM SAXONICUM:

A COLLECTION OF

Charters Relating to Anglo-Saxon History.

BY

WALTER DE GRAY BIRCH, F.S.A.,

Of the Department of MSS., British Museum, Honorary Secretary of the British Archæological Association; Member of the Committee of the Palæographical Society; Author of the "History, Art, and Palæography of the Utrecht Psalter", the "Fasti Monastici Ævi Saxonici," etc.

THE want of a new and comprehensive edition of the well-known "Codex Diplomaticus Ævi Saxonici" of the late Mr. John M. Kemble, published by the English Historical Society, 1839-1848, has been long felt by students and writers, not alone of English, but of European, Ecclesiastical and Political History. Since the publication of that work, the "Diplomatarium Anglicum Ævi Saxonici," by the late Mr. B. Thorpe, 1865; the "Facsimiles of Anglo-Saxon Manuscripts", by Lieut.-General J. Cameron, R.E., C B., F.R.S., 1878; the four volumes of "Facsimiles of Ancient Charters in the British Museum", edited by Mr. E. A. Bond, F.S.A., Principal Librarian, 1873-1878; the "Councils and Ecclesiastical Documents relating to Great Britain and Ireland", by Rev. A. W. Haddan, B.D., and Professor Stubbs, 1869-73; and other kindred works, have brought to light many new and important documents which should have had a place in it. To these, not a few may be added from Astle's Collection, lately acquired by the British Museum from the Earl of Ashburnham; the publications of the Master of the Rolls, the Deputy Keeper of Records, the Historical MSS. Commission ; and the Transactions of Antiquarian and Archæological Societies, and some are even yet unpublished.

It is intended in the proposed work to arrange all the documents in a general series, and according to order of chronology, the text of each deed being preceded by a short *précis*, and collated with the oldest and best copies, either manuscript or printed. The variations will be placed in foot-notes. At the foot of each deed will be given a summary of the principal sources from which the text and various readings are derived, so as to form a Bibliography of Saxon Diplomatics.

From a careful calculation it has been considered that the "Cartularium" can be contained in about twenty-five parts, embracing between two and three thousand documents—in many cases printed from the original and contemporary manuscripts—in a series which, it is hoped, will form a standard of reference to all matters connected with the early diplomatic history of England, as written in the charters, from the fifth century to the termination of the Saxon dynasties on the advent of the Normans. The work will be closed with copious Tables and Indexes.

As this work cannot be carried on without the support of subscribers, and as the impression is limited, it is requested that those who desire to subscribe to the work will signify their names at an early opportunity to the publishers,

Messrs. WHITING & CO., Limited,
30 & 32, SARDINIA STREET, LINCOLN'S INN FIELDS, W.C

Now Ready, Demy 8vo., Cloth, Price Six Shillings,

Older England:

ILLUSTRATED BY THE

ANGLO-SAXON REMAINS AT THE BRITISH MUSEUM,

IN A

COURSE OF LECTURES.

BY

J. FREDERICK HODGETTS,

LATE EXAMINER IN ENGLISH TO THE UNIVERSITY AND DISTRICT OF MOSCOW, PROFESSOR OF THE ENGLISH LANGUAGE AND LITERATURE IN THE IMPERIAL COLLEGE OF PRACTICAL SCIENCE, AND IN THE USATCHEFFSKIE TSCHERNYAFFSKIE COLLEGE AT MOSCOW.

Nearly Ready, Second Edition, with numerous Additional Illustrations, Price One Guinea.

SALAMINIA:

(CYPRUS)

THE HISTORY, TREASURES, AND ANTIQUITIES OF SALAMIS.

BY

ALEXANDER PALMA DI CESNOLA, F.S.A.,

MEMBER OF THE BRITISH ARCHÆOLOGICAL ASSOCIATION; MEMBER OF THE SOCIETY OF BIBLICAL ARCHÆOLOGY, LONDON; HON. MEMBER OF THE ROYAL MEDICAL ACADEMY, TURIN; ETC., ETC.

With an Introduction by

SAMUEL BIRCH, Esq., D.C.L., LL.D., F.S.A.,

KEEPER OF THE EGYPTIAN AND ORIENTAL ANTIQUITIES IN THE BRITISH MUSEUM.

With upwards of Seven Hundred Illustrations of the vast variety of valuable Objects in Gold, Silver, and Bronze; Gems, Cylinders, Precious Stones, Ivory, and Terra-cottas. Among which may be mentioned Finger-rings, Ear-rings, Necklaces, Leaves of beaten Gold-foil for head-attires or to cover the features of the dead; Masks, Swords, Knives, and other Weapons; Coins, Pins, Alabastra, Toys, Urns of large size adorned with geometrical patterns, other Urns of sepulchral use, finely modelled Statuary groups and Statuettes, portable Hand-warmers, and numerous Inscriptions, of the highest value to the Archæologist and Historian.

WHITING & CO., Limited,
30 & 32, SARDINIA STREET, LINCOLN'S INN FIELDS, W.C.
And all Booksellers.

www.ingramcontent.com/pod-product-compliance
Lightning Source LLC
Chambersburg PA
CBHW032024220426
43664CB00006B/354